ASTROLOGY

ASTROLOGY

A recent history
including the untold story of its role
in World War II

by

ELLIC HOWE

WALKER AND COMPANY
NEW YORK

K.C.

ASTROLOGY

A recent history
including the untold story
of its role in World War II

PRINTED IN GREAT BRITAIN

For Elsa, who shared the adventure

URANIA'S CHILDREN

Astrologers suppose that they are particularly subject to the influence of the planet Uranus and that their art is therefore 'Uranian'.

'It is a most remarkable circumstance, that whatever he [Uranus] produces or signifies, is of a *strange, romantic,* and *unexpected* kind; that portion of the individual's fate over which he rules being *decidedly extraordinary, most unlooked for, and totally at variance with the general current of such events, to the majority of those who are born under a different sway.* Indeed there is such an appearance of *magic* about the circumstances, that the person so influenced is induced, at times, to think that the *wand* of the *enchanter* has *metamorphosed his state. All looks like fairyland,* and reflection is at a loss to determine whether it is not the delusive representations of a *dream* rather than waking reality.'

John Corfield in *The Urania*, No. 1, June 1814.

Contents

PART I

The Historical Background

PART II

Karl Ernst Krafft

Illustrations

Acknowledgments

Of the many people who have given me invaluable help in connection with this book I would like to express my warm thanks to: M. C. Amacker (Geneva), Miss June Bainbridge, Professor Hans Bender (Institut für Grenzgebiete der Psychologie und Psychohygiene, Freiburg i. Br.), M. Louis Bévand (Geneva), Herr W. Bischoff (Berlin), M. Gustave-Lambert Brahy (Brussels), Dr Hans Buchheim (Institut für Zeitgeschichte (Munich), Dr. C. J. Burckhardt (Vinzel/Vaud), M. Th. Chapellier (Brussels), Mlle G. Charton (Lausanne), Mr C. J. Child, Professor R. Danneel (Bonn a. Rh.), Mr D. S. Delmer, Mr Peter Dorp, Dr G. Franz (Freiburg i. Br.), Fräulein F. Frey (Zürich), M. Michel Gauquelin (Paris), Herr F. G. Goerner (Mannheim), Mr Lionel Hale, Herr Werner Hamerski (Münster), Dr Otto Kellner (Hamburg), Countess Goedela Keyserling (Innsbruck), Dr W. Koch (Göppingen), Professor H. H. Kritzinger (Achern), Herr G. Lucht (Brandau im Odenwald), the late E. Hans Mahler (Zürich), the Hon. Ewen Montague, Q.C., Dr W. Mrsic (Munich), M. Roger Munsch (Pommeuse, S. et M.), Mrs P. I. Naylor, Mlle M. Panchaud (Lausanne), M. André Tanner (Lausanne), Herr Felix Tappolet (Zürich), the late Herr Paul Walser (Winterthur), Mr Stephen Watts, Mrs Ilse R. Wolff (The Wiener Library), Herr W. Th. H. Wulff (Hamburg), and finally the library staff of the Warburg Institute, University of London.

I am particularly grateful to Mr V. V. Tilea, C.B.E., for lending me four letters written to him by K. E. Krafft in 1939–40, also for talking to me at length about his relationship with Krafft and the late Louis de Wohl.

London, 3 February 1967   Ellic Howe

I
Encounter with Astrology

The first astrologer I met—later there were to be many others—was introduced to me early in 1943 by Sefton Delmer, who was by far the most imaginative and skilful exponent of 'black' psychological warfare techniques that I encountered during close on four years' employment at the Political Warfare Executive. There were two sides to the department's output: BBC broadcasts to Germany and enemy-occupied Europe, also leaflets bearing the imprint of H. M. Government and dropped by the Royal Air Force, were all 'white'. 'Black' operations, however, never indicated their British origin. Various 'black' broadcasting stations skilfully gave the impression that they were being operated inside Germany, and great pains were taken to ensure that 'black' printed matter looked as if it had actually been produced there. 'Black' material was not delivered to Germany in bulk by the RAF but was conveyed by underground channels, hence in relatively small quantities.[1]

Delmer's tame astrologer was the late Louis de Wohl, a tall, flabby elephant of a man who peered at me through tortoise-shell rimmed spectacles. He wore a well-tailored uniform and was apparently an army captain with a General List commission. He took some papers from a large and very expensive crocodile-leather brief-case and a cigar from a container made from the same material. 'The crocodile is my favourite animal,' he remarked. Delmer had already left. De Wohl sat there staring at me and I felt as if I were just about to be devoured by a crocodile. He asked me to repeat my name and how to spell Ellic. He spoke exceptionally good English but with a slight German accent. Then, without lowering his persistent gaze, he took a pencil in each hand and simultaneously wrote 'Ellic Howe', normally with his right hand and in mirror or reversed handwriting with his left one. I felt that he was trying to hypnotise me and looked away. That broke the tension and we got down to business.

De Wohl told me that Delmer had commissioned him to write the text for a faked issue of the German astrological periodical *Zenit*. He asked if we would be able to provide the necessary types for the signs of the zodiac and the planets. He pointed to them in his manuscript, and although I knew nothing about astrology I recognised them and said that they could easily be obtained for printing purposes. My first meeting with de Wohl was quite brief and I only met him on two or three other occasions, always in connection with a 'black' astrological project of Delmer's.

[1] Sefton Delmer's *Black Boomerang*, 1962, contains an authoritative account of British 'black' activities against Germany during the Second World War.

Apart from several issues of *Zenit* we also produced an attractive little booklet containing prophetic verse quatrains in the style of those written by Michel Nostradamus, the famous French 'seer' who lived in the sixteenth century. I will have more to say about these publications later. Here, however, I must mention the fact, which was unknown to me at the time, that our Nostradamus booklet was inspired by the knowledge that Karl Ernst Krafft, the Swiss astrologer who was supposed to be Hitler's adviser, had been using Nostradamus material for psychological warfare purposes. Nostradamus was now to be 'played back', as it were, to the Germans.

Krafft's connection with Hitler made him the object of our kind attentions. De Wohl certainly had a hand in the manufacture of a letter that was concocted above a forgery of Krafft's signature during the summer of 1943. Neither Delmer nor myself can remember very much about this letter except that Krafft was alleged to have informed his correspondent that Germany would lose the war and Hitler would die a violent death, or words to that effect. The plan was to manoeuvre the letter into the hands of the Gestapo. Then, if all went well, Krafft would be arrested and Hitler would lose the services of his presumably invaluable astrologer. I have no idea whether the document ever reached its intended destination, but with hindsight realise that it would have amused certain people in Heinrich Himmler's *Reichssicherheitshauptamt* (Head Office for State Security) because Krafft had been their prisoner since the summer of 1941.

After 1945 I soon forgot about much of my work for Delmer and other people in the department. Again, I hardly gave a thought to astrology until the spring of 1958 when my curiosity was aroused by references to the subject in various books by C. G. Jung. I was surprised to discover that Jung himself obviously took astrology seriously. In 1931, for instance, he observed that 'the cultural philistines believed until recently that astrology had been disposed of long since and was something that could safely be laughed at. But today, rising out of the social deeps, it knocks at the doors of the universities, from which it was banished some three hundred years ago.'[1]

Again, in his essay on 'Flying Saucers: A Modern Myth of Things seen in the Sky' he wrote: 'For those of my readers who are unaware of these things and think I am exaggerating, I can point to the easily verifiable fact that the heyday of astrology was not in the benighted Middle Ages but is in the middle of the twentieth century, when even the newspapers do not hesitate to publish the week's horoscope. A thin layer of rootless rationalists read with satisfaction that in the year 1723 Mr So-and-so had a horoscope cast for his children and do not know that nowadays the horoscope has almost attained the rank of a visiting card.'[2]

[1] C. G. Jung, 'The Spiritual Problem of Modern Man' in *Civilisation in Transition*, Collected Works, Vol. 10, 1964, p. 86.
[2] C. G. Jung, *Civilisation in Transition*, p. 370.

Finally, I came across the 'An Astrological Experiment' chapter in Jung's *The Interpretation of Nature and the Psyche*, 1955, in which he discussed astrology in relation to his 'synchronicity' theories.

So I decided to have a look at astrology, although with no very clear purpose in mind. It did not occur to me that the subject would preoccupy me for any longer than a month or two. I began by purchasing a copy of *Prediction*, a mass-circulation periodical, in which I read the advertisements of professional astrologers who offered 'advice on any specific question concerning marriage, finance, business, health, travel, removal, etc.' for two guineas or so. For the same modest sum one could obtain 'one year's detailed forecast with exact dates of all future events'. Astonished that a precise knowledge of the future could be had so cheaply, I turned to the editorial pages and to various contributions written in an incomprehensible technical jargon. For instance, of the horoscope of a film star it was stated that 'Mercury is shown to have a trine aspect to Mars, which is in Taurus. Taurus is ruled by Venus, which means that the action of Mars is subordinate to the ruler's function.' I could make nothing of this arcane statement.

The magazine also contained predictions for the month of issue arranged under each of the twelve signs of the zodiac. Thus everyone born under the sign Aries, for instance, would presumably be subject to identical short-term astral influences or have the same 'fate'. This did not make sense.

I had a look at *Horoscope*, the French equivalent of *Prediction*. Its contents were almost identical except that there were far more astrologers' advertisements and the French practitioners mostly offered a whole range of mantic specialities, such as palmistry, cartomancy (the mysterious *Tarots égyptiens*) and sometimes clairvoyance. The British astrologers for the most part conducted an exclusively postal business, but their French colleagues expected to receive their clients for personal interviews.

My next step was to commission a two-guinea horoscope reading from one of the 'wise ones' who advertised in *Prediction*. I sent the gentleman the date of my birth and informed him that the actual time of the event was unknown. He then asked for details of important events in my life and explained that these particulars would enable him to attempt a 'rectification' of my horoscope, meaning that he would attempt to deduce the birth time from the constellations prevailing on the dates in question. In due course his delineation arrived, together with the horoscope chart. I read his remarks with interest. He had decided that I was born at approximately 1.30 a.m. In later years half a dozen famous German astrologers tried to identify my birth hour but all suggested quite different times. Lest it be supposed that I henceforth squandered my substance upon horoscopes, I must explain that my German friends did not charge for their labour.

My astrologer sent me five pages of typescript. In the first paragraph he made a strikingly accurate observation about one of my more pronounced personality traits. This was very much to the point and I was impressed. He also offered a number of vague short-term predictions, e.g. I would do well financially in June, meet with unexpected obstructions in September and would travel abroad in October. I was never conscious that any particular prediction had been fulfilled, but I did go to France at short notice in November.

His unexpectedly percipient first paragraph persuaded me to go a little further. This was due to a passing interest in what the Germans call *Charakterologie*. I had recently read Jung's *Psychological Types*, Kretschmer's *Physique and Character* and other works of this kind by German writers. *Charakterologie*, it should be noted, is very much a German preoccupation. Furthermore, I had discovered that Jung himself was accustomed to study his patients' horoscopes, not in order to predict their futures, but because he believed that a natal horoscope could provide useful information of a purely psychological nature: for instance, why a given individual might be latently susceptible to a particular kind of neurosis. Hence there was presumably a brand of Jungian 'psychological astrology' and I hoped to discover the appropriate literature. A glance at the books currently on offer at the Atlantis Bookshop in Museum Street was sufficient to tell me that the knowledge or instruction I required would not be easily forthcoming.

And yet the stars were on my side. At that time my wife and I used to attend lectures at my relative Dr Eric Graham Howe's 'The Open Way' circle in the Harley Street district. There the audience included medically-trained psychologists, lay therapists and ordinary laymen such as ourselves. Dr Howe was interested in every conceivable manifestation of human behaviour and belief, so nobody was surprised when a lecture on astrology was announced. It was given by Mrs Phyllis Naylor, a professional astrologer whose name will not be found in the London telephone directory, let alone the advertisement pages of any periodical. She read a cautious paper on 'Astrology and the Problem of Precognition'. I soon made her acquaintance and this was the beginning of an enduring friendship.

In February 1959 Mrs Naylor taught me how to cast a horoscope and the elements of interpretation. The mathematical side was easily learned but I could not match Mrs Naylor's skill in describing the psychological characteristics of the people (whom I knew well) whose horoscopes I produced for her inspection. She had no idea of their identity. By degrees, however, I became fairly adept at this 'blind diagnosis' business. Most of my attempts at 'prediction' were wide of the mark and I imagine that my few successes in this direction—one or two of them were quite impressive—were achieved more by chance than virtuosity.

I fared better with 'prediction in reverse', meaning the identification of past events from a person's horoscope. The late Arthur Gauntlett, a well-known professional astrologer, challenged me to tell him what had happened to him on two specific days of his life. He said that none of his professional colleagues had succeeded in describing the events in question. In order to solve this puzzle I used the German 'Hamburg School' system, which is mentioned later in this book, and succeeded far beyond our respective expectations. Some years later Mr Gauntlett sent me a 'testimonial' which read: 'On the 30th January 1961 you gave me the answers to my questions, and you were so extraordinarily close to the actual events that, had I not known otherwise, prior knowledge might have been suspected.' I could not guarantee to repeat the performance today and cannot explain why I succeeded in 1961.

It was about this time that the problem of astrology's truth or falsehood ceased to interest me. By all accounts my alleged 'successes' should have been sufficient to convince me of the validity of the astrological thesis and make me one of astrology's band of true believers. Nevertheless, I felt that this 'messing about' with horoscopes, at least as far as I was concerned, was a waste of time. I was prepared to accept that there was more in astrology than the sceptics would be willing to admit, but at that point my personal involvement ended. By now I was beginning to realise that the answers to the questions that interested me most—these questions had nothing to do with the validity or otherwise of astrological beliefs—would not be discovered by casting horoscopes, but only by a process of historical research.

What puzzled me was the phenomenon of astrology's survival in the form in which I had encountered it, and above all its persistent, almost obtrusive presence in the twentieth century. Jung himself had drawn attention to this, but accurate information about the phenomenon's short-term historical background did not appear to be available. The scholars had carefully investigated countless aspects of astrology's earlier history, i.e. from its Babylonian origins up to the time when astrological beliefs ceased to be fashionable in Europe towards the end of the seventeenth century, but nobody had thought it worthwhile to examine the later period from *c.* 1700 onwards.

The reason for this neglect is easily explained. During close on two millennia, from pre-Hellenistic times until the very end of the Renaissance era, astrological ideas pervaded many departments of knowledge and intellectual speculation in the west. Astronomy and astrology were twin sisters, cosmological theories had an astrological basis and there were traditionally close links between astrology and medicine. During the present century, therefore, men working in a diversity of academic fields have inevitably encountered and commented upon astrological beliefs, traditions and traces. However, their interest ceases when, in terms of historical perspective, astrology loses its hitherto respectable status during the seventeenth century. In effect, why waste time studying the modern history of a disreputable superstition?

Aby Warburg (1866–1929) and his pupil and colleague Fritz Saxl (1890–1948), two of this century's most distinguished cultural historians, thought otherwise and laid the foundations of the important collection of twentieth-century *Astrologica* now at the Warburg Institute, University of London. Warburg made a close study of astrological symbolism in Renaissance art and Saxl traced and catalogued the major medieval astrological manuscripts. At Hamburg before the First World War Warburg began to collect contemporary astrological pamphlets and textbooks— modern publications of this kind were then a novelty in Germany— because for him they represented the surprising survival of the pagan beliefs that he had already identified in the Renaissance era. Indeed, for Warburg these publications had an entirely historical significance. Saxl continued to add to the collection after Warburg's death. I discovered these books very soon after I commenced this inquiry and soon had good reason to respect the memories of those who assembled them.

It was an essay on 'The Revival of Late Antique Astrology' by Fritz Saxl that set me on my subsequent path. Turning from the past to the present he mentioned the unexpected revival of astrological beliefs in Germany shortly before the First World War. He equated this with a widespread interest in fortune-telling which, he thought, began about 1910 and might be considered as one of the omens of that war.

'Since then it has increased considerably', he wrote. 'A great number of periodicals devoted entirely to astrology have sprung up, and quite a considerable literature has been printed—textbooks, prophecies, reprints of astrological classics and so on. A mass movement always has deep roots in psychology, and although we may find from a purely logical and scientific standpoint that the conclusions are wrong, the imaginative or, as I may venture to call it, the religious background of the mass-movement is of the greatest importance; and scholars do not degrade themselves, I think, by investigating it . . . It would be most interesting, to my mind, to see more clearly into this development, to know its leaders and its followers, its methods and its religious tendencies. Clearly we cannot understand our own times unless we pay heed to its unscientific tendencies.'[1]

Saxl's main theme in this essay was astrology's reappearance in the west during the twelfth century, when Arabic translations of much earlier Hellenistic Greek texts were translated into Latin for the first time. I was impressed by the following passage because it reminded me of something rather similar that I had recently read in Jung's 'The Spiritual Problem of Modern Man'. Saxl wrote: 'The twelfth century, which first saw paganism come back into its own in the garb of astrology, must have borne some

[1] F. Saxl, *Lectures*, 1957, Vol. 1, p. 73.

resemblance with our own time. The period of the crusades must have been filled with a degree of unrest such as exists today . . . It must have been, like ours, a period when the Christian religion seemed no longer completely able to satisfy the spiritual side of man, and there was room for paganism to slip in, as we see it doing today.'[1]

Jung thought that the astrological 'ferment' that has been a feature of the present century reflects 'Gnostic' influences and referred to 'the widespread and ever-growing interest in all forms of psychic phenomena, including spiritualism, astrology, Theosophy, parapsychology and so forth . . . The world has seen nothing like it since the end of the seventeenth century. We can only compare it with the flowering of Gnostic thought in the first and second centuries after Christ. The spiritual concepts of our time have, in fact, a deep affinity with Gnosticism.'

My task, as I saw it early in 1961, was to attempt a piece of research on the lines indicated by Saxl. It was already apparent that much of my material would be German. This statement requires explanation. I had noticed contemporary but unconnected revivals of interest in astrology in Great Britain and France in the 1890s. But whereas astrology had had a continuous although 'underground' history in Great Britain since the end of the seventeenth century, the recent French revival had no easily identifiable historical background. The German revival began even later than the French one and, as Saxl surmised, in c. 1910. In German-speaking countries astrology had been almost as completely forgotten as in France. The new German movement, however, was in many respects a by-product of the British revival of the 1890s.

What intrigued me most was the peculiar but still obviously uncharted history of the German astrological movement during the period between the two World Wars, because here the clues, if they could be discovered, might lead in the direction of Hitler and his astrologers, of whom Krafft was possibly one. The German preoccupation with astrology at that time was unparalleled in any other European country or the U.S.A. Indeed, the Germans literally took astrology to pieces in their attempt to discover what makes it 'work' or 'not work'. Nevertheless, Jung's supposition that astrology was 'knocking at the doors of the universities' was based upon an over-optimistic assessment of the influence of German *Akademiker* who happened to be deeply interested in astrology during those two decades. In any case, their raps on the gates of learning were faint and unheard. Again, Jung's proposition that 'the horoscope has almost attained the rank of a visiting card' referred to a specifically German situation during the

---

[1] Warburg made the same point in his *Heidnisch-antike Weissagung im Wort und Bild*, Heidelberg, 1920, where he suggested that the gods of classical antiquity had survived in Europe as 'cosmic daemons' and that the Church had silently tolerated a pagan cosmology in the form of astrology.

early 1930s. However, if we make allowances for some exaggeration on Jung's part, there was an identifiable German 'obsession' with astrology and, following Saxl's suggestion, I have attempted to indicate its historical background and subsequent course.

I was also curious to know about Karl Ernst Krafft's involvement in the German astrological scene. He, after all, was the only astrologer whose name had so far been positively connected with Hitler's. The following questions presented themselves: Did Hitler believe in astrology? Did Hitler employ Krafft? Who was Krafft?

Thus I found myself pursuing two parallel lines of inquiry. The first was purely historical and related to the immediate origins of the modern British, French and German astrological movements. The second concerned Krafft. A hunch rather than logic suggested that if I could assemble sufficient facts about Krafft's career I would not only have the material for an interesting, possibly unique case-history, i.e. relating to a well-known professional astrologer, but that Krafft himself would eventually lead me in the direction of the top Nazis who had some obscure connection with astrology.

I must admit that I have often despaired of contriving a satisfactory structure for this book. It is not an astrological manual and anyone requiring detailed information about astrological techniques must look elsewhere. Again, since I cannot 'explain' astrology I have refrained from attacking or defending it. It will be evident, however, that my attitude to the astrologers themselves is not as reverent as many of them would desire. If I am to be blamed for failing to offer more positive conclusions, I can only observe that a prolonged sojourn, such as I have made, in the 'underworld' of the astrologers, can be compared to an endless journey through a swamp. The expression 'underworld' possibly provides the best clue as to the nature of this particular *milieu*. It is not highly respected nor, generally speaking, are its denizens. And yet I would not wish to tar all the astrologers with the same brush because some of the many I have encountered have become close friends.

Finally, while both astrology and those who practise it continue to puzzle me, I believe that the symbolism they use, but so rarely appear to understand, has a certain objective beauty, even logic. The possible meaning of the symbols, in their ever-varying combinations, can sometimes be sensed in the course of a subjective, incommunicable experience. The magic spell is broken the moment one tries to translate everything into ordinary, everyday words. Hence my theory that astrology would be fine without the astrologers.

A Minimum of Astrological Theory

The astrological Tradition, in the form in which it is normally encountered in the west today, consists of a vast collection of empirical rules and procedures, many of them dating back to the first centuries of the Christian era, which have been transmitted from one generation of astrologers to another, copied from manuscript to manuscript, later from book to book, and amended and re-stated by successive astrological writers. There is no ultimate authority nor, for that matter, any supremely authoritative work or source. Every century, and latterly even every generation, has produced its own astrological canon, written in a contemporary idiom. The twentieth-century literature is enormous. Indeed, it is likely that more has been published on the subject during the past seventy years than throughout the previous twenty centuries.

A typical astrological manual has two purposes: to instruct the reader how to cast a horoscope, and then how to interpret it. Such books usually also contain chapters on predictive techniques, the 'rectification' of a horoscope when the birth-time is not accurately known and other topics of more interest to astrologers than to laymen.

A horoscope is simply an objective statement of astronomical facts and represents a geocentric 'map' of planetary positions—the astrologers include the Sun and Moon among the planets—in relation to the zodiac.[1] It is erected for a specific date and, above all, exact moment of time, and in relation to a given geographical co-ordinate. A chart can apply to a human birth, a country (e.g. a horoscope cast for the date and time of its independence, the signing of its constitution or any other significant event), a ship (its launching), or any unusual happening such as an earthquake, a railway accident or an assassination. In the absence of the necessary information it is impossible to know whether the horoscope applies to a man or a woman, a genius or an idiot, a pet animal or a gorilla, or an event.

The arithmetical calculations, which are made with the help of an ephemeris (annual tables of planetary motions with details of their respective positions at noon or midnight for every day of the year) and other

---

[1] The zodiac is a notional band of sky representing the Sun's annual path through the fixed stars. This ancient measuring device consists of twelve sectors each measuring thirty degrees. The sectors themselves are named after certain fixed star constellations, i.e. Aries, Taurus, Gemini, Cancer etc. With the exception of Pluto, the Moon and all the planets have their orbits within about $9°$ of the centre of this band of sky and hence move in the same apparent path as the Sun. The zodiac is a Babylonian invention, probably not earlier than $c.$ 500 B.C.

labour-saving tables, are quite simple. The 'magic' begins when deductions, based upon the traditional rules or their modern equivalents, are made on the basis of an analysis of the zodiacal positions of the individual planets, certain angular relationships between any two or more planets, the respective positions of the planets in the twelve Houses, and the zodiacal positions of the Ascendant or 'rising sign' and its related *Medium Coeli* or Midheaven. The above represents a very summary account of what is involved.

When Krafft taught himself how to cast a horoscope in 1919, he probably began by erecting his own, because this is what almost every novice does. Krafft's horoscope will provide a convenient working example. First he had to familiarise himself with the signs of the zodiac (see Fig. 1) and the approximate date when the Sun enters each of the successive 30° sectors.

Aries	(♈)	21 March	Libra	(♎)	23 September
Taurus	(♉)	20 April	Scorpio	(♏)	24 October
Gemini	(♊)	21 May	Sagittarius	(♐)	23 November
Cancer	(♋)	22 June	Capricorn	(♑)	22 December
Leo	(♌)	23 July	Aquarius	(♒)	20 January
Virgo	(♍)	23 August	Pisces	(♓)	19 February

Fig. 1 The Signs of the Zodiac.

Krafft was born at Basle on 10 May 1900 at 12.45 p.m., Central European Time, and his Sun sign was therefore Taurus.[1] Everyone else born that year between 20 April and 21 May was also 'born under Taurus'. A generalisation of this kind is of no great interest to an astrologer who is normally only concerned with a strictly individual horoscope, meaning one calculated for a given day, time and place.

[1] In a letter written to Dr Maurice Faure, of Nice, on 11 November 1933 he stated the official time, as recorded in his birth certificate, but added 'at 12.50 p.m. to be very precise'. He had obviously 'rectified' his own horoscope.

Since all the information contained in an ephemeris is calculated for noon (or midnight) Greenwich Mean Time, Krafft had to convert CET to GMT by subtracting one hour, giving a birth time of 11.45 a.m. GMT. At noon (GMT) on 10 May 1900 the planetary positions were as follows:

Sun	(☉)	19° 21′ Taurus	Jupiter	(♃)	8° 8′	Sagittarius
Moon	(☽)	2° 17′ Libra	Saturn	(♄)	4° 30′	Capricorn
Mercury	(☿)	29° 8′ Aries	Uranus	(♅)	11° 22′	Sagittarius
Venus	(♀)	4° 20′ Cancer	Neptune	(♆)	25° 21′	Gemini
Mars	(♂)	24° 49′ Aries	Pluto	(♇)	15° 30′	Gemini

Fig. 2 *Krafft's horoscope with the planets inserted.*

During the 24-hour period between noon on 9 May and noon on 10 May 1900 the respective planetary movements were:

Sun	0° 58′	Jupiter	0° 6′
Moon	11° 55′	Saturn	0° 2′
Mercury	1° 40′	Uranus	0° 2′
Venus	0° 53′	Neptune	0° 2′
Mars	0° 45′	Pluto	less than 1′

It should be noted that during any 24-hour period only the Moon 'moves' to any appreciable extent and passes into a new zodiacal sector after *c.* 2½ days.

Simple rule-of-three calculations or the use of logarithms indicate the planets' actual positions at any given *time* during a 24-hour period. Krafft was born so close to noon (GMT) on 10 May that with the exception of the Moon one could work on the basis of the actual noon positions as given in the ephemeris. His horoscope at this stage, as shown in Fig. 2, would still apply to everyone born on 10 May 1900. When a birth-time is un-known, the astrologer must content himself with erecting a chart on the basis of the noon positions. A complete horoscope, however, must include the Ascendant and *Medium Coeli* and these points can only be calculated upon the basis of a known time.

Diagrammatically (see Fig. 3) a horoscope expresses, among other things, the idea of the Sun rising in the east, i.e. ascending above the eastern horizon at dawn; culminating or reaching its highest point in the heavens at noon; setting in the west in the evening and invisible below the horizon during the night hours. Thus, given an Ascendant and *Medium Coeli*, which will be explained immediately, one has only to glance at the Sun's position in a horoscope to be able to assess the approximate time of birth.

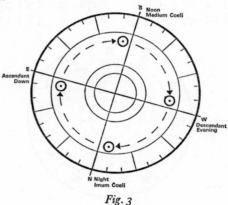

Fig. 3

The Midheaven is the degree of the zodiac that is culminating at any given minute. During any 24-hour period every one of the 360 degrees successively culminates at the MC. Every MC has its related Ascendant, i.e. the degree of the zodiac simultaneously rising on the eastern celestial horizon. The actual degree will vary slightly within small limits according to the latitude north or south of the equator. Roughly speaking, a new sign rises on the Ascendant every two hours.

When Krafft was born 1° 43' Virgo was on the Ascendant and the MC was 24° 2' Taurus. In order to discover these facts he had to make some simple calculations and refer to the appropriate tables. Fig. 4 shows his horoscope with the addition of the Ascendant-Descendant axis and the related *Medium Coeli–Imum Coeli* axis. These are the 'angles' of the horoscope and are said to be vitally important points in the chart. They can only be established on the basis of a known birth time.

We now come to the division of the horoscope into twelve Houses or sectors. The House sectors are not the same as the zodiacal sectors. The boundaries of the first and seventh Houses are determined by the Ascendant-Descendant axis, while those of the tenth and fourth Houses relate to the MC-IC axis. The boundaries of the so-called intermediate Houses will vary slightly according to the mathematical system of House division employed, e.g. Placidus, Regiomontanus, Campanus, Dr Koch's system and so on.

It is necessary to emphasise that House division is not founded upon astronomical data, but upon a choice of curious mathematical speculations or fictions. The average astrologer could no more tackle the necessary calculations, which require an expert knowledge of spherical trigonometry, than fly, and takes his information from Tables of Houses. The Placidus tables are the ones most widely used, but more by an historical accident than because they are necessarily superior to rival systems.[1]

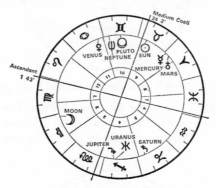

Fig. 4 Krafft's horoscope with the 'angles'

Although astrologers emphasise that it is necessary to calculate the degree of the Ascendant with punctilious accuracy, it must be mentioned that the majority of birth times, if recorded at all, are only known within plus or minus 15 minutes. Hence most Ascendants are hypothetical at least within *c.* 5° and any inaccuracy will therefore affect *all* the House boundaries. This is an anomaly that most astrologers prefer to ignore.[2]

Fig. 5 shows Krafft's horoscope with the addition of the twelve (Placidus) Houses. It will be observed that their areas are not equal but vary.

Finally, there are the so-called 'aspects', i.e. certain angular distances, expressed in degrees, between any two or more planets. The aspects mainly considered are:

Conjunction	(☌) 0°	Sesquiquadrate	(⚼) 135°
Opposition	(☍) 180°	Trine	(△) 120°
Square	(□) 90°	Sextile	(✳) 60°

[1] The house division problem, which is in any case insoluble, has preoccupied a minority of astrological polemicists since the beginning of the seventeenth century. Cf. Richard Gibson, *Flagellum Placidianum, or a Whip for Placidianism*, 1711. After 1920 the Germans quarrelled unceasingly on the subject; see F. Wiesel, *Das astrologische Häuser-Problem*, Munich, 1930, where fourteen competitive systems are described. See also Dr Walter A. Koch, *Horoskop und Himmelshäuser*, 1959, and *Regiomontanus und das Häusersystem des Geburtsortes*, 1960, published by the author at Göppingen. Both his books contain useful historical material.

[2] Birth times are officially recorded in most Continental countries and are therefore available on birth certificates.

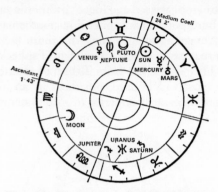

Fig. 5 Krafft's horoscope with the twelve Houses

Fig. 6 shows Krafft's horoscope with the addition of the most prominent aspects. Note, for example, Moon square (90°) Venus and Saturn, and sextile (60°) Jupiter. Venus opposition (180°) Saturn and sextile (60°) Ascendant.

Fig. 6 Krafft's horoscope with 'aspects,' e.g. Moon square (90°) Venus and Saturn and Venus opposition (180°) Saturn.

To sum up, a horoscope erected upon the basis of a known birth time contains the following factors:

Twelve 30° zodiacal sectors (12 × 30 = 360°).
Ten planets in their appropriate zodiacal positions.
Twelve Houses, the boundary of the first being the Ascendant.
Four 'angles' (specially 'sensitive' points): Ascendant, MC, Descendant, IC.
The angular relationships between any two or more planets.

We are now confronted with the hypothesis that a horoscope contains an 'astral' record of a moment of time, but expressed in a symbolical code which must be deciphered. The astrologer works on the basis of a number of assumptions:

1. That each planet works or operates in a different way. To explain this one need only refer to such commonly used adjectives as martial (Mars), mercurial (Mercury), saturnine (Saturn) and jovial (Jupiter).

2. That a planet in some way reflects the qualities of the zodiacal sign in which it is posited. Hence Mars in Leo will be different to Mars in Pisces.

3. That a planet will operate according to its House position. Hence Venus in the tenth House will mean one thing, while Venus in the fifth will suggest something quite different.

4. That angular relationships will 'temper' the respective influences of any two or more planets. For instance, Venus conjunction Mars (o°) might conceivably accentuate sensuality and/or sensitivity, while Venus square (90°) Mars might hinder love's pleasant course. Venus trine (120°) Mars would possibly promote it.

The art of interpretation involves the adroit *combination* of all the available evidence. If the reader protests that the evidence itself is highly unsatisfactory, for the purpose of this chapter we must assume that a horoscope can actually be made to reveal some kind of information. A major problem is one of vocabulary, if only because an expression such as 'Sun conjunction Mars in Capricorn in the seventh House square Saturn in Aries in the tenth House' is so difficult to translate into prose that is at once literate and sensible. One can, of course, refer to one or other of the innumerable astrological 'cook-books' that contain every conceivable interpretative permutation and combination, write down the 'answers' and then attempt a synthesis. This is, in fact, what the majority of astrologers do. Alternatively they repeat, rather like parrots, simple statements or ideas that they have committed to memory. Both methods will produce results of a kind, in the sense that more than 50 per cent of the propositions in an interpretation will appear to be more or less correct.

While many astrologers never get far beyond the mechanical reproduction of the traditional lore, there are some who can contrive more interesting results. They simply look at the chart and begin to talk and much of what they say can be startlingly apposite. I know this from my own experience but must mention that virtuosos of this class are seldom encountered. My friend Mrs Naylor certainly never refers to a 'cook-book'. My conclusion, therefore, is that certain individuals can make a horoscope 'speak' on the basis of intuitive deductions. It is possible that the horoscope itself represents some kind of focusing point, i.e. like a skryer's crystal.

Ignoring, for the moment, astrology's mantic side, I am willing to admit that its symbolism, considered as a whole, represents a marvellously constructed collection of analogies representing a wealth of ideas relating to the cyclical nature of human life (birth, growth and death), human typology, psychology and so on. These hypothetical *schemata* can be studied without the necessity for casting horoscopes and all the rest of it and they do, in fact, contain an immense *corpus* of traditional ancient wisdom. In this context the appeal is aesthetic rather than utilitarian.

The astrologer, however, is not greatly concerned with aesthetics and wants to put his knowledge to practical use. In the event that he is no longer dependent upon 'cook-books' he will be familiar with an extensive range of planetary and zodiacal analogies. In order to express these he will require a working vocabulary, possibly in the form of a range of 'key-words' that can be applied to the various factors in the horoscope. His ultimate synthesis will be based upon a purely subjective understanding of whatever his vocabulary happens to mean to him. Some typical 'key-words' are given below. They have no scientific validity but at least provide some kind of basis for an astrological delineation.[1]

THE PLANETS

Sun: the living being, the physical body, psychic energy, the male principle.

Moon: the soul or psyche, fantasy and feeling, change and fluctuation (cf. tides and months).

Mercury: intelligence, reason, associative or connective function, movement. Cf. Mercury as the messenger of the gods.

Venus: love, art, physical attraction, sentimentality, sexual aberration.

Mars: action, energy, impulsion, aggressive function, *libido*; Mars the god of war.

Jupiter: expansion, richness (material or metaphysical), health, humour (jovial!), developing function.

Saturn: limitation, contraction, concentration, inhibition, separation, maturity, loss (cf. death), saturnine temperament, restrictive function.

Uranus: suddenness, revolution, violence, transmutation (magic, alchemy, the occult arts), creative function.

Neptune: susceptibility, fantasy, romanticism, mysticism, deception and self-deception, psychism.

Pluto: power, dictators, demagoguery, metamorphosis, the masses.[2]

---

[1] Unfortunately for English-speaking readers the most helpful books on this area are all by German authors. See Dr H. A. Strauss, *Psychologie und astrologische Symbolik*, Rascher Verlag, Zürich, 1953, written by a Jungian psychologist; Thomas Ring, *Astrologische Menschenkunde*, Rascher, Verlag, Zürich, 2 vols., 1956–9; H. von Kloeck-ler, *Grundlagen für die astrologische Deutung*, Astra Verlag, Berlin, 3rd edit., 1952. These books reflect an intellectual level unknown in British or American astrological writing.

[2] The last three planets have all been discovered since the end of the eighteenth century, hence long after the development of the traditional analogies for the first seven: Uranus in 1781, Neptune in 1846 and Pluto in 1930. In each case the astrologers have contrived empirical 'interpretations' that have been eventually accepted as

THE SIGNS OF THE ZODIAC

Aries: courage, impetuosity, energy.
Taurus: patience, persistence, obstinacy.
Gemini: progressiveness, cleverness, instability.
Cancer: inspiration, sensitivity, evasiveness.
Leo: dignity, breadth of mind, pretentiousness.
Virgo: reason, exactitude, pedantry.
Libra: harmony, evaluation, trivialities.
Scorpio: profundity, insistency, roughness.
Sagittarius: justice, propriety, sophistry.
Capricorn: independence, abstraction, stubbornness.
Aquarius: spirituality, conviction, illusion.
Pisces: compassion, tolerance, indolence.

THE TWELVE HOUSES

1. Development of personality, environment, childhood, physical constitution.
2. Material possessions and money.
3. Family relationships, communication.
4. Parental home, hereditary characteristics.
5. Procreation, sexuality, pleasure, speculation.
6. Servants, health.
7. The community, partnership, marriage, open enemies.
8. Accidents, death, inheritances, the wife's or husband's money.
9. Spiritual life, philosophy, religion, travel.
10. Vocation, profession, public life.
11. Wishes and hopes, friendships.
12. Secret enemies, seclusion (hospitals, imprisonments), obscure difficulties.

Suppose, for example, that someone has Sun conjunction Mercury in Virgo in the third House. Theoretically one might look for a person (Sun) whose intellectual make-up (Mercury) would be logical, precise or even pedantic (Virgo) in matters connected with family relationships or communication (the latter in a very broad sense—third House). In the absence of further information relating to the native's *milieu*, education, trade or

---

authoritative. I have identified the following prototype formulations: J. Corfield in *The Urania*, June 1814, for Uranus; 'Professor' J. Ackroyd in the 1890 edition of W. J. Simmonite's *Complete Arcana of Astral Philosophy* for Neptune; Fritz Brunhübner in *Zenit*, May, 1932 for Pluto. In the case of Uranus and Neptune almost half a century passed before astrologers unhesitatingly included the new planets in horoscopes. Herr Brunhübner knew enough about Pluto to be able to publish a 138-page book, *Der neue Planet Pluto*, as early as 1934. 'I feel justified', he wrote, 'to say that Pluto can be called the cosmic aspect originating the Third Reich.'

profession, the astrologer cannot be certain whether the horoscope refers, for example, to a clerk who conscientiously maintains a vast card index or a scholar capable of the most painstaking and accurate research. These examples are so jejune as to be discouraging but if one analyses *all* the factors in the horoscope something interesting or even apparently valid often emerges.

It once occurred to me to consult the formulations printed in an old manual, John Gadbury's *The Doctrine of Nativities*, 1658, and apply them to Krafft's horoscope. They worked rather well. A few are reproduced below.

Krafft's Moon was in the second House. 'Moon in the second', wrote Gadbury, 'makes the Native sollicitous about Riches, and the Goods of Fortune; yet never setled Riches succeed to any upon such a Position; but the Native is still wavering, now Rich, now Poor; soon Prosperous, soon Unhappy; sometimes in Favor of great Persons, and much Gain thereby; other-times cast below all probable Hopes.' All this applied to Krafft, who was always 'solicitous' about money, earned it and spent it, inherited it and lost it. He knew many important people and sometimes benefited from these connections but experienced marked ups and downs.

His Saturn was in the fifth House. 'When Saturn is located in the fifth House, he portends, either no Issue to the Native, or the Death and Destruction of those he shall have . . . he destroys the Native's Pleasure, and stirs up Contentions and Strifes between him and Messengers or Ambassadors; and presages an adverse or cross Fortune in all his Negotiations.' Krafft had no children and experienced his fair share of 'Contentions and Strifes'.

'Mars in the Ninth makes the Native purely superstitious and Frothy in his Profession; Unstable, Vain-glorious, and often changing his Religion; never stable nor fixed therein; his Dreams will be frivolous and false, and he much puffed up and conceited thereby: his Journies many and cross . . .' It may be argued that Krafft's extreme identification with astrology and prophecy (cf. his obsessional interest in Nostradamus) reflected a superstitious attitude. The irrational certainly had a far greater appeal for him than the merely rational. Again, his desire to play an important part behind the scenes in the Third Reich can be interpreted as a 'frivolous and false' dream.

'Mercury in the ninth House declares the Native to be experienced in occult and obscure things, and the choicest of Arts, as Astrology and the Mathematics . . .' This certainly applied to Krafft.

Finally there is the whole area of 'prediction'. As I have already suggested, with the exception of the twelve Houses a natal horoscope is at least based upon astronomical data, even if there is no scientific proof that the planets 'influence' human beings and their affairs. With the exception of the 'transit' theory, which I will describe below, predictive techniques have no astronomical basis. A variety of methods all require the individual factors in a horoscope to be 'progressed' in accordance with one or other of a choice of empirical 'keys'. The so-called 'day for a year' and 'degree for a year' systems are two that are widely used, largely because they are relatively simple to operate.

Suppose, for example, that a hypothetical Mr Smith was born on 1 January 1935. In the autumn of 1974 he visits an astrologer and asks for information about his prospects throughout 1975. The astrologer consults his ephemeris, not for 1975, but for 9 February 1935, i.e. forty days after the birth date ('day for a year' system), inserts the planetary positions for that day on the chart and then investigates the angles formed by the 'progressed' planets in relation to those in the natal horoscope. Alternatively, in the case of the 'degree for a year' formula the 'progressions' are made on the basis of 40°. There is also the Naibod system, named after a sixteenth-century astrologer-mathematician, which is based upon the Sun's daily average arc of 59' 8". Some practitioners use so-called Primary Directions, which require exacting mathematical calculations. These are not widely employed in this age of 'instant astrology'. In any case they are far too complicated for elderly ladies who dabble with horoscopes in suburban back parlours.

Finally there are the 'transits', which at least have an astronomical basis. The astrologer examines the current or future positions of the planets, i.e. by referring to an ephemeris, and 'interprets' the angles they form with those in the natal horoscope. For example, a certain Mr X. was born on 13 September 1930 with Sun in c. 19° 58' Virgo (noon position). His wife committed suicide on 14 December 1965. On that day Uranus in 19° 34' Virgo was transiting his natal Sun or, as astrologers would express the situation: Uranus t conjunction (0°) Sun r (radical). Traditionally a transit of this kind could presage a sudden or dramatic event. I have kept a casual eye upon my own transits, but without ever coming to any particular conclusion.

The question is whether or not more or less accurate predictions can be made by the application of any of the available methods. In this respect it is a waste of time to look for the kind of proof that would satisfy anyone requiring scientific evidence. As might be expected, a careful analysis of all the circumstances connected with any random sample of predictions would probably indicate that a proportion of them would appear to have been fulfilled. Thus the problem is to isolate examples which seem to indicate genuine prescience. The score or so that I have recorded—none of them refers to myself—are interesting, but I have never been able to investigate all the relevant circumstances.

A cautious astrologer does not claim to be able to make forecasts other than those of a very general nature, e.g. the possibility of a period of emotional or physical tension, or the reverse; a change of circumstances such as employment, residence and the like; even the possibility of marriage or divorce. The shrill assertions of those who claim to be the indispensable advisers of business magnates and film stars are best disregarded. Indeed, as a general rule it is safe to ignore any professional astrologer who uses or covets overt publicity of any kind.

Contrary to my expectations, an examination of a large cross-section of the more serious astrological journals published in Great Britain, France and Germany since 1900 has revealed that the astrological *cognoscenti* have published surprisingly little on the subject of prediction. Many amateur astrologers seldom attempt predictive work on the grounds that the whole area is so unsatisfactory, and restrict their activities to so-called psychological astrology or *Charakterologie*.

The average member of the general public who takes the trouble to consult a professional astrologer is not greatly interested in *Charakterologie* but wants information about the future. Mrs Naylor once told me that there are two stock questions: 'Will I inherit any money?' and 'When do you think my husband/wife will die?' She also remarked on one occasion: 'What people want is an inexpensive act of magic, preferably one that does not cost more than a guinea or two!'

3
Astrology's Survival and Revival in Great Britain

Whereas astrology literally had to be rediscovered in France in the 1890s and in Germany during the early 1900s, the British astrological revival that took place in the 1890s merely represented a more vigorous continuation of a social phenomenon that had already had an uninterrupted domestic history since the end of the seventeenth century. Indeed, during a period of close on two hundred years, from c. 1700 until 1890 or thereabouts, in the West astrology was remembered and practised only in Great Britain. On the Continent it remained well underground or was almost completely forgotten.

The English only began to be deeply interested in the subject when it was already ceasing to attract the attention of cultured Europeans. This was during the second half of the seventeenth century when the London production of manuals and prognostic ephemera exceeded the combined output of all the main European publishing centres. While there was a noticeable decrease of interest during the first two or three decades of the eighteenth century, many educated Englishmen still continued to practise the art. Their number gradually declined but at no time during the eighteenth century was astrology completely forgotten and there was always a nucleus of faithful practitioners. In the meantime the demand for new astrological textbooks had diminished to such an extent that less than half a dozen new manuals were published between 1700 and 1780. The authority of the old seventeenth-century writers remained unchallenged until the late 1820s.

The general public's misinformed and superficial interest in astrology was maintained throughout the eighteenth century. It was still widely believed that astrologers could predict the future. Most country towns had a quack doctor or two who used astrology for diagnosis and whose herbal remedies were prescribed on the basis of their supposed planetary affinities. Astrology's survival on a popular level was largely due to the perennial appearance of the annual almanacs published by the Stationers' Company, one of the many medieval craft guilds that continued to flourish in the City of London.

The Stationers' Company, a trade association of printers, booksellers, bookbinders and stationers, had been granted an almanac publishing monopoly as far back as 1603 and profited financially from the increasingly large market for predictive almanacs that developed after c. 1650. All the successful publications of this kind were originally compiled by well-known professional astrologers, such as William Lilly, John Gadbury, William Salmon, William Andrews, John Partridge *et alii*. The shareholders in the Company's co-operative publishing business therefore had a vested interest in encouraging and supplying the demand for this kind of ephemeral literature. Thus when the last of the famous seventeenth-century almanac writers died one by one during the first two decades of the eighteenth century, their respective publications continued to appear with unchanged title-pages. Again, since it was the exception rather than the rule for the Company to announce the death of any particular astrological worthy, some of these men achieved a fictitious immortality. In this connection Francis Moore (*c.* 1657–1715), whose *Vox Stellarum* almanac was published by the Company until as late as 1896, provides an outstanding example.[1]

The number of predictive almanacs gradually decreased throughout the eighteenth century and by 1803 all the old publications had disappeared with the exception of John Partridge's *Merlinus Liberatus*, Vincent Wing's *Olympia Domata*, Henry Season's *Speculum Anni* and Francis Moore's *Vox Stellarum*.

The immense success achieved by 'Moore' at the expense of all the other Stationers' almanacs is inexplicable. I have searched in vain for evidence of brilliantly fulfilled predictions or any other feature that would commend this particular almanac rather than any other. In the absence of any sales figures prior to 1768 it is impossible to say when *Vox Stellarum* began to achieve the status of a best-seller. In that year close on 107,000 copies were sold. Partridge came a poor second with 5,600 copies, and five other predictive almanacs could only muster a combined sale of *c.* 13,000 copies.

By 1803 the print order for 'Moore' had risen to 393,750 copies, while the three other surviving predictive almanacs sold only 7,750 copies between them. *Vox Stellarum* reached its nineteenth-century peak in 1839 when 560,000 copies were disposed of. Thereafter its fortunes suffered a gradual decline, so that when the Company ultimately sold the copyright in 1927 its circulation had fallen to *c.* 16,000 copies. If one considers the sales of 'Moore' in relation to the population level (10.5 million in 1801; 17 million in 1835) the extent of its dissemination was impressively wide. It was this annual ration of predictive almanacs that kept belief in astrology alive at a popular level in Great Britain long after it had been more or less completely forgotten in Europe.

There was a revival of interest in the actual practice of astrology in Great Britain in the 1780s. The available evidence indicates the existence

[1] The present Foulsham edition, which claims to have been published without nterruption since the beginning of the eighteenth century, appears to be the successor to a pseudo *Vox Stellarum* or 'Old Moore's Almanac' first published in 1844. During the period 1897–1927 the Company's *Vox Stellarum* was handled by a commercial publisher on a royalty basis.

of a small but lively group of enthusiasts. Most of them were amateurs but there were also some professionals. Throughout the previous fifty years there had always been a small number of obscure professionals in London and elsewhere, although little is known about them. There was, for example, 'Mr Creighton, a gentleman, and a scholar, who about thirty or forty years ago [c. 1750], used to be followed by great numbers, on account of his skill in astrology, and the medical art. He resolved [answered] questions a few doors from Ludgate-hill, on the right-hand side of the way.'[1] A cutting, dated 1770, from an unidentified London newspaper contains an advertisement inserted by an anonymous professional astrologer who resided at 62 Old Bailey, not far from Mr Creighton's address. He charged 5s. 3d. for predictions 'that will be in writing, sealed up, and may be sent for by any person the next day, naming the year and day of the month they came for'. In the 1780s there was the apparently well-known Mrs Williams, who may well have been one of the first of her sex to practise astrology professionally.[2] She plied a seasonal trade at such fashionable spas as Bath and Bristol Hot-Wells and when in London could be consulted 'by ladies only from ten in the morning until eight in the evening, at her house, the Artificial Flower Warehouse, Store Street, Bedford Square. Ladies will be pleased to observe, it is a small house, with green shutters.'[3]

The small-scale astrological revival that began in the 1780s coincided with a new and in many respects antiquarian or romantic preoccupation with ancient Hermetic beliefs such as magic and alchemy. At the same time there was another class of devotee for whom astrology represented, above all, a predictive *science* founded upon severely mathematical principles, hence without any occult or magical nimbus. From now on the astrologers can be divided into two camps: those for whom its appeal is Hermetic or esoteric (cf. the Theosophical astrologers after c. 1890) and those who regard it as a science. The man in the street has never been conscious of these fine distinctions.

It was by chance rather than design that *The Conjurer's Magazine* (No. 1, August 1791) became the first periodical in any language to cater for the interests of astrologers. Initially its contents mainly consisted of chatty little articles on 'Philosophical and Ingenious Amusements', such as conjuring tricks and kitchen-table experiments in chemistry, although there was some astrological features. The latter were mostly contributed

---

[1] *The Astrologer's Magazine*, August, 1793.

[2] One Sarah Jinner, who described herself as a 'Student in Astrology', was the author of *An Almanack or Prognostication* for 1658. The only known copy is in the Guildhall Library in the City of London.

[3] Cutting from *The Morning Herald* dated October 1786. In 1805 a Mrs Corbyn, who did not restrict her services to members of her own sex, also advertised her astrological prowess. She lived at 8 Charlotte Buildings, Gray's Inn Lane (undated newspaper cutting).

by William Gilbert, who wrote under the pseudonym 'B'. The astrologers soon adopted the publication as their own and when its title was changed to *The Astrologer's Magazine* in August 1793 the editor expressed his thanks to 'our numerous Friends and Subscribers who have enabled us to contribute to the revival of Astrology; a science which was studied by Patriarchs of the first ages, but which, by the craft or ignorance of Pretenders, has been exposed to much calumny and error'. The use of the word 'revival' is significant, since it indicates a recent increase of interest in the subject.

The majority of the periodical's contributors used pseudonyms, and it is unlikely that we will ever learn the identities of Astrologus, Mehmet, Mercurius of Bath, Tarantabobus, Hampton Court Observer and all the others who aired their knowledge or squabbled about obscure points of theory or practice in its pages. Most of those who supported *The Coniurer's Magazine* appear to have been more interested in 'scientific' astrology than its occult counterpart. An exception was William Gilbert, mentioned above, a professional occultist of 11 Devonshire Street, Queen Square, who specialised in the preparation of magical talismans.

'The manufacture of talismans *is a great art*,' he wrote, 'which I have completely mastered after many struggles and oppositions . . . And any person who may want my assistance, and will apply for it, will not meet with a rebuff, but satisfaction as amply as he can conceive.'

Mr Gilbert did not work for nothing. 'I will therefore be PAID, and paid HANDSOMELY. The matter is very short—if they *want* ME, and can get nobody else to achieve what I can, they will do what is necessary—otherwise they will not. A few choice friends I accept.—B.'

In another article he explained the traditional connection between talismans and astrology: 'The reasons why talismans fail is, either because they have not been undertaken under the proper planetary position, or else, if this has not been attended to, that person's mind has not been ripe for (that is, has not wholly been given to the intended effect).'

Gilbert advertised his charges for private instruction in 'Astrology and Spirit, with the nature and use of Talismans' in the May 1792 issue of *The Conjurer's Magazine*.[1] His proposed fees, ranging from £20–£150 per annum according to the class of tuition required, were surprisingly high in relation to the current value of money. 'The instruction is to be epistolary or personal, according to circumstances,' he announced, 'either at the Pupil's own house, or at Mr Gilbert's; who, as soon as £200 are subscribed, will provide a proper place to receive Pupils either publicly or *privately*, as may best please . . . No Talismans will for the future be made for any but Pupils, *and I will stop the operation of all* but those which are made through my direction, or by myself.'

A better-known astrological authority had arrived in the person of Dr

[1] The sense of the word Spirit is obscure. It might mean necromancy.

Ebenezer Sibly (1752–99), an eccentric gentleman who took a medical degree late in life. He was the author of *The Complete Illustration of the Celestial Art of Astrology*, of which the first part was published in 1784. The work eventually grew to four parts and more than a thousand pages. Contemporary astrological pundits, and the 'scientific' astrologers in particular, had their own good reasons for disliking the *Complete Illustration*. In the words of one critic: 'We only esteem it a very quack performance, very unequally executed, by a head incompetent to the task of either composing or compiling it; for in it we discover all the faults of old John Gadbury [1627–1704] introduced without correction or distinction in the very language of Bedlam.'[1]

Sibly extensively plagiarised the works of seventeenth-century authors because he had nothing new to say about astrology. Again, if the book sold reasonably well and was reprinted within two decades of his death, it was because it was the only easily available major treatise on the subject. Sibly's compilation is of historical interest for two reasons: firstly because it demonstrates that the old astrological Tradition had become completely fossilised; secondly because it included a lengthy dissertation on magic. Connections between astrology and magic can be established as far back as the beginning of the Christian era. Manuscript copies (in Latin) of *Picatrix*, a tenth-century Arabic astro-magical treatise, were coveted by 'adepts' during the sixteenth and seventeenth centuries. It is unlikely that Sibly or his generation knew this work, but magic still had a strong appeal for those who liked to believe that the secret knowledge of ancient Egypt still survived in an obscure but nevertheless authoritative Hermetic tradition. Indeed, this supposition is still alive today.[2]

Sibly's name was widely known long after his death on 30 October 1799, not on account of his astrological writings or hack medical works (he edited an edition of Culpeper's Herbal), but because of the enduring popularity of 'Dr Sibly's Re-animating Solar Tincture, or Pabulum of Life', a nostrum of his own invention which was still on sale in the 1830s.

The Astrologer's Magazine ceased publication after its seventh issue in January 1794 and there was comparatively little astrological writing or publishing during the next thirty years. The sad experience of John Corfield, who attempted to publish an astrological periodical in 1814, indicates that there was still no satisfactory market for literature of this kind. His *The Urania* appeared in June and immediately died. The British Museum copy contains a pathetic marginal note in Corfield's handwriting: 'I was promised great assistance by pretended Lovers of the Science in the

---

[1] *The Conjurer's Magazine*, March 1792.
[2] The text of *Picatrix* has only been printed twice: in Arabic (1933) and in German as '*Picatrix*', *das Ziel der Weisen von Pseudo-Magriti*, translated by H. Ritter and M. Plessner, London, The Warburg Institute, 1962. The best available study of Renaissance Hermetism is Frances Yates, *Giordano Bruno and the Hermetic Tradition*, London, 1964.

execution of this work, but all failed me; and being left with the editing and expence thereof, it consequently fell to the ground . . . The letters in it are written by myself to myself for the want of correspondents.'

Another astrological magazine had a brief existence in 1814. This was *The London Correspondent* (eight numbers, January–August), which contained articles of interest to amateur astronomers and astrologers. One of its contributors was James Wright, who practised astrology professionally in London. He identified some of the anonymous writers whose articles had been published in *The Conjurer's Magazine*. W.E., for instance, was William Elder (1739–c.96) who had claimed in May 1792 that 'if a birth is sent to me within an hour and a half of truth, I can, without further information, gain a true time [i.e. by 'rectification'] within a few minutes; and having done so, can give a true description of the complexion, colour of the hair, private marks and moles, temper &c.' Wright revealed that H.D., another contributor, was John Lambert (1757–1809) who 'took to drinking the most ardent spirits in large quantities, which greatly accelerated his end'.

The French Revolution and the Napoleonic Wars might have been expected to have produced a rash of astrological speculation but this was not the case. Two studies of Napoleon's horoscope were published in 1805 and another in 1814. These were *The Nativity of Napoleon Bonaparte*, which was handsomely printed at High Wycombe in 1805. Its authorship has been ascribed, but probably incorrectly, to its printer, Thomas Orger. John Worsdale's *Napoleon Bonaparte's Nativity* appeared in the same year and was followed in 1814 by John Corfield's *Destiny of Europe!!! The Nativity of Napoleone Buonaparte, Emperor of the French*. Nobody knew Napoleon's birth time and there was some inspired guessing on the basis of so-called rectification techniques.[1] More than a century later the German astrologers produced a number of different horoscopes for Adolf Hitler, whose birth hour was at least approximately known.

John Worsdale, mentioned above, might have become better known if he had lived in London rather than Lincolnshire, where he spent the whole of his life. He was born at Fulbeck, ten miles north of Grantham, on 2 December 1766.[2] When a young man Worsdale was parish clerk at Fulbeck, but after living successively at Spanby and Donington Northope,

---

[1] Orger, or whoever wrote the book, proposed 11.40 a.m. on 14 August 1769. Worsdale preferred 10.9 a.m. and Corfield offered 11.28 a.m. Thomas White, the Bath astrologer, who referred to the horoscope in his *The Celestial Intelligencer*, Bath, 1810, suggested 9.41 a.m.

[2] Throughout the eighteenth century there was a coterie of astrologers and almanac writers in the Grantham-Stamford district. e.g. several generations of the Wing family, Edmund Weaver (*fl.* 1724–49), Richard Saunders (*fl.* 1683–1736), Robert White (1693–1773) and Thomas Wright (*fl.* 1769–92). Henry Andrews, for many years editor of the *Vox Stellarum* almanac until his death in 1820, was born at Friestone, only a mile or two from Worsdale's birthplace at Fulbeck. The significance of this regional group requires further investigation.

two Lincolnshire villages, eventually moved to Lincoln where he practised astrology professionally until his death there in *c.* 1826. In his *Astronomy and Elementary Philosophy*, [1820], he advertised that 'those Persons afflicted with Disorders of various denominations, may, if they think proper, communicate the Time and Place of their Birth, by Letter (post paid) to the Author of this Work, in the City of Lincoln, in order that the Nature and Origin of the Disease may be truly ascertained, and a Remedy prescribed for all curable Disorders, by the Ancient Rules of Elementary Philosophy'. He also pledged himself to 'point out, and ascertain the time and quality of every important event during the life of any individual, both past, present, and to come'.

Worsdale would have had no use for either William Gilbert or Ebenezer Sibly and their occult preoccupations. For him astrology was essentially a predictive science founded upon painstaking mathematical procedures. The book by which he was remembered by a later generation of astrologers was his *Celestial Philosophy, or Genethliacal Astronomy*, [1828], which was published two years after his death. (It was seen through the press by his son John, who appears to have succeeded to his astrological practice at Lincoln. His decease was not announced, probably to avoid the loss of clients.) This book is of more than passing psychological interest because it indicates the pathological pleasure that Worsdale derived from acquainting clients, or others who had offended him, with the date they might expect to die. Each of the thirty horoscopes analysed in *Celestial Philosophy* relates to the phenomenon that Worsdale euphemistically called 'dissolution'.

At Lincoln there lived Richard White, a hairdresser, who was born there on 25 April 1792 at 3.45 a.m. 'On Monday the 8th of September, 1817, he requested me to calculate his Nativity, which I undertook to convince him of the Truth of this venerable Study, being at the same time *aware* that no Man was a greater *enemy* to this Science than himself, neither could any persons pass more *scurrilous reflections*, and *unbecoming Language* on the power of the Celestial Hosts, than himself, and his Relatives . . . I then computed the time when the Native's Death might be expected, but in pointing out that solemn period, my Judgment was traduced, by the *hardened Infidel*, the *censorious Critic*, and the *Vulgar.*'

Worsdale predicted that White would die at the age of thirty-three. '. . . according to the Judgment I publicly delivered seven Years before his demise, the truth of which can at any time be proved; he died on the 18th April, 1825, at Noon, aged thirty-three Years nearly.'[1]

The case of Mary Dickson (*b.* 1 February 1798 at 3.48 a.m.) is of particular interest because of the possibility that her death by drowning might not have occurred if Worsdale had not suggested it to her. 'On the fifth of August, 1822, she, (in company with some of her Female Friends,)

[1] John Worsdale, *Celestial Philosophy*, [1828], pp. 109–18.

came to my House, and requested me to answer a few questions on her Nativity; she produced the correct time of her Birth, and observed, that she did not place confidence in such things, as she had never known any *proof* to give satisfaction; she asked me if I could inform her of the time of her Marriage, and whether she was likely to live happy in that State, to which I answered, that I was confident she would never enter into the Matrimonial Union; she said she was sorry that I should give such a false Judgment, as she expected to Marry in the ensuing Spring; my reply was, that I had substantial reasons (though they were of an *important and delicate nature,*) to prove the truth of my affirmation, which in a few Months would be verified . . . I then informed her that *something* of an *awful nature* would occur, before the Month of March, then next ensuing, which would destroy Life . . . she *laughed immoderately*, and said, she placed no confidence in my observations; I told her that it was with *deep regret* that I beheld the *terrific Astral Causes* in her Geniture, the *Effects* of which were fast approaching, but none of my admonitions had any influence on her Mind . . . before she left me she said in a *jocular way*, that as I had given my Judgment on the shortness of her Life, (if she thought proper to believe it), she wished to be informed of the quality of Death; I told her that it appeared to me, that *Drowning* would be the cause of her Dissolution.'[1]

Two weeks later Worsdale sent her a message warning her to be careful, but Miss Dickson treated it with derision. However, on 7 January 1823, when on her way from Lincoln to Boston by boat on the River Witham, she fell overboard, 'and when taken out, Life was extinct'.

There was no visible increase of interest in astrology until after 1825. Then it was largely due to the successive efforts of Robert Cross Smith and Richard James Morrison, both of whom were born in 1795. The old-established *Vox Stellarum* almanac was selling in very large numbers (it had an average annual sale of 270,000 copies between 1825–30), but by this time its editor was not above printing predictions taken at random from earlier issues. Indeed, there was hardly a line in *Vox Stellarum* that could have conceivably persuaded anyone actually to study astrology. Smith and Morrison made their mark as astrological publicists because they offered the public a new and more attractive kind of predictive almanac.

Smith was the first to appear on the scene. Of modest antecedents, he arrived in London from Bristol in *c.* 1822 and found employment, probably as clerk, with a builder in Upper Thames Street. He had already been interested in astrology for some years. One of his earliest acquaintances in London was G. W. Graham (*b.* 1784), who was soon to make his mark as a well-known professional balloonist. Graham, who was the contemporary equivalent of a champion motor-racing driver, pursued

[1] Ibid., pp. 120–1.

unconventional interests, including alchemy and astrology. He took a fancy to Smith, introduced him to his friends and encouraged him to become a professional astrologer. Indeed, he gave him financial assistance for a period while he was building up a connection.

Smith observed in Graham's horoscope 'an inclination to abstruse studies . . . the native having gone to very considerable lengths in occult philosophy, particularly in the *alchemical art and the transmutation of metals*, in which science I have been witness to some very curious experiments of his performing.'[1]

In 1822 they collaborated in writing a strange little 24-page tract on geomantic fortune-telling. This was *The Philosophical Merlin*, 'being the translation of a valuable manuscript formerly in the possession of Napoleon Bonaparte'. Smith was in the habit of 'discovering' pseudo-Napoleonic manuscripts, and was as assiduous in attributing occult interests to Napoleon as a later generation was in connection with Adolf Hitler. Their pamphlet was dedicated to 'the Famous and Renowned Mademoiselle Le Normand', a notorious Parisian fortune-teller.[2]

It was more by accident than design that Smith became the founder of modern popular astrological journalism. It happened in this manner. On 3 June 1824 an unidentified publisher and editor brought out the first number of a new weekly periodical called *The Straggling Astrologer* (16 pages for 4*d*.). The idea of a weekly journal exclusively devoted to astrology was completely novel. No. 4 bore the publishing imprint of William Charlton Wright, of 65 Paternoster Row, who reduced the price to 3*d*., probably in order to stimulate an already flagging circulation.

Smith appears to have been appointed editor towards the end of July. No. 9 (31 July) contained an announcement to the effect that the magazine had been 'honoured with some astrological MSS. appertaining to the lot of individuals of the highest rank by Her Royal Highness the Princess of Cumberland . . . who has, we are persuaded, been most unjustly persecuted'. The 'Princess' was the eccentric Mrs Olivia Serres, whose claim to be the legitimate daughter of the Duke of Cumberland, George III's brother, was never officially recognised. Astrology's later annals record the names of many bogus 'Doctors' and even a 'Countess' or two, but Mrs Serres provides an unique example of an Astrologer Princess. Readers who may have looked forward to intimate disclosures of high life in court circles were to be disappointed, for the lady's articles were very dull.

Smith hoped to hit a popular note. Thus the third instalment of 'Astrological Observations founded on the Testimony of Ages, relative to Marriage and Procreation' (No. 11, 14 August) enabled the reader to

[1] [R. C. Smith], *The Astrologer of the Nineteenth Century*, 7th [*sic*] edition, 1825, p. 440.
[2] Marie-Anne Adélaïde Le Normand (1772–1843). See A. Marquiset, *La célèbre Mlle. Le Normand*, Paris, 1911.

'discover if the female you are about to wed be a virgin'. This was too much for W. C. Wright who announced in the next issue that 'the Publisher regrets that several objectionable articles have, inadvertently, during his absence from town, crept into the preceding numbers. Care will, in future, be taken, that nothing offensive to the dignity of the Fair Sex will ever be inserted.'

No. 12, published on 21 August, was presented to the subscribers with a new style of title and the announcement of a veritable regiment of editorial collaborators. *The Straggling Astrologer of the Nineteenth Century* was now alleged to be conducted by 'the celebrated Mademoiselle Le Normand, of Paris, H.R.H. The Princess Olive of Cumberland, the Members of the Mercurii, the Editor of The Prophetic Almanack, and other Celebrated Astrologers'. The mixture, however, was much the same as before: the Princess contributed further prosy 'Astrological Fragments' and a brief analysis of George III's horoscope was signed 'by Raphael'. This was the first appearance of Smith's subsequently famous pseudonym. There was nothing from the pen of Mademoiselle Le Normand. She was probably not even aware that her illustrious name was being used. The Mercurii belonged to a small astrological society of which Smith was president.[1]

A more notable innovation was 'The Weekly Astrological Calendar: founded on Celestial Influence', with headings for Love and Marriage, Business and Gain, and Travel. This was the first *weekly* predictive feature in the history of astrological journalism.

When *The Straggling Astrologer* ceased publication on 30 October 1824, W. C. Wright still had a sizeable stock of unsold sheets on his hands. These were bound and issued in book form in 1825 as the sixth (!) edition of *The Astrologer of the Nineteenth Century*. In the meantime he commissioned Smith to prepare a so-called seventh edition of the same work. This was also ready in 1825 but owing to temporary financial difficulties Wright was obliged to transfer the publication to Knight & Lacey. The new book contained a lot of material that had already been published in *The Straggling Astrologer* with the addition of chapters on such topics as magical charms and ceremonies, geomancy and ghosts. Smith was one of the first of a long succession of hack writers on occultism that have abounded since the beginning of the nineteenth century. His current journalistic and literary activities found little favour among the contemporary 'scientific' astrologers, who objected to his efforts to present their art in a popular form. One of them suggested that it was highly desirable to 'prevent a rational and valuable science from being confounded with the thing called by certain persons Popular Astrology',

---

[1] 'The members thereof are at present but few and select . . . The place where these scientific gentlemen at present meet must, as yet, remain a secret.' (No. 22, 30 October 1824.)

adding that 'we have certainly no wish to injure any person in the public opinion, but when we have a parcel of nonsense palmed on the public as Astrology, we consider ourselves justified in exposing the situation'.[1]

Discouraged by the failure of *The Straggling Astrologer* and the criticisms of his astrologer colleagues, Smith 'resolved on abandoning the science of Astrology altogether, and was accordingly about taking a coffee-house in Poland Street, but owing to the lack of pecuniary finance he was compelled to abandon this project'.[2]

In the meantime W. C. Wright was back in business again and commissioned Smith to write a new predictive almanac. This was *The Prophetic Messenger*, of which the first issue (for 1827) was published in November 1826.[3] Wright disposed of the first printing of the *PM* within a week and immediately ordered a fresh supply. During the remainder of Smith's lifetime—he died in 1832—the almanac's circulation steadily increased. Nevertheless, by comparison with *Vox Stellarum* it still represented a small-scale publishing operation. The reason for its success was that its contents largely consisted of astrological predictions, the most important novelty being forecasts for every day of the year. In this respect it offered far more than *Vox Stellarum*.

Henceforth Smith achieved a modest measure of fame under his pseudonym Raphael, which appeared on the *PM*'s title-page, and his professional astrological practice developed in a satisfactory manner. At the same time he was an industrious writer.[4] John Varley, the famous water-colour painter, who was devoted to astrology, introduced him to William Blake shortly before the latter's death in August 1827.[5]

When Smith died on 26 February 1832 there was an immediate and even unseemly interest in the future of *PM* since the copyright, which had been his property, already had a modest value. An astrologer by the name of Dixon immediately approached Smith's widow and was informed that

[1] Preface to the bound edition of *The Spirit of Partridge*, 1825. This short-lived periodical was published in opposition to *The Straggling Astrologer* by members of The London Astrological Society (17 numbers, 5 August 1824–15 January 1825).

[2] *The True Prophetic Messenger for 1833*, p. 88.

[3] The *PM* derived its title from *The Prophetic Almanac*, a property which Wright had acquired in 1824. Four issues had previously been published by Baldwin, Craddock & Joy. Wright was responsible for the 1825 edition. The publication then passed to Knight & Lacey and died.

[4] Raphael's publications included *The Manual of Astrology*, 1828, *The Familiar Astrologer*, 1828, and fortune-telling books such as *The Royal Book of Fate*, 1829, *The Royal Book of Dreams*, 1830, and *Raphael's Witch*, 1831.

[5] Varley was the author of a *Treatise on Zodiacal Physiognomy*, 1828. It was his intention to issue the work in four parts but only the first was published. It contains descriptions of the alleged physical characteristics of persons born under Aries, Taurus and Gemini, also the well-known 'Ghost of a Flea' engraving by John Linnell after a drawing by William Blake. 'The Ghost of a Flea', according to Varley, 'agrees in countenance with a certain class of persons under Gemini, which sign is the significator of the Flea, whose brown colour is appropriate to the colour of the eyes of some full-toned Gemini persons.' See the illustration facing p. 52.

'two pupils of her late husband had offered their services to write the *Prophetic Messenger* for 1833'. Dixon was astonished for, as he subsequently wrote: 'On hearing this statement I could not forbear smiling at the idea that two young men, who had received only a few lessons from Raphael, shortly previous to his illness, should have the temerity in writing on so intricate a subject as that of mundane affairs.'[1]

The interlopers were John Palmer, who was employed in a chemist's shop in Duke Street, Piccadilly, and P. Moody, a messenger at the House of Lords. Palmer, like Smith, was a native of Bristol and was born there on 28 May 1807. He had recently returned from Paris where he claimed to have studied under Nicolas Vauquelin (1763–1839), the distinguished professor of chemistry at the Ecole de Médecine.[2]

Palmer and Moody were quickly off the mark as far as Mrs Smith was concerned, because Raphael can hardly have been laid in his coffin before Moody sent her a peremptory note. It read: 'I object to a mask being taken of Smith's face—*because it will give his death too great a publicity at present*—the full grounds I stated last night. Mrs Smith will use her own discretion after this; at any rate I should not agree to a cast being taken of his whole head.' They had good reasons for preventing the news of Smith's death from becoming too widely known: Smith had departed but it was intended that Raphael should survive. Dixon hoped to become Raphael the Second but Palmer and Moody had already staked their claim.

Dixon decided to write a *Prophetic Messenger* for 1833, 'in order to prevent the public from being so grossly imposed upon, as I understand it is the intention of the two aforesaid young men to write the "Prophetic" for 1833, for W. C. Wright, which publication will be *said* to be written by Raphael! I thought it proper to premise this much, and put the public in possession of the facts, in order to prevent the dissemination of such trash as cannot fail to emanate from the hands of those who have yet to learn their ABC in astrology.'[3]

For 1833, however, there were not two but *three* rival almanacs incorporating the word 'Prophetic' in their titles, although the third was not a serious competitor to those produced by the Palmer-Moody partnership and Dixon. This was *The Royal Prophetic Annual*, an eight-page catchpenny publication issued by John Catnach, a well-known manufacturer of popular chap-books. True to his usual form, Catnach promised his readers 'Awful Predictions' on the title-page. Dixon's was *The True Prophetic Almanac* for 1833 'by Raphael'. Its contents closely resembled

---

[1] Mundane affairs: general as opposed to personal predictions, e.g., relating to nations or states.

[2] Brief autobiographical information relating to John Palmer will be found in the 1837 edition of *The Prophetic Messenger*. Moody was an Extra Door Keeper at the House of Lords in 1833 and eventually became Head Messenger. He died in *c.* 1876.

[3] *The True Prophetic Messenger for 1833*, p. 90.

those of previous editions of the authentic *PM*, even to the extent of copying the titles and typographical style of the first Raphael's principal editorial features. At this point Dixon disappears from the contemporary astrological scene.

There is nothing to distinguish the first *PM* edited by Palmer from those produced by his predecessor. Nor is there anything in the 1833 or subsequent editions to suggest that Moody collaborated with him. On the title-page Palmer described himself as 'Professor of Chemistry and Mathematics'. The 1833 almanac contained a brief announcement of Raphael I's death and the statement that the present edition had been published for the benefit of his widow and children. Palmer died in 1837. By this time W. C. Wright appears to have purchased the copyright. He continued to publish the almanac until he died in 1858.

The representative astrological publicist during the first four decades of the Victorian era was undoubtedly Richard James Morrison, who used the pseudonym Zadkiel. Like R. C. Smith he was born in 1795, which was a vintage year for astrologers—Smith was born on 19 March, Dixon on 28 March and Morrison on 15 June. He was of genteel birth. His male grandfather had been a sea captain in the service of the East India Company and his father, Richard Caleb Morrison, was for many years one of George III's gentlemen pensioners. R. J. Morrison joined the Royal Navy in 1806 at the tender age of eleven, was on active service against the French fleet in the Mediterranean in 1810–11, received a lieutenant's commission in March 1815 and retired on half-pay in 1817. In 1827–9 he was an officer in the Coast Guard but left the service when he married a niece of Sir R. Joshua Paul, an Irish baronet, by whom he had nine children.[1]

Morrison was on friendly terms with R. C. Smith and was a member of The Mercurii in 1824. His first contribution to astrological literature, a letter signed 'John Partridge junior', was published in *The Spirit of Partridge* (No. 8) in the same year. He was living at Liverpool when he became a professional astrologer in 1830. Realising, from Smith's example, the publicity value attached to a successful predictive almanac, he began to publish *The Herald of Astrology* (its title was changed to *Zadkiel's Almanac* in 1836) in competition with Raphael's *Prophetic Messenger*. He was the sole proprietor of this publication, which was soon to have a larger annual sale than the rival *Prophetic Messenger*.[2]

[1] For details of Morrison's career see *The Dictionary of National Biography* and Christopher Cooke, *Curiosities of Occult Literature*, 1863.

[2] Successive price reductions enabled *ZA* to achieve a circulation lead over *PM*. Morrison initially charged 2s. 6d. for 72 pages. *PM*'s price was then 2s 9d. In 1835 he reduced the price to 1s. for 48 pages. A further reduction in 1847 enabled *ZA*'s readers to buy the almanac for 6d. and by 1870 they were receiving 84 pages for this modest sum. Raphael's *PM* did not compete in price until 1877 when it was sold for 6d. without the annual ephemeris or 1s. if the purchaser required the latter.

The sociological importance of these two almanacs should not be underestimated. Their combined circulations never approached *Vox Stellarum*'s 1839 peak of 560,000 copies, but they were in any case reaching a different market. By the 1830s nobody who wanted to know 'what the stars foretell' would have consulted *Vox Stellarum* because the 'genuine' information, compiled by acknowledged experts, was offered in far greater detail by Raphael or Zadkiel. What must be emphasised is that year after year, indeed decade after decade, these popular publications provided a perennial reminder of astrology's survival. Publicity of this kind brought new recruits to the ranks of the amateur practitioners and clients to the professionals.[1] I have already mentioned that this enduring public awareness of astrology was an exclusively British phenomenon, since these predictive almanacs had no counterparts elsewhere.

The contents of 'Zadkiel' and 'Raphael' followed a well-defined pattern. There were the indispensable 'predictions', always so vaguely worded that some of them were inevitably 'fulfilled'; accounts of the current astral prospects of members of the royal family or eminent persons in the public eye; also articles of a more general nature. In the latter context *Zadkiel's Almanac* is of particular interest because here the fruits of Morrison's peculiar, even eccentric, erudition are to be found cheek by jowl with hazardous predictions and strange cosmological theories.[2] Morrison was familiar with many recondite subjects and undoubtedly contributed to the education of some of his readers. It must be remembered that the almanacs were carefully read in many humble homes, particularly in country districts, at a time when little public entertainment was available. Morrison evidently supposed that some of his readers had a working knowledge of Latin, Greek, Hebrew and higher mathematics. Thus it is possible that *Zadkiel's Almanac* played a more important part in the field of adult education during the Victorian era than has been generally realised. Whatever the case may be, the almanac's contents, considered as a whole, vividly reflected its proprietor's unconventional personality.

Morrison was more concerned than any of his predecessors with the social standing of astrology and its professional practitioners. There were two reasons: firstly his awareness of a growing undercurrent of opposition to professional astrology, which was naturally equated with fortune-telling; secondly his own anomalous position, which compelled him to walk a perpetual tight-rope between respectability and illegality. As Lieutenant Morrison, R.N., a highly-educated man with a wide range of

---

[1] In 1960 I asked the late E. H. Bailey, then a very elderly man and formerly a well-known professional, how he had discovered astrology. 'I used to read "Zadkiel" when I was a boy,' he replied.

[2] See Morrison's *The Solar System as it is, and not as it is represented*, [1857] and *The New Principia, or The True System of Astronomy*, 1868. He supposed, for instance, that the Earth is the stationary centre of the solar system and the Sun only 365,000½ miles distant.

rational and irrational interests, he became well known in London society and was welcomed in a good many fashionable houses until the circumstances of the Morrison *v.* Belcher libel action in 1863, which he won, tarnished his reputation. The role of Zadkiel, the professional astrologer and editor of a popular predictive almanac, had to be played with discretion. It is likely that the majority of those who were acquainted with Morrison had no idea that he was Zadkiel.

He moved from Liverpool to Gloucestershire in 1834 and for the next ten years resided in the neighbourhood of Gloucester and Cheltenham.[1] The local inhabitants soon became aware of his astrological interests. His 1837 almanac mentioned a recent 'public discussion, held before some hundreds of respectable persons', at Cheltenham. An increasing volume of local chatter about the Lieutenant and astrology led to an attack by T. H. Moody, the author of a tedious *Refutation of Astrology*, Cheltenham, 1838, who objected to astrological beliefs on religious grounds. Moody mentioned that he had been 'informed by two gentlemen well known to Lieutenant Morrison, that the minds of several people in Cheltenham have been rendered unhappy by astrological predictions, and because the works of that gentleman are publicly vended in our town and other parts of England'. Twenty-five years later the *Daily Telegraph* was to complain that Zadkiel's prophecies were 'calculated to alarm the timied and mislead the credulous'.

Much as Moody deplored Morrison's activities, he found those of Philip Wood, who lived nearby at Stroudwater and who called himself 'Professor of the Divine and Celestial Science in accordance with Scripture, reason and mathematics', even more reprehensible. In the *Cheltenham Free Press* (31 October 1835) Wood advertised 'Celestial articles, viz. talismans, vigils [sc. sigils], and amulets prepared according to the genuine principles of Divine and celestial magic, for the removal or mitigation of the malignant influences of the heavenly bodies'.[2]

Morrison was never greatly worried by the criticisms of people like Moody because he, too, felt himself to be a good Christian. Scientific objections to astrology were something different and required answering. Hence objective proof could best be supplied, in his opinion, by demonstrating that planetary influences affected weather conditions. Here he followed in the footsteps of his seventeenth-century predecessors, such as John Gadbury who wrote about weather astrology in his *Nauticum Astrologicum, or the Astrological Seaman, directing Merchants, Marriners, &c., how (by God's blessing) they may escape divers Dangers which commonly happen in the Ocean*, 1691. Astro-meteorology was studied by Morrison and

---

[1] In the meantime he had published *The Grammar of Astrology*, 1833, and nineteen issues of *The Horoscope: A Weekly Miscellany of Astrology* (8 pages for 1½d., 1834).

[2] Similar but 'unconsecrated' articles at prices ranging from £6–£20, i.e. Sun, Venus, Runic and other talismans, are currently advertised by the Hermann Bauer Verlag at Freiburg i. Br., Germany.

other British astrologers until it ceased to be fashionable towards the end
of the nineteenth century. He became a member of the orthodox London
Meteorological Society and was elected to its council in March 1840.

In February 1843 J. Bradshaw, a Manchester astrologer, was prosecuted
for fortune-telling. In order to raise funds for his defence and similar
contingencies Morrison announced in his 1844 almanac the foundation of
the British Association for the Advancement of Astral and Other Sciences,
and a year later claimed 107 subscribers. Bradshaw was probably more
or less respectable or Morrison would not have wished to come to his
assistance. By this time, however, a number of disreputable charlatans
had appeared on the astrological scene.

'To those numerous parties who complain to us of the failure of
Astrologers to whom they have paid five shillings for a nativity, or half a
crown for a question,[1] we would once and for all say that no man of
education would stoop to receive such beggarly remuneration as that. All
the large towns of the Kingdom are full of ignorant fellows, who pretend
to know astrology, but who cannot even write their own names, or do a
rule of three sum . . . In the meantime we advise our friends to shun
every thing in the form of an Astrologer who cannot produce a Diploma
printed on parchment, and bearing the seal of the British Association for
Astral Science, which every educated and respectable Astrologer in the
Kingdom now possesses.'

The Association cannot have had a long life, since he did not refer to it
again in the almanac. This is the first known attempt to 'organise' astrologers on a professional basis. There were to be many more, particularly
in Germany, almost a century later.

Morrison moved from Gloucestershire to London in 1846–7. (He had
latterly resided at Shepscombe House at Painswick, a village about six
miles south-east of Gloucester. The house is still there.) Between the
years 1848–62 his approximate location can be traced from the current
address in the almanac of a fictitious Mr Samuel Smith.[2]

From 1847 onwards the almanac's cover and title-page stated that its
author was 'Zadkiel, Tao Sze'. According to Christopher Cooke, 'the
word Zadkiel or Zedekiel, means the Angel of Genius of the planet
Jupiter. Tao Sze means Doctor of Reason.'[3] An earlier but isolated use of

---

[1] 'Half a crown for a question': the reference is to *horary* astrology, in which a
horoscope is cast for the actual moment that a question is asked or received, i.e. by
mail. It was widely used until the end of the nineteenth century when it fell into dis-
favour. Alan Leo described it as 'the curse of the science and the ruin of the astrologer'.
(*Modern Astrology*, November 1896.)

[2] Smith's addresses: 1848, 11 Dudley Place, Paddington; 1849, Acre Lane, Clapham;
1850, 23 Middle Street, Cloth Fair, Clerkenwell; 1851, Reading; 1853–61, Post Office,
Brompton. The 1849 almanac stated 'Personal interviews declined', but when Zadkiel
was living at Reading he advertised his willingness to receive pupils wishing to learn
astronomy and astrology as guests in his house for a few weeks.

[3] Christopher Cooke, *Astrology in a Nutshell*, 1862, p. 27.

THE

𝖘𝖙𝖗𝖆𝖌𝖌𝖑𝖎𝖓𝖌 𝕬𝖘𝖙𝖗𝖔𝖑𝖔𝖌𝖊𝖗

OF THE NINETEENTH CENTURY;

(Late " The STRAGGLING ASTROLOGER ;")

OR, MAGAZINE OF CELESTIAL INTELLIGENCES:

CONDUCTED BY THE CELEBRATED

MADEMOISELLE LE NORMAND,

OF PARIS,

H. R. H. THE PRINCESS OLIVE OF CUMBERLAND,

𝕿𝖍𝖊 𝕸𝖊𝖒𝖇𝖊𝖗𝖘 𝖔𝖋 𝖙𝖍𝖊 𝕸𝖊𝖗𝖈𝖚𝖗𝖎𝖎,

THE EDITOR OF THE PROPHETIC ALMANACK,

AND OTHER CELEBRATED ASTROLOGERS.

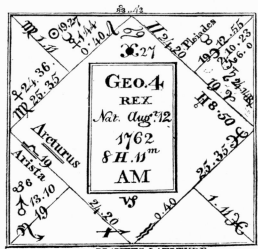

PLANETS LATITUDE.

ℍ 0.40. S. ♄ 2.383. ♃ 1⁹8. ♂1.26 S.♀0 45 N. ☿ 1.30 S. ☊ 0.30 N

HIEROGLYPHIC—No. XII.

HOROSCOPE OF HIS MAJESTY GEORGE IV.

CONTENTS.

PUBLISHED EVERY SATURDAY, BY WILLIAM CHARLTON WRIGHT,
65, PATERNOSTER ROW, LONDON.

Printed by A. SWEETING, 21, Aldersgate Street.

No. 12. *August* 21, 1824.—*Three-pence.*   N

1. The first weekly astrological periodical to
be published in any language (London, 1824).

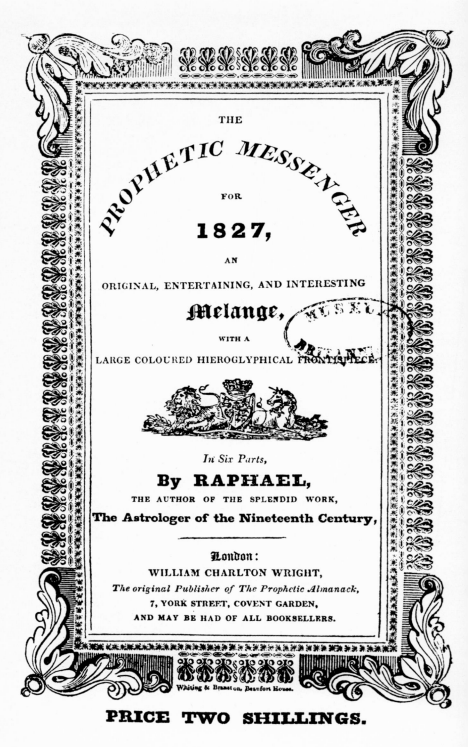

THE

PROPHETIC MESSENGER

FOR

1827,

AN

ORIGINAL, ENTERTAINING, AND INTERESTING

Melange,

WITH A

LARGE COLOURED HIEROGLYPHICAL FRONTISPIECE.

In Six Parts,

By RAPHAEL,

THE AUTHOR OF THE SPLENDID WORK,

The Astrologer of the Nineteenth Century,

London:

WILLIAM CHARLTON WRIGHT,

The original Publisher of The Prophetic Almanack,

7, YORK STREET, COVENT GARDEN,

AND MAY BE HAD OF ALL BOOKSELLERS.

Whiting & Branston, Beaufort House.

PRICE TWO SHILLINGS.

2. The first astrological almanac to contain 'predictions' for every day of the year (London, 1827).

the title Tao Sze can be found in the preface to the 1844 almanac, together with a swastika symbol.[1]

It was the Copestick affair at Bath, involving the prosecution and imprisonment of Francis D. Copestick, a local professional astrologer, that brought Christopher Cooke, a young London solicitor, into close touch with Morrison, and to his own lasting disadvantage.[2] Cooke first encountered Morrison at a phrenologist's consulting room in Piccadilly in 1847, but apparently did not have any conversation with him, heard him lecture on astrology in the same year and soon acquired a second-hand volume of the first (1834) series of Zadkiel's periodical *The Horoscope*. He later wrote that 'the book explained the connection supposed to exist between phrenological science and Astrology . . . and, as I had paid some attention to Phrenology, or rather to Physiognomy, as explained in the works of Dr Combe and Mr G. Combe, and in other publications, my interest in "The Horoscope" was increased.'[3]

Cooke applied to Zadkiel for a delineation of his horoscope in 1849 and received two 'readings', for which he paid £10. (The fee was high in relation to the contemporary value of money. At that time a journeyman compositor, traditionally a highly-paid craftsman, earned about £2 per week.) In October 1851 he received yet another delineation and during the same month wrote twice to Zadkiel for answers to 'horary' questions. Whether or not he ever sent Zadkiel a lock of his hair is not known. Zadkiel's 1849 almanac contained an interesting proposition relating to applicants for 'horary' information: 'If a lock of hair be sent by the querent, it renders the sympathy more decided, for it is a part of his person, and is equivalent to a personal application.' The links between modern radiesthetic ('The Box'!) theories and old magical traditions are closer than one might expect.

By the autumn of 1851 Morrison must have been aware that Cooke was a solicitor. A few weeks later the Copestick case, with all its implications as far as the legal position of professional astrologers was concerned, was absorbing much of his time. Francis Copestick had a small bookselling business at Bath. The recent publication of *Copestick's Prophetic Annual*,

---

[1] The earliest literary allusion to the swastika symbol in the *Oxford English Dictionary* is dated 1871. The 'esoteric' significance of the swastika does not appear to have been discussed in Germany until *c.* 1895, e.g. by Alfred Schuler (1865–1931). See his *Fragmente und Vorträge aus dem Nachlass*, with an introduction by Ludwig Klages, Leipzig, 1940. The Nazis adopted a symbol already well known in *völkisch* circles.

[2] Christopher Cooke was educated at Harrow School and admitted as a solicitor in 1844. He lived with his mother at 2 Upper Grosvenor Street, a fashionable address, and practised at 12 Southampton Buildings, Chancery Lane.

[3] Christopher Cooke, *Curiosities of Occult Literature*, 1863, p. 5. It was largely through George Combe (1788–1858) and his younger brother Andrew (1797–1843) that the teachings of F. J. Gall and, in particular, of K. K. Spurzheim attracted widespread attention in Great Britain after 1820. Phrenology was not only fashionable in the 1850s, but far better known than astrology. It is now almost forgotten although there is still a British Phrenological Society (founded in 1886).

Celestial Intelligencer and Weather Guide had attracted the attention of the local police, for in it he advertised 'the whole of the directions, trigono-metrically calculated for life' for £2, meaning a set of long-range predic-tions.   A plain-clothes police officer, accompanied by a woman *agent provocateur*, visited him at his home, requested him to answer some horary questions, paid him with marked money and then charged him under the Vagrant Act of 1824.[1]   The case was tried by the Bath magi-strates in December 1851.   Copestick was sentenced to a month in prison but was released pending an appeal before the Recorder at the next Quarter Sessions.   The Recorder confirmed the sentence on 10 January 1852.   Morrison went to Bath to give evidence in Copestick's favour.

At this time Morrison had recently moved to London from Reading and was living at 1 Milborne Grove in the Boltons district of Fulham.   He was now in close touch with Lord Robert Grosvenor, with whom he had become acquainted when the latter was President of the London Meteoro-logical Society, and discussed the Copestick business with him.   Grosvenor and William Ewart, a radical liberal, agreed to present a petition, which Morrison had drafted, to the House of Commons requesting certain amendments to the Vagrant Act.   This was done but nothing resulted. Morrison hoped to make it legal for *resident householders*, as opposed to 'idle and disorderly persons', to practise astrology professionally in their own homes.   In that event his own unsatisfactory position would at last have been regularised.

Cooke's personal acquaintance with Morrison began on 1 April 1852 when he visited Milborne Grove for the first time.   'The Seer', as Cooke often called him, had also invited William Sharp Cross, a barrister who was deeply interested in astrology.[2]   Cooke now became Morrison's close associate in a number of risky business ventures.   A decade later, when he heartily regretted that he had ever become acquainted with Morrison, he explained that the latter had completely convinced him that public recogni-tion of astrology's truth and, if necessary, legality was only just round the corner.   The disillusioned Cooke wrote: 'If he [i.e. Morrison] had never been an astrologer his position in society would have been higher than it is . . . I was impressed with the idea, which the experience of years has shown to be erroneous, that Astrology was more understood and more in vogue than really was or is the case.   Lieutenant Morrison's sanguine

[1] The astrologers had never forgotten the unhappy fate of Thomas White, also of Bath, who was arrested in much the same circumstances in the Isle of Wight in 1813. White was sentenced to prison for a year and died at Winchester gaol.

[2] W. S. Cross (1812–61) was sixth Wrangler at Cambridge in 1835. He contributed a number of articles to the second series of Zadkiel's *The Horoscope*, 1841, under the pseudonyms 'Scrutator' and 'Herschel', and was the author of *Reasons for Belief in Judicial Astrology*, 1849, which was published anonymously. Unlike his legal colleague Cooke, he had the good sense to be discreet about his astrological interests. A. G. Trent (i.e. Richard Garnett) wrote a biographical sketch which was published in *The Horo-scope*, Vol. 1, No. 3, 1903.

correspondence misled me in this respect, for even in October 1851 he stated that he daily found "persons of education and of good standing in society" including (*mirabile dictu!*) the editor of a London periodical, "to take up the science" and feel interested in its progress.'[1]

In 1853 Cooke began work on his book *A Plea for Urania* and subsidised its publication to the extent of £200 in 1854. It failed to sell more than 250 copies—he asked only 5s. for 388 pages—during the next six years and the sheet stock was jobbed off by his publisher for $4\frac{1}{2}d$. a copy without his knowledge or consent while he was in the U.S.A. in 1859. Cooke deserved a greater success for he had, in fact, written the first *readable* account of the astrological thesis to be published during the nineteenth century.

At the time that Cooke was busy writing *A Plea for Urania* he was also heavily involved as solicitor, investor and intermediary in various company promoting activities in which Morrison played a leading role. In the preface to *Curiosities of Occult Literature*, 1863, he said that he had not published 'a twentieth part of the correspondence connected with the three public companies mentioned in this volume . . . these companies, by reason of the astrological principle connected with them, and which might be elucidated by evidence, are removed from the ordinary track of speculations, in my opinion'.

Unfortunately Cooke never defined the nature of the 'astrological principle' behind The Wellington Telescope Company, the Emperor Life Assurance Society, or the coal-mining ventures in south Wales in which he speedily lost two-thirds of his own modest capital of £10,000. As for Morrison's part in these enterprises, today he would hardly escape prosecution for fraudulent misrepresentation. A combination of naïvete, optimism and excessive self-confidence, and possibly the inability to read his own stars, led the Lieutenant astray.

I have no room for a detailed account, as told by Cooke, of the history of the three companies mentioned above. The Wellington Telescope Company project, which was never realised, involved the manufacture and subsequent erection of a very large telescope in the vicinity of the Crystal Palace at Sydenham. Morrison was particularly anxious that Lord Brougham (1778–1868), the statesman, should lend his name to the enterprise. He had good reasons for not wanting to approach Brougham himself and employed Cooke as an intermediary. Brougham refused to become involved and Cooke later realised that his negative attitude sprang from his awareness that Morrison was identical with the anonymous Zadkiel who had published some disobliging remarks about him in *The Horoscope* as long ago as August 1834.

---

[1] The editor was William Charles Kent (1823–1902), who became proprietor of the *Sun* evening newspaper in 1850. On 19 January 1852 he published a leading article condemning the prosecution and imprisonment of Copestick.

'The evil Saturn in the ascendant', wrote Zadkiel, 'causes a great deficiency of personal beauty; in fact the native's face is what might be called plain. The Infortune in the ascendant causes also some defect in the *face* and this is the case. His Lordship has a nervous catching or twitching, which rarely allows him to be many minutes without drawing up the muscles of the face and mouth in a peculiarly disagreeable manner. Having repeatedly sat in his Lordship's company, we can vouch for the reality of this statement.'

The Emperor Life Assurance Society was in due course promoted and eventually achieved a precarious solvency. By this time Morrison, who had been its first chairman, had long since disappeared from the scene and Cooke had been obliged to spend countless unprofitable hours on the company's business. The coal-mining venture, in which a large sum of money had been invested by Morrison's friends, was hopelessly bankrupt by 1856, but this fact did not deter Morrison from advertising that 'any person with £4,000 might make £6,000 a year without risk'.

Cooke abandoned his never very satisfactory legal practice in 1859 and went to the U.S.A. for some months. When he returned to London he was soon in touch with Morrison again. The Lieutenant was still hoping to make astrology socially and scientifically acceptable and was endeavouring to found yet another society for this purpose. His current plan for a Congress of Astronomers and Friends of Astral Science came to nothing, but during the summer of 1860 he and W. H. White, who had been secretary of the now defunct London Meteorological Society, founded the Astro-Meteorological Society, which held its inaugural meeting at Cooke's rooms at 58 Pall Mall on 29 November. In the meantime Cooke had renewed his practising certificate and had agreed to act as the Society's solicitor. The new society flourished mildly throughout 1861 but, according to Cooke, during the autumn 'some persons left the Society because they maintained that it was connected with astrological science, which was an undeniable fact, although some refined attempts were made to prove the contrary'. The society was dissolved in March 1862 by the unanimous votes of those who attended its final meeting. By this time Morrison had become involved in a major scandal and the remaining astro-meteorologists presumably thought it advisable to sever any public connection with him. Cooke, who had greater reason to be wary of Morrison than most others, also broke with him at this point. 'Circumstances had occurred recently to bring to my mind the annoyances which had resulted from my personal connection with the past schemes of the Lieutenant,' he wrote. The circumstances in question were related to what Cooke called 'The Affair of the Crystal', and involved Morrison in unwelcome publicity of a kind that he had courted for years past but had hitherto always managed to avoid.

The crystal ball used by Morrison for various 'spiritualistic' experiments came into his possession in *c.* 1849. It had previously belonged to the notorious Lady Blessington, who died in Paris in that year. 'Having tested its powers,' he wrote in his 1851 almanac, 'I have resolved on giving my readers an account of this wonderful mode of communicating with the spirits of the dead.' It must be mentioned that Morrison's interest in such communications coincided with the early stages of what Frank Podmore described as 'the classic period of English spiritualism'. Public interest in alleged paranormal phenomena and psychism was beginning to be wide-spread.[1]

Spiritualist trance mediums did not use crystals and may not have been particularly aware of their historical significance in the context of magic and occultism. Morrison was well versed in this area and thought that his own crystal might have been the one used by the famous Dr John Dee during the reign of Elizabeth I. Morrison's crystal was a particularly large one. 'I have been shewn some others,' he wrote, 'but with the exception of the one shewn me by Lord S., they are much smaller. These are said to be consecrated to the Angels of the planets, and are, therefore, far less powerful than Lady Blessington's Crystal; which, being consecrated to the Archangel of the SUN, *Michael*, may be consulted during four hours each day, whereas the others can generally be used only for a very brief space of time; nor can very potent spirits be called into them or made to render themselves visible.' He stated that 'in this large crystal spirits appeared without being "called", as is usual . . . They gave us most *important information of the actual existence of the soul after death, and of the state in which it exists and will exist until the Judgment* . . . [but] *Astrology* is a much better guide than they [the spirits of the dead] can be. Still, as regards the future affairs of *Nations* they know much.'

Christopher Cooke, who claimed to have been present when 'remarkable visions' were seen in the Blessington crystal, explained the connection between skrying and astrology: 'This subject is connected with astrological science, as it is believed that the moon influences crystals, and that crystals should be used according to the planets to which they are consecrated, and which influence, or are supposed to influence, a certain day of the week, and hour of the day and night. This subject is also connected with Astrology because persons born under certain planetary configurations have the gift and power to divine by this mode of divination; and the remark applies to both sexes, although the power is comparatively rare with men. It is common with children—boys and girls.'[2] As to the 'charging' of crystals, he mentioned that 'the general idea is to consecrate the crystal by means of certain invocations or prayers, and to give the charge on the day and in the hour when the planet, or rather the influence

[1] A useful historical analysis will be found in F. Podmore, *Modern Spiritualism: A History and a Criticism*, 2 vols., 1902.
[2] Christopher Cooke, *Curiosities of Occult Literature*, 1863, p. 123.

of the planet to which it is intended to dedicate the crystal, rules'.[1]

Morrison himself was not able to summon 'the spirits of the crystal' and first used children as skryers, e.g. one of his own small sons and the grandson of Admiral Sir Thomas Ussher. The 1851–2 almanacs contain lengthy accounts of 'Visions seen in Lady Blessington's Crystal'. A spirit calling himself Orion appeared. 'A tall man with a helmet on, and in armour; a large club in his hand; a bear on its hind legs near him. He is fierce-looking but has a pleasant smile.' Morrison wrote down all that Orion was supposed to have said and two successive almanacs contain no less than twenty-five pages devoted to the platitudes that are typical of such communications. There was no further reference to the crystal until the 1862 edition (written in 1861) when he mentioned that he had experienced difficulty in finding 'seers' but had 'recently been so fortunate as to obtain four excellent adult seers; three of them are ladies and one a gentleman'.

In the early 1850s, however, Morrison could not keep his excitement to himself and wrote to *The Athenaeum* about the skrying experiments. His letters aroused interest and he 'received numbers of letters from the nobility asking for a sight of the crystal ball'. Crystal-gazing sessions were subsequently held at Morrison's house and elsewhere, with his own son and young Ussher acting as skryers. Among those present at various times were the Countess of Erroll, Baron Bunsen (the Prussian ambassador), Admiral Fitzclarence, the Marchioness of Ailesbury, the Bishop of Litchfield, the Earl of Effingham, Lady Egerton of Tatton, the Earl of Wilton and Sir Edward Bulwer Lytton, the famous novelist, who had a great penchant for the occult. The repercussions came a decade later.

For as long as most people could remember Zadkiel, whoever he might be, had been publishing his annual batch of predictions. However, what Cooke described as 'the Seer's free and easy remarks about persons and things in general', were not invariably welcomed by the people concerned. The astrological prospects of the royal family had provided almanac writers with useful copy since time immemorial and this was the case with Zadkiel, who also regularly discussed the current 'directions' of such worthies as the Duke of Wellington, Lord Palmerston, Lord Brougham and other prominent members of the establishment.

In the early 1840s Lord Robert Grosvenor was willing to act as an intermediary between Morrison-Zadkiel and the Prince Consort. Thus on 14 November 1840 Grosvenor wrote to say that he had been 'commanded to convey to you the Prince's thanks for Zadkiel's Almanac for the year 1841. H.R.H. does not know the exact moment of his own birth, but I have taken steps to find out, and if I do I will make it known to you; I trust under a happy influence.' Princess Victoria, the Queen's eldest child, was born on 21 November 1840 and Morrison calculated her

[1] Ibid., p. 127.

nativity. Grosvenor informed him that 'His Royal Highness has been pleased to accept the Horoscope of the Princess Royal, and has ordered me to thank you for it.' Writing from Windsor Castle on 10 December 1842 a Mr Anson acknowledged the receipt of 'the copy of *Zadkiel's Almanac* which has been presented to His Royal Highness by Lord Robert Grosvenor'.[1] Soon, however, Queen Victoria took exception to Zadkiel's annual attentions and under the heading 'Nativity of Her Majesty' the 1847 edition contained the following remark: 'I have said little on this subject lately, because I was informed, from a high quarter, that my predictions have given some uneasiness to a personage for whom I have no other than the highest respect and affection.'

The troubles that descended upon Morrison in 1862–3 were due to the accuracy of certain predictions concerning the Prince Consort and the Prince of Wales that were published in the 1861 almanac, the text of which was written during the summer of 1860. He suggested, for instance, that Saturn's stationary position during 1861 would be 'very evil for all persons born on or near the 26th August; among the sufferers I regret to see the worthy Prince Consort of these realms. Let such persons pay scrupulous attention to health . . .' And for the Prince of Wales: 'The lunation at the end of November, 1860, gives warning of some suffering at hand, but let us hope it will not be violent; 1861 is evil for the father of the native.'

Nor were Lord Palmerston's immediate prospects very cheerful since an eclipse due on 31 December 1861 would be 'very close to the place of the Moon at the birth of Lord Palmerston; the latter can hardly fail, if he live so long, to succumb to fate under such circumstances.' There was also a reference in a similar vein to Lord Brougham. Considering that Palmerston was then about seventy-seven years of age and Brougham past his eightieth birthday, forecasts of this kind were not too foolhardy, but the Prince Consort (*b.* 26 August 1819) was only forty-two and might have been expected to live for a good many more years.

These predictions would probably not have attracted much attention if the Prince Consort had not unexpectedly died on 14 December 1861, and if a certain Alderman Humphery, sitting as a magistrate at the Guildhall, had not happened to mention them in the course of hearing a case that had nothing to do with astrology. His remarks were quoted in a number of London newspapers and Zadkiel was attacked in a leading article in the *Daily Telegraph* of 31 January 1862.

There is a fellow who calls himself Zadkiel, and who for thirty-two years, it seems, has been suffered to publish annually a farrago of wretched trash which he calls an almanac, and in which, pretending to interpret the 'voices of the stars', he gives vent to a mass of predictions on public affairs. Once in every five years or so, one of Zadkiel's prophecies, which are

[1] *Zadkiel's Almanac*, 1864.

generally the stupidest jumping at probable eventualities, may by an accident come true; whereupon the seer goes into raptures of the 'Right again!' description, and sells his almanacs, we are sorry to learn, by thousands. Very recently the public were scandalised to hear that a London alderman, in the very performance of his magisterial functions, had so little respect for the dignity of the Bench as to call the attention of the newspaper reporters to one of Zadkiel's predictions for 1861, which had a hazy kind of coincidence with the death of the Prince Consort. The Almanac has gone up prodigiously in the market, we are told, since Alderman Humphery's ill-advised escapade; but it now becomes the duty of the press to apply a corrective to aldermanic folly, and to expose this Zadkiel in his true colours. Our witty contemporary *Punch* has more than once transfixed the impudent knave with the shafts of his sarcasm; and it shall not be our fault if this mischevious deluder is not in the long run morally tarred and feathered, and has not his ears nailed to the pump.

The leader writer concluded:

We might pass this rubbishing pamphlet by with contempt; but the publicity it has recently attained demands that it and the author, whoever he may be, should be exposed and denounced. The one is a sham, the other is a swindler. The Almanac is no mere harmless catchpenny; its contents are calculated to alarm the timid and to mislead the credulous; and as to the allusion to Lord Palmerston, and the speculations as to the probable duration of the life of that illustrious statesman, we regard them as disgustingly and unspeakably wicked. Who is this Zadkiel, and are there no means of ferreting him out, and hauling him up to Bow-street under the statute as a rogue and a vagabond?

The answer to the question 'Who is this Zadkiel?' arrived at the offices of the *Daily Telegraph* the same day. It was signed 'Anti-Humbug' but was written by Rear-Admiral Sir Edward Belcher. It read:

Sir,—in your impression this day you ask, 'Who is this Zadkiel?' and, 'Are there no means of ferreting him out and hauling him up to Bow-street under the statute as a rogue and a vagabond?' I will aid you on the scent by first informing you that he stands as a Lieutenant in the *Navy List*, seniority 1815; next that he has his admirers about Greenwich Hospital, who fancy him as a prophet A1; and that his mischievous propensities are not solely involved in that foolish publication *Zadkiel's Almanac*. More, I think he gave his name not long since as president of some peculiar society connected with astrology (R. J. Morrison).[1] A friend of mine reminds me that 'the author of *Zadkiel*' is the celebrated crystal globe seer, who gulled many of our nobility about the year 1852'. Making use of a boy under 14, or a girl under 12, he pretended, by their looking into the crystal globe, to hold converse with the spirits of the Apostles—even our Saviour, with all the angels of light as well as darkness, and to tell what was going on in any part of the world. Drawings were made of the objects seen in these visions. One noble lady gave the boy £5 to give her intelligence regarding her boy, who was in the Mediterranean. That boy 'peached'—let the cat out of the bag. Of course the information was false. He took money, if he be really the same, for these profane acts, and made

[1] I.e. the Astro-Meteorological Society.

a good thing of it. If it were deemed sufficiently important there can be no doubt that he could be satisfactorily ferreted out. As to his position as a naval officer, excepting in the Coast Guard he has not served afloat since 1815.

Morrison immediately instructed his solicitor to apply to the *Daily Telegraph* for the name of 'Anti-Humbug' and this was divulged. He demanded that Belcher should publish a retraction in the *Daily Telegraph*, but since no notice was taken he brought a libel action against the Admiral. The case should have been heard in May 1862 but Belcher's lawyers contrived one delay after another in the hope of making the affair so costly for Morrison that he would be obliged to abandon the action. Finally a judge made a special order for the case to be dealt with without further delay and it was heard at the end of June 1863.

At this point, when the Admiral's letter was still being widely discussed early in 1862, Christopher Cooke felt obliged to intervene, not on Morrison's behalf but because, as he subsequently pointed out in *Curiosities of Occult Literature*, 'if Zadkiel and his doctrines were merely an imposition and a chicanery, my costly attempt to make his fraternity respectable and legal, during ten or twelve years of my life, clearly was an act of simple inutility . . . The only justification which I could offer for allowing my name to be connected with such imprudent speculations as the Glamorgan Coal Company, and the Emperor Life Assurance Society in its original state, in conjunction with Lieutenant Morrison—was the testing of the truth of the astrological principle; and if this principle was to be plainly denied . . . all my thirteen years' work was labour lost.'

In March 1862 Cooke quickly wrote a 28-page pamphlet, *Astrology in a Nut Shell, in a Letter to Mr Alderman Humphery on Occult Phenomena connected with the Death of H.R.H. Prince Consort*, where his name appears on the title-page. Although this cautious defence of astrology and analysis of its contemporary legal standing attracted little attention, its publication probably did him more harm than good. He then began work on his book *Curiosities of Occult Literature*, which contained a fairly detailed account of his relationship with Morrison during the past decade and was intended, it would appear, to defend his own somewhat equivocal position. It can hardly have been to Morrison's advantage that it should have been published (at its author's expense) just before his lawsuit against Belcher came up for hearing, since it did not present him in any very favourable light.

The case of Morrison *v.* Belcher was tried by the Lord Chief Justice sitting with a special jury in the Court of Queen's Bench, Guildhall, on 29 June 1863. It was fully but unobjectively reported in *The Times* of 30 June and more fairly in the *Morning Advertiser*. Morrison denied that he had ever received money for showing the crystal or that £5 had been given to the boy. Although *The Times* suppressed their names, nearly all the titled people mentioned on p. 42 appeared as witnesses on Morrison's behalf and confirmed that he had never asked them for money. The Admiral's counsel called no witnesses for the defence but attacked the plaintiff on the score of his predictions in the almanac. The Lord Chief Justice was obviously hostile towards Morrison—there is nothing in *The Times* to suggest that he ever tried to stop the frequent laughter in the courtroom—and in his summing up indicated that he did not consider that Admiral Belcher could prove fraudulent imposture, but nevertheless gave the jury a strong hint that if they found in Morrison's favour the damages awarded to him need not be very great.

Morrison won his case but the jury only gave him 20s. damages and the judge refused him a certificate for costs. However, whereas the print order for the 1861 almanac containing the famous prediction relating to the Prince Consort had been for 38,000 copies, Morrison claimed one of 58,000 copies for the 1864 edition. It was sent to press soon after the court proceedings so the affair was not without its publicity value.

It was unfortunate for Morrison that his final effort to establish an astrological periodical coincided with the publication of Admiral Belcher's letter in January 1862, for in that month he published the first and only issue of Zadkiel's *Voice of the Stars*, which was intended to appear quarterly. It is likely that he was too preoccupied with the Belcher business to continue it. In 1861 he published the first part of Zadkiel's *Handbook of Astrology*, but the second volume did not appear until 1864. This small octavo manual replaced his old *Grammar of Astrology*, which was still in print but no longer his property.

During the final decade of his long professional career Morrison-Zadkiel was little in the public eye. The 1862 almanac was the last in which Zadkiel advertised his willingness to accept professional work and Samuel Smith made his final appearance in 1863 when Zadkiel stated that 'all letters or applications on any subject whatever' were to be sent to his *alter ego* at Brompton post office.

In the 1870 almanac, which was published in the autumn of 1869, he failed to predict the outbreak of the Franco-Prussian War, but announced the existence of The Most Ancient Order of the Suastika, or Brotherhood of the Mystic Cross. The subscription for an 'Apprentice Brother' was a modest 10s. 6d. Not to be outdone, Mr Sparkes, who edited the rival Raphael almanac, advertised The Society of the Most Ancient Magi, 'instituted for the especial purpose of advocating astrology in its purity, and for the spreading of Occult Knowledge'.[1]

With memories of his own unfortunate coal-mining experiences, Morrison may well have smiled when the London newspapers reported on 13 May 1873 that the miners at the Wynnstay collieries at Ruabon had

---

[1] Mentioned in *Zuriel's Voice of the Stars; or Scottish Prophetic Messenger* for 1871. The proposed foundation of the Scottish Astro-Philosophical Society was announced in the 1872 edition of this short-lived almanac.

refused to work because Zadkiel had predicted a calamity in North Wales for the previous Saturday. A colliery explosion took place in Nova Scotia, Canada, on 13 May itself, so honour was partially saved.

Christopher Cooke ceased to practise as a solicitor in 1862 and retired into private life. 'I find that connexion with astrological and mystic science is a bar to business,' he wrote, 'so I have discontinued my practice again, probably for ever.'[1] A lifelong bachelor, he died at the London Hospital on 18 April 1882 and left an estate of £15,000. To Harrow School he bequeathed a small legacy for a prize for proficiency in the English language, 'preference being given to the works of Dr Samuel Johnson and Dr Oliver Goldsmith'. The Christopher Cooke Prize is still awarded. Since his own literary style was far more readable than that of contemporary astrological writers, it is unfortunate that his *Complete Guide to Astrology* was never published. The manuscript was in the possession of P. Powley, a Hull astrologer, in 1889-90. Publication was announced but the book never appeared.[2]

While Morrison was certainly the central figure on the early Victorian astrological stage, he was by no means the only active British astrological publicist of his generation. There were others whom I will mention, although only briefly.

During his long lifetime Morrison saw four Raphaels come and go after R. C. Smith's death in 1832. I have already referred to John Palmer (Raphael II), who died in 1837. Raphael III's identity is unknown. He charged from 20s. to £5 for a 'horoscope of the whole life' but 5s. was sufficient for an 'horary figure for any passing event'. He also taught astrology and sold 'correct copies of curious ancient MSS. on Alchemy, Magic &c., and all branches of the Occult Sciences'. He ceased to edit *PM* in c. 1846 when he was succeeded by one Medhurst (Raphael IV), who had formerly been a naval schoolmaster on board H.M.S. *Victory*. He was the first to use the pseudonym Edwin Raphael, a practice that was intermittently followed by his successor. He died in 1853.

Raphael V was a certain Mr Sparkes (1820-75), who edited *PM* for the next twenty years. He was 'a very good astrologer but negligent with his customers'.[3] He lived in the Elephant and Castle district south of the River Thames, advertised all the usual astrological services and sold his own special anti-dyspeptic pills, 'a purely *vegetable production*, the result of long study and observation on the effect of various herbs on the digestive organs'. He edited two issues of an ephemeral periodical: *The Oracle; A Monthly Journal of Inductive and Predictive Philosophy, Meteorology, Medical Botany, Science and Art*, May-June 1861.

---

[1] Cooke, *Curiosities*, p. 225 *n*.

[2] See *The Astrologer*, edited by P. Powley, Vol. 3, November and December 1889.

[3] Raphael VI, i.e. R. T. Cross, in *Raphael's Private Instructions in Genethliacal Astrology*, a cyclostyled publication issued in 1881.

Next to R. J. Morrison the most influential astrological publicist of the early Victorian era was undoubtedly William Joseph Simmonite, of Sheffield, the leading practitioner, teacher and writer in the north of England. Whether or not he was a native of Sheffield is not known, but he is first mentioned in White's Sheffield Directory for 1837 in connection with the Bethel Academy, a day school for boys and girls in Coalpit Lane. In the early 1840s he was active in promoting adult education at Sheffield, and in 1845 was conducting the Sheffield British Institution for the Education of Young Gentlemen and Ladies.[1]

Simmonite was also a well-known medical herbalist. In the preface to his *Medical Botany or Herbal Guide to Health*, [1848], he mentioned that he had practised 'Botanic Treatment' for the past nine years and would 'still continue to compound Herbs, for the cure of all Diseases—and to forward to all parts of the United Kingdom his far famed Jupiter Pill, of which more than 9,000 Boxes at One Shilling each have been sold during the period of his private practice'. In 1856 he advertised that 'the famous Astro Botanic Physician, Dr W. J. Simmonite, may be consulted from 10 a.m. to 6 p.m. at his Medico-Botanic Dispensary on any diseases with which the constitution may be afflicted', and to his patients offered a wide choice of herbal medicines ranging (alphabetically) from Anti-Cholera Powder to a preparation discreetly named Woman's Friend.[2]

In addition to teaching and his medical work Simmonite also found time to conduct an extensive astrological practice and to write a succession of astrological works, some of which appear to have been widely circulated among serious students of the subject. He did not share Morrison's interest in cosmological speculation or crystal-gazing diversions nor, like some of the Raphaels, did he traffic in so-called alchemical and magical manuscripts. To the readers of his books he offered a solid, sober 'scientific' astrology on a careful mathematical basis and without any occult frills. I have the impression that he was the first nineteenth-century writer who did not merely reproduce the old seventeenth-century formulations.

Like Morrison he was a keen astro-meteorologist. He was elected a member of the London Meteorological Society in May 1839 and to its council at the same time as Morrison in March 1840. His most widely-read book is best known by the title of its second edition, namely *W. J. Simmonite's Complete Arcana of Astral Philosophy*, which was published in 1890 by J. Story, also of Sheffield. This was an advance on any previous manual because of the skill with which Simmonite organised his material.

---

[1] See his *Plans and Rules of the Sheffield Young Man's College in connection with the Sheffield Scientific and Philosophical Society. Established October 1842* (12 pages, Sheffield Public Library). A vast range of subjects, including Astro-Philosophy, was taught by a small staff at the Sheffield British Institution, which was a privately-owned establishment.

[2] Advertisement in *Dr Simmonite's Meteorologist . . . and Almanack for the Eventful Year 1856*, 18th yearly edition.

He expected much of his readers, e.g. that they should understand the principles of spherical trigonometry and be able to calculate House cusps without reference to tables. His purpose was obviously not to make astrology easy and he would have been appalled at the superficiality of many later publications.[1]

By 1851 Simmonite was apparently no longer practising astrology professionally and was passing commissions to a gentleman who called himself Mercurius Herschel, F.R.S. The name of Dr Smith Ashpe appears in the 1853 and 1856 editions of his *Meteorologist* almanac: 'Those who wish to consult the Astrologer, Smith Ashpe, may safely commit their requests to Dr Ashpe, Astronomer, Sheffield, by whom *alone* the Profession is carried on, *by letter only*, as *all interview*, except for Medical Advice is declined.'

Simmonite died in 1861–2. His brother Henry announced his own astrological practice in the 1862 edition of the *Meteorologist* almanac and was still conducting the Reform Medico–Botanic Dispensary in 1865–6.

Thomas Oxley and Edward Vaughan Williams can be dealt with together since they were master and pupil. I have selected them for brief mention because both were 'scientific' astrologers and uninterested in occultism. Again, both were specialists in the design, manufacture and sale of planispheres, which, in this context, were mathematical instruments used for calculating directions, i.e. predicting. There are fairly frequent references to planispheres in the nineteenth-century literature but no one appears to have used them after *c*. 1890 and the Germans, who were to be the major astrological experts after 1920, were seemingly unaware that they had ever existed.[2]

Oxley was living at Liverpool in 1830 when Morrison was there and then moved to London where he taught mathematics and astrology, advised inventors and speculators in connection with new patents and made working models for them. In the last of his publications (1848) he claimed to be the inventor of the patented American land-clearing machine, the patented self-reefing and unreefing paddle wheels and expanding and contracting screw propellers. He died in the early 1850s.[3]

---

[1] Simmonite's principal works include *The Quarterly Celestial Philosopher*, issued in parts, No. 1, January 1844 (second edition as *Complete Arcana* in 1890); *The Scientific and Literary Messenger*, issued in parts 1841–2; *The Astro-Philosopher and Meteorologist*, quarterly *c*. 1844–8.

[2] The first reference to the use of a planisphere in connection with astrology is in *The Astrologer's Magazine*, August 1793, where the one designed by a certain Mr Ranger is mentioned. Oxley wrote in 1848 that Ranger 'never published an account of his discovery but turned it to his pecuniary advantage by calculating the Nativities of the nobility and wealthy gentry, by whom he was well remunerated'. Oxley first heard of the instrument in *c*. 1809 and refused to pay one of Ranger's pupils a fee of five guineas to explain it to him. He proceeded to make one of his own design.

[3] Thomas Oxley was the author of *The Celestial Planispheres, or Astronomical Charts*, Liverpool, 1830, which was dedicated to Raphael I and The Mercurii. In a supplement to this work (1833) he accused R. J. Morrison of plagiarising material from

Oxley's astrological practice was continued at his old address (3 Elizabeth Place, Westminster Road) by Edward Vaughan Williams. The latter's *Astrologer's Magazine and Philosophical Miscellany*, 1857–8, was inexpertly edited and indifferently printed. There is an interesting passage in his *The True Celestial Almanac* for 1861. In his 'Terms for Nativities' he stated that his fees were 'entirely to pay for the time and extensive labour required in the necessary astronomical calculation of a Nativity, for the Astrological judgment is given gratuitously'. This stratagem would obviously provide a useful alibi if the police happened to trouble him.

When R. J. Morrison died at his house at Knight's Park, Kingston-upon-Thames, on 8 February 1874 he bequeathed his two campaign medals, his watch and chain, his 'magic crystal' and the copyrights of his books to his son Robert. The copyright of *Zadkiel's Almanac* was held in trust for the benefit of his third wife, Louisa Morrison. The editorship of the almanac now passed to Mr Sparkes, an old friend of Morrison's who had assisted him for some time past and had written the rival Raphael almanac since *c.* 1853.

When the 1875 issue of *Zadkiel's Almanac* was published in the autumn of 1874, no reference was made to the death of the publication's founder, his successor taking evasive action by announcing that 'Zadkiel begs emphatically to state that for the future *no correspondence* whatever with the readers of his almanac can be carried on, as the whole of his time is devoted to the work.' Nevertheless, the news of Morrison's death became known and an article in the Glasgow *North British Daily Mail* of 7 October 1874 pointed out that 'upon the principle that in constitutional monarchies, the sovereign never dies, Zadkiel still flourishes for the benefit of mankind and of the almanac business, which—alas for human credulity—is said to be a profitable speculation . . . We are afraid, however, that Zadkiel the First has left but a small portion of his mantle behind him, for in the predictions for 1875 there is a greater ambiguity of language and a more cautious anxiety to "hedge" than in previous almanacs.'

Sparkes' death in May 1875 made it necessary for the Morrison family to find another editor for the almanac. Their choice was Alfred James Pearce (1840–1923), who was to edit the publication for an even longer period than its founder.[1] Pearce had been 'destined for the medical

---

his lectures in the 1832 edition of *Zadkiel's Almanac*. His *The Gem of the Astral Sciences*, 1848, was dedicated to Sir Robert Peel, which makes one wonder if this politician was one of his clients.

[1] He was the son of Charles Thomas Pearce (*d.* 1883), a homoeopathic physician who was honorary secretary of the British Homoeopathic Association, founded in 1845, of which Lord Robert Grosvenor was the president. Pearce's conviction in 1849 on a charge of manslaughter created great indignation in homoeopathic circles. He had unsuccessfully treated his brother, R. D. Pearce, who died of cholera. Pearce practised

profession . . . but financial difficulties prevented him from completing his medical course, so that he never took a London degree, but he practised as assistant to other medical men for many years'.[1] At that time unqualified assistants were still common in the medical profession.

A. J. Pearce was still a youth when he first became interested in astrology, and was a member of Morrison's short-lived Astro-Meteorological Society soon after his 21st birthday in 1861. His first book, *A Defence and Exposition of the Principles of Astrology*, 1863, was dutifully dedicated to Zadkiel, 'who has done so much for the science of astrology, by clearing it of the superstitions formerly associated with it'. A passage in the chapter on medical astrology indicates that he was 'practising' medicine within a week of his majority. A sick child was brought to him and he cast a horary chart. 'Venus being in the 10th [House], and partly ruling the Ascendant, the author looked for a remedy suitable to the diseased state, under her domination; as Venus rules all *white* metals and minerals, he prescribed the *phosphate of lime*, in small doses.'[2]

The average reader would not have noticed many changes in *Zadkiel's Almanac* after 1875, although a careful examination reveals that Pearce gave the articles, as opposed to the essentially popular predictive material, a somewhat different slant. As he wrote elsewhere in 1880: 'We draw the line at magic and spiritualism.'[3] He was a well-read man, not in the occult field so dear to Morrison, but in a more scientific direction. It was not untypical of Pearce that he should have given the readers of the 1877 almanac a summary account of Francis Galton's famous book *Hereditary Genius*, 1869 (reprinted as a paperback in 1962). It was his business to 'predict', because that it was what the public expected, but he was more cautious than Zadkiel I. While he regularly published primary directions for Queen Victoria and the Prince of Wales in the late 1870s, he identified neither of them by name and was content to refer to them as 'Eminent

---

homoeopathic medicine in the West End of London during the 1860s. He believed in astrology and made a careful note of his son's birth time, 9.20 a.m. on 10 November 1840, which Pearce rectified as 9ʰ 18ᵐ 4ˢ a.m.

[1] Obituary notice in *The British Journal of Astrology*, July 1923.

[2] Empirical remedies of this kind are still used by astrologers who dabble with medicine today. See, for example, Dr Friedbert Asboga, *Astromedizin und Astropharmazie*, 1931, second edition 1954; Dr George Washington Carey and Inez Eudora Perry, *The Zodiac and the Salts of Salvation*, an American publication (second revised edition 1948) which discusses 'the relation of the mineral salts of the body to the signs of the zodiac and an esoteric analysis and synthesis of the zodiacal signs and the physicochemical allocations'; Dr William M. Davidson, *Medical Astrology and Health*, Astrological Bureau of Consultation, New York, 1959.

In 1961 a German astrologer from Hamburg who had no medical qualification, dangled a pendulum over my wife's hand and forthwith prescribed a neo-Paracelsian concoction with the attractive name of Arcanum 7. At Frankfurt am Main in January 1965 a certain Herr E. informed me that he had successfully treated a number of cases of cancer with medicines possessing an alleged affinity to the planet Neptune.

[3] In his periodical *Urania*, September 1880 (nine issues, January–September 1880).

Personages'. The almanac increased its circulation during the early years of his editorship, but not on the basis of sensationalism. An annual sale of 140,000 copies was claimed during the 1880s, but from 1891 onwards no figures were printed. *Zadkiel's Almanac* ceased publication in 1931, Pearce having edited it for forty-eight of the past fifty-six years. His *Text-Book of Astrology*, 2 vols., 1879–89 (second edition 1911) was the last of the major Victorian manuals.

Owing to Sparkes' death a new editor was also required for *Raphael's Prophetic Messenger* almanac. In this case Sparkes' successor was even younger than Pearce, for Robert T. Cross (*b*. 15 May 1850, *d*. 1923), was only twenty-five years old when he began to edit the *Prophetic Messenger*.[1] A native of East Anglia, he published his own horoscope in the Raphael ephemeris for 1913 where he wrote: 'Nothing has prospered with me except Astrology. I have tried many things, but all have ended in failure or loss. In Astrology, however, I have succeeded beyond my expectations, and my life as a whole leaves me much to be thankful for.' His *Guide to Astrology*, 2 vols., 1877–9, a pocket-sized elementary manual, was widely used by students for many years. He does not appear to have practised astrology professionally, but in the almanac provided the names of astrologers to whom applicants for horoscopes could apply, e.g. Mr Didaskolos, of Coleford, near Bath in 1889, J. W. Herschel, of Frome, in 1893, and George Wilde, of Halifax, in 1904.

Pearce and Cross were members of a generation of astrologers that must have found it difficult to imagine the possibility of a widespread increase of interest in their art. It is true that their respective almanacs sold reasonably well since each had an annual circulation of more than 100,000 copies and they were undoubtedly read by many times that number. However, nobody could learn very much about astrology's technicalities from an almanac. Nor, during the first twenty years of their respective editorships, was there any noticeable increase in the number of people who were prepared to study astrology seriously. Astrological beliefs were as far from achieving an aura of respectability as in the past and R. J. Morrison's proposition that astrology would soon be recognised as a science was as illusory in the 1880s as it had been thirty years earlier when he misled Christopher Cooke. However, one unanticipated result of the Victorian Education Acts was the appearance of working-class astrologers, especially in the north of England where earnest artisans, although not very many,

---

[1] William Charlton Wright, *PM*'s original publisher, died in 1858. The property was acquired by the firm of Piper, Stephenson and Spence (1858–60), and was then successively controlled by T. T. Lemare (until 1872), and Catty and Dobson or J. E. Catty until 1886 when the imprint of Messrs Foulsham, the present publishers, first appears. Foulshams do not own the copyright but distribute *PM* and other Raphael publications, some of them direct descendants of the fortune-telling books written by R. C. Smith (Raphael I) in the late 1820s, on behalf of the present generation of the Cross family.

3. *Above :* R. J. Morrison (Zadkiel)
1795–1874.

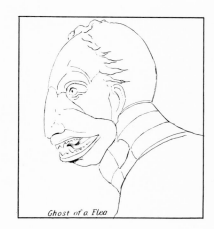

Ghost of a Flea

4. *Right :* 'The Ghost of a Flea,'
symbolizing the 'Gemini' type—
engraved by John Linnell after
a drawing by William Blake (see
note on page 31.)

5. Hugo Vollrath and others at the Leipzig Astrologers' Congress, 1923. *Left to right:* Theobald Becher, A. M. Grimm, A. Ulkan, Hugo Vollrath and M. E. Winkel.

now industriously studied the available nineteenth century manuals. Any public connection with astrology was so *declassé* that when a man of the intellectual distinction of Richard Garnett professed his belief in it, even his friends found it difficult to take him seriously.

Richard Garnett (1835–1906) was an illustrious, even famous, member of the staff of the Department of Printed Books at the British Museum and a well-known man of letters. He became interested in astrology in the 1870s. Samuel Butler, the author of *Erewhon*, learned of his friend's eccentric preoccupations in June 1883, when he wrote to his father to ask whether he was born 'in the early part of the day of December 4th, 1835, or the latter part . . . My reason for asking is this. My friend Mr Garnett of the British Museum has, or pretends to have, a craze about astrology.' Butler had just encountered Garnett at the Museum and complained that he was suffering from a cold. Garnet said: 'I was afraid you might be ill and was thinking of writing to enquire.' Butler asked why. Garnett 'rather hummed and ha'd, and at length explained that, if I was born in the latter part of December 4th, 1835, I should be suffering from the transit (I think he said transit) of Saturn, as the Queen and two or three more people were. If, however, I was born in the early part of the day it would not affect me.'[1]

Garnett's occasional essays upon astrological topics were published under the pseudonym A. G. Trent, an anagram of Garnett. The best known of these was 'The Soul and the Stars', of which the first version was printed in *The University Magazine*, March 1880. Later he recalled that the piece 'grew out of a controversy between two able contributors to the magazine on the topic of Reincarnation, which the present writer ventures to deem susceptible of illustration from an entirely different point of view'.[2]

Garnett outlined his own conception of astrology in 'The Soul and the Stars' where he wrote: 'It is . . . necessary to insist on the strictly empirical character of astrology, inasmuch as it is generally regarded as an occult science. The astrologer is regarded as a kind of wizard, and allowed the alternative of divination or imposture. The fact nevertheless remains, that astrology with the single exception of astronomy, is, as regards the certainty of its data, the most exact of all exact sciences . . . [The astrologer's] calculations are performed by no more cabalistical process than arithmetic.

[1] Carolyn G. Heilbrun, *The Garnett Family*, 1961, pp. 46–47.
[2] A revised and enlarged version of 'The Soul and the Stars' was published in G. Wilde and Joseph Dodson, *A Treatise on Natal Astrology*, Halifax, 1894. G. Wilde (1860–1916) was employed by one of the northern railway companies before he became a professional astrologer. J. Dodson, who was in practice as a solicitor at Stainland, near Halifax, was a prominent supporter of the Occultists Defence League. The members of this organisation were mostly professional fortune-tellers, mainly phreno-logists, although the membership also included palmists, physiognomists, psycho-metrists, trance mediums and a few astrologers. See the League's *Directory of Occult Practitioners*, 1901, compiled by J. Dodson and Ida Ellis (copy at British Museum).

The influences he attributes to the heavenly bodies may be imaginary, but are in no sense occult, unless *occult* means *that which is not generally admitted*!'

Astrology was not exactly dying on its feet in Great Britain in the 1880s, but it was not attracting very much attention. However, a period of expansion lay ahead. This was almost wholly due to the impact of Theosophical teachings and esoteric speculations during a period of about thirty years from *c.* 1884 until the outbreak of the First World War. These thirty years are of the greatest importance in relation to the history of all modern 'underground' movements.

The United States of America, where the links with the old European Hermetic tradition were tenuous and even artificial, was the birthplace of the two most important 'occult' movements of modern times: Spiritualism and Theosophy. The Theosophical Society was founded in New York City in 1875 by Helena Petrovna Blavatsky, Colonel Henry S. Olcott, William Q. Judge and others who were primarily interested in spiritualism and its phenomena. Madame Blavatsky and Olcott moved to India in 1879 and the Society's headquarters were ultimately established at Adyar, near Madras, in 1882. A London branch had been formed in 1878 but there was little public interest in Great Britain until 1884 when A. P. Sinnett, a newspaper editor who had been one of Madame Blavatsky's converts in India, published his *Occult World*, 'with its remarkable account of strange phenomena and yet stranger claims in respect of the Russian seeress'.[1]

In its early days the Theosophical movement was in many respects a by-product of the Spiritualist one. When H. P. Blavatsky, who was born at Jekaterinoslav in the Ukraine in 1831, arrived in New York City in 1873 she earned her living as a medium. 'An unknown Russian woman, she plunged into the Spiritualist movement, then so powerfully affecting America, and in a less measure many other countries.' Her self-appointed mission, however, was to demonstrate the existence of 'an age-old knowledge of the deeper laws of life, studied and guarded by those who could use it safely and beneficiently; persons who in their higher ranks were called "Masters", though other titles were used for them—Adepts, Chohans, Elder Brethren, the Occult Hierarchy, and so on.'[2]

Although there were many who supposed that Madame Blavatsky was a vulgar fraud, her followers regarded her as an inspired Teacher and, indeed, as the visible representative of the Hidden Masters. Her *Isis Unveiled: A Master Key to the Mysteries of Ancient and Modern Science*, first published in New York in 1877 (and later translated into French,

---

[1] A. E. Waite, *Shadows of Light and Thought*, 1938, p. 86.
[2] Biographical sketch of H.P.B. in the fourth (Adyar) edition of her *The Secret Doctrine*, London, 1938, p. 15. This compendium of eastern and Western occultism, first published in two volumes in 1888, has attracted an enormous readership during the past eight decades.

German and other languages) created a minor sensation. A. E. Waite (1857–c.1940), one of the more respectable British occultists of his generation, read it when he was a young man and 'hated its anti-Christian bias', but found it 'helpful as an *omnium gatherum* of esoteric claims and pretences, a miscellany of magic and its connections, with the sole exception of alchemy'.[1]

Theosophy, Madame Blavatsky's new *ersatz* religion, had an immediate appeal for many who were dissatisfied with conventional Christian beliefs. The recipe was adroitly contrived: to a chaotic synthesis culled from the vast barrel of ancient European Hermetism she added a liberal dose of Buddhist and Hindu elements and in the process gave a large number of Americans and Europeans a superficial acquaintance with Eastern religious and mystical traditions, not to mention a lot of nonsense of her own invention.[2] For many the most fascinating novelty was the teachings she claimed to have received from various invisible 'Mahatmas', one or other of whom were alleged to have instructed her in Tibet, a country which it is unlikely that she ever visited, although she may have reached its borders.

The scandals that afflicted the Theosophical Society during the early 1880s centred round Madame Blavatsky's mediumistic activities and, in particular, the mysterious arrival—out of thin air, as it were—of the so-called 'Mahatma Letters', which were said to contain communications written personally by members of the Occult Hierarchy and delivered to her by invisible messengers.

The publication of A. P. Sinnett's best-selling *Occult World* in 1884 conveniently coincided with Madame Blavatsky's return to Europe. With the exception of a brief visit to India in 1884–5 she remained in the West, mainly in London, until her death there in 1891. The presence of the mysterious H.P.B. provided a magnificent advertisement for the Theosophical Society, whose membership now grew rapidly. 'Theosophy was in the forefront in those days,' A. E. Waite recalled. '. . . I remember very well the strange crew that filled Sinnett's drawing room at Theosophical gatherings: the astrologers, the mesmerists, the readers of hands and a few, very few only, of the motley spiritualist groups.'[3]

Apart from the crackpots who inevitably swarm round any new occult honey-pot, the Theosophical Society also attracted a large number of respectable members of the *bourgeoisie*, including a useful quota of wealthy or titled ladies. The Press, in its turn, gave the Society an immense volume of publicity, since Theosophical personalities, wrangles and

[1] A. E. Waite, *Shadows of Light and Thought*, 1938, pp. 66, 68.
[2] In this respect she was surpassed, after her death, by Annie Besant and the Rev. C. W. Leadbeater. Their speculations on such subjects as the 'astral plane', 'occult chemistry' and semi-divine beings known as Avatars, who were even higher in the spiritual hierarchy than H. P. B.'s hypothetical Mahatmas, attained a degree of absurdity that was at once pathetic and comic.
[3] A. E. Waite, *Shadows of Light and Thought*, 1938, p. 87.

scandals provided editors with an almost perennial abundance of news-worthy copy. The historical and social implications of this strangely influential 'esoteric' movement should not be underestimated.[1]

Madame Blavatsky's works contain frequent allusions to a Theosophical cosmology with a vaguely astrological basis. Theosophists were there-fore aware of astrology's existence, although only a relatively small number bothered to learn its technicalities. However, there were to be sufficient to form the nucleus of a new and identifiable astrological movement.

The Victorian astrologers and their predecessors mostly regarded astrology as a predictive science. Their approach was utilitarian rather than esoteric or mystical. Hence astrology was an end in itself. In an article published in 1903 Alan Leo, who was mainly responsible for the creation of the new Theosophical version of astrology, wrote: 'It is no exaggeration to say that all the astrologers I met at the commencement of my career were satisfied with the *horoscope alone* . . . it was clear that the *meanings of the symbols* found in the horoscope were not properly understood by them . . . it was not until the light of the Wisdom Religion [Theosophy] gave illumination to the ancient symbology that a few astrologers, turning the rays of that life upon astrological symbols, were able to penetrate behind the veil of the horoscope.'[2]

Astrology now achieved a spurious respectability by attaching itself to Theosophy's apron strings, at least as far as the Theosophical astrologers were concerned. Its traditional associations with fortune-telling were conveniently rationalised, or ignored, since the horoscope could be re-garded as a kind of esoteric document and its interpretation an occult exercise. The Law of Karma satisfactorily explained many of astrology's obscurities, because Madame Blavatsky had made it all crystal clear in *The Secret Doctrine*: 'Those who believe in Karma have to believe in *destiny*, which from birth to death man is weaving round himself as a spider weaves his web; and this destiny is guided either by the heavenly voice of the invisible prototype, or by intimate *astral* or inner man who is but too often our evil genius.'

Theosophical astrology was not created overnight. In fact its develop-ment was a relatively slow process. First it was necessary for a few astrologers with a sense of mission to acquire the necessary Theosophical background. The most important of these pioneers was Alan Leo, an obscure commercial traveller who was to become this century's first major astrological publicist and, furthermore, the first astrologer of all time to

---

[1] For a helpful analysis of the intellectual and religious implications see C. G. Jung, 'The Spiritual Problem of Modern Man' in *Civilisation in Transition*, Collected Works, Vol. 10, 1964. A. H. Nethercott's massive biography of Annie Besant contains a detailed and lively account of contemporary Theosophical politicking (*The First Five Lives of Annie Besant*, 1961, *The Last Four Lives of Annie Besant*, 1963).

[2] *Modern Astrology*, 1903, No. 4.

practise his art on a large and well-organised professional scale. The manner in which a man like Leo can emerge is not without interest.

In June 1887, a few months after Madame Blavatsky finally settled in London, 'Professor' P. Powley, of Hull, published the first issue of a new monthly periodical, *The Astrologer*. There were no encouraging precedents for its success, for during the previous twenty-five years only three astrological journals had seen the light of day in Great Britain and none had survived for longer than a few months. There was a market for popular predictive almanacs but astrological adepts were still too few or too scattered to support a specialist publication. That Powley's *The Astrologer* lasted for three years was largely because the new working-class astrologers made it possible. The correspondence columns—this was a novel feature in astrological journalism—indicate the kind of public that was reading the periodical. There was, for instance, the lady who signed herself 'A Working Man's Wife' and who wrote: 'I know several females who are studying astrology. I am pleased to say that I am a student and a firm believer myself.' She wanted astrologers to wear a distinctive badge for the purpose of mutual recognition. Then there was the gentleman who wrote from Sheffield: '. . . there are plenty of working men in this country who would spare twopence a month [for *The Astrologer*] that would not spend sixpence on an almanac at one time . . . I am a subscriber to Raphael's Almanac. I find at my next birthday something awful is going to occur. A word through your invaluable monthly would be esteemed very much by me, and would be information for others'.

Nothing resembling an organised astrological movement existed at that time in Great Britain. Indeed, the same applies today when there are three astrological societies in London. However, small local societies were now being formed, chiefly in the north of England, and Powley regularly published letters announcing that a group had been established in this or that town. Early in 1888, for example, he printed four letters from individuals who wished to contact fellow workers in the astrological vineyard in their own particular district. One of them was from F. W. Lacey, who resided at 23 Corrance Road in the London suburb of Brixton. This letter was read by William Frederick Allen, a commercial traveller, who lived not very far away at 12 Lugard Road, Peckham.[1]

Alan Leo—astrology never knew him as W. F. Allen—was born in London on 7 August 1860. His father served in India as a private soldier in a Highland regiment at the time of the Mutiny, was discharged in *c*. 1858 and found employment in the dispensary of a London hospital. He left his wife and disappeared without trace when Leo was still a small child.

---

[1] The small terrace houses in Lugard Road and Corrance Road must have been fairly new in the 1880s. Both Brixton and Peckham were working-class districts, mainly inhabited by artisans and lowly-paid clerks. Today these streets are almost exclusively occupied by West Indians and have become slums.

Mrs Allen was a zealous member of the sect of Plymouth Brethren and her husband had become weary of her bigotry.

Leo described the circumstances of his early life in a letter published in *The Astrologer* (February 1890), in which he discussed the untoward workings of the planet Uranus, although without revealing that the information referred to himself.

'I have before me the natus of a man who will not quickly forget his experience, for it is indeed remarkable. Born 6h. 10m. a.m. August 7th, 1860, with Uranus alone in the *Medium Coelis* [i.e. the 10th House] . . . the 10th House represents the Native's honour, trade and profession, and all matters connected with his mother; now he could never agree with his mother, in fact there was not a particle of sympathy between either. He was bound apprentice to three different trades—Drapery, Chemistry and Grocery respectively—the first he only remained three months, and at the second, six months, and at the latter he served two years out of seven, indentures being cancelled by mutual consent. At 16 years of age he found himself in Liverpool without a penny, and also without a friend, he was driven to sleep in the streets; 12 months later saw him holding a splendid position in that town. At 18 years of age he was again reduced to the greatest poverty in another large town, but his fortune changed just as suddenly, for at 20 years of age he was his own master, employing a number of hands, again to fall as low, for at 22 he found he was ruined by the dishonesty of his manager, who had robbed him to the utmost limit.'

He was about 18 years old when he found employment in a sewing machine factory. After a time he went on the road for this firm. According to *The Life and Work of Alan Leo*, 1919, a collection of memorial essays by different writers which was published by his widow after Leo's death in 1917: 'At the age of twenty-one, his employer died and Alan went to live in Manchester, where a brother of his late employer had two grocers' shops, and he was offered the position of Manager of the larger of the two, with an excellent salary. It was in that city about three or four years afterwards [*c.* 1885] that he heard of Astrology for the first time.'

Leo eventually became manager of both businesses, and was presumably deceived by whoever was left in charge of one of the two shops. Continuing Leo's own story: 'He came to London friendless and penniless, and on the verge of starvation. Again mark the influence of Uranus's sudden nature, at 25 he was Manager of one of the largest firms in the City of London, loved and respected by all; but such is the treacherous nature of Uranus that once more he slid down the ladder, and is again working up to the top of the tree.'

'One of the largest firms in the City of London' was a firm of sewing machine manufacturers. Leo was unemployed when he first met Lacey in the spring of 1888, but soon found a position as a traveller for confectionery. He had learned the elements of astrology at Manchester from a certain 'Doctor' Richardson, a herbalist in the Simmonite tradition who had treated him for some minor complaint or other. 'The old man and the young one grew fast friends, and in a short time Dr Richardson declared that Alan knew more about it [astrology] than he did . . . And so time passed on, with practical business days but the nights devoted to Star lore. For the time was rapidly approaching when he would be drawn again among his own people of the past, Occultists he had known and worked with in former lives.'[1]

Leo's membership of Lacey's little group brought him into touch with an eccentric young man by the name of Walter Richard Old, who later called himself Walter Gorn Old and whose pseudonym, Sepharial, became well known to all English-speaking students of astrology. W. R. Old was born at Handsworth, near Birmingham, on 20 March 1864 and was about 24 years of age when he first met Leo. He was educated at King Edward's School, Birmingham and at a very early age began to study astrology and the Cabala. 'At twenty-one he broke down with hyperaesthesia.[2] He had been burning the candle at both ends for some considerable time and the wicks all but met. Practical Occultism and Psychology engaged his attention for several years during which he attended lectures for the medical course and did some dispensing. He tried a variety of coats, but none of them fitted him, and he threw them off one after the other. Orientalism took him in his grip, and from the Hebrew he went to Coptic and the Hieroglyphics, then to the Assyrian, and finally to Sanskrit and Chinese. As a student he was not a disgrace, and he had passports for business capacity, but is of the opinion that, left to himself, he would wreck the best business that was ever founded inside twelve months.'[3] However, it would be unwise to overestimate the standard of these linguistic attainments.

Old moved from Birmingham to London in 1889 and immediately found himself in the very centre of Theosophical activities. In spite of his youth he was a member of Madame Blavatsky's so-called Inner Group, the dozen specially-favoured 'Initiates' who resided with her at 19 Avenue Road, St John's Wood, when she moved there in October 1889.[4] Alice Leighton Cleather, who was also a member of the party, wrote in 1923: 'H.P.B. used to call him "the astral tramp", on account of his habit of "roaming about in his astral body at night", as she put it.'[5]

[1] Bessie Leo in *The Life and Work of Alan Leo*, 1919.

[2] In the 1880s hyperaesthesia meant 'excessive and morbid sensitiveness of the nerve centres'. After 1920 the term had parapsychological applications. See S. G. Soal, *Preliminary Studies of a Vaudeville Telepathist*, University of London Council for Psychical Investigation, 1937.

[3] C. Sherburn in *Old Moore's Monthly Messenger*, November, 1913.

[4] 'The Inner Group were sworn so solemnly to secrecy that even after forty years, G. S. R. Mead, who had by then long split from the Society, felt himself bound by his oath that he would not divulge their rites or occult experiments.'—A. H. Nethercott, *The First Five Lives of Annie Besant*, 1961, p. 347.

[5] A. L. Cleather, *H. P. Blavatsky as I knew her*, Calcutta and Simla, 1923, pp. 23–24.

Old took Leo to the Theosophical meetings that were held at Madame Blavatsky's residence at Lansdowne Road, near Notting Hill Gate, and later at Avenue Road. Leo became a member of the Society in May 1890—three months before W. B. Yeats resigned from it—and remained faithful to the Theosophical cause for the rest of his life.

Powley's periodical *The Astrologer* was in financial difficulties at the end of 1889 and both Lacey and Leo were aware that it could not hope to survive for much longer. Although there were no encouraging precedents pointing to the success of a publication of this kind, Lacey proposed that they should publish their own magazine. They met to discuss the proposition on Thursday 21 November 1889 and decided to go ahead. According to Lacey: 'A "radical election" figure was taken, and the testimonies for success were exceptionally good.' The 'election' horoscope was cast in order to discover a propitious publication date. There is a record of yet another talk about the project on the top of an omnibus in Broad Street in the City of London in May 1890.[1] Powley announced the forthcoming publication in the penultimate issue of *The Astrologer*, May 1890, where it was stated that the first number of *The Astrologer's Magazine* would be published on 1 August.

W. R. Old, or rather Sepharial, had also entered the field. His little periodical *Fate and Fortune* appeared in July but did not survive more than four issues. For the time being Lacy and Leo were unworried by competitive publications, although before long four new ones were on the market.[2]

Neither Leo nor Lacey had any journalistic experience nor, for that matter, had either of them anything new or startlingly interesting to say about astrology. The initial success of *The Astrologer's Magazine* can be largely ascribed to the free horoscopes with very brief delineations which were offered to subscribers who remitted their payments direct to the proprietors. Payment in advance for two years was rewarded with a personal astrological forecast covering the same period. Powley had previously tried the 'Great Free Offer' gambit, but only undertook to provide the answer to a question, i.e. by casting a horary chart, and to print a brief reply in a future issue of *The Astrologer*. For this purpose a 'No Fees Astrological Coupon' was printed on the back cover of each issue.

[1] *The Life and Work of Alan Leo*, edited by Bessie Leo, 1919, p. 30, where the planetary positions for the 'election' horoscope are given. I estimate that it was cast shortly before midnight. Leo then presumably had an hour's walk 'across country' from Corrance Road back to Lugard Road. The conference on the omnibus is mentioned in Leo's *Modern Astrology*, February 1902.

[2] *The Future*, February 1892–July 1894, 26 issues, edited by A. J. Pearce (Zadkiel); *Coming Events*, October 1896–1901, edited by J. W. Herschel, of Frome, Somerset until *c.* July 1897 and thereafter by Sepharial (W. R. Old); *Star Lore and Future Events*, January 1897–March 1903, edited by Zadkiel (A. J. Pearce). None of these periodicals had a large circulation. *The Horoscope*, October 1902–July 1904, a quarterly edited by Rollo Ireton (i.e. the Hon. Ralph Shirley), was decently printed and included occasional contributions by A. G. Trent (Richard Garnett). Shirley was for many years editor of *The Occult Review*, No. 1, January 1905.

During the four years that Leo and Lacey were in partnership their 'free horoscope' idea secured a good many new subscribers, but there was little financial profit and the preparation of the horoscopes required incessant work at week-ends. During this period (1890–4) they dispatched more than 4,000 of these productions.

Business commitments obliged Lacey to withdraw from the partnership upon the completion of the fourth volume in July 1894 and Leo now became the periodical's sole proprietor. In August 1895 he changed its title to *Modern Astrology* and rented a small office, probably one room at 1–2 Bouverie Street, a turning off Fleet Street. Since he was still employed as a commercial traveller he was unable to attend there very regularly.

In September 1895 he married Bessie Phillips, the illegitimate daughter of Michael Phillips, a member of the Jewish faith who lived at Southampton. Her previous very brief marriage to a phrenologist had been annulled a year earlier, and she only consented to marry Leo on condition that no consummation would be demanded. Bessie Leo (1858–1931) was an ardent Theosophist who had latterly been in practice as a professional palmist, phrenologist and physiognomist at Southampton. She was a regular contributor to *Modern Astrology* from 1898 onwards and it was her turgid articles that henceforth gave the periodical a markedly Theosophical complexion. C. E. O. Carter, who knew her well, many years later described her in unflattering terms: 'She was possessed by an itch for power but she was totally incompetent and very indolent. This led to an attitude of constant ineffectual interference.'[1] She appears to have been an unpleasant woman.

In the November issue of *Modern Astrology* Leo advertised for an 'apprentice', although what he really required was an office boy who would work for nothing, or even pay for the privilege. 'He must be over 14 and under 21 years of age, and be willing to assist in the publishing office when required. In exchange for his services astrologically in a general way, I will undertake to make him a competent astrologer in three years from the date of his apprenticeship. This is an offer that is unique, and an opportunity that has not occurred for centuries . . . A premium will be required, but should a special case arise it may be dispensed with.' It is not known whether any foolhardy youth applied.

Leo eventually became a full-time professional astrologer in 1898. He had already moved to a spacious house at 9 Lyncroft Gardens, a turning off the Finchley Road in Hampstead, and was soon receiving more commissions for paid astrological work than he could conveniently manage. Many of his early clients were members of the Theosophical Society who, in their turn, recommended him to their friends. Rather than turn work

[1] C. E. O. Carter, 'The Astrological Lodge of The Theosophical Society' in *In Search*, Vol. 2, No. 1, New York, 1959. There is an interesting autobiographical sketch in Leo's *Esoteric Astrology*, 1913, pp. 207–26.

away, he decided to employ people to assist him and began to recruit a small staff: two or three astrologers to do the mathematical calculations and as many clerks to write out the delineations, which he mostly dictated himself, and to attend to the clerical work connected with his now multifarious astrological activities. These included his periodical, book-publishing, correspondence courses and an astrological society. By 1903 he was employing no fewer than nine people, not counting his wife Bessie who played an active part in running the business.

Leo's astrological firm—there had never been anything like it in the past—was in a flourishing state in the early 1900s. The Modern Astrology Publishing Company, of which he was the sole proprietor, had branches in Paris and New York, although neither was in existence for very long.[1]

The success of Leo & Co. was largely founded upon the mass-production of cheap horoscopes, but first the sales and manufacturing techniques had to be evolved. Leo's principal clerk found the solution. He had been in the habit of making copies of all the delineations that Leo dictated to him and now pointed out that 'in all cases where treating of the same rising sign [Ascendant], or lunar position, etc., there was a similarity of style and matter—the sheets were in fact virtual *fac-similies*'.[2] This was not surprising since Leo had obviously been dictating the same kind of astrological 'patter' time and again. The sensible solution, therefore, was to use a duplicating machine or similar apparatus for the preparation of stocks of prefabricated horoscopes. Suppose, for example, that an applicant wrote to say that he was born on 1 July, a set of sheets for 'Sun in Cancer' could be quickly collated and mailed. These so-called Test Horoscopes, for which Leo charged 1s., were baits and were intended to attract commissions for more conventional and remunerative astrological work. Within three years of the inception of the Test Horoscope scheme Leo & Co. had mailed 20,000 of these primitive horoscopes. The idea was soon plagiarised by rival although less successful professional astrologers.[3]

There is an amusing account of a typical morning at 9 Lyncroft Gardens in E. H. Bailey's periodical *Destiny* (June 1904–October 1905). Bailey was a leading member of Leo's staff and detested both his employer and his wife. A brief quotation will suffice: 'The morning mail had just been delivered and Albanus Leon [i.e. Alan Leo] was busily engaged in sorting out a large pile of letters of all shapes and sizes . . . Most of them con-

[1] Leo's Paris branch was run by Leopold Mieville, who had translated some of his early works into French. The 'office' was probably wherever Mieville's desk happened to be located. It is unlikely that the New York office at 1 Madison Avenue was any more important.

[2] 'The History of the Test Horoscope' in *Modern Astrology*, December 1903.

[3] There was an earlier but unsophisticated precedent for the production of prefabricated horoscopes. In the 1840s 'Doctor' C. W. Roback, of Boston, Mass., engaged a lithographic printer to run off thousands of identical horoscopes. See R. J. Morrison in *Zadkiel's Almanac*, 1852. For a highly-suspect account of Roback's career see his own *Mysteries of Astrology and Wonders of Magic*, Boston, Mass., 1854.

tained money orders, for Leon had an immense clientele, and the income from his business had now reached four figures a year and bid fair to greatly increase as time went on. The mail this morning was an exceptionally heavy one and the pile of postal and money orders was rapidly mounting up. It was true that the great majority were only for a shilling [i.e. for Test Horoscopes], but these, with the five and ten shilling orders, and three or four for a pound, as well as various cheques for various amounts, made up a very goodly sum.' The data for the Test Horoscopes was then handed to 'Harold Stratton, the chief assistant and confidential secretary to Albanus Leon. He wore glasses and there was a dreamy, inert look about his face suggestive of a pronounced lunar influence; he was in fact born with the first decanate of the sign Cancer rising.' What could be more descriptive?

Leo's employees became increasingly restive at this irreverent prostitution of their art and there was a mass walk-out in 1903. Leo ascribed this unfortunate event to his own malefic constellations. 'During the whole of the present year I have been under the influence of Sun in opposition to Neptune and Mercury', he wrote. 'This has caused the breaking up of the staff during the summer months and the closing of the New York office.'[1] These untoward astral circumstances and the Law of Karma satisfactorily explained everything.

Leo never found it difficult to reconcile his Test Horoscope racket with his high-minded Theosophical principles for, after all, even a shilling horoscope was better than none if it brought one more recruit to the ranks of those who believed in astrology.

He found nothing inconsistent in his dual existence: there was Mr Leo the professional astrologer and Mr Leo the earnest esotericist. In the May 1907 issue of *Modern Astrology* he wrote: 'I must admit that I have been swinging very much in the direction of the esoteric side of the science, for, to speak candidly, it is the only part of the science that really interests me.' Six years later he published his book *Esoteric Astrology*, 1913, in which may be found such gems as: 'The planet Jupiter represents the body, which term is here meant to include the etheric double as well as the dense physical . . . The Auric Egg itself, regarded as a vehicle, is under the dominant influence of Jupiter, as are all the finer substances composing the inner vehicles of Consciousness.' High-minded jargon of this kind gave astrology a satisfying aura of respectability in muddled but enthusiastic Theosophical circles.

Leo's subsequent career until his death on 30 August 1917 can be dealt with very briefly. He visited India twice before 1914 and made dutiful pilgrimages to Adyar, the headquarters of the Theosophical Society. He was prosecuted for fortune-telling in May 1914 but was acquitted on a legal technicality. At the trial it was stated that his current charges for

[1] *Modern Astrology*, October, 1903.

horoscopes ranged from 5s. to 5 guineas, the latter for a forecast covering the next ten years. He was prosecuted again in July 1917. This time, however, his stars were unpropitious and he was fined £25. Prosecutions of astrologers were infrequent at this period, but the City of London police had been keeping a watchful eye upon him since c. 1911.

His ambitious series of textbooks—the collection eventually grew to seven quarto volumes—has served countless novice astrologers since the first of them was published in the early 1900s. They were all translated into German in the 1920s and most of the original English editions are still in print. It is symptomatic that the title of the first volume and, indeed, of the complete series, was *Astrology for All*. His Victorian predecessors, such as W. J. Simmonite and A. J. Pearce, had never thought it necessary to write about astrology in a highly-simplified manner, but Leo purposefully brought the subject within reach of any lower middle-class lady with sufficient intelligence to master a few elementary arithmetical calculations and copy the seemingly appropriate 'cook-book' interpretations from one or other of his works. Indeed, for many the task of extracting information from a horoscope was no more difficult than mixing the ingredients for a cake. His *Esoteric Astrology*, from which I have quoted above, was the only one of his books that was more apt to bewilder than instruct.

Leo never published a predictive almanac. Hence the man-in-the-street, who automatically associated astrology with the names of Messrs Raphael and Zadkiel, whose almanacs could be bought at any bookstall, probably never heard of him. He was essentially an 'underground' character, more influential than might be expected but unknown to the average member of the general public. However, the moment that anyone took the least step in the direction of the study of astrology, they would have immediately encountered his name. He was, as I have said, this century's first major astrological publicist.

Despite Leo's capacity for making money, it has been exceptional for twentieth-century professional astrologers to be able to support themselves solely on the basis of fees received for horoscopes. Thus it was necessity rather than desire that compelled W. R. Old to write one worthless book after another on a variety of occult subjects, and to contribute his monthly quota of hack journalism to *Old Moore's Monthly Messenger* (October 1907–September 1914) and its successor *The British Journal of Astrology*.[1]

It was Old who had introduced Leo to Theosophy. Whereas Leo's allegiance to Theosophical teachings never wavered, Old's official connection with the Theosophical Society ceased soon after Annie Besant

---

[1] The British Museum catalogue lists about forty-five books by Old, most of them written under his pseudonym Sepharial. A few typical titles include *Kabbalistic Astrology*, *A New Manual of Astrology*, *Second Sight*, *The Kabbala of Numbers*, *Your Fortune in Your Name*.

jostled her way to the top soon after Madame Blavatsky's death. Like others who had been close to Helena Petrovna Blavatsky—he was present when she died—Old had little affection for the new President of the European Section.[1] Nor had he much use for Leo's mystical Theosophical astrology. In an announcement for his forthcoming book *The Law of Values*, 1914, which he described as 'an exposition of the primary [astrological] causes of stock exchange fluctuations', he proposed that 'the sooner we bring the science down from the clouds where the would-be esotericists have incontinently harried it, the sooner will it gain a proper recognition in the practical world'.[2]

Old's theory was that astrology could be used for severely practical purposes, such as making money. He was convinced, for example, that commodity (e.g. cotton and wheat) and stock exchange prices were subject to planetary influences and could therefore be predicted. K. E. Krafft, who was far more intelligent than Old, thought the same twenty years later. Old, who was a financial simpleton, was confidently inviting subscriptions to his private Market Forecasts at 5 guineas per circular, as early as 1898.[3]

Old's, or rather Sepharial's, best-selling lines were undoubtedly his various astrological horse-racing systems, such as his 'Golden Key', 'Apex' (this cost £50 in 1920) and 'Snapshot' systems. His new 'Simplex' system, first advertised in 1921, made the tiresome work of casting horoscopes unnecessary, since it worked 'on Acceptance Weights only by simple arithmetic, showing the wonderful value of the Power of Numbers. No Maps or Astrology. Price £20.' The 'Simplex' system was largely based upon the theories of an oriental gentleman who called himself Sheik Habeeb Ahmad. The Sheik's *magnum opus*, *The Mysteries of Sound and Number*, first published in 1902, was still in print as late as 1930. Mr Ahmad is said to have been a highly-successful punter.[4]

W. R. Old died on 23 December 1929, eight months before the editor of the London *Sunday Express* discovered, probably not without surprise, that there was a mass-readership for feature articles on astrology. The

[1] Annie Besant (1847–1933) was Madame Blavatsky's most outstanding convert. Formerly, as vice-president of the National Secular Society and a close associate of Charles Bradlaugh, she had been a vociferous advocate of free thought and agnosticism. Soon after meeting H.P.B. in 1889 she abandoned rationalism for esotericism. Her identification with Indian nationalism began in the early 1890s.

[2] *Old Moore's Monthly Messenger*, November 1913.

[3] Advertisement in *Coming Events*, December 1898. A somewhat similar service was announced in 1915 when the monthly subscription was 20s. (*British Journal of Astrology*, November 1915).

[4] The earliest reference to astrological horse-racing systems may be in 'Professor' John Ackroyd's pamphlet *Astrology: Egyptian Astronomy*, Rochdale, 1878, where there is an advertisement for the author's forthcoming *Treatise on Astrology applied to Speculation on the Turf*, 'whereby a fortune may be made in a short time'. There is no evidence that it was ever published. Powley included a few articles on the subject in *The Astrologer*. I have typescripts of most of Sepharial's systems but have never put them to the test. Copies will be supplied to astrologers in return for a donation to any appropriate society for the suppression of gambling.

invention of popular newspaper astrology appears to have been a specifically British development. Having nurtured belief in 'the stars' during the long period when it was practically dormant on the Continent, we now gave the topic the widest possible publicity. Neither Lord Beaverbrook, who controlled the *Sunday Express*, nor John Gordon, who edited the paper at that time, cared a fig for astrology. For them the only important factor was that given the necessary expertise, in terms of journalistic skill and editorial presentation, it helped to increase circulation. It soon became clear that popular astrological journalism was ripe for exploitation, and readers' letters proved the point within a day or two of the publication of R. H. Naylor's first feature article.

At this point, before discussing the impact of newspaper astrology, I must mention that the post-Leo era, as far as Great Britain is concerned, is of little interest to a historian of this recondite subject. In Europe, after 1920, the most important centre of astrological activity and endeavour was Germany, where the preoccupation with astrology was on a scale never matched in Great Britain nor, for that matter, in any other country. Having produced Leo, whose name was well known in international astrological circles—W. R. Old's importance was negligible by comparison —the British rested upon their astral laurels. When the Germans eventually got to grips with astrology after *c.* 1920, they did so with the thoroughness that is said to be characteristic of their national character. The British astrologers, comparatively few in number and well content with the unsophisticated traditional or esoteric astrology that they had inherited from the Victorians and Leo and his generation, were hardly aware of what was afoot in Leipzig, Munich, Düsseldorf, Hamburg and other centres of Teutonic astrological endeavour.

So far I have said nothing about astrology in the United States of America. It is inconceivable that the early settlers arrived without a copy of one of the seventeenth-century manuals, and the ephemerides published annually by the Stationers' Company must have found their way across the Atlantic. However, there does not appear to have been a domestic American astrological literature until the 1840s, when Thomas Hague, of Philadelphia, published a periodical, *The Horoscope* (1840–4 with several minor changes of title), which was followed by *Hague's Horoscope and Scientific and Prophetic Messenger*, Philadelphia, 1845–8. The circulation of these publications must have been very small.

The most energetic nineteenth-century American astrological publicist was undoubtedly Luke Broughton (1828–99), who migrated from Leeds to Philadelphia in *c.* 1855. His father had practised medicine and astrology at Leeds and so, too, had his uncle Dr Mark Broughton. The latter was probably the author of *The Sidereal Atlas, or Messenger of Astrology* almanac for 1845. Both the elder Broughtons appear to have been qualified physicians. Luke Broughton's two elder brothers, Mathew and Mark, had preceded him to Philadelphia, where both practised astrology. Luke took a medical degree there in *c.* 1863. He had already commenced the publication of *Broughton's Monthly Planet Reader and Astrological Journal* (No. 1, April 1860) which he continued in New York City when he moved there in 1863. His *Elements of Astrology* [1898] seems to have been the first ambitious textbook to be published in the U.S.A. One of his pupils was the astrologer 'Professor' W. H. Chaney (*b.* 1821), whose illegitimate son, by the musical spiritualist Flora Wellman, later became the well-known novelist Jack London.

American astrologers were largely dependent upon British manuals until soon after the First World War, although a large domestic literature was subsequently created. I speedily dispossessed myself of the works of Messrs Max Heindel, Nicholas de Vore, Lewellyn George, Evangeline Adams, Manly Palmer Hall, Marc Edmund Jones and all the other American *cognoscenti* without feeling their loss. They and other twentieth-century American astrologers closely resemble most of their European counterparts which means, in effect, that they confidently reproduce the same old traditional fodder. Again, as in Europe, the leading American publicists are members of an 'underground' movement that can only be loosely defined. They have, however, been responsible for a widespread and successful dissemination of astrological beliefs. In 1941, for example, the U.S.A. could provide sufficient readers to support no less than seven mass-circulation astrological monthlies.[1]

[1] See Marcia Moore, *Astrology Today, A Socio-Psychological Study*, New York City, Lucas Publishing Co., 1960 (typewriter fascimile), offered as a B.A. thesis at Radcliffe College. This contains an analysis of a questionnaire sent to 900 astrologers. The publication was sponsored by the late Alice A. Bailey's Lucis Trust. Mrs Bailey was the author of a series of inflated 'esoteric' works, for the most part 'dictated' by a discarnate gentleman called 'The Thibetan'. The curious are referred to her autobiography, *The Unfinished Memoirs of Alice A. Bailey*, Lucis Press, 1951. Her protégé Dane Rudhyar's *The Astrology of Personality: A Re-Formulation of Astrological Concepts and Ideals, in Terms of Contemporary Psychology and Philosophy*, New York City, Lucis Publishing Co., 1936 (recently reprinted) represents a serious attempt to define modern astrological concepts. This book has undeniable soporific qualities. *In Search* (12 issues, 1958–61) published by the now defunct Astrological Centre, New York City, is one of the more interesting English-language periodical publications. Sydney Omarr's *Henry Miller: His World of Urania*, 1960, is a useful guide to the many allusions to astrology in Miller's books. See also Henry Miller's *Big Sur and the Oranges of Hieronymus Bosch*, London, 1958, for its entertaining chapters on Conrad Moricand, the French astrologer.

4

Newspaper Astrology in Great Britain

The 'predictions' published by a large number of European and North American mass-circulation newspapers and women's magazines have become such a commonplace feature of everyday life that the singular nature of the phenomenon has been obscured by its familiarity. What is so bizarre is that these publications, which claim to be as modern as the hour, should perpetuate the survival of beliefs that originated in pre-Christian Babylon and Hellenistic Greece. This is possibly the strangest feature of all.

Most who read or glance at these prognostications regard them as a harmless form of entertainment. Nevertheless, it is this daily or weekly ration of astrological speculation that has persuaded millions to infer, however vaguely, that the stars in their courses might conceivably influence human destinies. Again, popular astrological journalism is undoubtedly responsible for the fact that a surprisingly large proportion of adults not only know their zodiacal (Sun) sign but, in addition, something about the 'astral' qualities attributed to it. There is also a considerable market for monthly periodicals whose contents consist almost entirely of astrological forecasts and information.[1]

The London *Sunday Express*, which was the first important newspaper to publicise astrology on a large scale, became aware of its journalistic possibilities entirely by chance. Princess Margaret Rose, the younger daughter of the Duke and Duchess of York and sister of the present Queen Elizabeth II, was born at Glamis Castle in Scotland on 21 August 1930. Since the news was already two or three days old when the issue for Sunday, 24 August was being prepared, the editor decided to give it a fresh angle by publishing a short article about the Princess's horoscope.

R. H. Naylor (1889–1952), a London professional astrologer, was invited to erect the chart and to supply the necessary commentary. Mr Naylor did all this and, furthermore, added some brief information about the current astrological prospects of people whose birthday anniversary lay in the week ahead. This article was published as a half-page feature. An immediate flood of appreciative readers' letters persuaded the editor that it might be profitable to add astrology to the traditional recipe of crime, sex, sport and scandal, and another article ('Were you born in September?') was commissioned for publication on the following Sunday. This, too, was received with acclamation and Naylor was asked to provide

---

[1] Cf. *Prediction* (Great Britain), *American Astrology* (U.S.A.), *Horoscope* and *Astres* (France), *Das Neue Zeitalter* (Germany), and many others. No circulation figures are available but all these publications have a nation-wide distribution and can be purchased at bookstalls.

a series of contributions. The first of these was scheduled to appear on Sunday, 5 October.

By noon that morning at least several hundred thousand of the newspaper's million purchasers must have read Naylor's prediction to the effect that British aircraft were prospectively in serious danger. Confirmation was soon forthcoming when the BBC announced that the R-101 airship, which was on its maiden flight from Cardington to India, had crashed in northern France. A week later the *Sunday Express* gave the forecast a lot of publicity and henceforth allowed Naylor a full page for his weekly articles which now became one of its permanent features. Naylor became famous almost overnight and wrote for the *Sunday Express* until the wartime shortage of newsprint.

It was not long before *The People*, the *Sunday Express*'s most important rival, jumped on to the astrological band-wagon with a weekly article by Edward Lyndoe.

An astrological publicity stunt staged by the *Sunday Dispatch* for circulation promotion purposes in 1936 deserves commemoration, if only because of its farcical nature. It has been described by Mr W. J. Tucker in his *Autobiography of an Astrologer*, 1960.[1] In 1936 Mr Tucker was a comparatively new recruit to the ranks of the professional astrological publicists, but was subsequently to achieve a certain prominence.

William Joseph Tucker, the son of a London policeman, was born on 19 November 1896 and left school at the age of fourteen. After his demobilisation from the army in 1919 he was employed in the fur trade until 1931, but during his spare time took correspondence courses in civil engineering and chemistry. Mr Tucker was, in fact, a scientist *manqué*. He also tried his hand at journalism and contributed film reviews to various cinema journals and local newspapers. He became interested in astrology in 1930 when he was writing his first book, *The 'How' of the Human Mind*, but objected to the evidently unscientific approach of all the well-known astrological pundits. Now his self-appointed task was to clean out astrology's Augean stables: '. . . my scientific training insisted upon the restoration of order out of the existing chaos, the aim being to reconstruct Chaldean Astrology within a scientific framework'. This laudable objective was quickly achieved and in 1933 he founded the Scientific (Anti-Occult) Astrological Company. He and a partner in this progressive enterprise employed a staff of canvassers to obtain orders for astrological work. This novel approach soon brought a visit from the police but Mr Tucker was able to assure the authorities as to the scientific nature of his methods and he was left undisturbed.

In April 1935 he published the first issue of a new periodical, *Science*

---

[1] This and about two dozen other books by Mr Tucker, all printed on a duplicating machine, are obtainable from their author at Pythagorean Publications, 45 Penshurst Avenue, Sidcup, Kent.

and Astrology. Within a few months its circulation had risen to about 36,000 copies, of which no less than 30,000 were exported to the U.S.A. In the meantime his own newly-formed publishing company had issued half a dozen of his own books, including *The 'How' of the Human Mind*. Unfortunately for Mr Tucker *Science and Astrology* came to an abrupt end in November 1936 when its American distributors refused to pay for the August and September issues on the grounds that the paper covers had cracked and come apart. This disaster, which Mr Tucker's own horoscope had apparently failed to reveal, occurred at the very time when he was heavily engaged in work for the *Sunday Dispatch*.

His connection with the *Sunday Dispatch* operation began on Wednesday, 23 September 1936 when he received an urgent telephone call from the editor. When they met the following day Mr Tucker was invited to contribute a weekly feature article, under the pseudonym 'Scorpio', to be called 'Your Future in the Stars', also to supply *Sunday Dispatch* readers with personal horoscopes at the unusually low price of 1s. 6d. each, of which 6d. was to be retained by the newspaper. The scheme was announced only three days later, namely in the issue for Sunday, 27 September, so very little time was available for the necessary preparations.

Neither Mr Tucker nor the editor knew how many people would rush to buy 1s. 6d. postal orders during the next few weeks but they budgeted on the basis of an initial weekly demand for 5,000 horoscopes. Most astrologers would have been aghast at the prospect of having to erect even fifty charts in such a short time, but Mr Tucker was undeterred.

'It was necessary to find immediate office accommodation with sufficient space to house several hundred workers,' he wrote. 'And since a *personal* horoscope chart of the nativity of each applicant had to be compiled with calculated aspects, this meant I would need to find competent astrologers for the work.' He managed to engage six whom he described as 'fairly competent' but required at least sixty. Hence it was necessary to train people to do the work in a completely mechanical fashion on a 'production line' basis.

Mr Tucker's horoscope factory was soon in full swing. He had quickly compiled what he described as 'code-books controlling the horoscope assembly' and at the same time began to train the staff. Its members were divided into three groups: there were those who calculated the natal charts, those who 'coded' the horoscopes, and finally those who assembled 'complete horoscopes from the furnished codes'. The operation was completely successful. There was a 'torrential flood of applications' and for a while Mr Tucker and his helpers were inundated with work. The *Sunday Dispatch*'s great 1s. 6d. horoscope scheme ran for a few weeks and was then quietly allowed to disappear.

I have before me the prospectus for the second (1962) edition of *The 'How' of the Human Mind* by Wm. J. Tucker, D.Sc., Ph.D. 'which gained for its author a degree of Doctor of Science from each of two universities'. These academic distinctions were bestowed upon Mr Tucker late in 1937. In his own words: 'Early in 1936 I made the acquaintance of Dr Henry Chellew, one-time lecturer on Psychology to the University of London . . . it was my book *The 'How' of the Human Mind* which specially engaged the doctor's attention. It succeeded in evoking from him vociferous praise. He asserted vigorously that the book had not received the attention which its merit deserved, and declared his determination to see that honour should be bestowed where it was due. At all events, it was through the very good offices of Dr H. Chellew, supported by that well-known scientist, Professor A. M. Low, that my book was brought to the attention of the American universities with the special recommendation of its sponsors. As a result, both the American Institute of Applied Psychology and The Temple Bar College, each accepted *The 'How' of the Human Mind* as a thesis, and each conferred upon me the degree of Doctor of Science.'[1]

Within a month or two Mr Tucker became thrice a Doctor. The Temple Bar College degree was awarded on 15 November 1937, while that of the American Institute of Applied Psychology was granted only two days later. The latter institution of higher learning made him a Doctor of Philosophy early in 1938 and at the same time appointed him a member of its European Board of Regents. Dr Tucker must be one of the few men alive today who has gained three doctorates within as many months.[2]

There is, of course, a difference between full-page feature articles, such as those that R. H. Naylor used to write in the 1930s, and the dozen very brief paragraphs that represent the current astrological pabulum in British and other daily newspapers. Contrary to the generally-held belief that these 'predictions' are composed by any available member of the editorial staff, who could obviously no more cast a horoscope than fly, they are generally supplied, at least in Great Britain, by professional astrologers. During the early 1960s 'Lord Luck', of the *Daily Express*, was paid about £15 per week for his trouble. The engagement of his predecessor had been speedily terminated because he had rashly predicted: 'Today is specially propitious for stock exchange speculations' on a public holiday when the stock exchange was closed. The incongruity had not been noticed, but a score of readers' letters soon drew attention to the gaffe.

---

[1] W. J. Tucker, *Autobiography of an Astrologer*, 1960, pp. 305-6.

[2] Dr Tucker does not seem to have been aware that his friend Mr Chellew never had any connection with the University of London. The late Henry Chellew was obliged to acknowledge this fact in writing on 28 June 1954. (Information communicated to me by the Secretary of the Senate.) The late A. M. Low's claim to the title of Professor was, to say the least, unsatisfactory. See Lord Brabazon of Tara's Introduction to Ursula Bloom's biography *He lit the lamp*, 1958. The American Institute of Applied Psychology ceased to exist in the early 1940s, while The Temple Bar College (Seattle) was closed by order of the Federal Trade Commission in July 1947.

5
The French Revival

One may search in vain for the French equivalents of R. J. Morrison, W. J. Simmonite, A. J. Pearce and others who kept astrology alive in Great Britain during the nineteenth century. In France it had to all intents and purposes been forgotten. Even as late as 1891 Papus confidently asserted that 'astrology is one of the ancient divinatory sciences whose rules have been completely lost today.'[1] Papus was the pseudonym of Dr Gérard Encausse (1865–1916), whose monumental *Traité méthodique de science occulte* was published in 1891 when he was only 26 years old. The French astrological revival began soon after the appearance of this book and was a by-product of the widespread popular interest in occultism that Encausse himself did so much to foster in France.

France was the centre of a kind of Romantic Hermetism. Any study of the latter's origins inevitably leads in the direction of the French *Illuminés* of the period just before the French Revolution, e.g. Martines de Pasqually, Louis-Claude de Saint Martin ('*le philosophe inconnu*'), J.-B. Willermoz and others, most of whom had connections with contemporary continental freemasonry. Here all the strands met.[2]

The mature French occultist movement, which reached its apogee in the 1890s (*fin de siecle*!), and which gave birth to the revival of astrology in France, was created by an extraordinary galaxy of students of magic, alchemy, the Cabala and what they imagined to be Rosicrucian tradition. The authoritative recent sources of hidden knowledge were thought to be available in the writings of Fabre d'Olivet (1767–1825), Hoëne Wronski (1778–1843) and Eliphas Lévi (i.e. Abbé Louis Constant, 1810–75), with the Cabala as the ultimate repository of arcane wisdom. Papus wrote: 'All the alchemists are cabalists, all the religious or militant secret societies [e.g. the original Templars] that have appeared in the West—Gnostics, Rosicrucians, Martinistes [i.e. followers of Louis-Claude de Saint Martin] and Freemasons—are linked with the Cabala or expound its theories . . . the Cabala, as we see it, is the most

---

[1] Papus, *Traité méthodique de science occulte*, 1891, p. 1043.

[2] See A. Viatte's important *Les sources occultes du romantisme, 1770–1820*, 2 vols., 1928. Of the more recent publications see *Aspects de l'illuminisme au 18me. siècle*, edited by R. Amadou, Les Cahiers de la Tour Saint-Jacques, 1960, also Serge Hutin, *Les sociétés secrètes*, 1960, which includes a useful check-list of books on the history of French freemasonry. Details of the publications of many obscure nineteenth-century Frenchmen who wrote on various departments of occultism will be found in Papus, *Traité*, 1891. See also A. L. Caillet, *Manuel bibliographique des sciences psychiques ou occultes*, 3 vols., 1912.

complete version of the mysteries of Egypt that has reached us.'[1]

The Cabalist texts, commentaries and theories that fascinated the French occultists had very little connection with those of the Jewish esoteric schools that began to flourish in the south of Spain and Provence during the thirteenth century. Renaissance humanists such as Pico della Mirandola and Johannes Reuchlin were interested in the Cabala because it incorporated familiar Pythagorean and Neoplatonic ideas. As in astrology and, indeed, all other departments of Hermetism, there was the attractive concept of a universal Law of Correspondence, hence the basis of a system by which the nature of Man in relation to the Cosmos could be explained and understood. A later and less respectable development of the so-called Christian Cabala, namely the version created by non-Jewish humanists, was the supposed connection between the Cabala and magic, typically in the form of Gematria, which still survives as Numerology, a method of divination in which the letters of the alphabet are related to numbers. Cabalist symbolism, which permeated every department of late renaissance Hermetic and magical theory, also became part and parcel of the theoretical apparatus of alchemy and traces can also be found in masonic literature.[2]

In France in the 1880s there was little or no interest in early Cabalist writings. The authority who exercised the greatest influence upon Papus and his generation was Eliphas Lévi, who suddenly emerged during the 1850s as an occult publicist of the first rank.[3] His *Dogme et rituel de la haute magie*, 1856, was reprinted no less than three times before 1903 and is still available in French, English and German. It is one of those books that the innocent mistakenly purchase in the expectation that it contains arcane knowledge of the highest quality. This is by no means the case.

According to Jules Bois, who explored its highways and by-ways in an elegantly cynical manner, e.g. in his amusing *Le monde invisible*, 1902, the French occultist movement of the 1890s began to take shape in *c.* 1884. The fact that Madame Blavatsky was in France for a while in 1884 may be regarded as coincidental. She recruited a small but enthusiastic following there, but by comparison with its British counterpart the French branch of the Theosophical Society was neither influential nor important. This was because Madame Blavatsky's 'message' had very little appeal for such

---

[1] Papus, *Traité*, pp. 480–2. The myth that western Hermetism originated in ancient Egypt is refuted in Frances A. Yates, *Giordano Bruno and the Hermetic Tradition*, London, 1964.

[2] Modern Cabalist works by such occultists as Dion Fortune, *The Mystical Qabala*, 1935, and Israel Regardie, *The Tree of Life*, 1932, can be safely ignored. Will-Erich Peuckert, *Pansophie: Ein Versuch zur Geschichte der weissen und schwarzen Magie*, 2nd edit., Berlin, 1956, contains an authoritative account of magical Cabalism in the sixteenth and seventeenth centuries. See also G. Scholem, *Major Trends in Jewish Mysticism*, 1941, and his masterly *Ursprunge und Anfänge der Kabbala*, 1962.

[3] See Paul Chacornac's biographical study, *Eliphas Lévi, rénovateur de l'occultisme en France*, 1926.

sophisticated young occultists as Encausse and his friends Stanislas de Guaita (1861–97) and Josephin Péladan (1859–1918). Schoolboys when Eliphas Lévi died in 1875, fifteen years later they were the leading French exponents of occultism. All of them were Cabalists and Neo-Rosicrucians.[1] During the 1880s, at any rate, it is unlikely that any of them would have known very much about astrology for the very good reason, as Encausse observed in 1891, that astrology itself had been completely forgotten in France.

In 1890 little or nothing on the subject had been published in France for more than two centuries. J. B. Morin de Villefranche's monumental *Astrologia Gallica*, 1661, the last of the major French manuals was not as scarce in the 1890s as it is today, but would-be astrologers who could read Latin must have been *rarae aves*. Nevertheless, there were a few, but very few, practitioners of a curious kind of Cabalist astrology that was unknown outside France. Its principal exponent was Paul Christian (i.e. J.-B. Pitois, 1811–77), a well-known student of occultism who was a contemporary of Eliphas Lévi.[2]

The first of the modern French astrological treatises was Ely Star's *Les mystères de l'horoscope*, 1887, which describes an onomantic or Cabalist astrology resembling Christian's. 'Doctor' Ely Star (i.e. Eugène Jacob, 1847–1942) was one of those curious persons who abound in occultist circles. The son of a farmer at Neufchâteau, Vosges, he came to Paris during the late 1870s, was enthused by Lévi's and Christian's magical works and in due course became secretary of the Cercle des Études Psychologiques, whose members were mainly interested in spiritualism and animal magnetism. He appears to have earned his living by the sale of magical amulets and medical practice of a dubious nature. His wife practised cartomancy professionally. He was prosecuted for fraud in 1914 and was sentenced to a short term of imprisonment.[3]

Star's *Les mystères de l'horoscope* is of interest because it contains the first modern reproductions of the designs of the twenty-two major Tarot

[1] See Oswald Wirth, *Stanislas de Guaita, Souvenirs de son secrétaire*, Paris, 1935; Philippe Encausse, *Papus (Dr Gerard Encausse), sa vie, son oeuvre*, Paris, 1932; R. G. Abrun, *Péladan*, 2nd edit., Paris, 1904, also articles about him in *Nouvelle Revue du Midi*, Nimes, December 1924.

[2] The 'system', which is quite unlike conventional astrology, is described in Christian's *L'homme rouge des Tuileries*, Paris, 1863; 2nd edit., [1937], also in his *Histoire de la Magie*, 1870 (English translation as *The History and Practice of Magic*, edited and revised by Ross Nichols, 2 vols., London, 1952). Paul Chacornac, *Éliphas Lévi*, 1926, refers briefly to Christian's *Carmen Sibyllum, Prédiction de las naissance du fils de Napoleon III par les Arcanes du Magism égyptien consulté le 3 avril 1850*, Paris, 1854. Chacornac mentions two other Frenchmen who were interested in astrology before 1890: Dr Henri Favre (1827–1916), editor of *France Médicale* from 1863, who was an exponent of both astrology and physiognomy, and Eugène Ladois (1822–1904), the author of several physiognomical works.

[3] See Jules Bois, *Le monde invisible*, 1902, p. 291, and *Zentralblatt für Okkultismus*, Leipzig, vol. viii, 1914–15, pp. 150–2.

trumps, the so-called *Arcanes majeures*, which he took from the copper-plate engravings in the eighth volume of Court de Gebelin's *Le monde primitif*, 1781. De Gebelin was the first to ascribe an occult or mantic significance to these cards. The theme was subsequently developed by Eliphas Lévi and Paul Christian, but it was clearly Papus and his friend Oswald Wirth who were responsible for much of the nonsense that is currently ascribed to Tarot symbolism. Indeed, I cannot sufficiently emphasise the artificial nature of the Tarot's alleged connection with traditional Hermetism.[1]

There is no evidence that anyone outside France was familiar with the principles of onomantic astrology as outlined by Christian and Star. However, the French soon rediscovered astrology's traditional rules and, furthermore, in a respectably 'classical' form. The father of the new French astrological movement was F.-Ch. Barlet (i.e. Albert Faucheux, 1838–1921), who was well known in occultist circles and a prominent member of Stanislas de Guaita's Ordre Kabbalistique de la Rose-Croix. Barlet had acquired a working knowledge of conventional astrology as early as 1886—he seems to have been familiar with the contemporary British literature—and subsequently taught the art to Abel Haatan (i.e. Abel Thomas), a pharmacist whose shop was in the rue d'Aboukir. Haatan was also an enthusiastic alchemist.[2] He was the author of a little *Traité d'astrologie judiciaire*, 1895, which was followed two years later by Fomalhaut's *Manuel d'astrologie sphérique et judiciaire*, Paris, 1897, in which astrology's mathematical procedures, but little else, were presented with immense care. This book also contains a section describing possible analogies between the Tarot trumps, the planets and the signs of the zodiac. Furthermore, more than thirty years before the discovery of the planet Pluto, Fomalhaut confidently stated on p. 316: 'There is a planet beyond the orbit of Neptune and its name is Pluto.' Fomalhaut, however, was none other than the Abbé Charles Nicoullaud (1854–1925), a priest

---

[1] The first full-scale Tarot manual was Papus, *Le Tarot des Bohémiens*, 1889, in which the twenty-two Major Trumps were accorded a Cabalist significance. A. P. Morton's English translation was published in London in 1892 and was followed by A. E. Waite's *Pictorial Key to the Tarot*, 1911. The first German manual, E. Kurtzahn's *Der Tarot*, did not appear until 1920. The only more or less satisfactory history of the Tarot is G. van Rijnberk's *Le Tarot*, Lyons, 1947.

[2] There was no corresponding interest in alchemy in Great Britain. Among the leading nineteenth-century French *amateurs* were Louis Lucas (1816–63), a pupil of Hoëne Wronski, author of *La médecine nouvelle*, 2 vols., Paris, 1861–3, and Saint-Yves d'Alveydre (i.e. Joseph-Alexander Saint Yves, 1842–1910). Jules Bois wrote a witty account of his one and only meeting with the latter, who informed him that he had written 1,400 pages in three days, the material being transmitted to him telepathically by the Grand Lama of Tibet. For an account of his extraordinary sociological theories, apparently inspired by or plagiarised from Fabre d'Olivet's *Histoire philosophique du genre humain*, 1824, see Barlet's *Saint-Yves d'Alveydre*, Paris, 1910. The French preoccupation with alchemy continues. See L. Pauwels and J. Bergier's best-selling *Le matin des magiciens*, Paris, 1960, and the fascinating 'Dossier Fulcanelli' by R. Ambelain and E. Cansliet in *Parapsychologie*, Les Cahiers de la Tour Saint-Jacques, ix, [1962].

who was the *curé* of a large Parisian parish. His book is still in print.[1]

Neither Haatan's nor Fomalhaut's manuals attracted much attention in French occultist circles during the 1890s and astrology was still unknown outside a small sector of that particular *milieu*. Jules Bois, for instance, was surprised to discover an astrologer, a certain Gévingey, above the Café Voltaire in the Place de l'Odeon. 'Who would still have hoped to find astrologers in Paris?' he asked in 1902.[2]

Nevertheless, an expansion of interest in astrology was imminent. It began during the early 1900s with the publication of Henri Selva's *La théorie des déterminations astrologiques de Morin de Villefranche*, 1902, and the first of Paul Choisnard's books. In Great Britain, where there was a fair choice of manuals published since 1850, Alan Leo and his contemporaries were content to ignore the seventeenth-century textbooks which were regarded as old-fashioned. They uncritically accepted the Tradition in the form in which it had reached them. In France, however, it was still necessary to identify the classical Tradition, and preferably in as pure and authoritative a form as possible.

Henri Selva (b. 1861) supposed that he had achieved this when he translated and edited a number of chapters in Morin de Villefranche's vast *Astrologia Gallica*, 1661, which contained the most highly-synthesised and, indeed, sophisticated instructions for horoscope delineation so far achieved by any of the old authors. This book, which for Selva had the merit of being written by a compatriot, was known in England towards the end of the seventeenth century but in the meantime had been completely forgotten there. The Morinus 'system' as presented by Selva has noticeably influenced the modern French approach to astrology.[3] It was adopted by many German astrologers after 1920 but is still practically unknown in Great Britain.

Throughout the nineteenth century the majority of the British astrological writers were at the same time professional practitioners. In France, however, practically all the authors whose works were published during the period 1890–1920 preserved a more or less amateur status. Selva was employed on the Paris stock exchange while Paul Choisnard (1867–1930), whose early books appeared under the pseudonym Paul Flambart, was a graduate of the famous École Polytechnique and an artillery officer. Choisnard's name deserves commemoration because he was the first to make a serious attempt to establish the existence of astral influences on

---

[1] Nicoullaud was the founder of the anti-masonic periodical *Revue internationale des sociétes secrètes*. He was also a Nostradamus expert (see p. 161 infra). Another Roman Catholic priest who was interested in astrology was the Abbé Eugène Vignon (1864–1936), whose *Petit manuel pratique de l'astrologie* was published under the pseudonym A. de Thyane in *c*. 1908.

[2] Jules Bois, *Le monde invisible*, Paris, 1902, p. 281.

[3] See J. Hiéroz, *L'astrologie selon Morin de Villefranche*, 2nd edit., Paris, 1962, and other books by this author.

human individuals on the basis of statistical evidence. The Tradition suggested to him that he might expect to find certain features in the horoscopes of several members of the same family, e.g. a parent with Sun in Leo and a child with a Leo ascendant. Nobody had previously subjected collections of horoscopes to statistical analysis, although A. J. Pearce had already foreseen something of the kind in 1880.[1]

Hence Choisnard's *Preuves et bases de l'astrologie scientifique*, Paris, 1908, which was based upon two earlier works (*Influence astrale*, 1900, and *Étude nouvelle sur l'hérédité*, 1903) represents a landmark in this particular literature. Choisnard himself was satisfied that he had furnished adequate proof of his thesis but it must be emphasised that he worked with limited material and that his statistical techniques were undoubtedly primitive. Official science, as might be expected, ignored his supposed findings. His astrological *confrères* in France gratefully acknowledged his authority while their counterparts in Great Britain do not appear to have been aware of his existence. At this time (*c.* 1908) the Germans had yet to rediscover astrology.

The historical pattern of the French astrological revival after 1900 is much the same as in Great Britain, except that no professional practitioner or publicist of Alan Leo's calibre emerged. Again, there was no marked extension of interest in the subject until after the First World War, when a large domestic literature was produced. The general public did not begin to become aware of astrology through the daily press and such popular periodicals as *Votre Destin* (1935) and *Sous le Ciel* (1936) until after *c.* 1930.

Unlike their German contemporaries, the French astrologers were never greatly interested in the 'organisation' of their movement, hence there was a comparative absence of internecine strife, although there were frequent and noisy quarrels on points of doctrine. The French appear to have been completely ignorant of all that was happening on the astrological scene in other countries, but this insular attitude was equally evident in Great Britain and Germany. There has never been anything corresponding to a European, let alone a world-wide, astrological movement.

In 1944 the Vicomte Charles de Herbais de Thun (*b.* 1862), a Belgian astrologer, published a massive biographical *Encyclopédie du mouvement astrologique de langue française* (456 pages), containing details of the careers and book and periodical publications of *c.* 170 French-speaking astrologers from *c.* 1890 onwards. Buried in this mass of data, for the most part relating to unimportant or very obscure people, there is nevertheless a large amount of interesting although unsynthesised material. The *Encyclopédie* is a notable work in a bibliographical context, although decades may pass before a candidate for a Ph.D. thesis will bless the Vicomte's memory.[2]

[1] See 'Vital Statistics and Astrology' in *Urania*, March 1880.
[2] Copies of de Herbais de Thun's *Encyclopédie* were still available in 1966 from Monsieur G.-L. Brahy, 107 Avenue Albert, Brussels, Belgium.

6
The German Revival

Throughout the eighteenth and nineteenth centuries astrology was as much underground in German-speaking countries as elsewhere in Europe. The fact that Julius Pfaff (*b.* 1774), professor of mathematics at the University of Erlangen from 1818 until his death in 1835, was interested in it has latterly been misinterpreted. It is claimed by contemporary German astrologers that Pfaff taught astrology at Erlangen, seemingly upon the fallacious assumption that since he was a university professor and had a working knowledge of astrology, he cannot have failed to have lectured on it. This is unlikely. Astrology was only one of Pfaff's many extra-mural preoccupations, e.g. the history of ancient religions, egyptology and philology. His astrological publications included *Astrologie*, Nürnberg, 1816, a collection of aphorisms culled from the works of old authors, and the first complete translation into German of the *Tetrabiblos* of Claudius Ptolemaeus.[1]

A handful of pamphlets represents the total output of German astrological literature during the half century after Pfaff's death, suggesting that the subject was only of interest to a few eccentrics who had access to the older literature.[2]

The origins of the modern German astrological movement are to be found close to the Theosophical Society in the 1880s. Madame Blavatsky arrived in Europe from India in the spring of 1884 and spent the next few months in Paris and London. It was then that she first met Frau Gebhard. Marie Gebhard (1832–92), the daughter of Major Thomas L'Estrange, of Dublin, was the wife of Gustav Gebhard, a well-to-do manufacturer at Elberfeld. She was a devoted student of the Cabala and *Haute Magie* and a pupil (mainly by correspondence) of Eliphas Lévi, whom she visited almost annually for instruction in Paris from 1865 until the Master's death a decade later. After the Franco-Prussian war Lévi spent a few weeks at Elberfeld and no doubt admired the 'Occult Room' which she had specially furnished at her handsome residence at Platzhof 12. The German Section of the Theosophical Society was founded in the 'Occult Room' on 22 July 1884, with Dr Wilhelm Hübbe-Schleiden as its President. Two

---

[1] The translation was published in his *Astrologisches Taschenbuch für das Jahr 1822* and continued in the edition for 1823. The co-editor of the *Taschenbücher* was his colleague G. H. Schubert (1780–1860), a pioneer parapsychologist in the field of animal magnetism, clairvoyance and dreams. His *Nachtseite der Naturwissenschaften*, 1808, 4th edit., 1840, was widely read in its day.

[2] See Dr Adolph Drechsler, *Astrologische Vorträge gehalten zu Dresden im Winter 1854–5*, Freiburg i. Br., 1855 (88 pp.) and J. A. Mensinga, *Über alte und neuere Astrologie*, Berlin, 1871 (40 pp.).

weeks later Madame Blavatsky came to Elberfeld and was the Gebhards' guest until shortly before she returned to India at the end of October.

Dr Hübbe-Schleiden (1846–1916) was already well known as an advocate of German colonial expansion but henceforth played an important part in the development of the German Theosophical movement, which soon attracted a fair number of recruits. In 1885 he began to publish *Die Sphinx*, a monthly journal devoted to Theosophy and occultism. One of his contributors was Karl Kiesewetter, who was the first to write about astrology in any modern German periodical.[1]

Madame Blavatsky was in Europe again in the spring of 1885 and never returned to India. One of her companions on the voyage back was Dr Franz Hartmann, a German who had just made a lengthy sojourn at the Society's headquarters at Adyar. Franz Hartmann (*b*. Donauwörth 1838, *d*. 1912) was a student of pharmacy and medicine at Munich during the early 1860s. He had not yet completed his studies when he spent a summer holiday in Paris in 1865. He made an excursion to Le Havre and, acting upon a sudden impulse, applied for the post of ship's doctor in a vessel that was just about to sail with emigrants to the U.S.A. Forty-two days later he disembarked in North America where he remained for the next seventeen years. Here it is sufficient to record that he acquired a medical degree at St Louis, became an American citizen and practised medicine in many different parts of the U.S.A. He was interested in spiritualism and joined the Theosophical Society after reading H. P. Blavatsky's *Isis Unveiled* sometime after 1877. In 1883 he made his way via Japan to the Theosophical Society's headquarters at Adyar where he met Madame Blavatsky. He was to be deeply involved in the Theosophical Society's affairs and politics, at first in India and after 1885 in Europe until his death in Germany in 1912.[2]

Hartmann was one of the most prolific writers of his generation on Theosophy, magic and occultism. He was also familiar with Hindu and Buddhist literature and was respected by Theosophists as an authority on these subjects. Madame Blavatsky's attitude to him was ambivalent. In a letter to A. P. Sinnett (September 1885) she exclaimed: 'Poor Hartmann. He *is* a bad lot, but he would give his life to the Masters [i.e. the invisible 'Mahatmas'] and Occultism . . . but *I* cannot trust him.' In short, Hartmann was one of the many extraordinary and, it must be said, unsatisfactory people that abounded in the Theosophical *milieu* during its pre-1914 heyday.

In *c*. 1899 Hartmann recruited a disciple and secretarial amanuensis in the shape of a university student by the name of Hugo Vollrath (*b*. 11

---

[1] Karl Kiesewetter (1854–95) was the author of *Geschichte des neueren Occultismus*, 1891, a standard work on modern occultism that was published in the same year as Papus' *Traité*. The two books cover much the same ground. Kiesewetter's early death at Meiningen was caused by poisoning from drugs taken to induce clairvoyance.

[2] See F. Hartmann's autobiographical *Denkwürdige Erinnerungen*, 1898.

April 1877). They were a strange couple: Hartmann, whom the British Theosophists nicknamed 'Dirty Franz' because of his unwashed appearance, and Hugo Vollrath, forty years his junior, a quick-witted rascal with a penchant for occultism. Vollrath now abandoned his studies in order to accompany Hartmann on his incessant lecture tours and quickly discovered that there was a market for occult 'knowledge' although some years passed before he entered the field as an independent operator. If I have introduced Vollrath, who was to be a key figure in the subsequent development of the new German astrological movement, via Madame Blavatsky, Dr Hübbe-Schleiden and Dr Hartmann, it is to show that in Germany after c. 1910 as, indeed, in Great Britain during the 1890s, the revival of interest in astrology had a specifically Theosophical background.

In 1907 Hugo Vollrath was 30 years old and without a settled profession. His university career had ended when he became Dr Hartmann's *chela*, but this did not deter him from calling himself Herr Dr Vollrath.[1] The Leipzig Theosophical group had latterly allowed him to take charge of its library, only to discover that he had conjured up a so-called 'Literary Department' of the German Section of the Theosophical Society, complete with a panel of honorary members or patrons whose names were used with neither their knowledge nor consent. The 'Literary Department' soon gave birth to the Theosophical Publishing House at Leipzig with Vollrath as its proprietor. The local Theosophists, who mistrusted both the man and his motives, complained to Dr Rudolf Steiner, the General Secretary of the German Section. The 'Vollrath Affair', with all its recriminations and polemics, was not least of the causes that led to the eventual resignation of Steiner and many of his followers and the foundation in 1912 of the rival and, indeed, later far more influential Anthroposophical Society.

Steiner expelled Vollrath from the German Section in 1908. The indignant Vollrath who, after all, had just launched a Theosophical publishing firm and realised that his expulsion would be bad for business, appealed over Steiner's head to Annie Besant in London. While she was prepared to accept Steiner's decision as far as Germany was concerned, she confirmed Vollrath's continued membership of the international Theosophical organisation and soon appointed him as the German representative of her Order of the Star of the East, the grotesque 'society' whose function was to announce the presence of the long-awaited 'World Teacher' in the shape of the Hindu youth Krishnamurti. All this was too much for Steiner, who in any case was never a Theosophist of the traditional Adyar variety, and was another factor that led to his secession from the Society. The parting would in any case have come sooner or later.

When matters came to a head in 1912 Vollrath was already fairly well

---

[1] It is likely that he was compelled to abandon his fraudulent academic title in August 1914. See *Nachrichtenblatt der Astrologischen Zentralstelle*, September 1933, p. 9.

established as a Theosophical and occult publisher at Leipzig. He was not the only operator in this highly-specialised field for there was already Max Altmann, also at Leipzig, who had been active before Vollrath appeared upon the scene. In July 1908 Altmann published the first issue of a new monthly periodical, the *Zentralblatt für Okkultismus*. Vollrath thereupon decided to launch a rival publication and in October 1909 produced the first issue of *Prana*, which he described as a 'Journal for Experimental Secret Sciences'. The names and addresses of potential subscribers were easily procured. He engaged one of Altmann's employees, who brought the *Zentralblatt's* mailing list with him. And, adding insult to injury, he imitated the *Zentralblatt's* typographical style so closely that it was difficult to distinguish one periodical from the other. Furthermore, his editor was Karl Brandler-Pracht, who had previously edited the *Zentralblatt* for Altmann. At this time (1908–9), Karl Brandler-Pracht was one of the very few people in Germany who knew anything about astrology. Furthermore, in many respects he was to be the founder of the modern German astrological movement. Vollrath, in his turn, was the first German publisher to develop a strong astrological list. Hence their pre-1914 collaboration is not without a certain historical importance, if only because there was no question of an astrological revival in Germany in the absence of the necessary technical literature, and for the latter both a writer and a publisher were required.

The first of the actors upon the German astrological stage are now gathering in the wings. Apart from Brandler-Pracht there were Alexander Bethor, Otto Pöllner, Albert Kniepf, Ernst Tiede and Wilhelm Becker, all of whom played a significant role in reviving interest in astrology in Germany before 1914.

Karl Brandler-Pracht, the most active publicist in this small group, was born at Vienna on 11 February 1864 at 5.21 a.m. or, more exactly, 31 seconds later.[1] His parents proposed a business career but he became an actor and in due course arrived in the U.S.A. where he played in his own language to audiences of German emigrants. He was in Europe again by *c.* 1900 and might have continued to act in minor provincial theatres in Germany and Austria had he not attended a spiritualist seance at Basle. Upon this occasion a 'spirit' informed him that his predestined mission was to spread the astrological gospel. It is probable that he had already

[1] It must not be inferred that the time was actually recorded with such impressive accuracy. The record or memory of most births is to the nearest quarter of an hour, or is an approximation, such as 'at about 20 minutes past 4 in the morning'. When astrologers produce data to the nearest minute, the horoscope has almost invariably been 'rectified' or 'corrected'. Indeed, when seconds are mentioned this is always the case. The 'rectification' of a horoscope is based upon the dates of important dates in the native's life and is intended to produce an accurate Ascendant. The calculations are laborious, the mathematical procedures at best empirical, and the whole time-consuming exercise totally unscientific.

learned the elements of the science in America, and his knowledge of English now made it possible for him to translate and adapt material for use in Germany. His first book, an elementary manual, was published by Max Altmann in 1905.[1]

Since there was only a very limited market for professional astrology before 1914, Brandler-Pracht turned to occult journalism, which brought him into touch with Altmann and then with Vollrath. He persuaded Altmann to support the only organised astrological group existing in Germany at that time. This was the Cosmos Society of German Astrologers, which cannot have had many members, of which the President was P. Reinhart, of Bremen, who appears to have had a medical qualification.[2] The *Zentralblatt für Okkultismus* now became the Society's official organ.

Reinhart's association was not an exclusively local group at Bremen but had members elsewhere in Germany, notably at Munich, where a small nucleus of enthusiasts was beginning to appear. Its leading lights were Alexander Bethor (i.e. Aquilin Backmund, 1876–1938) and Otto Pöllner (*b.* 1864). Bethor, who was then about 30 years of age, was well-educated and financially independent. 'He was the only contemporary German astrologer with any pretensions to being a gentleman.'[3] His friend Otto Pöllner, a humble engraver by trade and a staunch Theosophist, learned sufficient English to be able to study the books in Bethor's library. In 1909 Bethor began the monthly publication of *Zodiakus*, which was the first German periodical to devote itself exclusively to astrology. Very few contributors were available and practically all the articles were written by the half dozen men whose names I have already mentioned. Bethor managed to keep *Zodiakus* alive for three years until it ceased publication for lack of support.

Brandler-Pracht's propagandist activities were the more effective since he was constantly on the move and made a point of contacting local Theosophical groups, which provided ready-made and receptive audiences. (Alan Leo had done the same in Great Britain during his commercial travelling days in the 1890s.) He was in Vienna in 1907, where he founded the First Viennese Astrological Society, and then in Munich (1908–9), where he organised yet another society with the help of Bethor and Pöllner. During this Munich period he fell foul of Rudolph Steiner

[1] Two insignificant textbooks had been published during the previous fifteen years, although neither of them can have attracted more than minimal attention: Ernst Mayer, *Handbuch der Astrologie*, 1891; Gustav Gessmann, *Katechismus der Sterndeutkunst*, 1896. Gessmann was a hack writer and the author of many books on chiromancy, hypnotism, magnetism and graphology.

[2] In the first number of Bethor's *Zodiakus* (1909) Reinhart advertised 'comparative physiognomical studies' based upon the inspection of a photograph, a specimen of handwriting, hand-prints made with printer's ink (for chiromantic purposes) and a horoscope. This combination of divinatory techniques was very rare at the time and is uncommon today.

[3] Dr Walter Koch, of Göppingen, in a letter to the author.

and the Countess Pauline von Kalkreuth, who had just opened a 'Hall for Art and Music', a Theosophical centre, and who vehemently disapproved of the primitive brand of occultism that Brandler-Pracht peddled alongside his astrology. Hence he was inevitably driven in the direction of Vollrath, who had no love for Steiner.

Vollrath required an editor for his new periodical *Prana* and enticed Brandler-Pracht away from Altmann. Brandler-Pracht moved to Leipzig where he founded the German Astrological Society. Vollrath allowed him to produce a monthly supplement to *Prana* in the shape of the *Astrologische Rundschau*, which subsequently became an independent publication and one of the most important German astrological journals until the Nazis closed it down in 1938. Vollrath launched yet another periodical with an astrological department in April 1910. This was *Theosophie*, with a supplement edited by Ernst Tiede.

Brandler-Pracht did not stay long in Leipzig and successively edited *Prana* and the *Astrologische Rundschau* from Hamburg-Altona (January–August 1911), London (September–December 1911) and Berlin-Charlottenburg (January 1912–March 1914). He and Vollrath parted company in the spring of 1914—there was the inevitable quarrel—and Ernst Tiede now became editor of the *Astrologische Rundschau*. By this time, however, Brandler-Pracht had written the first four or five volumes of Vollrath's 'Astrological Library' series, which later became an ambitious publishing project.

The last notable member of the pre-1914 group of German astrological pioneers was Wilhelm Becker, who began to practise astrology professionally at Berlin in 1910. He had just returned from a lengthy stay in London, where he had been one of Alan Leo's pupils. He had acquired the German translation rights of half a dozen of Leo's minor works—those for the more important books eventually went to Vollrath, much to Becker's disgust—and it was he who was initially responsible for making Leo's name widely known and, indeed, admired in German astrological circles.

It would be incorrect to suggest that there was an identifiable German astrological movement before 1914, and so far very few Germans outside the Theosophical or occultist *milieu* can have been more than vaguely aware of its existence. The few who knew anything about the subject still supposed that the British were the great experts. Astrology was never mentioned in the newspapers and it is doubtful whether one German in fifty thousand knew the name of his or her zodiacal (Sun) sign.

The 1914–18 war interrupted further progress on the astrological front. Brandler-Pracht moved to Switzerland where he founded astrological societies at Zürich and St Gallen. Vollrath lay low at Leipzig until he was picked up by the military police, court-martialled and sentenced to a brief term of imprisonment for evading military service. In 1914 there were no portents suggesting the widespread interest in astrology that was to be evident in Germany only a decade later. However, once the Germans really got to grips with it, they displayed all their traditional qualities of thoroughness.

A surprisingly large number of Germans, including many well-educated men and women, began to study astrology in the early 1920s. The reason for this sudden preoccupation with a hitherto unfashionable, even mildly disreputable area, is not difficult to discover. The aftermath of military defeat, with all its problems and uncertainties, including a runaway currency inflation which was only brought under control at the end of 1923, persuaded many to look to 'the stars' for information and portents of better times to come. Before 1914 the comparatively few German astrologers were mostly Theosophists or occultists or both. They regarded astrology as an essentially Hermetic science. However, a large proportion of the newcomers were interested in neither Theosophy, its offspring Anthroposophy, nor traditional occultism, and preferred to think of astrology as a science in its own right which, given time and the breakdown of traditional prejudices, would be widely accepted as such.

I now return to Hugo Vollrath, who was quickly in action again as an astrological publisher. By 1923 his 'Astrological Library' series already amounted to close on a score of titles. His virtual monopoly in this field was soon to come to an end since many other publishing firms, most of them very obscure, now entered this new and profitable field. By 1923–4 there was a substantial market for astrological literature, and the German output of manuals, tables, predictive almanacs and other *Astrologica* became enormous by comparison with that of any other European country.

Some entertaining revelations on the subject of Hugo Vollrath were contributed to the *Zentralblatt für Okkultismus* by Dr Johannes Balzli, a physician, throughout 1920–1. Vollrath had previously published Balzli's lectures on occultism in his 'Prana Collection' but they had quarrelled and Balzli was now paying off old scores. It appears that as early as 1913 Vollrath had invented an *alter ego* whom he called Walter Heilmann. Soon after the war Heilmann appeared as the Secretary of a fictitious Rosicrucian Society in Germany, and collected subscriptions from gullible people, mostly women, who received impressive diplomas and 'esoteric instruction' in the form of 'Master Letters'. Many tried to meet the mysterious Herr Heilmann but none succeeded. Heilmann-Vollrath gave birth to yet another mythical character called Dr Johannes Walter, who had a cover address at Berlin-Friedenau.

The Rosicrucian 'Master Letters' were not written by Vollrath, but consisted of material translated from the pseudo-Rosicrucian nonsense published in California by yet another 'initiate' who called himself Max Heindel. He, too, was an unsatisfactory person. As Max Grashof, which seems to have been his real name, he had attended Rudolf Steiner's Theosophical lectures in Berlin in the early 1900s. He then emigrated to the U.S.A. where he joined Kathleen Tingley's Universal Brotherhood, which was a schismatic Theosophical sect. His next move was to found the 'Rosicrucian Fellowship', whose members purchased his 'Rosicrucian Letters of Instruction'. The contents of these was based upon material he had purloined from Rudolf Steiner, whose arcane pronouncements were eventually 'played back', as it were, to the Germans via Vollrath's German version of Heindel's English texts which were founded upon Steiner's talks which were originally delivered in German.[1]

Nor was Heilmann-Vollrath a respecter of literary property. He had received for his personal use certain manuscript instructions for 'Occult Exercises' from a gentleman who called himself Bô Yin Râ, and distributed copies (in return for payment, of course) to his own pupils.[2]

Vollrath allowed brief particulars of his various connections to be published in the 1925 edition of the astrological year book published by his own Theosophical Publishing House. 'In the Gnostic movement he was a friend and colleague of Abdul Bahai, while Bô Yin Râ enrolled him in The Brothers of Light. He was for many years a friend of Dr Hanisch and a member of the Mazdaznan movement.'

It is unlikely that Abdul Bahai was connected with the well-known Bahai sect founded in Persia in 1835 and which now has followers in Europe and the U.S.A. Vollrath's friend was The Metropolitan Abdul Bahai, head of the Gnostic Church (its headquarters were at Haifa), who appointed him Bishop of Erfurt and 'handed him a consecrated cedar-wood cross'.[3] The Mazdaznan movement was founded in c. 1900 by Otoman Zar-Adusht Ha'nish, who claimed to have been born at Tehran in 1844. The Master's real name was Otto Hanisch and he was born at Posen in 1854. Formerly a compositor at Leipzig, he emigrated to the U.S.A. and later founded the Mazdaznan movement, which preaches strict vegetarianism and the practice of 'esoteric' breathing exercises. Hanisch died at Los Angeles in 1936. His movement is still in existence.

The Bishop of Erfurt was not without a sense of humour. Theobald Becher, who was for many years in charge of the astrological side of his publishing activities, once told my friend Dr Otto Kellner that Vollrath was accustomed to wear a fez at his office. 'It keeps my aura in place,' he remarked.

Ernst Tiede, who had succeeded Karl Brandler-Pracht, resigned from the editorship of Vollrath's *Astrologische Rundschau* in the autumn of 1920,

[1] See G. Wachsmuth, *The Life and Work of Rudolf Steiner*, New York, 1955, p. 190. Dr Wachsmuth is the author of *Kosmische Aspekte von Geburt und Tod*, Dornach, 1956. This anthroposophical-cum-astrological treatise on 'Cosmic Aspects of Birth and Death' is described as 'Studies in Karma Research'.

[2] Bô Yin Râ, who claimed to be a member of a mysterious 'White Lodge', was Joseph Schneiderfranken (1876–1943), a painter who was the author of a series of singularly cloying books on 'self realisation', some of them published by Vollrath, that were widely read in Germany during the 1920s.

[3] See *Nachrichtenblatt der Astrologischen Zentralstelle*, September 1933, p. 9.

probably because of Balzli's revelations. His successor was yet another of the extraordinary individuals who flit across these pages. The new editor was none other than Rudolf Freiherr von Sebottendorff, who had achieved a certain notoriety as a prototype Nazi shortly before Hitler made his first public appearance at Munich.

The Freiherr's real name was Adam Alfred Rudolf Glauer. The son of a railway engine driver, he was born at Hoyerswerda, between Dresden and Cottbus, on 9 November 1875. It is likely that he was an apprentice in an engineering works in the neighbourhood of Görlitz before going to sea as a stoker in *c.* 1898. Later he deserted his ship in Australia in order to prospect (unsuccessfully) for gold. He then found his way to Turkey (*c.* 1900) where he remained until 1913, apparently working as an estate manager or engineer in the region of Bursa. He became a Turkish citizen in 1911. While in Turkey he interested himself in occultism and esotericism and was probably familiar with the appropriate Sufi and Islamic literature. He is said to have taught himself astrology from English textbooks. He claimed to have been adopted under Turkish law by Baron Heinrich von Sebottendorff, which explains how Adam Glauer became a 'nobleman'. Upon his return to Germany he was involved in the fruitless attempts to interest the General Staff in a prototype armoured vehicle, apparently a kind of tank, invented at Breslau by Friedrich Göbel.

Von Sebottendorff soon became a prominent member of the Germanen Order (founded in 1912), an anti-semitic secret society organised on pseudo–Masonic lines. At the end of 1917 he was appointed head of the Order's Bavarian Province and moved to Munich where, requiring a suitable cover for the Order's activities, he founded the Thule Society which soon had about two hundred active members. Acting on behalf of the Germanen Order in July 1918 he purchased the Franz Eher Verlag, a Munich publishing business, and with it the *Münchener Beobachter*, an obscure and run-down local weekly newspaper. The *MB* henceforth became an anti-semitic scandal sheet and the Thule Society's official organ.

The Freiherr and his fellow members of the Thule were up to their necks in the involved and violent Bavarian political scene during the first five months of 1919, the year which witnessed the swift rise and fall of the Bavarian Soviet Republic (7 April–2 May) and the foundation (on 5 January) of an obscure right-wing nationalist (*völkisch*) group that called itself The German Workers' Party. It need only be added that von Sebottendorff was obliged to make a hurried departure from Bavaria in *c.* July 1919 and that he played no further part in political life. It is necessary to mention, however, that on 9 August 1919 the *Münchener Beobachter* changed its name to *Völkischer Beobachter* and a month later Corporal Adolf Hitler became a member of the German Workers' Party and of its committee. At that time Hitler was employed as a *Reichswehr* intelligence agent at Munich, his function being to report on the activities of local political groups. While the German Workers' Party had a number of close links with the Thule Society, there is no evidence that Hitler and von Sebottendorff ever met, but Hitler was undoubtedly acquainted with many of the Freiherr's connections.

By the summer of 1920 Hitler, who had returned to civilian life, was the undisputed leader of the German Workers' Party which had meanwhile become the National Socialist German Workers' Party. The Party acquired the *Völkischer Beobachter* from a group of people who had been close to von Sebottendorff in December 1920. Now, only a few weeks before the negotiations for the transfer of the *VB* were completed, von Sebottendorff, who had moved to Bad Sachsa, a small spa in the Harz region, suddenly appears as the editor of the *Astrologische Rundschau* and for a short period becomes one of Germany's most prolific and, indeed, widely read astrological authors. During the next few years he wrote or edited half a dozen books for Vollrath's 'Astrological Library', including a German translation of Max Heindel's *The Message of the Stars*, which had achieved a considerable success in the U.S.A. His *Geschichte der Astrologie* (*History of Astrology*), 1923, reveals his admiration for Guido von List (1848–1919) and G. Lanz von Liebenfels (1874–1954), whose influences may be discerned in certain aspects of National Socialist racial ideology. While the Freiherr's name soon became a household word in German astrological circles he lived and worked in the strictest privacy and avoided all personal contacts. Indeed, such veterans of the German astrological movement as Dr Wilhelm Mrsic and Herr Wilhelm Wulff told me that they never set eyes on him. In any case, he returned more or less permanently to Turkey in 1923.[1]

Von Sebottendorff was not a shareholder in the Franz Eher Verlag at the time the *Völkischer Beobachter* was sold to the NSDAP in December 1920 but his sister had a modest holding and so, too, had Dr Wilhelm Gutberlet (1870–1933), a Munich physician who was not only a member of the Thule Society but had been present at the very first meeting of the German Workers' Party that Hitler himself had attended on 12 September 1919. Walter Schellenberg, one of the leading members of Himmler's circle during the war years, met Gutberlet towards the end of his life and

---

[1] I hope one day to publish a separate study of von Sebottendorff. In the meantime the reader is referred to his *Bevor Hitler kam*, 1933, 2nd edit., 1934, which was suppressed at Hitler's or the Party's instructions. He was in Munich for a while in 1933 and was arrested early in 1934. (Document in Bayer. Hauptstaatsarchiv Abt. IV.) He was released and returned to Turkey where he met his death by drowning in 1945 (information supplied by Dr G. Franz-Willing). His autobiographical novel, *Der Talisman des Rosenkreuzers*, [1925] is of considerable interest. See also G. Franz-Willing, *Die Hitler Bewegung*, Vol. 1, 1962 and Werner Maser, *Die Frühgeschichte der NSDAP*, 1965. D. Bronder, *Bevor Hitler kam*, 1964, is untrustworthy as far as von Sebottendorff, the Thule Society and National Socialism's supposed occult connections are concerned.

recalled conversations with him on the subject of Hitler's pathological racial mania. 'I discussed this several times with Dr Gutbarlett [*sic*] . . . who belonged to Hitler's intimate circle. Gutbarlett believed in the sidereal pendulum and claimed that this had given him the power at once to sense the presence of any Jews or persons of partial Jewish ancestry and to pick them out in any group of people. Hitler availed himself of Gutbarlett's mystic power and had many discussions with him on racial questions.'[1]

Gutberlet was a keen astrologer and his name appears in a list of a score or more German medical men who were interested in the subject that was published by Dr Korsch in *Zenit* in May 1931. Thus we can account for at least one astrologer, but no more, in Hitler's milieu in the early 1920s.

Frau Elsbeth Ebertin, who was responsible for an astrological 'prophecy' concerning Hitler that caused much discussion in Munich in 1923–4, met the Führer briefly at the end of a crowded political meeting there during the autumn of 1923, but it is unlikely that he was aware of her identity. She was by far the most accomplished German astrological publicist of her generation. Indeed, I doubt whether anyone else, with the possible exception of the late R. H. Naylor, has ever matched her skill in presenting astrology to the general public. She was unknown in German astrological circles before 1914 but a decade later already enjoyed a considerable reputation as a Sibyl. Furthermore, she was the first woman in Germany to make a name for herself as a professional astrologer.

Elsbeth Ebertin was born at Görlitz on 14 May 1880 and in her younger days was a professional graphologist. During the early 1900s there was already a widespread public interest in graphology in Germany (but not in Great Britain) and hence a wide, although poorly remunerated, demand for the graphological articles she contributed to newspapers and magazines. For 4 Pfennigs a time she composed countless four-line delineations of specimens of handwriting sent by readers for publication in 'Our Graphological Corner' and similar features.[2] All her early books—she was always an extraordinarily prolific writer—were for the popular graphological market. She might have continued quite happily as a graphologist if she

[1] See *The Schellenberg Memoirs*, p. 113. This book was published in England in 1956 and the *Memoiren* in Germany in 1959. The texts are approximately the same but not identical. Only the English version mentions Dr Gutberlet by name.

[2] According to R. Saudek, *The Psychology of Handwriting*, 1925, the word Graphology was unknown until 1871 when it was coined by the Abbé H. Michon, the founder of the modern French graphological movement. Cf. his *Le mystère de l'écriture*, 1872, with a preface by A. Desbarolles, the famous palmist, who was a friend of Eliphas Lévi. Until *c.* 1895 the German graphologists were wholly under the influence of the French school, as represented by Michon and his better-known pupil J. Crépieux-Jamin (*d.* 1940; see Count Hermann Keyserling's illuminating obituary in *Der Weg zur Vollendung*, June 1941). Scientific graphology was developed in Germany by W. T. Preyer (1841–97), a pioneer child psychologist, H. Busse, a criminologist and founder of the Deutsche Graphologische Gesellschaft (1896) and, above all, Ludwig Klages (1872–1956). The latter's *Handschrift und Charakter*, 1917, reached its 23rd impression by 1949.

had not encountered astrology and arrived at the conclusion that it offered more exciting and, indeed, rewarding possibilities. This only happened after a false start. In 1907 she received an appreciative letter from Russia in which the writer expressed his opinion that she would be well advised to study astrology, adding that he had requested Vollrath's bookselling department to send her a copy of Brandler-Pracht's manual. When the book arrived she gave it a quick glance, could not make head nor tail of it, put it aside and forgot about it.

At Görlitz three years later she had a puzzling meeting with a woman who claimed to be a graphologist but patently knew nothing about the subject. Frau Ebertin was surprised when she was asked for her own birth date as well as a specimen of her handwriting. However, in spite of her lack of graphological expertise the woman provided quite an impressive impromptu character delineation. Then the truth came out: the woman was an astrologer but masqueraded as a graphologist in order to avoid unwelcome visits from the police. Impressed by astrology's apparent possibilities, Frau Ebertin was anxious to learn more about it. The woman said she would provide some handwritten notes describing the Sun's 'influence' in each of the twelve zodiacal signs in return for a payment of RM.120. Frau Ebertin agreed to this although it was far more than she could afford at the time. A few days later she began to ask for astrological textbooks at bookshops, but in vain. She had forgotten about the book she had received from her Russian correspondent. Eventually she found the first volume of Brandler-Pracht's 'Astrological Library' series which Vollrath had just begun to publish at Leipzig. Only then did she discover that she had cheerfully paid a lot of money for an exact copy of a few paragraphs which had been taken directly from Brandler-Pracht's book.

At this stage someone told her that Albert Kniepf was doing professional astrological work at Hamburg. She wrote to him and was astounded when he asked RM.50–100 for a set of 'lifetime' predictions. It must have occurred to her, too, that astrology was well paid by comparison with graphology. Again, Kniepf's letter contained a remark that interested her. 'At the moment you are suffering from a pronounced suicidal mania and have to battle with excessively difficult conditions in your own life,' he wrote. This happened to be true and, furthermore, a deduction of this kind could never be achieved on the basis of conventional graphological evidence. She began to study astrology in order to equip herself for a new career as a professional practitioner.

The first of her many books and *opuscula* were published during the 1914–18 war.[1] The first annual issue of her subsequently widely-read

---

[1] *Sternblätter*, Nos. 1–10, Leipzig, *c.* 1915; *Königliche Nativitäten*, 1916 (a study of the current astrological prospects of Wilhelm II of Germany, George V of Great Britain and Nicholas II of Russia); *Die Nativität Hindenburgs*, 1917, a review of Hindenburg's horoscope.

annual prophetic almanac, *Ein Blick in die Zukunft* (*A Glance into the Future*), No. 1, 1917 (for 1918) made minor publishing history, for this was the predecessor of many similar publications, most of which were associated with the names of well-known German astrological publicists. In connection with the first two issues of this year book she was obliged to suffer objections and delays at the hands of the military censorship, where it was realised that astrological predictions might easily become the source of undesirable rumours.

In the past it had never occurred to any of her German contemporaries that it might be possible to write about astrology in a simple and, above all, interesting fashion. In this respect her ability was unique, but then she was a born journalist. When one reads her work there is the impression of looking over the shoulder of a highly-responsible, kindly and invariably overworked woman, incessantly harried by members of the public in quest of advice on personal matters or anxious to have their fortunes told. Nevertheless, there was nothing she disliked more than astrology's equation with vulgar fortune-telling and she regarded her 'art' with the utmost seriousness. Her literary style was a trifle cosy but at least the attention is held. By 1920 she had already established a considerable reputation, and the ex-King Ferdinand of Bulgaria, who was living in exile in Germany, was one of her most faithful and treasured clients.

By the spring of 1923, when she was busy writing the 1924 edition of *Ein Blick in die Zukunft* at her home at Görlitz, Hitler and his National Socialist German Workers' Party were conspicuous on the Bavarian political stage. Hitler's oratorical gifts attracted large audiences and his brown-shirted storm-troopers had already broken a fair number of skulls at rowdy meeting hall or beer cellar affrays. (Hitler's meetings were often held at one or other of the large Munich beer cellars.) Frau Ebertin was just about to compose a series of generalised predictions for persons born with their natal Sun in Aries when she received a letter from Munich from one of Hitler's many enthusiastic woman supporters. Her correspondent sent her Hitler's birth date (but *not* his birth hour) and asked what she thought of his horoscope.

Frau Ebertin published her answer, although without revealing Hitler's name, in the 1924 edition of her year book, which was on sale by the end of July 1923. 'A man of action born on 20 April 1889, with Sun in 29° Aries at the time of his birth, can expose himself to personal danger by excessively uncautious action and could very likely trigger off an uncontrollable crisis,' she wrote. 'His constellations show that this man is to be taken very seriously indeed; he is destined to play a "Führer-role" in future battles. It seems that the man I have in mind, with this strong Aries influence, is destined *to sacrifice himself for the German nation*, also to face up to all circumstances with audacity and courage, even when it is a matter of *life and death*, and to give an impulse, which will burst forth quite suddenly, to a German Freedom Movement. But I will not anticipate destiny. Time will show, but the present state of affairs, at the time I write this, naturally cannot last.'

None of this was complete nonsense. It will be noticed, however, that Frau Ebertin did *not* suggest any particular date in connection with her warning. Nevertheless, since her year book contained essentially short-term prophecies, the inference was that it would be unwise for this man born under the sign Aries, whoever he might be, to undertake any ill-considered course of action in the near future. Any Munich National Socialist who chanced to read *Ein Blick in die Zukunft* would have recognised Hitler without much difficulty, especially in view of Frau Ebertin's use of the expression 'Führer-role'. There was only one so-called 'Führer' in Germany and he was Hitler. Apart from the fact that Frau Ebertin's correspondent at Munich must have drawn attention to the passage, the authoress sent a copy of her year book to the *Völkischer Beobachter* as soon as it was published, and, as we will learn, it was shown to Hitler.

The prediction, such as it was, was soon fulfilled. On 8 November 1923 Hitler and his followers staged a badly-organised *Putsch* at a political meeting at the Burgerbräu beer cellar and the following morning there was the famous procession to the centre of Munich, headed by Hitler and Ludendorff who were accompanied by Hermann Goering, Julius Streicher and other subsequently notorious Nazis. Shots were fired by the police and some National Socialists were killed. Hitler fell, breaking his shoulder, and quickly made himself scarce but was arrested a few days later. He, Ludendorff and others were brought to trial in February 1924. Ludendorff was acquitted but Hitler and a dozen more were found guilty of conspiring to overthrow the Reich government. The sentences were passed on 1 April 1924. Less than nine months later Hitler, who had been sentenced to five years' detention, was released from Landsberg prison, where he had been busy writing the first volume of *Mein Kampf*.

These stirring events provided Frau Ebertin with some welcome personal publicity. She had been at Munich since the previous September, i.e. at least a month or two before the Beer Cellar *Putsch*. She mentioned in the 1925 edition of her year book, which was written during the spring and summer of 1924, that she went to Munich because she sensed that stirring events would take place there and wanted to experience them at first hand. This suggests that she now had a professional astrological interest in Hitler. However, in the same edition of *Ein Blick in die Zukunft* she inferred that when she wrote her Hitler 'prophecy' a year earlier in the spring of 1923, she knew little or nothing about 'the National Socialists and the *völkisch* movement in southern Germany'. She continued: 'When I write my almanac I make a point of not reading the daily newspapers and do not allow myself to be influenced. So I looked up the constellations [i.e. Hitler's] in order to be able to write a few quite impartial remarks about them. There was not time to write for his birth *hour*, so I cast a provisional horoscope for the day of his birth, looked at its main features and discovered that it concerned an unusual character who, no matter whether he was born in the morning or the evening, would not be favoured by good fortune—because of the coming Saturn–Sun opposition —were he confronted with a major action or allow himself to become involved in one.'

Frau Ebertin indicated that she had cast the horoscope on the basis of the Sun's position *at noon* on 20 April 1889. By midday, however, the Sun was already out of Aries and had passed into Taurus (actually 0° 34' 40" Taurus). Why, then, did she so pointedly suggest that Hitler was born with his Sun in the last degree of Aries? The answer, I believe, is that she was completely aware of his political significance and jumped to the conclusion that this turbulent, aggressive character *must* have his Sun in the fiery sign Aries rather than in the 'earthy' and presumably more docile sign Taurus.

During the weeks preceding the Hitler–Ludendorff trial, which began on 26 February 1924, together with L. Hoffmann, a Bavarian journalist who was interested in astrology, she wrote *Sternenwandel und Weltgeschehen* (*The Stars in their Courses and World Events*), one of this century's most fascinating astrological tracts. At least 20,000 copies were sold within a few weeks, and provided both Frau Ebertin and astrology with widespread publicity.[1] The first half of the pamphlet was written by Hoffmann and contains a partial record of his talks with Frau Ebertin at Munich on 21–24 January 1924. He had previously looked for her at a Home for Deaconesses, where she had found accommodation, but was informed that she had moved to a nearby pension, where he eventually discovered her. She told him that a famous Sibyl's life was by no means an easy one.

'My address soon became known,' she said, 'and as the political excitement grew in intensity, there were naturally a lot of people who wanted to learn what the stars revealed about the situation. They were continually asking the porteress for me and if and when I could be seen, or they telephoned, which naturally disturbed the house's peace and quiet. Apart from that, the whole of the autumn was a terrible time for me, full of upsets and disquiet. It was all caused by Saturn who, in my horoscope, too, threatened more than ordinary trouble and indicated a heavy burden of suffering, financial loss and possibly a period in a sanatorium or hospital, imprisonment, criminal lawsuits and financial damages, all through secret enemies. At the beginning of 1923 I already saw the dangers ahead, and of course considered how I might best diminish Saturn's influence upon

[1] Herr Reinhold Ebertin, her son, told me in 1962 that he believed that successive reprints amounted to at least 70,000 copies.

my destiny. I thought it advisable to look for solitude during the critical period and quietly get on with my literary work. After a long search I eventually found the convent-like little room at the Home for Deaconesses.'

After 8 November, she said, she had no peace at all, because she was now besieged by members of all the Munich political parties, right- and left-wing, all of whom wanted to know 'the future'. Hoffmann asked her if Hitler had been aware of the warning she had published in *Ein Blick in die Zukunft*.

'Of course,' she replied. 'During the summer I sent a copy of my year book to the editorial department of the *Völkischer Beobachter* and several good friends of mine showed Hitler the passage in question. I was told that in reply to my warning he impatiently exclaimed: "What on earth have women and the stars got to do with me?" I tried to explain to a number of Hitler's followers, whom I know personally, that their *Führer* would have very critical aspects in November, and do you know what they said? "At this moment, when he's got something so important ahead of him, the aspects can't be good enough!" '

Frau Ebertin told Hoffmann that meanwhile she had discovered the time of Hitler's birth, i.e. 6.30 p.m. at Braunau am Inn, which corresponds with the time recorded in the baptismal register there. This was the first occasion upon which this information, later to be of such interest to German astrologers, was mentioned in any publication.

She attended one of his meetings and had even been able to exchange a few words with him afterwards. Hoffmann suggested that he was probably rather vain, but she did not agree.

'No, in my view Hitler hasn't the *prima donna* vanity which the opposition newspapers ascribe to him. It seemed to me that he was rather shy when I spoke to him after the meeting when he was surrounded by people. It appears as if he is only in his element when he has a mass-audience that eagerly listens to every word he utters. On the platform he is like a man possessed, like a medium, the unconscious tool of higher powers.' With prophetic insight she added: 'It will turn out that recent events will not only give this [Hitler] movement inner strength, but external strength as well, so that it will give a mighty impetus to the pendulum of world history.'

Frau Ebertin was not the only German citizen who hoped to interest Hitler in astrological information during the summer of 1923. There was also Party Comrade Georg Kopper, of Landshut, who on 15 June dispatched a handwritten communication headed: 'To Adolf Hitler, the Führer of the German Freedom Movement'. This document contained particulars of a number of important dates in German history and their supposed astrological significance. For some obscure reason Herr Kopper's offering was not consigned to the wastepaper basket but was preserved in the Party archives. It survived the war and can now be inspected at the Federal Archives at Coblence.[1]

When O. A. H. Schmitz's *Der Geist der Astrologie* (*The Spirit of Astrology*) was published in 1922 it had an immediate appeal for those who would scarcely have been impressed by the literary performances of Karl Brandler-Pracht or Rudolf von Sebottendorff and who would have been unlikely purchasers of Elsbeth Ebertin's predictive almanac. This book, which bore the imprint of a well-known Munich publisher, was of particular interest to the well-educated middle-class public that was beginning to interest itself in astrology.

Oskar A. H. Schmitz (1873–1931) was a man of letters, not of the first importance, but certainly well known. A successful novelist, playwright and *feuilletonist* in many of the better-class newspapers, his name was familiar to the literate sector of the public. At Salzburg in 1917 he happened to meet a Baroness P. This lady, who was unaware of his identity, told him after a quick glance that he was born under the sign Aries, which was correct. The same day she cast and interpreted his horoscope and impressed him by the accuracy of her delineation. At Vienna a little later he encountered Friedrich Schwikert, formerly an officer in the Austro-Hungarian navy, who was the leading local astrological expert.[2] Schwickert lent Schmitz some books by Alan Leo and Henri Selva and he retired to a remote Styrian village where he industriously studied them. When he returned to Vienna Schwikert gave him a fortnight's intensive tuition.

As soon as it was possible for Germans to travel abroad again, Schmitz went to Zürich where he became acquainted with C. G. Jung. Fascinated by Jung's analytical psychology—I do not know if he was already familiar with Freud's work—he had a course of analysis. He next turned up at Darmstadt where Count Hermann Keyserling had recently (1920) founded his subsequently famous School of Wisdom and was lecturing to audiences that included many people of social and intellectual distinction. Keyserling's *The Travel Diary of a Philosopher*, 1919, had achieved an outstanding success and immediately made him famous. While the Count was disliked or mistrusted by the majority of academic philosophers—this was inevitable—he represented an important and, indeed, stimulating intellectual force in post-war Germany.

Schmitz, always an ardent and persuasive propagandist for any cause that interested him, talked to Keyserling about Jung's work and, of course, astrology. During the autumn of 1921 the Count submitted to a few

[1] Ref. NS/Vorl. 17a. I am obliged to Dr Werner Maser for drawing my attention to this document.

[2] F. Schwickert, (1857–1930) was a 'supérior inconnu' in the Martinist Order and a member of Lanz von Liebenfels' Order of the New Temple. A well-known professional astrologer, he was largely responsible for introducing the classical French 'Morinus' system to the Germans.

analytical sessions with him but never became deeply involved. Schmitz would have liked to attach himself to Keyserling and the School of Wisdom in some prominent capacity but the Count did not care for apostles and tactfully sent him back to Zürich and Jung.[1] Schmitz became Jung's most effective literary propagandist at a time when his name was still comparatively unknown in lay circles.[2]

Apart from Schmitz, Keyserling was acquainted with many who had taken up astrology during those hectic post-war years. The subject was never prominently on the agenda at the School of Wisdom but it was certainly not frowned upon. The Count's personal attitude to it was both objective and eclectic. If Keyserling had publicly condemned astrology as superstitious nonsense, the fact would undoubtedly have dissuaded many who took it up at that time.

The pre-1914 astrological societies had mostly ceased to exist during the war years. While a few local groups were formed after 1918, there was still no identifiable German astrological movement by the end of 1921. Its seeds were sown when the first important German Astrologers' Congress was held during the summer of 1923. The fact that a large number of astrologers met at Leipzig was largely the outcome of A. M. Grimm's activities at Munich during the past two years. Nevertheless, while Grimm could and, indeed, did claim to be the originator of the Congress idea, everything happened more by accident than design.

A. M. Grimm (1892–1962) was a native of Dresden. He taught himself astrology in 1910 and in 1914 founded a Central Office for Astrological Meteorological Information. Of course there was no 'Central Office' in the strict sense of the word and it is unlikely that any but a few gullible individuals subscribed to his so-called weather forecasts. Soon after the armistice Grimm emerged as an unusually prolific astrological writer and publicist at Munich, where he quickly produced a number of textbooks which he published himself. He was a singularly pure specimen of the *astrologue enragé*, one of those people who never know when to stop.

The Munich police first became aware of astrology shortly before 1914 when they prosecuted Otto Pöllner for fortune-telling. In April 1921 they made a determined effort to suppress local professional astrological activity and, as might be expected, were never able to distinguish between a 'scientific astrologer', which was what Grimm claimed to be, and the tatty

[1] For Keyserling's comments on Schmitz's 'apostle nature' see the important chapter on C. G. Jung in his autobiographical *Reise durch die Zeit*, Vol. 2, 1958.

[2] I do not know when Jung first became interested in astrology. He parted company with Freud in September 1913 and the two men never met again. According to Ernest Jones: 'For the past two years Jung had been delving deeply into the literature of mythology and comparative religions . . . Freud was already beginning to be unhappy at the direction of Jung's researches.' (*The Life and Work of Sigmund Freud*, abridged Pelican edition, 1964, p. 368.) Jung may well have been aware of astrology in 1913 but it is probable that his real 'conversion' was due to Schmitz in the early 1920s.

female fortune-tellers whom Grimm himself contemptuously described as 'planet hags'. The police visited his home on 18 April 1921, seized all his astrological books and papers and charged him with fortune-telling. Grimm went to insensate lengths to defend the case. Appeal followed appeal but the court of highest instance decided against him. While he obviously enjoyed his 'martyrdom' and the resulting publicity, he preferred to pay a small fine rather than go to prison. He now saw himself as a leader of public opinion as far as astrology was concerned, and decided to organise a European Astrologers' Congress. This three-day event, which took place at Munich in September 1922, was the first of its kind to be held in any country. The Congress was European only in name, since with the exception of a Frau Dr Martens from Switzerland most of those who attended were local people. Grimm presided and contributed a wonderful piece of half-baked nonsense on 'Astrology and Einstein's Theory of Relativity'. Brandler-Pracht and Otto Pöllner were both present but remained silent. So, too, did the 'observers' sent by the Munich police. They disclosed their identity a few days later when they visited the home of Ludwig Stenger, and confiscated his draft of the official report. Meanwhile at Leipzig Hugo Vollrath had kept himself well informed about Grimm's Congress and thought that it was now time for him to get himself into the act.

The Astrologers' Congress idea appealed to Vollrath for strictly practical reasons. He was the most active publisher of astrological literature, although competition was now growing, and the proprietor of the most widely-read astrological periodical. It was his growing financial stake in astrology that persuaded him that collaboration with Grimm might be advantageous. There were already signs of an appreciable extension of public interest in astrology and he hoped to be able to influence the course of events. The ordinary amateur astrologers, Urania's anonymous devotees, never realised the extent to which they were pawns in a game played by those who had a vested interest in astrology. Accordingly Grimm soon received a letter proposing that the next congress should be held at Leipzig.

In June 1923 about sixty persons, including many of the leading professionals, met at the Theosophical Society's lecture hall at Leipzig. This was the first of a series of annual congresses which were held without interruption until 1936. They had no counterpart in any other country and reflected the German passion for organisation.

The 1923 Leipzig congress, at which A. M. Grimm presided, was notable for ambitious plans and doctrinal quarrels. The major row was in connection with the revolutionary theories of the so-called Hamburg School, which I will mention later. The ambitious projects related to the proposition that if astrology was to be recognised as a science in its own right, certain necessary steps must first be taken. Dr Fritz Quade, a Berlin patent lawyer who was already well known as an investigator of psychic phenomena, proposed the creation of a Central Astrological Office, which would arrange all future congresses and function as a parent organisation for the astrological movement as a whole. He also suggested the creation of a Central Statistical Office, i.e. for the collection and analysis of data which could eventually be used in support of the claim that astrology was not a superstitious survival but a genuine science in its own right. It was agreed that the Central Astrological Office should be at Munich under the control of A. M. Grimm and Dr Wilhelm Mrsic (b. 1896), a young academic biologist who was a lecturer at the university of Zagreb in Jugoslavia. The Statistical Central Office was to be located at Leipzig under the direction of Theobald Becher and two others. Since Becher was Vollrath's right-hand man, the latter could expect to have a finger in the pie. Another small group at Hamburg, which included my friend Herr Wilhelm Wulff, was given the task of drafting a questionnaire for use in connection with the statistical project. By the autumn a programme of work for the statisticians had been prepared and it was decided to collect and analyse material in relation to the Ascendant Theory, 'Sensitive Points' (i.e. in a horoscope), the Pre-natal Epoch theory (an eccentricity inherited from the British and, in particular, from Sepharial and E. H. Bailey and now completely forgotten),[1] Transneptunian planets (i.e. planets outside the orbit of Neptune and still unidentified by astronomers, but very real to members of the Hamburg School), and finally Weather astrology.

Unity of purpose prevailed for at least two months and then there was the inevitable row. Grimm, who in any case had been an ineffective chairman, quarrelled with Vollrath, who had refused to submit the Congress minutes for his approval on the grounds that the Theosophical Publishing House had been responsible for all the administrative arrangements. Grimm huffily resigned from his presidency of the Central Astrological Office and was succeeded by Dr Mrsic. Having made his bid for the movement's leadership and failed, Grimm henceforth sulked in the background although, as we will discover, later made occasional ludicrous interventions. In 1924 the Statistical Office also came under Dr Mrsic's wing. There were many who were relieved to see it moved away from Vollrath's vicinity. Hence Vollrath's plan to control the movement was soon frustrated. Dr Mrsic quietly and efficiently organised five annual congresses until he surrendered the presidency of the Central Astrological Office in 1928.[2] The ambitious statistical project never made much headway owing to lack of time and money.

The majority of the local societies, whose number rapidly increased

[1] In Germany its leading protagonist was A. Frank Glahn (b. 1865). Herr Wulff, who knew him well, described him to me as 'a squinting Koot Hoomi with six toes on each foot'. Koot Hoomi was one of Madam Blavatsky's 'Mahatmas'.

[2] The congresses organised by Dr Mrsic in conjunction with local astrological societies were those held at Berlin (1924), Vienna (1925), Hamburg (1926), Magdeburg (1927) and Cassel (1928).

after 1923, were affiliated to the Central Astrological Office. At this point I must briefly refer to the Astrological Society in Germany, which was founded in May 1924. ASiG was controlled behind the scenes by Vollrath and was intended to supplant, if possible, the Central Astrological Office, which had evaded his clutches. ASiG's role was comparatively unimportant until 1933 when the National Socialist *Gleichschaltung* (integration) issue came to the front and Vollrath and his clique attempted to create a Nazi astrological movement.

More interesting than Vollrath's ASiG was the Academic Society for Astrological Research, which was founded in Berlin in June 1924 by Dr Quade and Dr F. Schwab.[1] For the next decade membership of this society, which could only have existed in Germany, was restricted to *Herren Doktoren*. Yet another 'academic' society, the *Deutsche Kulturgemeinschaft zur Pflege der Astrologie* (literally, German Cultural Association for the Cultivation of Astrology) was founded in March 1927 but was dissolved or became inactive a year or two later. Its membership included a number of surprisingly distinguished people, e.g. Professor J. Verweyen, the Bonn philosopher, Professor E. Dacqué, the well-known Munich palaeontologist, and Dr Theodor Lessing, yet another philosopher, who taught at the Technische Hochschule at Hanover, and who was murdered by German or Sudeten Nazis at Marienbad, Czechoslovakia, in August 1933.

The 'academic' astrologers did not bother to write textbooks and apart from occasional articles and a few short monographs published very little. Nevertheless, the existence of at least a hundred *Herren Doktoren* who publicly affirmed their belief in astrology cannot have been without its effect.

An individual German's attitude to astrology was conditioned by his or her social milieu, educational background, membership of this or that local group, an identification or otherwise with Theosophy, Anthroposophy or occultism, and a preference for any one of a wide choice of astrological systems. There was no such person as a typical German astrologer, nor was there any standard or universally accepted technique. The only common factor was the widely-held belief that valid deductions could be made from horoscopes.

The Germans, however, were the first to discuss the idea of what they called 'psychological astrology'. O. A. H. Schmitz, the enthusiastic disciple of C. G. Jung, suggested in 1922 that astrology was something for which psychology had been waiting. This was an exaggeration and the wish was father to the thought. It is easy to understand why Schmitz and others wanted to establish a link between astrology and psychology. It was because they sensed the intellectual sterility of the Tradition in the form in which it had reached them. Astrology, eternally fascinating, promised

---

[1] Dr F. Schwab was a physician. His *Sternmächte und Mensch*, 1923, 2nd enlarged edition 1933, contains interesting information about astrological typological theories.

so much but in reality performed so little. It could certainly not furnish consistently accurate predictions and the whole area was cluttered up with unsatisfactory features, e.g. its identification with fortune-telling, its close association with the messier side of occultism, and the inability of those who practised it to demonstrate any scientific basis for their beliefs.

The question, then, was whether astrology could be made to perform any useful contemporary function. Character analysis appeared to offer the most fruitful possibilities. The astrologers had in any case been attempting this kind of thing since time immemorial, although in an unsophisticated manner. There were obviously a number of strictly practical applications, such as guidance in the choice of a career or a marriage partner, the assessment of a person's suitability for a given employment and, more ambitious, the diagnosis of an individual's latent disposition to a particular kind of neurosis. There was a need, then, for a new, more sophisticated, and more scientific kind of astrology, and therefore the necessity for astrologers to provide something more impressive than conventional 'cook-book' interpretations of horoscopes. Unfortunately very few could achieve anything more than the delineation of a horoscope on traditional lines, hence with the usual indifferent results. Again, very few of these would-be psychologists knew very much about psychology.

Schmitz, of course, was acquainted with the principles of Jungian analytical psychology. It is unlikely that more than a handful of his astrologer *confrères* shared his knowledge, although the Baroness Olga von Ungern-Sternberg, who was both an astrologer and a medically trained psychologist, would have been familiar with the corpus of psycho-analytical literature. It must be remembered, too, that members of the general public were not then as superficially conversant with the theories of the various psychoanalytical schools as they are today. Thus when the Germans now began to talk about 'psychological astrology', they almost invariably related it to *Charakterologie*, i.e. the study of so-called psychological types. This already existed as a speculative department of academic psychology or psychiatry and had no close connection with, for example, Jungian or Freudian analytical psychology.

The principal sources of the astrologers' inspiration can be identified. The first German editions of C. G. Jung's *Psychological Types* and E. Kretschmer's *Physique and Character* were both published in 1921. These books were known to well-read laymen. In addition, many were familiar with Ludwig Klages' theories (in the field of *Ausdrucksdeutung*, i.e. the interpretation of expression) because of the wide sale enjoyed by his graphological works.

The most effective pioneer in the field of 'psychological astrology' was undoubtedly Herbert Freiherr von Kloeckler (1896–1950). This aristo-cratic ex-regular army officer studied medicine for a while after his demobilisation but abandoned his intention to qualify as a doctor when the currency inflation of 1922–3 left him penniless. He became a professional astrological writer and consultant at Leipzig. Indifferent to the movement's internecine warfare and petty politics, also to its Theosophical and occultist sector, he was the first to jettison much of astrology's medieval ballast and to attempt to formulate a version more compatible with twentieth-century requirements. His *Grundlagen für die astrologische Deutung* (*Foundations of Astrological Interpretation*), 1926, is by one of the most illuminating guides to the subject and at the time of its publication set a new standard in astrological writing.

Von Kloeckler's Leipzig group included many of the local intellectuals who were interested in astrology. One of them was my friend Dr Otto Kellner, then a youthful member of the editorial staff of the renowned Thieme-Becker *Künstlerlexicon* (*Dictionary of Artists*), whose *Charakterkunde und Astrologie*, 1927, represented an early attempt to show how a combination of graphology and astrology might be used for 'characterological' investigations.

I mentioned above that von Kloeckler got rid of some of astrology's medieval ballast. At Hamburg Alfred Witte threw the lot overboard and invented a new kind of astrology, so revolutionary and in many respects so complicated that it could hardly fail to attract a modest following. It must be emphasised that there was plenty of room for a von Kloeckler, who was cautious and conservative, for a Witte who was apparently neither, and for a small regiment of other astrological theorists and innovators. There were many different roads to a knowledge of the stars.

Alfred Witte (1878–1941) was a minor employee in the city surveyor's office at Hamburg and first became interested in astrology when Brandler-Pracht was preaching the gospel there in 1910. While serving on the Russian front during the 1914–18 war Witte attempted to predict the times of Russian artillery barrages on the basis of a careful astrological record of previous ones. Given this or that combination of cosmic factors, then the Russian guns might be expected to open fire at a given moment. That, at least, was the theory. Witte, however, was puzzled by the fact that Russian shells frequently exploded in the Russian lines when, *pace* the stars, they should have remained silent. Intrigued by this illogical state of affairs, he sought for an answer. Eureka, it was found. These inexplicable manifestations could only be due to the influence of a planet or planets, as yet unidentified, beyond the orbit of Neptune. This deduction led to the 'discovery' of a hypothetical planet which was subsequently named Cupido. Later he and his friend Friedrich Sieggrün found seven more Transneptunian bodies which they called, in the order of their presumed distance from the Sun, Hades, Zeus, Kronos, Apollon, Admetos, Vulkanus and Poseidon. The next task was to calculate ephemerides so that astrologers could incorporate these hypothetical planets in horoscopes.

I have no idea how this was done, but reference to a Hamburg School ephemeris for 1961–70 indicates that as I write these lines Cupido is in 18° 15′ Libra, Hades in 14° 46′ Taurus and retrograde, and Kronos in 4° 46′ Gemini. It was eventually possible, then, for Witte and his followers to cast horoscopes that included eight planets whose existence was (and still is) unknown to astronomers. Furthermore, the nature of the respective 'influences' of these planets was defined and in due course published in the *Regelwerk für Planetenbilder*, a fabulous astrological cook-book that has been the Hamburg School's holy writ since the first edition appeared in 1928.[1]

I must confess my inability to describe even the broad outlines of Witte's Hamburg School system in a few paragraphs. It is perhaps sufficient to say that one prepares data resembling mathematical equations, always involving groups of planets in a specific angular relationship, and often with as many as a dozen or even a score of planetary combinations in a single equation. One then refers to the indispensable *Regelwerk* for interpretations and attempts to synthesise the information. A succession of rather laborious calculations is required; it is necessary to know how to operate and read a dial-like instrument and the hours pass happily by. A sensation of being engaged upon a demanding scientific exercise has undoubtedly appealed to many who use the Hamburg School and one tends to be hypnotised by line after line, sometimes page after page, of planetary equations. However, this extraordinary system, which bears no resemblance to any traditional one, can be made to produce quite baffling results. I used it in 1961 to identify the events in Mr Gauntlett's past life.[2]

It was as a result of the Gauntlett experiment that I read L. Stuiber's pamphlet *Überzeugende astrologische Experimente* (Convincing Astrological Experiments), 1955, with more than ordinary care. The late Ludwig Stuiber (1888–1963) was a Viennese engineer who claimed to be able to deduct past events from horoscopes with particular accuracy by using Hamburg School methods.

According to his pamphlet, on 5 January 1952 he visited some people who posed the following question: 'What happened in the street on 16 July 1927 at 5 p.m. to someone who was born at Vienna on 18 August 1901?' No birth time was given. The following morning Herr Stuiber set to work and that same evening informed his friends that the event was 'Death by shooting—murder'. He was informed that this was correct. The man had been shot by the police, apparently by accident. Herr Stuiber had arrived at a probable birth time by the process of 'rectification',

[1] A fifth revised and enlarged edition was published by Ludwig Rudolph (Witte Verlag), Hamburg, in 1959. An English version, *Book of Rules for Planetary Pictures* was published privately by Hans Niggemann at New York City in 1960 (typewriter facsimile).
[2] See p. 5.

i.e. deductions on the basis of specific events in the native's past life, of which he had been given particulars.

In the meantime a member of the family had recalled that her brother was born at about 8 p.m. Herr Stuiber had estimated 7.52 p.m. as the time. This was all very fascinating but I was still unable to deduce from Herr Stuiber's text *how* he had arrived at his correct result. It is true that he could have visited a public library and searched the Viennese newspapers published on 17 July 1927 for possible clues. However, he mentioned quite casually that the question had been posed on a Saturday evening and that he had solved the problem on a Sunday, when the libraries would have been closed. As for this and other examples in Herr Stuiber's pamphlet, one can either accept or reject his various statements.

Witte wrote a long series of articles about his system that were published in Vollrath's *Astrologische Rundschau* during the early 1920s. It is difficult to believe that many could make head or tail of them. The system itself did not attract much attention until Friedrich Sieggrün read a paper about it at the Leipzig congress in 1923. This caused an immediate uproar, largely provoked by A. M. Grimm, whose neutrality as chairman left much to be desired, and Wilhelm Becker, Alan Leo's erstwhile pupil, who angrily attacked Witte's heretical theories. Becker suggested that something like black magic must surely be involved. It never occurred to him that the whole business of casting and interpreting a horoscope is, in fact, a kind of magical operation.

For those unsympathetic to von Kloeckler or Witte there were plenty of alternative sources of instruction. For instance, Friedrich Schwickert and Dr Adolf Weiss produced a modernised version of the seventeenth-century Morinus system in four volumes in 1926-7. In France Henri Selva had rediscovered the *Astrologia Gallica* of Morin de Villefranche some twenty-five years earlier. This classical system now became widely known in Germany. Vollrath soon followed with translations of all of Alan Leo's major works in seven handsome volumes. Many more new astrological manuals appeared in quick succession.

A rough estimate suggests that during a period of two decades after 1921 at least four hundred books and pamphlets intended for astrologers were published in Germany, the majority of them before 1935. During one five-year period (1926-31) there were no less than twenty-six different astrological year books or predictive annuals, most of which were edited by professional astrologers who appreciated their publicity value. By 1928 half a dozen specialist monthly or bi-monthly periodicals were currently catering for the interests of those who actually practised astrology. These published contributions furnished by literally scores of contributors.

The evidence suggests that the post-war proliferation of interest in astrology was specially marked during the years 1923-8, when recruits to the cause were exceedingly numerous. Again, for every astrologer who delighted to see himself in print, there were hundreds more who quietly studied in the privacy of their homes and never joined a society or study group. It was they who provided the market for the multitude of books and pamphlets that were published at this time, not to mention ephemerides, tables, horoscope forms and so on. Dr Otto Kellner told me that Vollrath's *Astrologische Rundschau*, which was probably never even seen, let alone read, by members of the general public, achieved a monthly circulation of 6,000 copies.

Yet another notable feature of this period was the speed with which new experts, acknowledged or self-appointed, appeared upon the scene. By 1927 the views of well-known or long-established professional astrologers were no longer regarded as specially authoritative. The well-educated amateurs, the *Herren Doktoren* in particular, were now setting the pace. Hence the 'old guard' professionals who, after all, had pioneered astrology in Germany, felt at a disadvantage *vis-à-vis* these learned and sometimes condescending gentry. Eventually, as the next chapter records, their indignation at this state of affairs boiled over.

It is reasonable to ask whether astrology had by now achieved an aura of respectability in Germany. The answer is: no. The allegiance of a few university professors and a couple of hundred *Herren Doktoren* was hardly sufficient to redeem the notorious Madame Urania's badly-tarnished reputation. Astrology had nevertheless created widespread interest and the *Süddeutsche Monatshefte*, a highly-respectable literary and cultural monthly review, even devoted a special issue to its pros and cons in May 1927.[1]

[1] Dr Karl Bayer, *Die Grundprobleme der Astrologie*, 1927, written by an 'academic' astrologer, contains a well-documented account of the contemporary 'intellectual' sector of the German astrological movement and its associated literature.

7
The German Astrologers and the Third Reich

Dr Hubert Korsch (1883–1942) was a Düsseldorf lawyer who specialised in company work, hence his expert knowledge of board and committee procedure, e.g. the drafting of resolutions and minutes and the conduct of meetings. His first appearance on the astrological scene was at the 1926 Hamburg congress when he proposed that the Central Astrological Office should organise tests for astrological proficiency and adroitly manoeuvred himself on to the committee appointed to devise them. He was also an active member of Vollrath's ASiG. My friend Dr Otto Kellner recalled Korsch's bustling interventions at an ASiG congress held at Leipzig in 1927 in one of his letters: 'Vollrath opened the proceedings with a typically soapy address, complete with the usual Theosophical platitudes. Dr Korsch was soon on his feet like a fighting cock and briskly advised Vollrath to get on with the agenda. The esoteric waffle quickly ended.'

Dr Korsch was conspicuous at the CAO's 1928 Magdeburg congress. Indeed, he made such a nuisance of himself that W. Feuerstake, the new President, resigned in a huff and Dr Mrsic was obliged to act as chairman. The CAO was now without a President and Dr Mrsic ironically asked Dr Korsch if he would like the job. This led to his election at the 1929 Nürnberg congress a year later. Dr Mrsic proposed the motion and Wilhelm Becker seconded it, much to the latter's subsequent regret. A pike was now swimming happily in a pond of astrological minnows.

Dr Korsch, who was then 46 years of age, was neither an esoteric nor an occultist. For him astrology represented a science and his self-imposed task was to persuade the general public and, if possible, conventional scientists that this was the case. This ambitious aim could not be achieved without first cleaning out astrology's Augean stables. The implication was that the professional astrologers, many of whom were rather unsatisfactory people, would have to dance to Dr Korsch's tune. There was talk of the necessity for official diplomas for those considered worthy of them and stern measures against the charlatans who sold prefabricated horoscopes. While some of the well-educated professionals were prepared to support Dr Korsch, there were others who viewed his incessant activity with distaste. His opponents were mainly long-established practitioners who had been on the scene long before anybody had even heard of him.

Hitherto the Central Astrological Office's membership had consisted exclusively of affiliated local societies. The rules were soon altered so that individual astrologers could now become members. This policy adversely affected Vollrath's Astrological Society in Germany at Leipzig, which was not an exclusively local society and which soon began to lose subscribers who happened to have more faith in Dr Korsch than in Vollrath & Co. Vollrath's plan to gain control of the German astrological movement had been frustrated in 1923 but he still hoped that ASiG would eventually supplant the CAO. With Dr Korsch's arrival this project appeared increasingly unlikely.

Dr Korsch's next step was to publish a new monthly astrological periodical. This was *Zenit* (January 1930–December 1938). While it ostensibly functioned as the CAO's official organ it was Dr Korsch's own property and was supported by a useful subsidy from a wealthy Düsseldorf businessman whose identity was not revealed. *Zenit* presented an immediate threat to the profitability of all the other astrological journals, including Vollrath's long-established *Astrologische Rundschau* and Wilhelm Becker's *Die Astrologie*. *Zenit* was certainly the best astrological periodical that had so far been published in any country and Dr Korsch quickly succeeded in attracting the collaboration of most of the leading amateurs, particularly the *Akademiker*. It was the amateurs rather than the professionals who were investigating every conceivable aspect of astrological theory with tremendous industry. An anti-Korsch movement was soon organised by the 'old guard' professionals with A. M. Grimm and Wilhelm Becker at their head.

Their first public protest was staged in June 1932 when a Congress of Astrological Pioneers was held at Erfurt. This event was organised by Reinhold Ebertin, the son of Elsbeth Ebertin. Brandler-Pracht, Becker and Grimm all held forth, but the most stirring address of all was given by Christian Meier-Parm, a young man from Hamburg who had recently achieved a certain notoriety in astrological circles.[1] It was useless, he said, for astrologers to expect any benevolence from the representatives of official science. Nor should 'rationalists' such as Dr Korsch presume to represent their interests. What was needed was an autonomous University of Astrology which would confer its own degrees and doctorates. This suggestion was greeted with acclamation. Those who attended the Erfurt congress closed the proceedings by founding an *Astrologische Zentralverband* which, they hoped, would soon replace Dr Korsch's organisation. This project died almost as soon as it had been conceived.

The attacks on Dr Korsch continued. During Dr Mrsic's era the Central Astrological Office had refused all commissions for astrological

---

[1] See his evocative autobiographical fragments in Reinhold Ebertin's *Kosmobiologie*, February 1967. He attended Dr Korsch's Wiesbaden congress in 1931 but disliked its snobbish and stuffy Victorian 'plush sofa atmosphere'. His recent article on 'The horoscopes of thirty-five girls in brothels', which von Kloeckler published in *Sterne und Mensch*, had apparently caused many raised eyebrows in that conventional *milieu*. According to Meier-Parm these people would never have deigned to cast the horoscope of a proletarian.

work and was not prepared to recommend the services of any particular astrologer. This rule had now been changed and in the September 1932 issue of *Die Astrologie* Wilhelm Becker published an article about a horoscope that Dr Korsch was alleged to have supplied to a woman client. It was alleged that Korsch (or the CAO) had charged RM.110 for a horoscope that had been incorrectly calculated. Hence the twenty-two pages of typescript containing the delineation were said to be worthless.

A month or two later Becker published a letter from an anonymous correspondent—he undoubtedly wrote it himself—who suggested that Korsch was a Jesuit spy with close connections with the criminal police and that it would be revealed one fine day that his mission was to lead the astrological movement astray and at a propitious moment deliver it into the hands of its executioners. The writer added that several people at the Erfurt congress supposed that Korsch was playing the role of an *agent provocateur*.

Dr Korsch's counter-attack appeared in *Zenit* (February 1933). He printed an article alleged to have been written by a certain Dr Fleck—Becker suspected, probably correctly, that Korsch had written it—who revealed that he had in his possession a horoscope delineation consisting of sixty-five typewritten pages. The first sheet contained a horoscope chart, the client's name, the usual birth data and the astrologer's signature. The remaining sixty-four sheets had been printed on a duplicating machine. The denouement followed: the horoscope had been supplied by Becker. For Dr Korsch and all serious astrologers there was nothing more heinous than the traffic in prefabricated horoscopes.

Becker retaliated in an 'Open Letter to Dr Korsch' which was published as a four-page supplement to the March 1933 issue of *Die Astrologie*. It was also circulated a month or two later with Vollrath's *Astrologische Rundschau* and hence gained a wide readership. In the course of a scurrilous and unintentionally funny document Becker suggested that Dr Korsch must be short of remunerative legal work and was using the CAO as a shopfront for the sale of expensive and second-rate astrological delineations. He emphasised that Korsch's attitude to the professional astrologers was well known: Korsch thought that they were a crowd of fatheads and claimed that he and the other *Akademiker* were superior to them. He said, too, that there was a perfectly reasonable explanation for the horoscope in Dr Korsch's possession. Until 1916, according to Becker, astrology was not a proper profession. Then the public interest greatly increased and orders for astrological work piled up to such an extent that he was unable to cope with them. So he employed the system that he had learned from Alan Leo, and used a duplicating machine for the preparation of pre-printed sheets until 1924 when he reverted to individual horoscopes. In any case, he added, he was convinced that his own prefabricated delineations were greatly superior to anything that Dr Korsch had to offer.

Becker's 'Open Letter' was written in February 1933. At that time very few people in Germany, let alone the astrologers, could have realised the full implications of an event that had taken place as recently as 30 January. On that day Adolf Hitler became Chancellor of the German Reich.

The Reichstag fire occurred almost a month later on 27 February. The next day Hitler persuaded President Hindenburg to sign a decree 'for the Protection of the People and the State' which suspended seven sections of the constitution that guaranteed individual and civil liberties. There was now a prescribed National Socialist attitude for every conceivable human activity. Almost every adult German became emotionally involved, because no matter whether he or she was for or against Hitler and the National Socialist German Workers' Party, there was no escape from the impact of National Socialist ideology and propaganda.

The astrologers, and particularly the publicists who claimed to represent their interests, were in a difficult position. The State or the Party— henceforth the two could not be easily distinguished—might be expected to 'supervise' astrology and its practitioners as, indeed, they quickly showed signs of wanting to control everything else. The nature of this control, in the interests of the so-called National Socialist *Weltanschauung*, was not immediately apparent.

The astrologers, or rather their leaders, did not wait for the Party or the State to express an interest in their affairs, but were soon looking for some kind of protective umbrella which, it was hoped, would allow them to carry on without too much interference. However, there was no question of a united front and the subsequent individual 'negotiations' were part and parcel of an astrologers' dog-fight that was conducted without quarter on either side. The story of this *guerre des astrologues* adds nothing to our knowledge of astrology itself, but shows how a relatively small group of Germans reacted to a new and unprecedented political and social situation.

A detailed account of every phase of the contest between Dr Korsch and Vollrath & Co. for the leadership of the German astrological movement would require far more space than can be afforded in this book. Here the reader will find only the broad outlines of a saga that is documented at wearisome length in the contemporary periodical literature.[1] The most extraordinary feature of all was the persistence with which all the leading protagonists fought for possession of a corpse.

I will begin by introducing Herr Engineer Martin Pfefferkorn, the would be 'Führer' of a National Socialist astrological movement. He was born at Leipzig on 14 July 1904 and was therefore in his twenty-ninth year when Hitler became Chancellor. He had been an active member of Vollrath's ASiG for some years but was hardly known outside Leipzig astrological circles. During the autumn of 1932 he attempted to found an

[1] See the *Nachrichtenblätter* (News Letters) published by Korsch's CAO and Vollrath's ASiG, also many articles published in *Zenit* in 1933–4.

Arbeitsgemeinschaft Deutscher Astrologen (German Astrologers' Study Group) and applied for its affiliation to ASiG. I do not know why Pfefferkorn found it necessary to establish yet another astrological society. Subsequently he claimed that his ADA was intended to reflect a specifically National Socialist attitude, i.e. *before* the Nazis came to power, but the available evidence does not appear to support this contention. However, Pfefferkorn seems to have been a zealous Party member well before 30 January 1933. In any event, his application for ADA to be accorded official recognition by ASiG was rejected by the latter's committee, which included Vollrath and the faithful Theodor Becher, on the grounds that ADA as yet had neither members nor a constitution. Indeed, ADA might have been stillborn if the advent of Hitler and the National Socialists had not radically altered the situation early in 1933.

The President of ASiG was Dr Gerhard Naumann, a schoolmaster at Wurzen, a small town about twenty miles east of Leipzig. He was joint editor with Theodor Becher of Vollrath's *Astrologische Rundschau* and had translated the seven large Leo books for Vollrath's Theosophical Publishing House. His wife Irma was also a member of the ASiG committee and well known in local astrological circles. The fact that the Naumanns had never disguised their dislike for Hitler and the Nazis was now to be greatly to their disadvantage. Party Comrade Pfefferkorn had lost no time in renewing his application for ADA's affiliation with ASiG. It was opposed by the Naumanns, also by my friend Dr Otto Kellner, who was also a member of the committee, but now strongly supported by Vollrath and Becher, who sensed the direction in which the political wind was blowing. Neither of them was a convinced Nazi but their own commercial interests had to be protected since ASiG was run as a useful appendage to the Theosophical Publishing House. It was therefore clearly advisable to appease Pfefferkorn.

It is uncertain whether the Naumanns voluntarily resigned from ASiG or were hounded out. In any case their long-standing connection with it was abruptly ended about the middle of March 1933, only a fortnight or so after the Nazis seized Germany by the throat. Naumann made a half-hearted attempt to found a rival society but nothing came of this plan and Vollrath and Pfefferkorn were left in possession of the field. Dr Kellner resigned at the same time as the Naumanns. Pfefferkorn was not yet top dog in ASiG but his ambitions in this respect were soon to be fulfilled. In the meantime he began to make his voice heard by contributing wordy articles to the ASiG Newsletter.

His first article, its title was 'Combat Astrological Charlatanry', is of interest because of his allusions to recent discussions of Hitler's horoscope in periodicals that were read by members of the general public rather than by serious students of astrology. The Führer's horoscope was rarely mentioned in the astrological journals and predictive almanacs between

1924 and 1931, probably because it still appeared unlikely that either Hitler or his followers would ever represent anything more than a noisy nuisance. By 1931, however, his horoscope was beginning to attract attention again.

Karl Frankenbach, an Austrian Nazi, published an optimistic interpretation in *Zenit* (April 1931). Disagreement was expressed in the next issue by a writer who cautiously used the pseudonym 'Spectator'. He was convinced of the inevitability of Hitler's ultimate downfall but obviously had no idea when this would happen. It was as well that 'Spectator', who was Dr Korsch's friend Josef Schultz at Düsseldorf, concealed his identity because ten years later the Gestapo was most anxious to discover it.

It was generally supposed by astrologers that Hitler's horoscope should be calculated for a birth at Braunau am Inn on 20 April 1889 at 6.30 p.m. Immediately after he became Chancellor horoscopes based on a variety of different times, hence with a whole range of varying Ascendants, were being published in order to justify this or that conception of the *Führer* and his potentialities. For instance, a contributor to one low-class and sensational pseudo-occult publication, offered a new Hitler horoscope in which the birth time had been 'adjusted' by as much as twelve hours. Pfefferkorn complained that 'the "new" horoscope indicates destructive and rapacious tendencies . . . that his [i.e. Hitler's] followers do not admit'. In February 1933 Frank Glahn published yet another Hitler horoscope in his periodical *Astral Warte* with a 5.45 a.m. birth time (Ascendant 17° Taurus) and expressed his disbelief in Hitler's ability to form a viable government. A month later he found it advisable to retract this dangerous statement. According to A. M. Grimm in *Die Astrologie* (May 1933), Glahn found the 17° Taurus Ascendant, and hence the 5.45 a.m. birth time, by swinging a pendulum over the Führer's chart. Many astrologers 'corrected' the horoscope on the basis of past events in Hitler's life. Elsbeth Ebertin, for instance, proposed that his birth had taken place between 6.22 and 6.26 p.m. (*Ein Blick in die Zukunft* for 1934, written early in 1933).

Soon, however, astrologers who liked to see themselves in print began to use the utmost circumspection when discussing Hitler's horoscope. References to it ceased altogether after 1934, probably as a result of a confidential directive to publishers from the Propaganda Ministry. The veto also applied to the horoscopes of all the leading Nazis and any kind of astrological speculation on the subject of the Third Reich.[1]

[1] Hitler's horoscope continued to fascinate Germans who were not astrologers. There is a revealing passage in the autobiography of Hans Blüher, one of the founders of the *Wandervögel* youth movement. Soon after the Röhm *Putsch* of 30 June 1934 he invited Count Finckenstein, an astrologer friend of his, to tell him about the horoscope. They met at a Berlin restaurant. 'My friend Ulrich looked cautiously round to see if anyone was listening to us. Then he leaned towards me and whispered into my ear through a cupped hand: "He's a homicidal maniac!" Ever since then I knew that Germany had sold herself into the hands of a murderer.' (*Werke und Tage*, 1953, pp. 168–9.)

It was not long before Pfefferkorn was doing his best to make trouble for Dr Korsch in connection with an article by Dr Karl-Guenther Heimsoth that had appeared in *Zenit* in November 1932. I have never been able to understand all the implications of this highly-technical astro-political study and it is possible that many contemporary readers of *Zenit* were not much the wiser. The manner in which Pfefferkorn used Heimsoth's piece as a rod for Dr Korsch's back illustrates the tricky nature of the current situation when the Nazis were busy settling old scores.[1]

Dr Heimsoth was no common-or-garden astrologer. In 1919–20 he had been prominent in the paramilitary *Freikorps* movement and was acquainted with many of the leading Nazis during the Party's early days. At one time he had been a close friend of Gregor Strasser, the leader of the left-wing 'revolutionary' National Socialist faction. Strasser had broken with Hitler as recently as December 1932, hence all Strasser's friends, past and present, were suspect.

Dr Heimsoth had qualified as a doctor and specialised in psychology. Furthermore, he used astrology in connection with his medical practice. He was an active member of the Academic Astrological Society at Berlin, where he resided, and the author of *Charakter Konstellation*, 1928, a study of the horoscopes of homosexuals. Heimsoth was deeply interested in this subject because he, too, was an active homosexual. In view of all these circumstances it is hardly surprising that he was acquainted with Ernst Röhm, the notoriously homosexual chief of the *Sturm Abteilung* (SA), Hitler's Party private army.

In 1928–9 Röhm was a military instructor in the Bolivian army and corresponded with Heimsoth, who had just published *Charakter Konstellation*. There were frequent references in Röhm's letters to his lack of congenial homosexual company. 'You have only yourself to blame if your book has encouraged me to ask a favour of you,' Röhm wrote in one of them. 'You are obviously very skilled in judging horoscopes. Could you not have a look at mine? I was born at Munich on 28 November 1887 at 1 a.m. Then I might learn what sort of a person I am. Frankly, I don't really know. I suppose that I am homosexual, but only discovered this in 1924.'

Ernst Rohm, Gregor Strasser and Karl-Guenther Heimsoth were all murdered by the SS in June 1934 (Röhm *Putsch*). Heimsoth was the Nazis' first identifiable astrologer victim, but not the last.[2]

---

[1] Dr Korsch's membership of the *Reichsverband Deutscher Schriftssteller* (Party organisation for writers and editors controlled by the Propaganda Ministry) was cancelled on 21 June 1934 on the ground that articles published in *Zenit* before 30 January 1933 made his own political reliability appear doubtful. He was allowed to continue to edit *Zenit* pending further enquiries and was eventually readmitted to membership in April 1935. Although a Party member, Korsch's personal position was always insecure from the summer of 1933 onwards.

[2] The Röhm-Heimsoth correspondence was given wide publicity in the German anti-Nazi press in 1932. The letters were no longer in Heimsoth's possession and were

Hundreds of thousands of Germans made haste to join the Nazi party during the spring of 1933. Hugo Vollrath and Theodor Becher were among the new recruits. In the April issue of the *Astrologische Rundschau* Becher confidently stated that 'awareness of one's national heritage and blood ties with the aryan race are indivisibly bound up with astrological science,' and in the ASiG Newsletter a month later he urged the necessity for 'getting rid of parasitical, alien and subversive elements' in the astrological movement, adding that they would be judged in the light of their previous attitude to National Socialism. With the exception of Dr Korsch's *Zenit* many of the astrological periodicals began to publish articles which explained that astrology was essentially a nordic science, on 'Race and Astrology' and similar fashionable subjects.

In this respect the worst offender during 1933–4 was Reinhold Ebertin's *Mensch im All*, probably because his periodical was temporarily united with 'Professor' Ernst Issberner-Haldane's *Die Chiromantie*. Issberner-Haldane (*b.* 1886) was a well-known Berlin palmist who specialised in alleged medical diagnosis on the basis of deductions from the appearance of his patients' finger-nails.[1] He was also an astrologer and in 1933 published a short textbook (*Einführung in die Astrologie*). His autobiographical *Der Chiromant* (*The Palmist*), 1925, contains valuable source material for the student of the German occult 'underground'. In spite of its racial nonsense and anti-semitic allusions it was banned in 1934. Issberner-Haldane was a disciple of Lanz von Liebenfels, the Viennese founder of the Ariosophical Movement, which was at once occultist and pathologically anti-semitic. There is evidence to suggest that Hitler read Lanz von Liebenfels' periodical *Ostara* during his Vienna period before 1914.[2]

in the files of the public prosecutor's department at Munich. At this stage photographic copies were smuggled out of the latter's office. Dr Helmut Klotz, a renegade Nazi, reproduced them in a privately printed 16-page pamphlet (no title, Berlin, March 1932?). They were reprinted soon after Röhm's death in *Die Memoiren des Stabschef Röhm*. This volume of spurious memoirs was published at Saarbrücken by emigré Germans and copies were smuggled into the Reich. For Röhm's efforts to regain possession of his letters, see Herbert Heinersdorf, 'Akten zum Falle Röhm' in *Mitteilungen des Wissenschaftlichhumanitären Komitees, e.V.*, Berlin-Charlottenburg, No. 32, January–March 1932.

[1] His advertisement in *Mensch im All*, December 1933, contained the warning 'Beware of Charlatans!'

[2] A detailed account of Lanz von Liebenfels' career will be found in W. Daim, *Der Mann, der Hitler die Ideen gab*, Munich, 1958. Liebenfels was a learned astrologer and, according to Dr Daim, habitually gave a false birth date (Messina, 1 May 1872 instead of Vienna, 19 July 1874) in order to lead other astrologers astray. His enormous literary output included *Praktisch-empirisches Handbuch der ariosophischen Astrologie*, Berlin, 1933 (issued in parts and possibly not completed). It was published by his follower Herbert Reichstein, who issued a fair number of the Master's works. Reichstein was yet another member of the occult underground. In April 1933 he published the first number of the weekly *Arische Rundschau* (*Aryan Review*), an anti-semitic rag that included such choice items as 'The Cabalist Horoscope of Adolf Hitler'. Lanz von Liebenfels was forbidden to write for publication in 1938. By this time Hitler's 'Messianic' image made it necessary for a veil to be drawn over his early intellectual influences.

A leaflet received from the Professor in 1964 contained the surprising information that he had received 'priestly consecration in a Christian order' in 1929. The same source revealed that he was awarded the title of Professor *honoris causa* by an unspecified university in 1912 and became an honorary member of the Plasmogenic Society at Barcelona in 1926. 'He has refused all other honorary titles.'

Together with Ebertin and others in 1933 he founded *Die Geistige Front*, an association of professional *Charakterologen* which can only have had a brief existence. 'In principle the following are not accepted: Jews and other racially inferior persons, physically handicapped or crippled people (other than those wounded in the war), charlatans, quacks and such persons who must be regarded as unreliable.'[1] Issberner-Haldane's connection with Ebertin's periodical came to an end in September 1936.

In the meantime Herr Party Comrade Engineer Martin Pfefferkorn had been busy behind the scenes at Leipzig. His *Arbeitsgemeinschaft* had not only been affiliated to the Astrological Society in Germany, but was now a major force within ASiG itself. Vollrath and Becher were his obedient servants. His triumph was complete when an extraordinary general meeting of ASiG was held on 12 June 1933. This was attended by Dr Werner Schingnitz, representing the Party's Leipzig Cultural-Political Office, who was more than ready to engineer a *coup d'état* on behalf of Party Comrade Pfefferkorn.[2] Dr Schingnitz announced the immediate *Gleichschaltung*, i.e. 'National Socialist integration', of ASiG. The word *Gleichschaltung* was on everybody's lips in Germany at that time. It meant, in effect, the reorganisation of every activity on a National Socialist basis, hence the ruthless elimination of all individuals whose political sympathies were suspect.

Dr Schingnitz read a list containing the names of those who were to be 'elected' to the committee of ASiG. Party Member Martin Pfefferkorn was to be the new President, assisted by Party Member Theobald Becher (Vice President and Treasurer), Party Member Hugo Vollrath, Party Member Dr Paul Moebius and two others, including one who was not a Nazi but otherwise presumably harmless.[3]

Von Sebottendorff's *Bevor Hitler kam* was suppressed in 1934 because of its author's unwelcome emphasis that Hitler's ideology was a by-product of the spirit of the Thule Society.

[1] *Mensch im All*, October 1933.

[2] Dr Otto Kellner recalled Dr Schingnitz in a letter: 'Dr S. was a slender, dark-haired little chap, still very young, who looked like an ape. He was assistant to Professor Hans Driesch, the well-known philosopher. After 1933, if I am not mistaken, he ran the Leipzig branch of the Nazi Union of University Teachers.'

[3] Dr Moebius was ASiG's official representative in Berlin. A change of address notice published in *Die Astrologie* (October 1932) announced that he specialised in 'Biochemistry, Homoeopathy, Diets and Astrodiagnosis according to the system of Dr Heindel'. The latter was none other than Max Heindel, the Californian 'Rosicrucian' mystagogue who certainly never had a medical degree.

Pfefferkorn was completely convinced that he was now destined to become the leader of a united and National Socialist German astrological movement. This grand design, which necessitated the downfall of Dr Korsch and the collapse of the Central Astrological Office, was henceforth pursued with great energy and absolutely no sense of proportion.

Very conveniently for Pfefferkorn the CAO's annual congress was due to be held at Stuttgart about three weeks later, since this would be an excellent opportunity for showing the ASiG–ADA flag in the enemy's camp. His trump card was that he had already made contact with the *Kampfbund für Deutsche Kultur* (League for the Protection of German Culture), which was one of a multitude of busybody Party offices which all had more or less overlapping functions and which provided jobs for deserving Party members and a veritable regiment of political opportunists. The *Kampfbund* had written to him on 29 June 1933 and had authorised him to make it clear at Stuttgart that his prospective efforts to unite the German astrological movement would meet with its warm support.

Pfefferkorn, who led a delegation of about fifteen ASiG members, was much in evidence at the CAO's annual general meeting on 4 July. While Dr Korsch was able to deal successfully with most of the ebullient Herr Pfefferkorn's interventions, he knew better than to resist when the latter proposed that the 1934 congress could only be held at Munich, 'the city in which the Führer year after year fought his sternest battle'. It was discretion rather than unanimous respect for Adolf Hitler that produced a unanimous vote in favour of the motion.

Pfefferkorn returned to Leipzig having made a lot of noise but without 'liquidating' Dr Korsch. They were, however, to meet again in Berlin a few days later and this time Pfefferkorn won the round. Their next encounter took place on 14 July at the offices of the Party's *Verbindungsstab*, a bureau which provided liaison services with the various Reich ministries. Both were seeking official support, or perhaps merely tolerance, for their respective groups. Pfefferkorn was accompanied by Dr Moebius.

Pfefferkorn was summoned to someone's office and Korsch and Moebius remained together in an ante-room. Dr Moebius noticed that Dr Korsch was wearing a Party badge and enquired about his entitlement to do so. Dr Korsch said that he did not feel obliged to answer the question. After a heated argument a senior Party official was summoned who enquired when Dr Korsch had joined the NSDAP. Korsch said that he had become a member early in May and was informed that he should have been aware that individuals who had joined after 30 January 1933 were not permitted to wear the swastika badge or be addressed as Party Comrade until after the expiration of a probationary period of six months. He was also told that he was liable to arrest for this breach of the regulations. Dr Moebius did his utmost to take the matter further and it was not until four months later that Dr Korsch learned that the authorities had decided not to prosecute him.

Pfefferkorn's next move was an attempt to 'organise' the professional astrologers. For this purpose he used the services of A. M. Grimm who, although not a Party member, ostentatiously called himself *Reichsorganisationsleiter* (Reich Organising Leader, a typically Nazi title) of the League of German Professional Astrologers. Grimm was soon mailing peremptory circular letters, complete with swastika device, on the lines of: 'You are required to become a member of the League of German Professional Astrologers. Your failure to comply will reflect an anti-National Socialist attitude'. Dr Korsch wrote to the League for the Protection of German Culture to enquire if Grimm had received its authorisation. The League disowned Grimm and stated that it had no intention of intervening in the affairs of the astrologers because factional differences within the movement itself made any such plan impracticable. Grimm himself did not succeed in recruiting more than a handful of obscure professional astrologers and his association ceased to exist early in 1934.

The next anti-Korsch gambit—in this case I do not know who was responsible—was to spread a rumour that he was not of pure aryan descent. Dr Korsch felt obliged to emphasise his lack of Jewish ancestors in the October 1933 issue of *Zenit*.

Although the point was never made very clearly in the contemporary literature, it is evident that both Dr Korsch and Martin Pfefferkorn were worried about the future status of the professional astrologers. They were entirely willing to sacrifice the charlatans, of whom there were many, but hoped to protect the respectable practitioners. The problem in relation to the authorities, in so far as the latter were identifiable, was to persuade them to accept the validity of the diplomas that were now being offered by both camps to professional astrologers, also to amateurs, who were capable of passing stringent tests. Nobody of any great consequence thought it worthwhile to apply for the Leipzig diploma but a fair number of well-known professionals obtained the one offered by Dr Korsch's Central Astrological Office. Dr Korsch, however, was still unable to persuade the authorities that the possession of a CAO diploma was an automatic guarantee of competence, respectability and political reliability. Hence all the professionals, whose ranks included many who worked on a part-time basis, were still in a vulnerable position.

In the autumn of 1933, at the very time when the CAO was issuing its first batch of diplomas, the police presidents at Berlin, Hanover and Cologne instructed newspapers published within their jurisdiction to refuse all advertisements sent for insertion by astrologers. Since the reputable professionals never advertised their services, this only affected the small fry who serviced the popular end of the market with prefabricated horoscopes.

The situation became more serious during the spring of 1934 when the Berlin police president banned all forms of professional fortune-telling in the Berlin area. This ban naturally included astrology, and the sale of popular astrological periodicals, predictive almanacs and prefabricated horoscopes was also stopped. It would appear that similar preventive regulations were soon in force in other parts of the Reich but I have been unable to obtain precise evidence on this point. The professional astrologers, as a class, were obviously in a difficult position from the spring of 1934 onwards.

By the autumn of 1934 the Pfefferkorn versus Korsch battle was beginning to die a natural death, if only because Pfefferkorn realised that he had no chance of winning it. He retired from the fray altogether in October 1934 after nominating Theobald Becher to succeed him as President of the Astrological Society in Germany. The public explanation was that his Party and other duties made it impossible for him to continue in office. He had dutifully waved the swastika banner and had achieved nothing.

Dr Korsch made his final attack on Vollrath in the December 1934 issue of the CAO's Newsletter. He had been collecting material for his Vollrath dossier for years on end and now published one of his most spectacular documents. Prior to 1914 Vollrath had always called himself Herr Doktor Vollrath and, according to Dr Korsch, claimed to have been awarded his doctorate at Tübingen on the basis of an economics thesis. Korsch had made careful enquiries at Tübingen where the university authorities stated that there was no record that Vollrath had ever studied there. In those days all doctoral theses were printed, hence if Vollrath had ever been a Herr Doktor printed evidence must exist somewhere. The document itself was eventually discovered and its title-page was now gleefully reproduced in the CAO's Newsletter. The subject of Vollrath's dissertation was *The Development of Investment and Financial Trusts in England* and it was supposed to have gained him a doctorate in March 1905. Dr Korsch sent full particulars to Tübingen where they still denied any knowledge of either Vollrath or his thesis. The implication, therefore, was that the document was a fake and Dr Korsch invited to comment upon this proposition. Vollrath, however, preserved a discreet silence.

There were still no signs that the astrologers might now expect to be left in peace. In Berlin and elsewhere the police began to confiscate booksellers' stocks of astrological literature, apparently on a haphazard basis, and were just as liable to seize serious textbooks, which were of no interest to members of the general public, as less reputable works. These seizures provoked the movement's last major effort to establish a *modus vivendi* with the authorities. The story of the events of the autumn of 1934, which were accompanied by the customary intrigues and is too involved for detailed examination here. The end result, however tortuously contrived, nevertheless provided an interim solution.

Those who suffered most from the sporadic confiscations of astrological literature were not the astrologers at large but booksellers, publishers and authors who were remunerated on a royalty basis. A certain Herr Bohneberg, the proprietor of the Regulus Verlag at Görlitz, a publishing house with a considerable astrological and occult back-list, took the initiative by summoning the leading specialist publishers and booksellers, also many prominent members of the astrological movement, to a meeting at Berlin on 25 August 1934. This led to a further conference at Berlin on 27–28 October which was organised by Christian Meier-Parm, who hoped to succeed where both Dr Korsch and Martin Pfefferkorn had failed.

Meier-Parm's plan was to create a body representative of all sectors of the movement that could negotiate with the 'authorities' in order to get the ban on professional astrology lifted. He and his mentor Frank Glahn had already had discussions with the (Prussian?) Ministry of the Interior and the division in Dr Ley's powerful German Labour Front which dealt with the affairs of the so-called independent professions. At the same time, as a result of Herr Bohneberg's conference of 25 August, Johannes Vehlow, a Berlin professional astrologer who had written an extensive series of textbooks, had been having conversations with various unidentified ministries and the Berlin police. There was now talk of the creation of a Committee for the Organisation and Advancement of Astrological Research. What might be described as the 'Parm Plan' did not receive the support of Dr Korsch and the CAO, largely because Korsch was jealous of all independent attempts to negotiate on behalf of the astrologers.

Meier-Parm took the chair at the second Berlin meeting in October. For a while it seemed likely that he would be elected to represent the interests of all the parties present, but Dr Korsch was able to prevent this. The result was a stupendous row. Since Meier-Parm had completely lost control of the situation he was thrown overboard and old Wilhelm Becker, the senior astrologer present, was invited to take the chair. After interminable arguments about voting rights, two working committees were formed. Dr Korsch gained a seat on each of them but failed to secure his own election as chairman. In the meantime Meier-Parm, who had been excluded from the deliberations, was lying in wait for Dr Korsch outside the conference hall and when the latter emerged assaulted him, although probably without hitting him very hard. Three weeks later Dr Korsch and Major von dem Hagen, who was also representing the CAO, resigned from the Berlin committees in order to preserve their own freedom of action.

In spite of Dr Korsch's non-cooperation, a so-called Committee of Three (Wilhelm Becker, Johannes Vehlow and Emil Saenger) succeeded in getting something done. Discussions were now held with the Berlin police, the Prussian Ministry of the Interior, and the Publishers' and Booksellers' Associations. In the final analysis it was the Publishers' and Booksellers' Associations which came to the astrologers' rescue. Their representatives persuaded the Berlin police and the *Reichsschrifttums-kammer*, a Party office that dealt with the affairs of authors, writers and journalists, to sanction the creation of a Censorship Office for Astrological Literature under the direction of Karl-Friedrich Schulze. This gentle-man, who had been president of the Magdeburg Astrological Society, was not only a Party member but so inoffensive that even Dr Korsch made no public protest at his appointment.

At this point the turmoil that had beset the German astrological move-ment since the beginning of 1933 began to come to an end. Four more years to pass before the outbreak of war in 1939 and almost six before the movement itself was ultimately destroyed during the summer of 1941. Its great days, however, were over, and the battles of 1933–5 were followed by a gradual running down process. There was a curious anomaly. As from *c*. July 1935 full-time professional astrologers, graphologists, *Charak-terologen* and chirologists (palmists) were allowed to join the 'Independent Professions' section of the German Labour Front and were under the supervision of the indispensable Herr Karl-Friedrich Schulze. It seems that a distinction was made between 'reliable' and politically acceptable practitioners and their less satisfactory brethren. At the end of 1936 even one so well informed as Reinhold Ebertin was not completely clear about the current situation. In a review of the present state of the astrological movement which he published in *Mensch im All* (January 1937), he indicated that conditions varied from place to place. In some towns it was sufficient for a professional astrologer to give certain assurances to the local police. It would appear that professional work was sometimes tolerated on condition that an individual practitioner went about his business with the utmost discretion. It probably suited the authorities' purpose to keep everyone guessing. The uncertainty naturally led to all manner of rumours. Witte's Hamburg School *Regelwerk* was banned for a time but was later allowed to be sold in an amended version. Stories to the effect that the Hamburg School system itself had been banned were widely current among astrologers in 1937.

Dr Korsch was still fairly optimistic in 1935. The attacks mounted by Vollrath & Co. had withered away and the Central Astrological Office was still the most effective representative organisation. Hence Dr Korsch's decision to organise the most ambitious astrologers' congress so far staged in Germany, namely an international affair to be held at Düsseldorf in September 1936. It was officially announced in November 1935 after prolonged negotiations with the Propaganda Ministry and the Düsseldorf Gauleiter's office. This congress (1–7 September 1936) attracted as many as 400 visitors, including astrologers from sixteen countries outside Germany. Two senior Party officials representing the local Gauleiter and Kreisleiter spoke at the opening session and telegrams containing the astrologers' respectful greetings were sent to the Führer and Dr Goebbels. The subsequent receipt of a telegram expressing Hitler's best wishes for the success of the congress was later widely misunderstood by naïve astrologers who did not realise that Hitler's staff dealt with such communications on a purely routine basis. Twenty-one papers were read, including six in French and one in English, the latter contributed by Mr W. J. Tucker—the academic laurels referred to on p. 71 had yet to adorn his brow—who spoke on 'Aristotle, Kant and Basic Astrology'.

It is unlikely that anybody realised that this would be the last major German astrological congress. The one scheduled to be held at Baden-Baden in 1937 was cancelled without any public explanation at very short notice, presumably on official instructions.

The year 1937 also witnessed the suppression of the German branch of the Theosophical Society. Vollrath's Theosophical Publishing House was closed down, the *Astrologische Rundschau* ceased publication and ASiG, which now called itself the German Astrological Society, was liquidated. Vollrath retired to a country house (it appears to have been the property of the Theosophical Society) in the neighbourhood of Leipzig. Most of the rooms were occupied by the Hitler Youth, who were also the recipients of the Theosophical Society's grand piano. Whether or not he survived the war years is unknown.

Elsbeth Ebertin was another member of the old guard whose customary activities were coming to an end. The twentieth (1937) edition of her almanac *Ein Blick in die Zukunft* contained a cryptic passage in which she hinted that the suspension of its publication was due to circumstances outside her control. Wilhelm Becker's *Die Astrologie* also ceased publication in 1937.

The last of the pre-war congresses was held at Starnberg, an agreeable lake resort near Munich, at the end of August 1938. The following information has been provided by Herr Wilhelm Wulff and Dr. Kellner. The local arrangements were made by two leading members of the Munich Astrological Society: Georg Seidenschwang, a vintage Nazi and possessor of the Golden Party Badge, and Lorenz Mesch, an architect. They and Dr. Korsch had been officially warned that no printed record of the proceedings was to be published. Dr. Korsch was due to preside as usual but failed to arrive. He had been arrested on a charge of perjury and had already been in a Dusseldorf remand prison since 19 July. This fact was not widely known at Starnberg. Seidenschwang announced that Dr. Korsch was ill and according to Herr Wulff: 'a murmur went round the room'.

Apart from Seidenschwang, Mesch and Wulff very few of the participants were aware that the Munich Gestapo had proposed to arrest the lot of them out of hand. News of the plan had reached a senior member of Himmler's staff who happened to be an old friend of Mesch—in fact Mesch had once cast his horoscope for him—and he was able to prevent its fulfilment. Nevertheless, the authorities sent their watchdogs in the shape of Dr Kurd Kisshauer, who will be mentioned again later in this book, and Dr Kittler, from the *Reichsschrifttumskammer* the Propaganda Ministry department that supervised all literary and publishing activities. Astrological writers came under Kittler's wing and he himself was well versed in astrology. They both listened attentively and said nothing. Initially not many were aware of their respective identities. On the morning of Monday, 29 August 1938, Herr Wulff's wife telephoned him from Hamburg and said that the police had just searched his home. Dr Kellner recalled many years later that when he himself arrived at Starnberg that morning and greeted Herr Wulff, the latter looked anxious and withdrawn.

In many, but apparently not all, cases Messrs Kisshauer and Kittler made a careful note of who was present at Starnberg. Thus when Dr Kellner was arrested at Leipzig on 9 June 1941 he was reminded at the Gestapo headquarters that he had attended the congress. It is evident, then, that the authorities were already busy collecting information about prominent members of the astrological movement in 1938, but the day of reckoning did not arrive until three years later.

Dr Korsch's *Zenit* was published for the last time in December 1938. Hence the Astrological Central Office, if it continued to exist, had lost its official organ. Two periodicals survived until the spring of 1941: *Sterne und Mensch*, originally founded by Freiherr von Kloeckler but not edited by him since February 1935, and Reinhold Ebertin's *Mensch im All*. Neither of them contained even an oblique reference to the astral implications of the occupation of Czechoslovakia in March 1939 or, after September 1939, to the fact that Germany was once again involved in a major war. In many respects astrology had already been driven underground. It is certain, however, that a great many people in Germany who had some understanding of astrology were studying Hitler's horoscope more intently than ever in the past. Among them was the Swiss astrologer Karl Ernst Krafft, who was now living in southern Germany and hopefully waiting for a summons to serve the Third Reich and its masters.

PART II

8

The Quest for Krafft

I began to look for Krafft's trail soon after my first lesson with Mrs Naylor in 1959. In her library I noticed a copy of his *Traité d'Astro-Biologie*, which he published in 1939, and recalled his name and the faked letter business in 1943. Mrs Naylor lent me the book, which I read, or rather tried to read, with some interest because it was so unlike the tedious astrological manuals that I had so far encountered. Krafft claimed to have established the existence of cosmic influences on human individuals on the basis of large-scale statistical evidence. The *Traité* appeared to be a biometric rather than a strictly astrological treatise, and in any case there was scarcely a line in the book that would help any one to 'interpret' a horoscope. My lack of mathematical training did not allow me to follow, let alone check, Krafft's statistical arguments, but this unusual work nevertheless fascinated me. It seemed, in some inexplicable manner, to bring a vague and shadowy figure to life, and I was intensely curious to know more about its author and, in particular, his alleged connection with Hitler.

Krafft was clearly no common-or-garden astrologer. Hence it was quite conceivable, even logical, that Hitler should have employed a star performer, a scientific virtuoso of Krafft's apparent calibre, rather than a nonentity. Even at that time, when Mrs Naylor was teaching me the elements of astrology, I was more interested in Krafft than in astrology itself and sensed, rather than consciously realised, that anything that I might happen to learn about astrology would have some bearing upon the Krafft puzzle. There was this irrational feeling that *l'affaire Krafft* would continue to preoccupy me until I could discover the answers to a great many barely formulated questions.

I was soon hunting for a copy of de Wohl's *The Stars of War and Peace*, 1952, the book in which he stated that his own appointment as top secret astrologer for various unspecified British intelligence agencies was directly related to the assumption that Krafft was working for Hitler.[1] The evidence upon which this supposition was based appeared to be scanty. De Wohl referred to letters that a neutral diplomat accredited to the Court of St James's received from Krafft in 1939-40. It was the diplomat, according to de Wohl, who suggested that Krafft must surely be advising

---

[1] I was unable to find a copy of the English version and for the purposes of this book have used the Swiss edition, *Sterne, Krieg und Frieden*, 1951.

Hitler, while he himself had found the formula that ultimately persuaded the British to employ him. The diplomat had told de Wohl that he would not find it easy to induce the Foreign Office or anyone else in a position of authority to take this hypothetical Hitler–Krafft relationship very seriously. De Wohl's view, however, was that it was unimportant if certain highly-placed people in London were sceptical about astrology. The vital factor, he emphasised, *was that Hitler believed in it.* 'Hence, if I make the same calculations as Hitler's astrologer,' he told the diplomat, '*I* will know what kind of advice Hitler is getting from a man whose judgement he respects. It is only logical that this information will be extremely useful to the British!' According to his own account of the events of 1940, de Wohl was subsequently interviewed by a succession of important people and was in due course engaged to do secret astrological work. Later, he said, he was granted a commission in the British army.

What intrigued me, however, was de Wohl's apparent lack of curiosity about Krafft after the war. Apart from his book he published many internationally-syndicated articles that purported to describe his own wartime activities. Nevertheless, as far as Krafft was concerned he provided no fresh information. Nor, for instance, did he mention Krafft's death in a German concentration camp. I soon discovered that this fact was known to British astrologers who happened to be aware of Krafft's name. De Wohl's apparent indifference to the German side of the story aroused my suspicions, and I began to wonder if there was more in this than met the eye.

Krafft was a Swiss citizen and, as I eventually learned, did not move to Germany until 1937. At this stage it was necessary to ask why Krafft had left Switzerland and to find out what had happened to him between the time he arrived in Germany and his death early in 1945.

A week or two after I borrowed Mrs Naylor's copy of the *Traité* I visited Sefton Delmer at his farm in Suffolk and mentioned my new and unexpected interest in Krafft. Delmer suggested that I should try to uncover the facts about his connection with Hitler. I said that the evidence, if it existed at all, could only be found in Germany and that even the most elementary clues were lacking. I remember saying: 'It will be like looking for a needle in a haystack.'

Soon after my talk with Delmer I happened to attend a lecture at the Astrological Lodge of the Theosophical Society. There was a table upon which new and second-hand astrological literature was exposed for sale, and I purchased half a dozen old German astrological magazines. In one of them I found a short article about Krafft. The writer mentioned that a certain Dr X., who lived in London, had recently corresponded with his widow. It was easy to trace Dr X., who was well known in astrological circles, and to arrange to visit him. He was unable to give me any useful information but told me that Frau Krafft was living at the Villa Rose at

Commugny, between Geneva and Nyon. A telephone call to the Villa
Rose revealed that she had long since departed and that her present
whereabouts were unknown.

The Introduction to the *Traité* was written 'entre les bords du "Leman"
[the Lake of Geneva] et la Forêt Noire' in March 1939, while the acknow-
ledgements page was written that June at Urberg, a remote Black Forest
village not far from the Swiss frontier at Basle. There were no Kraffts in
the current St Blasien telephone directory, so my wife and I decided to
spend a few days at Lausanne and try to pick up Krafft's trail there. No
clues presented themselves at Lausanne, but I did meet a local astrologer,
a waiter at the *buffet de la gare*, who said that he specialised in tracing
missing persons by using astrological techniques. He was a delightful
man and I would have liked to have seen more of him. However, at one
moment at Lausanne, had I but known it, I was standing within a few
yards of Mlle Marguerite Panchaud's porcelain shop in the Galeries du
Commerce. She was an old friend of Krafft's and had helped to subsidise
the publication of the *Traité*, but we were not to meet until three years
later.

I made no further progress on the Krafft front until a week or two after
the successful Gauntlett experiment in January 1961. Thereafter, owing
to a succession of 'accidents' and coincidences, the pace became fast and
furious. The first important clue arrived in February 1961. I had noticed
what appeared to be a very early publication of Krafft's in a German
bookseller's catalogue. This was his *Influences cosmiques sur l'individu
humain*, Geneva, 1923. This particular copy had been inscribed by Krafft
on 7 July 1923 for Dr Martin Knapp, lecturer in astronomy at the University of Basle. Inside the book I found a long typewritten letter in which
Krafft described, in great detail, the begininngs and current progress of his
astro-statistical investigation. It was curious that this letter should have
unerringly found its way to one of the few people who might conceivably
want to read it.

A few weeks later I was busy transcribing a dozen more letters of
Krafft's, all of them written to Mrs Harold Butler, as she was then, during
the years 1935–8. It was Mrs Naylor who introduced me to Lady Butler,
the widow of Sir Harold Butler, who had been director of the International
Labour Office at Geneva before the war. Aware of Lady Butler's interest
in unconventional subjects and of her long residence at Geneva, Mrs
Naylor asked her if she had ever met Krafft. Lady Butler had known
Krafft very well indeed and Mrs Naylor soon arranged for us to meet.
Among the letters I found a copy, in Krafft's handwriting, of one dated 11
October 1935 that he had received from Count Hermann Keyserling, who
lived at Darmstadt. The Count noted that Krafft was due to lecture at
Mannheim, which is close to Darmstadt, on 31 October 1935 and invited
him to visit him. 'I would like to have a long talk with you,' the Count

wrote, 'Your interpretation of the language of Nostradamus appears to be completely right. It is one of the profoundest expressions of the character of prophetic expression that I have ever met.'

What interested me was that Keyserling, of all people, should have been so anxious to meet Krafft. The Count was one of the most renowned figures on the contemporary intellectual scene, although by 1935 the Nazis were beginning to silence him in Germany. I had met his widow in 1960 and wrote to ask if there was any Krafft correspondence in the Keyserling Archive at Innsbruck. The Countess kindly sent me copies of fourteen letters, three of them from her husband to Krafft and the remainder from Krafft to the Count, all of the period 1937–9. At this stage I was able to make a partial reconstruction of Krafft's life and movements during the years 1935–9, although a lot of information was obviously missing. I still knew very little about his early life, and nothing at all about his later connection with the Third Reich and the circumstances of his death.

One sentence in the copy of the old German astrological magazine that had led me to Dr X., and which I had missed in 1959, provided a vital clue. The writer briefly mentioned a gentleman whom he described as 'the astrologer Goerner' and who, he inferred, knew the facts about Krafft's final German period. By this time I was aware (from yet another German astrological periodical) that Herr F. G. Goerner, if he were still alive, was probably living at Mannheim. I traced Herr Goerner's address and wrote to him. It emerged that Herr Goerner, who described himself as a psychologist and psychotherapist, had known Krafft exceedingly well and had been imprisoned with him in Berlin in 1941–2.

Following a convention dear to astrologers we exchanged birth dates. Herr Goerner informed me that he was born at Bodenbach an der Elbe on 25 July 1898 'with an Ascendant in 3° 8′ Leo', but had lived at Mannheim for the past forty years. It appeared that the atmosphere and climate of Mannheim suited him particularly well, while Bodenbach, he explained, lay on a less favourable (magnetic?) axis between Berlin and Munich. 'In the era of the Third Reich,' he wrote, 'my arrest was ordered at Munich and I was in prison in or near Berlin.'

While Herr Goerner was evidently willing to satisfy my curiosity about Krafft, he hoped that I would take an informed interest in his own astrological investigations. I gathered that in collaboration with a certain Herr Georg Lucht, who had also known Krafft well, he had evolved procedures for making predictive graphs. He sent me a specimen of a *Lebenskurve* (life graph), but I could not fathom how it had been calculated. I learned, too, that together with Herr Lucht he prepared similar documents severally described as Dynamograms, Polarograms, Geograms, Nautograms, Aerograms and Psychograms. He explained that the Nauto- and Aerograms could be applied to naval and aeronautical situations, e.g. for predicting sinkings and crashes, and added that he would welcome a research grant from some well-disposed Foundation providing that his findings were restricted to the use of the North Atlantic Treaty Organisation.

In due course it was agreed that I should visit him at Mannheim one week-end in July 1961. During my three days there I spent about twenty hours with Herr Goerner and recorded parts of our conversation on a 'Minifon' machine. He had an excellent memory and precise dates and other details were recalled with apparent accuracy. My debt to him is considerable, since he gave me a detailed account of what had transpired in Berlin during the period from October 1941 to February 1943, when he and Krafft were in the custody of the Gestapo together. Herr Goerner did me yet another kindness. He asked his friend Herr Lucht to prepare a memorandum describing the circumstances of his collaboration with Krafft during the early months of 1940. This turned out to be a vitally important document.

Apart from Herr Goerner I had arranged to see two other gentlemen, namely Professor H. H. Kritzinger at Karlsruhe and Professor Hans Bender at Freiburg im Breisgau. I had not previously connected either of them with Krafft and had another reason for wanting to meet them. I had learned that both of them were interested in astrology. Were they 'true believers' or was there some other reason for their preoccupation with a subject that is by no means fashionable in academic circles? In England, at all events, the chance of encountering a real live Professor who knew anything at all about astrology would have been very remote.

One of my German contacts—by this time I was in touch with a surprising number of local astrological pundits—had told me that in his early days Professor Kritzinger had been an astronomer and had later turned to meteorology. It was also said that he had worked on ballistic problems connected with the German V-weapons during the Second World War. I knew, too, that he had achieved a certain measure of fame as the author of popular books on the borderland of science and occultism, a no-man's-land which a man in his position might discuss in public without causing too many raised eyebrows. However, I had not yet read any of them and was unaware of his long-standing interest in Nostradamus and the whole field of ancient prophecy. In a letter he wrote to me in December 1962 he mentioned that he was the anonymous author of a leaflet containing an interpretation of a Nostradamus prophetic quatrain (x, 51) which circulated among German soldiers in France in 1914.

The Professor, who was then in his seventy-fourth year but looked amazingly youthful, received me in his study, a small book-lined room with a widely-spaced network of wires suspended just below the ceiling. These wires were connected to an electrical control panel. He pressed a switch and explained that we were now sitting beneath a 2,000 volt electrical field and with undoubted benefit to our respective healths. I cannot say that it had any particular effect on me.

I had supposed that my conversation with Professor Kritzinger would be confined to polite generalities, but this was not the case. The local bush telegraph had already been at work and he knew about my interest in Krafft. Furthermore, he had been acquainted with him and had been largely responsible for his arrival in Berlin and his subsequent employment there. The substance of Professor Kritzinger's story will be found in chapter 11. Before I left he generously gave me some unique documents relating to Krafft's Berlin period.

According to the information then available to me, Professor Bender was the incumbent of one of Freiburg's two chairs for psychology and, in his capacity as director of the *Institut für Grenzgebiete der Psychologie* (Institute for the Border Areas of Psychology), a parapsychologist with an international reputation. I knew, too, that he had staged a series of 'blind diagnosis' tests with a number of German astrologers. When we met he told me that the first of these tests had been conducted with Krafft as long ago as 1937, when Dr Bender was on the staff of the Psychological Institute at the University of Bonn. I also learned from Professor Bender that it was he who had suggested a stay at Urberg to Krafft in 1937 when the latter was proposing to leave Zürich and settle for a while in southern Germany. Even the correspondence relating to this proposal had survived. My friendship with Hans Bender grew very quickly and led to regular visits to his Institute at Freiburg and occasional meetings in London.

In retrospect it was surprising how much information I managed to collect during that long week-end in Germany. There were immediate developments when I returned to London. The diplomat who showed de Wohl the letters he had received from Krafft was M. Virgil Tilea, at that time the Rumanian minister plenipotentiary in London. Only now did I discover that he had never returned to Rumania and was still in London. I telephoned him and said that I had just come from Germany with an interesting document (Herr Lucht's memorandum) written by the man who had actually typed the very last letter that he had received from Krafft. M. Tilea invited me to call upon him and produced the letter in question, which he allowed me to borrow and photostat. It now became possible to position a number of pieces in a complicated jigsaw puzzle.

A few weeks later I learned of another collection of papers relating to Krafft. A certain Dr Adolphe Ferrière had contributed a short chapter on 'Cosmobiology and Education' to Krafft's *Traité*. A search for other publications by Dr Ferrière disclosed that he was the author of *Typocosmie* (4 vols, Nice and Turin, 1946–55). When I read this work I realised that part of its contents must have been largely based upon lectures given by Krafft at Lausanne during the years 1934–8. Hence, since this was a post-war publication, some papers must have survived.

Dr Ferrière had recently died and an *Association des Amis de Dr Adolphe Ferrière* had been formed as a pious memorial. A leaflet inside one of the volumes of *Typocosmie* disclosed the address of the Association's honorary secretary in Paris. I wrote to ask if any correspondence between Krafft and Dr Ferrière was available and received a reply from M. Roger Munsch, the Association's president, who informed me that a lot of documents were at Geneva, that he was Dr Ferrière's literary executor, and that I would be able to inspect the material in Paris in September. I eventually met M. Munsch at his home near Pommeuse, Seine et Marne, where I was shown half a dozen bulky files covering the period 1924–41. A glance at these papers told me that here was the material that would effectivelly document the earlier part of Krafft's career. Some weeks later a complete microfilm record of the correspondence arrived in London.

Herr Goerner had already told me that during the early 1930s Krafft had been employed as an adviser on personnel selection—on the basis of graphology and, less publicly, astrology—by the important 'Globus' department store at Zürich. My wife and I now made our way there and lunched with the late Herr E. Hans Mahler, the managing director of the 'Globus' group, and the late Pastor Paul Walser. The latter had received his initial graphological training from Krafft and had succeeded him as the firm's graphological consultant when his association with 'Globus' ended in 1932. Herr Mahler was able to fill in a number of gaps in the Krafft story and explained how Krafft had been sent to him by Oscar Guhl, his father-in-law, a Zürich tycoon who had previously employed Krafft at the Orell Füssli publishing business, which he controlled, and the Guhl private banking establishment. Both Herr Mahler and Pastor Walser provided new documents.

The mass of material which I had now assembled, and the Ferrière microfilm in particular, kept me busy for the next year. In the meantime I gradually traced other people who had known Krafft and corresponded with them. I made another 'research journey' in September 1962 and obtained useful results at Munich, Lausanne and Geneva although I visited half a dozen other places. At Munich Dr Hans Buchheim, a distinguished historian and a member of the staff of the *Institut für Zeitgeschichte* (Institute for Contemporary History) kindly lent me his file on the 'Aktion Hess'. It was in the course of this Gestapo *razzia*, which was mounted a month after Rudolf Hess flew to Scotland in May 1941, that hundreds of astrologers, including Krafft and Herr Goerner, were arrested and the German astrological movement destroyed. Among Dr Buchheim's papers I found a couple of useful documents relating to Krafft's Berlin period which supplemented the information that I had already received from Herr Goerner and Herr Lucht. At Lausanne and Geneva I was able to meet half a dozen people who had known Krafft well, including Mlle Panchaud, whom I have already mentioned.

My journeys in quest of Krafft were almost at an end. The first of two meetings with Professor Rolph Danneel, director of the Zoological Institute, University of Bonn, took place in the autumn of 1963. He had been at school with Krafft at Basle and had subsequently remained in touch with him. Like Professors Kritzinger and Bender he was interested in astrology. Finally, as late as January 1965 a meeting at Brussels with M. Theodore Chapellier, who had been involved in an unsuccessful attempt to publish an early version of Krafft's *Traité*, led to further information and more documents.

The reader is entitled to ask whether my almost irrational expenditure of time and effort on Krafft was justified. I must admit that I enjoyed the detective work, the thrill of the chase, and the many unexpected encounters. What I learned from the Krafft story was how astrological beliefs, preoccupations and ambitions can dominate a human life and, in Krafft's case, ultimately destroy it. The pagan gods (or planetary daemons) still require an occasional sacrifice.

9
The Origins of an Obsession

Karl Ernst Krafft was of German rather than Swiss descent. His paternal grandfather, who built and owned the present Hotel Krafft in the Obere Rheingasse at Basle, was from the Wiesenthal district just across the frontier in the German province of Baden. Here the broad valley of the River Wiese runs north-east towards the Black Forest.[1] Grandfather Krafft married a Basle girl, a Fräulein Meier, who bore him two sons. Carl, the eldest (*b.* 24 November 1864) entered commerce and in due course became a director of the 'Cardinal' brewery at Basle. The second son, Dr Albert Krafft, was a chemist. The future brewery director married Anna Gebhard (*b.* 11 March 1867) who, like her father-in-law, was a German from the Wiesenthal region. Carl and Anna Krafft had two children, who were both born at Basle: Karl Ernst (10 May 1900) and Anneliese (18 September 1901).

Herr Felix Tappolet, of Zürich, who was at school with Krafft and a frequent visitor to his home, sent me his impressions of Krafft's boyhood days. He recalled, in particular, what he described as the 'oppressively bourgeois and stuffy atmosphere' that prevailed in the Krafft household. It is evident that he disliked the elder Kraffts, but his feelings were possibly coloured by Krafft's own ambivalent feelings towards them. He described the parents in the first of a long series of letters which he wrote to me in 1962: 'A pathologically despotic mother (but not ungifted) and a solid, thick-set father ("I hate Art!"), whose toothy physiognomy would have persuaded the Muses to take sudden flight, were responsible for the existence of two children.'

Professor Rolf Danneel, whose name is mentioned in the previous chapter, did not agree with Herr Tappolet's assessment of the father and said that Krafft senior was 'a very decent type of businessman', whom he had always respected. Of the mother, Herr Tappolet observed: 'She was always far too ready to malign any generally respected person, and heaven help anyone who dared to contradict her!' Professor Danneel also recalled her sharp tongue. Herr Tappolet: 'The parents were disagreeable bourgeois and bourgeois qualities are infectious. Krafft was not exactly a philistine, but almost as unbearable as one.'

In a letter to Mrs Harold Butler (1 May 1938), Krafft compared his mother with an irresponsible volcano or a burning oil well, which must either be left well alone or extinguished by throwing a bomb at it. Krafft's

---

[1] Members of the Krafft family are still to be found in the Wiesenthal, e.g. at Schopfheim.

early life appears to have represented a protest against his father's conservatism and his mother's tyranny. He never had much of a relationship with his father, but a 'love-hate' bound him willy-nilly to his mother. It was clearly from her that he inherited his own 'volcanic' qualities.

He entered the Humanistic Gymnasium at Basle shortly before his eleventh birthday in 1911 and remained there until he matriculated early in 1919. Herr Tappolet told me that he always managed to remain somewhere near the top of the class without too much effort. His school reports were satisfactory although on one occasion he was rebuked for being 'impertinent and above himself'.[1] Herr Tappolet remarked that he often did his homework during the short recreation break and was impressed, too, by his ability to write extremely fast and yet with admirable legibility. In later years Krafft developed a distinguished, almost calligraphic hand which has fascinated every graphologist to whom I have shown it. I have noticed, too, that Krafft's handwriting, which is illustrated opposite p. 180, appears to have influenced those of both Herr Goerner and Professor Danneel.

At school Krafft showed unusual promise as a mathematician. When his schooldays were nearing their end he hoped to go to a university and take a science degree. His father was against this on the grounds that scientists were two a penny and argued that a career in banking or insurance offered better long-term prospects. Krafft dug his heels in and after some acrimonious arguments was allowed to enrol as a science student at the university of Basle on 23 April 1919. His sister Anneliese died a week later.

Herr Tappolet liked her: 'Anneliese, a seraphic being, made her escape from that soul-destroying, oppressive atmosphere by her death (tuberculosis). It was intended that she should study the piano. Her brother managed to survive that murderous *milieu* because, apart from his sensitivity, he was endowed with a sufficient dose of ruthless defensive energy.'

Krafft claimed to have had a warning of his sister's death in a prophetic dream that he experienced in the autumn of 1917. 'It made a great impression upon me,' he wrote in English in 1935, 'so that I wrote it down at once in my diary, although I could only partially grasp its symbolism. Yet it proved to have foretold, with many details hidden in those symbols, events that took place about a year afterwards and which were of rather a tragic nature, concerning my own life and that of the people around me.'[2]

He was soon to be confronted with the spiritualist hypothesis of survival after death. Herr Tappolet wrote: 'The loss of their daughter, at least in the parents' opinion, was utterly undeserved. God had revealed himself

[1] The Gymnasium records of this period are in the cantonal and municipal archives at Basle. Dr Andreas Staehlin, a member of the archive staff, kindly inspected them for me.

[2] K. E. Krafft, 'My Approach to and my Wanderings through the Fields of Astrology' in W. J. Tucker's periodical *Science and Astrology*, London, 1937, p. 248.

as a robber! Seances were now held to make the Beyond return its prey.
But in vain.'

Krafft began to read the literature of spiritualism and this led him to
occultism. He 'devoured more than actually digested all the books on
occultism and similar subjects at the university library . . . my mind was
then turned rather towards experimental science and mathematics, yet I
felt urged to read one book of this type after another.'[1]

His preoccupation with spiritualism and occultism was temporarily
interrupted when he became liable for military service at the age of twenty.
He spent a brief period with a medical unit but was soon discharged on
health grounds. This experience coincided with an interest in telepathy,
and he experimented with some of his comrades. He was surprised and
even a little scared when he discovered that he could apparently convey
suggestions to them from a distance.

In the meantime during the summer of 1919 he had had a preliminary
look at astrology but soon abandoned it because it seemed to lack any
scientific basis. In his own words (in English): 'I gave up this study,
paying again more attention to chemistry, at the same time practising some
Yoga exercises.'[2]

Krafft senior was still trying to persuade him to abandon science for
something more 'useful', such as law or economics. Herr Tappolet recalled
his friend's accounts of heated arguments in the family circle. The father
threatened to show his recalcitrant son the door and make him fend for
himself. Karl Ernst was greatly relieved when he was eventually allowed
to leave the parental home and continue his studies at the university of
Geneva.

Herr Tappolet described Krafft at this time: 'One cannot imagine
anything more "Teuton" than the twenty-year old Krafft. But the
"Teuton" was neither tall, fair-haired, blue-eyed, nor endowed with an
impressive physique. On the contrary, he was short, dark-haired, dark-
eyed and with sharp, peering, pale features. For a long time he looked
more like a gnome than a human being. The way he dressed completely
reflected his highly personal mixture of defiant apartness and helpless
dowdiness. . . . You can assess the dowdiness and lack of social polish in
the Krafft *milieu* when I tell you that both father and son wore paper
collars!'

Others who met Krafft much later also recalled his gnomelike appearance. Countess Keyserling wrote in English: 'He was a queer little fellow,
looked like a gnome; very pale and with burning black eyes; rather deca-
dent like many Swiss people whose ancestors lived in a valley and inbred a
lot . . . There was some flame burning in him, but a cold fire, like one of
those dancing lights one reads about in books, which lead people astray in
a swamp.'

[1] Ibid.   [2] Ibid.

Dr C. J. Burckhardt, the distinguished Swiss diplomat and historian who was briefly acquainted with him in 1936—Count Keyserling had sent Krafft to see him—also remembered his 'brilliant, deep-set eyes and very pale complexion'.

As I was to discover, nobody who ever met Krafft remained unimpressed by those searching eyes. Nevertheless, according to Herr Tappolet, he had practically no sight in one of them.

A condensed version of Herr Tappolet's impressions follows. It must be emphasised that he did not see much of Krafft after the spring of 1925, although they spent six disastrous months together as graphological consultants in 1930. Krafft was clearly a major experience in Herr Tappolet's life, although a negative one.

'Krafft was a difficult, complicated man,' he wrote. 'He took pleasure in regarding himself as a [scientific] pioneer, and it flattered him down to his finger-tips that he enjoyed a certain measure of fame at one time or another. There were two Krafft "polarities"; his problem was the road between them. He began as a convinced materialist and ended as an ecstatic student of the Cosmos. His great questions were: "To be or not to be?" and "Will *I* win through?" He was an aggressive, dynamic person. His "Eros" represented the reverse of love's gentle course. Because of his inordinate ambition and desire for power he fulfilled himself despotically rather than erotically. Only gradually did it dawn upon him that there are "powers" and "spheres" with a deeper content, because they operate more tenderly. It was second nature with him to confuse his *vis-à-vis* and to drive him or her into a corner. He could be immensely tactless, and it was difficult to persuade him that someone's silence expressed repulsion rather than defeat.

'He shunned alcoholic drinks like the plague because he would have felt defenceless under the influence of strong liquor. For him defencelessness would have been the equivalent of suicide. I can hardly describe his hostility to the world at large. Hence his preoccupation with the Cosmos. He had no sense of humour at all; for him humour meant irony.' Herr Goerner, however, told me that Krafft, when he first met him in 1931, was a 'lively, light-hearted man'.

Mlle Germaine Charton, who was a member of his Lausanne lecture circle in the 1930s, wrote in a letter she sent me in 1962: 'Someone once described him as a man who would unfailingly act in an unpredictable manner. He had glimpses of genius, but sometimes behaved like a charlatan, and was misjudged by people who did not understand his complicated character. His own assessments of people could be vindictive to the point of being one-sided.' Dr J. B., also of Lausanne, wrote to me: '. . . I consider that my encounter with this man was the most ill-omened and regrettable of my life. . . .'

Most of the people whom I met, or with whom I corresponded, who had known Krafft, could only recall his negative qualities. It was as if, with the passage of time, they could only see the dark side of the mirror. Nevertheless, judging by many of his early letters to Dr Ferrière and, in particular, those to Mrs Butler, there was an attractive side to his character. To be just, one must remember his undoubted idealism, his enormous although largely fruitless (perhaps even futile) industry, and his undeniable sense of purpose. Karl Ernst Krafft was no ordinary mortal.

Krafft arrived at Geneva in November 1920. He lodged for a while with a widow at Grand Lancy, an unattractive suburb on the road to Annecy, but soon moved to the house of a Monsieur Bévand, a market-gardener, in the same district. Felix Tappolet visited him there and found him garbed in a loin cloth practising his yoga exercises. His suggestion that Krafft should abandon this solitary occupation and join a student's club was treated with contempt.

In the meantime he led a lonely existence and in the evenings began to study astrology again. I suspect that he wanted to learn, if possible, about his own future and, equally important, discover what his parents' horoscopes might reveal. In 1935 he told his Lausanne pupils how closely he studied their charts. 'The more they persecuted me, the better I understood the part they were destined to play in my life!'

He now experienced his first important human relationship. In 1921 he met a certain Madame R. at a lecture given by Inayat Kahn on his own particular brand of Sufi mysticism. There is a veiled allusion to Madame R. in Krafft's *Traité*: 'In 1921 there was an encounter of major importance with a woman. This relationship dominated my life for many years, involuntarily supplanting any "competition".' She is also mentioned in the transcript of one of his Lausanne lectures in 1935: 'In 1921 my progressed Venus was sextile to my radical Sun. During the winter of 1920–1 I noted this aspect. How would it turn out? According to the astrological manuals it was quite a favourable one. . . . I met someone who played a decisive part in my life for years on end. From a rational point of view this was love without hope, but nevertheless one of the most important meetings in my life in relation to my personal development and work.'

Herr Tappolet, who met Madame R., wrote: 'She rubbed a few of the rough corners off him. He now became a little less *gauche*, not so much the provincial Teuton from Basle. Of course he asked her to marry him, but she already had a husband who could keep her in fair luxury, which was more than Krafft could do. She was about five years older than Krafft; intelligent, good-looking and elegant, and with a penchant for esotericism.'

Krafft continued to follow a haphazard academic curriculum, but with no fixed purpose in mind. Many years later he told a correspondent that at Basle and Geneva he had studied physics, chemistry, mineralogy, mathematics, astronomy, botany, zoology and statistics. With the exception of mathematical probabilities and their application to statistical techniques his knowledge of all these subjects can only have been peripheral.

Krafft's current preoccupation with astrology produced a conflict between faith and reason. It appeared to 'work', but what the astrologers persisted in calling a science was clearly unscientific. In any case, the kind of evidence that would satisfy conventional scientists was conspicuously absent. With the exception of Paul Choisnard, twenty years earlier, the astrologers had never attempted to investigate the problem on a scientific basis. Krafft decided, therefore, to repeat Choisnard's statistical experiment, but on a far more ambitious scale. He clearly hoped to discover positive evidence of stellar 'influences', but this wish was discreetly rationalised. Indeed, it is most unlikely that he revealed his personal identification with astrology to Professor Liebmann Hersch, who taught statistical mathematics at the University of Geneva. The overall concept of his astro-statistical project was certainly discussed with Hersch.

Very little is known about the early stages of Krafft's ambitious plan, but its broad outlines can be deduced from his correspondence and publications. He sensibly decided to ignore the old astrological Tradition, with its mass of vague and often conflicting statements, and hoped to discover whether the objective statistical analysis of the factors in a large number of horoscopes would produce any data that was outside the law of mathematical probability. The presence of such data would not necessarily prove the validity of the Tradition but, he supposed, would at least indicate the existence of astral 'phenomena' as yet unknown to orthodox scientists. Hence it was not his purpose to establish, for example, that 'Moon in Libra in the sixth House' means this or that but, rather, to identify unexpected angular frequencies or equally unexpected groupings of planets in any small sector of the 360° of the ecliptic between 0° Aries and 29° Pisces. Finally, he hoped to discover whether there was any connection between what he called the 'mobile factors', meaning actual planetary positions on a given day, and the planetary positions in a natal horoscope.

The statistical approach indicated the necessity for a very large number of horoscopes. Again, while it was uncertain whether positive conclusions, if they could be established, would substantiate any part of the Tradition, prospectively the new science of Cosmobiology, to be pioneered by Krafft, who already saw himself as a second Newton, would presumably have far-reaching practical applications. The first stage of the investigation began in 1921 and continued until the spring of 1923. Much of the research material was laboriously assembled at the Geneva registry of births and deaths where Krafft spent countless hours copying data from the old registers from 1820 onwards. Then there was the wearisome and almost mechanical task of casting thousands of horoscopes and, far more exacting, the statistical analysis of tens of thousands of individually numbered 'observations'. Louis Bévand, his landlord's young son, who was still a student at a local commercial college, learned how to cast horoscopes and in his spare time was able to relieve Krafft of some of the drudgery.

Krafft began by repeating Choisnard's 'astral heredity' experiment, but in this case did not have a large collection of horoscopes. The hypothesis was that certain factors would repeat themselves in the charts of the members of several generations of the same family. The available material led Krafft to the confident conclusion that 'Man is not born into this world under a random planetary constellation, but under one that will bear a marked resemblance to those of other members of the same family.' He next turned to what he called 'cosmic influences on human temperament and psychology'. In order to limit the field of enquiry and, if possible, find a common pattern, he decided to study a large number of horoscopes relating to individuals with a common interest or profession, in this case musicians. The birth data of 2,800 musicians born since 1820 was extracted from biographical dictionaries and the subsequent analysis of *c.* 60,000 numbered observations led to his belief that there was an identifiable relationship between a birth constellation and musical ability and, in turn, to the statement that 'the birth constellation has a marked influence on the temperament and psychic constitution of a human individual'. Finally, he studied the possibility of 'cosmic influences on human physiology' and for this purpose selected the phenomenon of death. His hypothesis was that 'death does not occur in relation to any chance constellation, but is connected with current planetary transits over specific points in the natal horoscope'. A general conclusion was that 'the birth constellation determines, once and for all, an individual's physical constitution, also his predispositions and immunities . . . during the course of his life successive planetary transits influence his physical development, either stimulating it, or diminishing it (by illness) or ending it (by death)'.

These and other far-reaching deductions were published in 1923 in his pamphlet *Influences cosmiques sur l'individu humain*, and were repeated, but with the addition of the mathematical arguments in 1939 in his *Traité d'Astro-Biologie*. Professor Hersch had checked his statistical procedures and documentation and had declared himself satisfied. It was Hersch's insufficiently critical approval that led to the self-deception that was to influence the whole course of Krafft's later life. There is now little doubt that the whole of his so-called statistical evidence was completely worthless. In fact, the new science of Cosmobiology was a chimera from start to finish.[1]

On 31 May 1923, shortly before the end of his last term at Geneva,

---

[1] After Krafft's death M. Michel Gauquelin, a French scientist with no astrological affiliations, attempted to repeat Krafft's work on the basis of indications and material published in the *Traité*. Apart from the fact that M. Gauquelin's findings were gener-

Professor Hersch allowed Krafft to read a paper on 'Cosmic Influences on the Human Individual' at a statistical seminar held at the university. This was attended by a number of Hersch's colleagues, also by a few local medical men, who heard the Professor's surprisingly encouraging verdict: 'If there is a rational explanation of the relationship between cosmic and biological phenomena, the proof offered by Monsieur Krafft's statistics should be considered as conclusive.'

Others were not so forthcoming. The professor of botany said to Krafft: 'You can prove as much as you like, but your theory is complete nonsense', while the professor of astronomy advised him not to waste his time on such absurdities. Finally, a Basle mathematician, who at least took the trouble to examine his vast documentation, observed: 'The material and the method appear to be unassailable, but what I cannot fathom is how a Gauss or a Helmholtz could have overlooked such important facts. Hence my inference that your results are based upon some kind of self-deception that is difficult to pin down.'

Since neither Professor Hersch nor the Basle mathematician had faulted his statistical techniques, Krafft was sure that these adverse criticisms could only be ascribed to academic conservatism and was convinced that fame, and even fortune, were in the grasp of the founder of the new and epoch-making science of Cosmobiology. Even his sceptical father was temporarily persuaded that Karl Ernst had discovered something important and agreed to provide a small salary for Louis Bévand so that he could assist Krafft on a full-time basis.

A fortnight after his performance at the university Krafft delivered an expanded version of his original paper, this time illustrated by lantern slides, in two instalments at a lecture hall in the rue d'Athenée. There was no charge for admission but a collection was made to help cover the expenses. A summary of his conclusions was published as 'Influences cosmiques sur l'individu humain' in *Vers l'Unité*, a local periodical largely devoted to psychism. Krafft senior paid for some offprints, including fifteen printed on a superior *papier de Hollande*. It was one of the latter that unexpectedly came into my possession in 1961.

Krafft senior soon received an unpleasant surprise. Only now did he learn that his wayward son had nothing to show for four years at two universities except an enormous collection of horoscopes, a large statistical card index and a pamphlet. Krafft had returned to Basle with neither degree nor diploma. Furthermore, the academic authorities at Geneva had made it plain that they would not allow Krafft to submit a Ph.D. thesis based upon his astro-statistical investigations.

---

ally negative, he established that Krafft's statistical methods were at once primitive and misleading. Then, having 'demolished' Krafft, he decided to repeat the experiment on more scientific lines. The results, which were surprising, are briefly discussed in chapter 19.

It is not difficult to imagine the subsequent uproar at Basle. Krafft senior declared that his offpsring must forthwith abandon his astrological chimera and either find himself a job, preferably in banking or insurance, or resume his studies elsewhere and seriously read for a degree in law or economics. Krafft fought a successful delaying action and managed to convince his father that a 'Ph.D. (Cosmobiology)' might still be possible, and in London of all places. He had learned, probably from Dr Hersch, of Professor Karl Pearson's department at University College, and persuaded his nonplussed parent to allow him to go to England. Assuming that Cosmobiology would never be taken seriously unless presented to an amazed world by Herr Doktor Krafft, it was agreed that Karl Ernst should try his luck with Pearson.[1]

Krafft arrived in London early in January 1924 and found lodgings in West Hampstead. A week or two later he received a letter from a certain Dr Adolphe Ferrière, of Geneva, with whom he had not been previously acquainted. Dr Ferrière had just read his essay in *Vers l'Unité* and had felt compelled to write to him. Krafft was unaware at this time that his correspondent was a distinguished Swiss educationalist.[2]

Dr Ferrière had first become interested in astrology during the 1914–18 war and discovered that it appeared to 'work', although not in a completely satisfactory manner. He supposed, however, that it might be possible to use it for investigating the temperaments of difficult or backward children but became discouraged because he, like so many others who have tried it, experienced great difficulty in interpreting a horoscope. There were the symbols, but what did they really mean? There was no information on this point in Krafft's pamphlet because there was no bridge between traditional astrology and Krafft's supposed identification of planetary influences. Ferrière hoped, however, that Krafft's work might eventually lead to an elucidation of the age-old astrological puzzle.

[1] Karl Pearson (1857–1936), Galton Professor of Eugenics in the University of London, had an international reputation and the statistical methods which he improved or invented were applicable in so many different fields of scientific research that he attracted students from all parts of the world and his department was for many years the mecca of biostatisticians and geneticists. Theoretically this was the right place for Krafft, even if Pearson was initially unaware of the strange fish that he had landed in his biometric net.

[2] Adolphe Ferrière (1879–1960) was a member of a Protestant family long established at Geneva. He studied zoology at Geneva but turned to pedagogy when he met Hermann Lietz (1868–1919), the German educational theorist and founder of the 'New School' movement (country boarding schools on British lines). Ferrière founded the Bureau Internationale des Écoles Nouvelles in 1899, was awarded a doctorate of sociology at Geneva in 1902, and in 1912 joined the staff of the recently established Institut Jean-Jacques Rousseau at Geneva, which specialised in experimental research in education. He wrote many books on the theory of education and his work was extensively translated. His *Psychological Types and the Stages of Man's Development*, published in an English translation in Heinemann's 'Education Series' in 1958, owes more to his astrological interests, and even to Krafft, than the uninitiated reader might expect.

Krafft and Ferrière corresponded throughout the spring and summer of 1924. In a series of very lengthy letters Krafft told Ferrière that he was planning a gigantic research project, but inferred that Pearson, whom he described as a 'convinced Darwinite', was obviously sceptical about the validity of his cosmobiological theories. Krafft airily suggested that this was because Pearson could not understand his documentation, although the probable truth is that Pearson was too busy to spend much time listening to Krafft's speculations. However, Krafft did admit that he had learned more about statistical techniques during a month with Pearson than from Professor Hersch during a whole year at Geneva. Krafft's sojourn in London was not exclusively devoted to furthering the cause of Cosmobiology for, according to Herr Tappolet, he now had his first sexual experience. Herr Tappolet remarked that the young lady soon transferred her affections to someone less complicated.

Krafft was back at Basle in July 1924. The British climate had not agreed with him and his parents had suggested that he should return to Switzerland. The situation was further complicated by the fact that the authorities at the University of London were not prepared to take into account the terms he had already spent at Basle and Geneva and insisted that he would have to work for a further three years for a London degree. Krafft senior was still prepared to subsidise yet another period of academic endeavour but Karl Ernst rejected his offer on the grounds that it would be a waste of time. Still completely confident of the importance of his discoveries, all he wanted was to complete the research and present the results to an astonished world with as little delay as possible. His father's reaction was to say that the sooner he found himself a job the better. Karl Ernst had no desire to be shut up in an office and wrote to Dr Ferrière to ask if a niche could be found for him at the Institut Jean-Jacques Rousseau. He suggested that he could teach statistics and languages and, an additional attraction, organise a course on Cosmobiology. He was prepared to be patient, he added, because he knew from his horoscope that he would have to face many difficulties until c. 1928. Dr Ferrière scribbled in the margin: 'No money for this. What about the doctorate?'

Krafft senior retired from business during the summer of 1924 and when Karl Ernst returned to Basle early in July had just completed the negotiations for the purchase of a modest property, the Villa Rose at Commugny, a village behind Coppet, between Geneva and Nyon on the Lake of Geneva. Fortunately for Krafft preparations for the move temporarily delayed any detailed consideration of his own future. He spent his time copying thousands of dates of births and deaths at the Basle registry and early in August escaped to Geneva where the registry officials infuriated him by charging Fr.2 per hour for the privilege of using their dusty volumes. He met Dr Ferrière for the first time during this visit. He may have already known that the Doctor was completely deaf. The files contain many scraps of paper upon which Krafft scribbled replies to his questions about astrology and Cosmobiology.

The family was installed at the Villa Rose by 8 September 1924 and then Krafft's purgatory began. A few weeks earlier he was still under the impression that he might, after all, return to London, but Krafft senior had blocked this escape route. The arguments about his future continued. Herr Tappolet is the source of the following anecdote:

'What you want is a *Lebensstellung* (lifetime job),' Krafft senior said.

'What is a *Lebensstellung*?' Karl Ernst asked.

'A *Lebensstellung*', said his father portentously, 'is one you can die in!'

Winter followed autumn and Krafft was still at the Villa Rose. Indeed, he remained there, plodding away at his horoscopes and statistics throughout the remainder of 1924. Louis Bévand was still on the payroll and was working more or less full time at the house, returning to Geneva only at week-ends. Bévand took his meals with the family and recalled that Krafft, absorbed in his own thoughts, hardly spoke. Afterwards they retired to his room and the horoscopes. The academic calm was only disturbed by the sound of Frau Krafft shouting furiously at the cows who regularly found their way into the garden. At Basle Krafft had been able to escape after supper and visit his friends, but he knew no one at Commugny and to make matters worse his father expected him to join him in an evening game of cards or chess. This was the last straw.

I assume that he made sporadic and half-hearted attempts to find a job but nothing happened until December 1924 when he obtained part-time employment at the recently-established International Students Union at Geneva. Krafft regarded this as a set-back but could not propose any better solution. His modest administrative duties interrupted his private work, but he could at least see less of his parents.

Felix Tappolet was invited to spend the 1925 Easter holiday at the Villa Rose and found the atmosphere 'murderous'. One afternoon he amused himself with a little weeding in the garden. Frau Krafft soon arrived on the scene and angrily asked him what he thought he was doing.

'What's all this in aid of?' she screamed. 'So that you can tell them all at Basle that we have been making you work?'

Krafft, who was present, quickly made himself scarce. Later he remarked: 'The great thing about the Villa Rose is that it has five exits, not counting the chimneys!'

Letters written to Dr Ferrière at this time indicate that Krafft was having psycho-analysis, but details are lacking. He left the International Students Union during the summer of 1925 and became an assistant at Miss Storey's 'Quo Vadis?' bookshop at Geneva. She was a well-to-do English spinster, a Theosophist and a devoted disciple of Krishnamurti, Annie Besant's 'World Teacher'. Krafft appears to have been reasonably happy at 'Quo Vadis?' where he sold the works of Madame Blavatsky,

Annie Besant, the Reverend C. W. Leadbeater and other esoteric out-pourings. Herr Tappolet told me that Miss Storey sometimes found her helper a trifle overwhelming.

Krafft continued to work on his astro-statistics in his spare time and Louis Bévand laboured away at the Villa Rose or the Geneva registries. An immense amount of material had been collected but Krafft was obviously incapable of making a synthesis. Copies of letters written at this period to Dr Mrsic and Dr Kritzinger indicate that there were still ambitious plans for a *magnum opus*, but that was all. In the meantime Krafft senior was becoming increasingly impatient. There was a more than usually stormy scene on Christmas Eve (1925) when Krafft was told that he would have to leave the Villa Rose and fend for himself. There was an uneasy truce during the next couple of weeks and then Krafft senior acted. He saw his friend Oscar Guhl, a Zürich magnate who had a controlling interest in the Guhl Bank, the important 'Globus' department store and, possibly a recent acquisition, the Orell Füssli publishing firm. It was settled that Krafft should join Orell Füssli as a management trainee at a very modest salary. These parental dispositions were announced to a shocked and angry Karl Ernst during the third week of January 1926, together with the news that he would be expected to keep himself on what Guhl paid him.

For Krafft this ignominious exile to Zürich was the last straw. He described his outraged feelings in a hysterical letter—his handwriting betrayed his nervous tension—written to Dr Ferrière on 22 January 1926. In this pathetic document he complained of his parents' 'unjustifiable severity', his dismay that Louis Bévand was to be sacked at the very moment when tremendous scientific discoveries were on the horizon and, above all, of what he called his father's 'myopic desire for financial security up to the nth generation'. There were times, he said, when he thought of burning those thousands of horoscopes and beginning a normal life, complete with conventional career, wife and family, but now it was too late. If his parents wanted to 'cut off his hands', he would 'hang on with his teeth'. In the meantime he had made his will and had bequeathed all his papers to Dr Ferrière who, he hoped, would continue his work.

A week or two later Dr Ferrière suggested that he should visit Krafft at the Villa Rose before he left for Zürich. Krafft replied on 5 March 1926 and told his friend that he had received no visitors at his parents' house since 30 September 1925, and had resolved to see no one there during their lifetime unless they specially requested it.

Krafft boarded a train for Zürich on 20 March 1926. If Krafft senior supposed that he had put an end to his son's cosmobiological or astro-logical obsessions, he was mistaken. At this stage, however, the much-tried father makes his exit from this story.

10

An Unconventional Professional Astrologer

When Krafft arrived at Zürich he was a guest for a few days at Oscar Guhl's villa on the Zürichberg before moving to less luxurious lodgings. Almost two months passed before he found time to write to Dr Ferrière at any length and on 13 May 1926 he needed eight closely-typed pages to convey all his exciting news. He reported that Guhl had already increased his monthly salary by Fr.100 to Fr.500 (£20) and had promised him another rise in the autumn. Surely this refuted his father's conviction that he was 'not even capable of earning the money to pay for the water in his soup', he proclaimed. Now Guhl's good opinion of him proved otherwise. He said that during those two brief months at Orell Füssli he had learned more of value to his work—he meant Cosmobiology—than in all the years devoted to statistics and meditation. With a publishing organisation and printing facilities at his disposal, he now hoped speedily to complete his *magnum opus* and supervise its production himself.

Orell Füssli was then rather a pedestrian school-book and directory publishing firm with a subsidiary printing business. Krafft arrived when Guhl's policy of reorganisation and expansion was being implemented. At first he helped the head of the publishing department, but was soon given more responsible duties. In the autumn of 1926 he proudly informed Dr Ferrière that he would soon be promoted to deputy manager, 'not just for the publishing department but for the whole firm'. That October he was confidently writing to Dr Ferrière about Orell Füssli's projected German edition of the latter's *L'éducation dans la famille* and sent him a copy of a memorandum he had written for Herr Zutt, the firm's publishing director. It was composed in brisk, businesslike German. The adaptable Herr Krafft had quickly learned the language of commerce. As Herr Tappolet observed in 1962: 'Imaginative technical and commercial abilities lay fallow in Krafft.'

Soon, however, he was in hot water, although apparently not with Guhl, when his over-zealous interference led to the sacking of a fellow subordinate who also had a 'protector'. Indeed, at one moment it looked as if Krafft himself might have to go. In January 1927, less than a year after his arrival at Zürich, he was able to tell Dr Ferrière that he now 'occupied the old director's room and have definitely replaced him'. A fortnight later he wrote: 'Things are going better at business. My progressed Moon sextile Jupiter makes itself felt, although that's only what the Tradition says. . . . It's not my Cosmobiological work that has helped me in business, but rather my wide culture and mercurial adaptability.'

6. Karl Ernst Krafft—from a studio portrait made *c.* 1916.

7. *Above:* Karl Ernst Krafft—from a snapshot taken in a Zürich street *c.* 1932.

8. *Above right:* Karl Ernst Krafft—from a studio portrait made in London in 1924.

9. *Opposite:* Krafft and his wife in the cabin he built at Urberg in 1938. Local peasants gleefully informed the police that it was used for military espionage purposes. No trace of it remains today.

Die Weissagungen
des Nostradamus

Von
C. Loog

Johannes Baum Verlag, Pfullingen i. Württ.

37

10. C. Loog's Nostradamus commentary, published in 1921, containing a 'prediction' of the German invasion of Poland in 1939. It was Loog who indirectly gave Dr Goebbels the idea of using the prophecies of Nostradamus for psychological warfare purposes.

His Orell Füssli period ended as suddenly as it had begun, in the autumn of 1928. Speedy promotion and, no doubt, his own lack of tact, had stirred up the jealousy of 'some colleagues whom circumstances did not permit me to "behead"'. The use of that last word is symptomatic. There had been 'conspiracies, intrigues and abuse of confidence; the refined exploitation of some mistakes—inevitable for an active man'. Guhl did not return his protégé in disgrace to the Villa Rose but transferred him to his banking establishment and paid him well for part-time work. I have not been able to discover why Guhl took this unusual step. A little later he was also employed on a part-time basis by Hans Mahler, Guhl's son-in-law, at the 'Globus' department store.

This sudden transformation of Krafft's position was probably due to a combination of factors. He had recently begun to publish some of the results of his previous astro-statistical investigations and Mahler had become aware of his Cosmobiological theories. Furthermore, he was willing to allow Krafft to prove his contention that his knowledge and abilities, however unconventional, could be usefully employed within the framework of a large commercial organisation. It must be explained that Mahler, who was then in his early thirties, was deeply interested in experimental management techniques and in that respect was in advance of many of his contemporaries. In this context Krafft had something interesting to offer, for the statistician had now become a *Charakterologe*.

While Krafft's attitude to traditional astrology was always sceptical, and even condescending, his doubts did not inhibit him from practising it. Indeed, not long after he came to Zürich his knowledge of astrology made it possible for him to earn a little pocket money. There is a hint of prospective payment for a delineation in a letter written to Dr Ferrière in May 1926. In October 1928, soon after he left Orell Füssli, he informed the Doctor that he was 'obtaining very tangible results, and even some additional income, in the field of psycho-diagnosis, mainly based on graphology'. He referred to this activity again in January 1929 when he mentioned that his work as a *Charakterologe* was 'giving great satisfaction to all the interested parties'. He said, too, that he sometimes achieved 'really curious results, for instance the reconstruction of past events'. The latter remark infers the use of astrology rather than graphology. He paid a brief visit to Paris in April 1929 and told Dr Ferrière that 'they were very interested in my work as a *conseiller-psychologue-caractérologue* . . . there is the possibility of an arrangement that will allow me to leave the Bank at Zürich, but *not* "Globus". The latter ought to bring in about ten or twelve thousand francs a year. There may be a couple of trips to Paris every month.' It is possible that Mahler had given him an introduction to the 'Printemps' department store at Paris. He worked for this firm for a short time in 1932.

In August 1929 he informed Dr Ferrière that the 'Globus' direction had appointed him its psychological adviser. 'The work is graphological, i.e. for the engagement of staff and other matters. It requires a third of my time, but the pay is very generous.' He said, too, that there were prospects of a retainer from Orell Füssli, that he was still working for the Guhl Bank, but only for a few hours every week, and was able to use about a third of his time as he pleased. In September 1929 he told Dr Ferrière that his prospective annual income was now in the region of Fr.20,000 (£800). The nature of Krafft's work for 'Globus' is described in a letter written by Herr Mahler soon after we met in September 1962:

'Krafft worked at Orell Füssli within the framework of the technical direction on rationalisation problems, also in connection with an improved management organisation. He was particularly interested in security printing and apart from all this he was already preparing graphological studies. He then transferred to a private bank at Zürich whence he was "attached" to various concerns with which the bank was closely connected. His sphere of activity rapidly developed from work on organisation problems to pyschological counsel for the management. He became increasingly involved in personnel selection on the basis of graphological analysis, combined with astrological predictions based upon natal horoscopes. I gladly acknowledge that almost without exception the character analyses he prepared at that time of people with whom I am still acquainted have proved to be fundamentally correct.'

Krafft was soon to play quite an important role at 'Globus'. According to Herr Mahler: 'He was increasingly drawn into senior management conferences and was a member of an informal committee consisting of a fellow director and myself. The function of this committee was the systematic evaluation of the psychological factors relating to a fairly wide range of staff matters, e.g. selection and promotion and, most important, to establish whether or not two individuals would be able to work harmoniously together or whether there was the likelihood of a clash of personalities. He also did some economic forecasting and in this connection used his knowledge of "planetary cycles", rhythms and the like. Thus from a knowledge of the past he tried to predict the future. In many cases his market forecasts were correct but there were some "misses", which were nevertheless unavoidable. These "misses" used to puzzle him. However, I told him that I sincerely hoped that no one would ever succeed in obtaining an accurate knowledge of either his own destiny or that of the world at large, because if life's course could be accurately predetermined, it simply would not be worth living.'

By the autumn of 1929 Krafft had as much work as he could manage and there was room for an assistant. After an interval of some years he had recently encountered Felix Tappolet again. Herr Tappolet knew nothing about either graphology or astrology but Krafft believed that his intuitive gifts would help him to become an effective graphologist and invited him to spend a week with him at Zürich. When Herr Tappolet was in London in 1962 he told me that he was at that time thinking of emigrating to Canada, but Krafft persuaded him to stay. A partnership agreement was settled in December 1929. They rented an office which, according to Pastor Walser, was luxuriously furnished, and issued a prospectus for 'characterological studies based upon handwriting and other documents affording interpretation'. For personnel selection they offered to sift the most likely candidates for a minimum fee of Fr.20, while the tariff for a detailed individual report (8–10 sheets) was Fr.240–400 (£10–£15). The prospectus stated that an official birth certificate would be useful in all cases, and particularly when full-scale studies were required. They had carefully avoided any allusion to astrology, but Krafft could not cast a horoscope without the birth data.

Herr Tappolet's professional association with Krafft lasted for about seven months and for himself, at least, was a disastrous experience. Although he began to study the standard graphological textbooks by Ludwig Klages and Max Pulver, he could not apply what he learned from them. Herr Tappolet told me that he was a physical and nervous wreck when he left Krafft in June 1930.[1] The office was then vacated.

A letter to Dr Ferrière (3 January 1930) indicates how seriously Krafft took his work as a professional *Charakterologe*. He referred to the superiority of the 'psychological portrait' as compared with the mere description of 'character', and emphasised that a large-scale analysis resembled a painted portrait, was therefore a 'work of art' and was remunerated accordingly. He mentioned that he had charged a certain Mlle F. P. Fr.600 (£25) and that 30–40 hours of work were involved.

One such 'work of art' was the forty-page document presented to Oscar Guhl on the occasion of the latter's sixtieth birthday on 24 February 1930. Krafft mentioned it in a letter to Dr Ferrière and proudly announced that it was his most outstanding production to date. Herr Tappolet, on the other hand, described the essay on 'Oscar Guhl as the Embodiment of a Human Archetype' as a byzantine piece of flattery. 'It was a hard blow for Krafft', he continued, 'when Guhl never even referred to the document and did not utter a single word of thanks. Krafft was speechless, and that in itself was extraordinary.' My own assumption is that Guhl, like myself, could not make head nor tail of Krafft's masterpiece.

Krafft soon looked for someone to replace his erstwhile assistant. Once again he chose a colleague who knew nothing about graphology, but Pastor Walser was of tougher fibre than poor Herr Tappolet. Walser was already

---

[1] Herr Tappolet told me about an astrological prediction that Krafft made in *c.* June 1929. He forecast that one of the two people closest to Tappolet would die in mid-December 1931 or January 1932. He was working on a farm near Bordeaux in December 1931 when he received a telegram announcing that his younger brother had been killed in a riding accident.

mildly interested in astrology when he first met Krafft early in 1930. At that time he was in charge of a small parish near Winterthur. After Tappolet's departure Krafft arranged a meeting in Zürich and suggested that he should try his hand at graphology on a free-lance basis.

'I was astonished at Krafft's proposition,' Herr Walser told me. 'He was incredibly insistent and kept on saying: "You *can* do it; you *must* do it!" So I took some scripts home with me and studied them. Well, I began to write reports for "Globus" and Krafft discussed them with me, but from a *literary* point of view rather than a graphological one. In that respect he was a real schoolmaster and, in fact, an accomplished teacher. Of course I soon familiarised myself with the principles of scientific graphology. Krafft and I became friends, and while he was my teacher I became his father confessor. He was assailed by all manner of inner problems and difficulties and was a very complicated person, at once ascetic and sexually unsure of himself. He seemed to hover between complete chastity and quite extraordinary fantasies.'

When Pastor Walser appeared upon the scene in the autumn of 1930, Krafft had been at Zürich for more than four years. I must now take the reader back to the spring of 1926 and explain what had happened to the great astro-statistical project. During his first year at Zürich Krafft was still full of ambitious plans for the publication of an important scientific book. Indeed, a few chapters were set up in type at Orell Füssli but no further progress was made, either because he was too busy or, more likely, because of his innate inability to finalise any major literary undertaking. Instead the material was used during the years 1927–30 for a dozen articles, some of them in several instalments, which were mainly published in *Die Astrologie* and *Sterne und Mensch*. Hence he addressed himself to an astrological rather than a scientific audience. There were also two short books: *Influences solaires et lunaires sur la naissance humaine*, published by Editions Médicales Norbert Maloine at Paris in 1928 and, in the same year, *Astro-Physiologie*, which was issued by the Astra Verlag at Leipzig, an astrological publishing house. Krafft's name now became well known to all the serious German astrologers.

By the time that the last of the cosmobiological studies, with their involved and, to most readers, largely incomprehensible mathematical arguments, was published in 1930, Krafft had more or less lost interest in this field of enquiry. In November 1931 he suggested to Dr Ferrière that 'the whole "scientific farce" [i.e. Cosmobiology] of the past decade was merely a necessary reaction to certain hyper-rational dispositions in my natal horoscope'. Thus his ostensibly scientific attitude had merely camouflaged his fundamental preference for the irrational.

Now, in view of the unsatisfactory, indeed intellectually unacceptable nature of the old astrological Tradition, something better had to be found to replace it. The answer, which was gradually and even strenuously worked out after 1926, was the abstruse astro-metaphysical system which he called Typocosmy. The precise nature of Typocosmy is extremely difficult to define. According to Krafft it was the 'General Alphabet of the World of Phenomena'. He also referred to it as 'the natural order of the [planetary] archetypes'. In a letter (14 December 1933) to G.-L. Brahy, the Belgian astrologer, he said that 'the foundations of Typocosmy are much more scientific than you appear to grasp. The history of civilisations, the psychology of the unconscious, [planetary?] harmonics, general and specific symbolism and many facts already established by Cosmobionomy—such are the foundations upon which stands the edifice for which I daily find fresh confirmation. I have been able to achieve a basic reconstitution of ancient theo- and cosmogony in perfect harmony with the Typocosmic zodiac and the natural order of the archetypes.'

Typocosmy was at once a mystical, esoteric form of astrology and a private philosophical or cosmological system based upon Krafft's exalted visions of the macrocosm and the microcosm. My own conclusion is that it was an intellectual aberration from start to finish, although it appears to have fascinated the members of the small study groups who sat at Krafft's feet after 1933. Furthermore, since Typocosmy was a 'universal' system, it could also be applied to horoscope delineation. Indeed, Krafft firmly believed that in this respect it was greatly superior to conventional astrology. Once again he was obsessed by the idea that he had discovered something of epochal importance. The cosmic scientist had now become a cosmic philosopher.

At the end of 1929 Dr Ferrière was busy planning the foundation of an 'international committee for the study of individual psychology and human typology' and invited Krafft to become its president. This gesture indicates Dr Ferrière's great admiration for him. At this juncture it seemed advisable to enlist C. G. Jung's support and Krafft asked Dr Ferrière for an introduction to him. 'Could you mention, *if you have an opportunity*, my researches and work to Dr Jung? I have learned from several sources that he is fairly receptive to the idea of astrology, also that my work has been mentioned to him, but up to now we have not met for want of "neutral ground". However, it's not urgent.' (27 December 1929.)

And yet perhaps the matter was urgent, because Krafft referred to it again a week later: 'If a convenient occasion presents itself, can you let Jung have your own opinion of my Typocosmic and characterological work. He will then possibly feel more inclined to accept an invitation which one of his acquaintances intends to send him, so that our meeting can take place on "neutral ground".'

Krafft probably wanted the encounter to be arranged on 'neutral ground' because the prospect of having to go cap in hand to the famous Dr Jung was altogether too humiliating. On 13 January 1930 he informed Dr

Ferrière that he had sent copies of his two books and offprints of some of his articles to Jung.

By the end of March 1930 Dr Ferrière's international committee had recruited a few members, including Dr (later Sir Cyril) Burt, the British psychologist. The eminent Professor Eduard Spranger, of Berlin, had refused to join it and Jung had remained silent. Indeed, he had not even bothered to answer Krafft's letter. Krafft was beside himself with anger: 'In spite of numerous attempts on my part and special introductions, I have not achieved the desired personal contact with Jung, and for very good reasons. In his private life the author of *The Psychology of the Unconscious* does not appear to be the man whose idealism is reflected in the best pages of his books. His indifference towards his fellow human beings borders upon snobbishness . . . I have recently been able to compare Keyserling's attitude to my work as opposed to Jung's. On the one hand interest and warm thanks for an important book that I lent him, on the other hand indifference to the point of discourtesy, and the failure even to acknowledge the receipt of three or four letters and enclosures, the contents of the latter being at least interesting, if not valuable . . . On the basis of past experience, it will not be me who goes in search of Jung again.'

Dr Ferrière's international committee does not appear ever to have functioned effectively, but at least one publication appeared under its auspices. This was a little book by Ferrière and Krafft, *Caractérologie Typocosmique*, Geneva, 1932, which bore the imprint of Dr Ferrière's *Bureau de la Ligue Internationale pour l'Education Nouvelle*.[1]

Krafft sailed in moderately smooth waters between the summer of 1930, when Felix Tappolet left him, and the late autumn of 1931. Then, quite suddenly, he ran into financial difficulties. In a letter to Dr Ferrière (5 December 1931) he mentioned that it was a long time since he had been so short of money. Private clients had not paid their debts and recent stock exchange speculations had turned sour. Three weeks later he wrote: 'Damn the state of the New York market. The latest fall in share prices has cost me all I earned during the autumn and more besides.' He had learned about stock exchange operations at the Guhl bank and had been making speculative purchases of shares, probably on margin, on the basis of the supposed effects of planetary conjunctions and cycles.

At this point I encountered an unexpected gap in the Krafft–Ferrière correspondence. Dr Ferrière had apparently preserved every scrap of paper that he had received from Krafft from February 1924 onwards, but there was nothing written during 1932. Furthermore, Krafft published practically nothing during that year. A partial explanation was provided by Herr Mahler and Pastor Walser when I met them in Zürich in 1961, also by two letters written by Krafft to Dr Bender during the summer of

[1] My own copy is the one presented by Krafft to Dr Martin Knapp, the Basle astronomer. It is mercifully enlivened by Knapp's cynical marginal notes.

1932, which I did not see until 1963. I will first deal with Pastor Walser's story, which was recorded on a 'Minifon' apparatus.

'At "Globus" Krafft was an *eminence grise,*' Herr Walser said. 'An appointment, a promotion or an increase in salary could depend upon his confidential reports, hence he was feared. Again, because his perception could be uncanny, and because of his known association with astrology, he was widely regarded as a "magician". To make matters worse, his verdicts were sometimes harsh and he could be very ruthless. During the spring or summer of 1932 he was suddenly attacked by a *folie de grandeur* and told Mahler that his appointment to the board of directors of "Globus" was long overdue. Mahler found it difficult to take this seriously and said: "My dear Herr Krafft, your work for us is extremely useful, but I would not dream of proposing your election as a director!" Mahler had a genuine regard for Krafft, but latterly he had been poking his nose into matters that did not concern him, even to the extent of interfering in the private life of one of the directors. Mahler felt it advisable to terminate Krafft's connection with "Globus" and gave him notice on quite generous terms. However, the proposed compensation did not satisfy Krafft and he made a noisy scene in Mahler's office. In fact, he became so hysterical that the bewildered Mahler thought he had lost his reason. An ambulance was called and Krafft was taken to an asylum. Mahler asked me to visit him there and we had a long talk. He had calmed down by then and they let him out a day or two later.'

It is probable that this contretemps occurred in mid-March 1932. Too humiliated to remain at Zürich, where the story would not have remained a closely-guarded secret, Krafft made tracks for Holland and spent a few weeks with his friends the van der Koppels at Zeist, on the outskirts of Utrecht.[1] He was in Paris by 16 July when he wrote to Dr Bender, who was then a junior member of the staff of the Psychological Institute at the University of Bonn. He told Bender that he was just about to start work as psychological adviser to the 'Printemps' department store on the basis of twenty hours' work a month for a fee of 3,000 French francs (£33). He mentioned, too, that he was very short of money and asked for a loan of a few hundred Marks until the autumn. Krafft wrote to Dr Bender again on 25 July and said that while the 'Printemps' people had not offered him a contract, his prospects were fairly encouraging. 'The chances of my being able to return to Zürich are rapidly diminishing,' he added. However, his self-imposed exile was briefer than he had expected. He was in Zürich again by September 1932, although there were to be regular monthly visits to Paris throughout 1933–4.

[1] Krafft was introduced to Anna van der Koppel, his future wife, by a member of the Bircher-Benner family at Zürich in *c.* 1930. Her father also met Krafft and invited him to Holland. He took advantage of this offer when circumstances made Zürich unbearable in 1932.

Many letters and postcards contain a record of Krafft's and Dr Ferrière's relationship during 1933. At this point Dr Ferrière's own letters to Krafft begin to appear in the files. If, as was often the case, Krafft was too busy to reply to Dr Ferrière, he scribbled brief comments or replies to questions in the margin and mailed the letter back to him.

Krafft's father died on 16 January 1933 and a legacy—the amount is not known—temporarily relieved his financial difficulties. Unwisely he decided to test his cosmo-economic theories on a more ambitious scale and embarked upon a series of share transactions based upon his assessment of the presumed short-term effects of various periodicities, planetary cycles and sundry other astral indications. He also became the trusting Dr Ferrière's financial adviser. Twenty-seven letters and postcards written between 15 April and 21 October 1933 contain a partial record of their respective transactions. Unfortunately, the stars did not behave reliably. Dr Ferrière was lucky to escape with a comparatively small loss but Krafft appears to have dissipated all or most of his legacy. While all this was happening the tone of his letters to Dr Ferrière became increasingly nervous and sometimes offensive. When he was short of money during the autumn of 1933 he asked Dr Ferrière to lend him Fr.1500 (£85). Dr Ferrière was unwilling to comply with this request or proposed conditions that Krafft felt unable to accept. Whichever was the case, Krafft's intense and sometimes vindictive resentment smouldered until 1936.

Krafft's own assessment of himself at this time is vividly expressed in a letter written on 11 November 1933 to Dr Maurice Faure, a Nice physician who was investigating a supposed relationship between sun-spot activity and epidemics. 'Now you, who have met so many people, must have encountered others of this "bohemian" type,' Krafft observed. 'People who cannot be pigeonholed and who, in spite of themselves, live restless lives; people who are pushed around and pursued by their genii and their daemons (one is very much like the other); who always sow but scarcely ever reap, who are storm-tossed without mercy by a fate that seems to bear them in its arms, only to hurl them an instant later into the dark abyss of inner and material difficulties. . . . From a strictly rational point of view there is no "guiding line", either in my studies, research work or practical activities. . . . Thus every department of my life reflects something so "scrappy", so "wild", so "romantic", to say the very least, that when I am dead it would serve as material for a novel rather than a "scientific" work.'

Nevertheless, early in 1934 Krafft's tormented life entered upon a more peaceful phase, which was to last until the end of 1936. He continued his work as a 'psychological adviser'—in the letter to Dr Faure from which I have just quoted he referred to himself as a psychotherapist—and began to lecture to small groups, in return for modest fees, at Lausanne and

Zürich.[1] This, too, was a period of incessant, although always unconventional, intellectual activity. In so far as any pattern can be discerned, his main interests were Typocosmy, *Sprachgeist* (the 'spirit of language' or, as Dr Bender called it, 'Word Magic'), cosmo-economics, and the interpretation of the obscure prophetic verse quatrains of the sixteenth-century 'seer' Michel Nostradamus.[2] To analyse this *mélange* in any detail would require a book on its own.

Krafft claimed to have discovered correlations between cosmic cycles or periodicities, e.g. the Jupiter/Saturn conjunction (19.83 years), and economic fluctuations or crises. He had made a particular study of William Beveridge's 'Wheat Prices and Rain Fall in Western Europe' (in *Journal of the Royal Statistical Society*, May 1922) and H. L. Moore's *Generating Economic Cycles*, New York, 1923. Both these researchers had identified economic cycles but had not associated them with cosmic phenomena. Krafft felt sure that the latter must be present and made two large-scale investigations covering German wheat prices, 1800–1930, and American railway share prices, 1831–1932. All manner of previously unsuspected related planetary periodicities and sub-periodicities were found. In fact, Krafft being the man he was, it would have been surprising if he had not discovered them.

At 'Globus' Krafft wrote occasional *Wirtschaftsberichte* (Economic Bulletins). The first of these was prepared in 1931 and had a very limited circulation. He continued to produce these documents after he left 'Globus' and from December 1935 onwards they were duplicated, published bi-monthly, marked 'Confidential' and sold to subscribers. They normally consisted of at least a dozen sheets and it is likely that his average 'print order' was for about sixty copies.

Krafft's bulletins contain a surprising mixture of straightforward economic and political information, cosmic speculation, and articles on topics that happened to interest him, such as Freiherr Stromer von Reichenbach's eccentric 'historionomical' theories. Any casual reader would probably not have been immediately aware that the document in his hands had come from an astrological stable. However, one thing was evident, namely Krafft's increasingly negative attitude to his own country. This had a bearing upon his subsequent identification with the Third Reich.

Krafft's *Sprachgeist* theories are, I believe, nonsense from start to finish. He referred to them in a letter to Dr Faure as 'a far-reaching linguistic study, an analysis of the roots of the names of the planets and the ancient gods, which has led to a series of verifications and surprising discoveries, with tremendous implications both from the point of view of the

---

[1] Between 16 January 1934 and 5 February 1939 he lectured on *c.* 132 occasions at Lausanne. From September 1935 onwards his pupils met at Mlle. Panchaud's porcelain shop in the Galeries du Commerce. His Zürich lectures were mostly given at the homes of members of the Bircher family.

[2] He published half a dozen articles on Nostradamus in *Zenit* during 1935–6.

history of civilisations and psychological and philosophical applications'.[1]

Krafft met C. G. Jung at long last during the summer of 1934. In the postscript of a letter to Dr Wilhelm Mrsic (10 June) he wrote: 'I hope to see Jung again soon. He is very interested in *Sprachforschung*', i.e. linguistic research. (Herr Tappolet knew about this or another visit to Jung: 'Krafft was overjoyed when he returned from Jung's fine house at Küssnacht. The great man allowed the discussion to last for two hours and even accompanied the astrologer to the garden gate.') There is a typical example of *Sprachgeist* in a letter he wrote to Dr Irmgard Krieger, who lived at Stuttgart, on 8 April 1935: 'It's not *Life* that is rotten, but this Life (on earth) is! Dieses Kriechen des Körpers (Kopros-porcus-corpse!) dem wir immer wieder verfallen.' Only the first part of the sentence requires elucidation: This creeping/crawling of the (physical) body (Kopros-porcus-corpse): *Kopros*: excrement (Greek); *porcus*: pig (Latin); then *corpse* (English). The inference is that all three words derived from the same archetypal root, and had a relationship with *Körper*, the body. Krafft 'discovered' hundreds, if not thousands, of similar archetypal [*sic*] coincidences.

When Krafft wrote to *X* he often sent copies of his letter to *Y* and *Z*. Thus it was Pastor Walser who gave me a copy of Krafft's letter of 6 August 1935 to his friend F. G. Goerner at Mannheim. This document helped to determine Krafft's and Goerner's future relationship. It also had a connection with Count Keyserling's letter to Krafft of 11 October 1935 (see p. 122). Krafft had recently attended the annual German astrological congress at Wernigerode, and from there went to a similar but international event at Brussels.[2] On both occasions he lectured on Typocosmy but experienced different reactions from his audiences.

'When I compare the Wernigerode and Brussels congresses', he wrote, 'it is once again clear to me that the essence of Typocosmy can only be made comprehensible to the Germans . . . the Latins, with their preference for *quelque chose de clair et précis*, are getting further and further away from understanding it. Thus in the near and distant future I count more and more upon a growing understanding in the German-speaking countries. . . . Hence I come with even more pleasure to your suggestion that I should now make my first attempt to establish contact in southern

[1] For the theory of *Sprachgeist* see Krafft's *Typokosmie: über Urbilder und Sinnzeichen; vom Walten des Sprachgeistes*, Verlag der Zenit, Düsseldorf, 1934. Krafft thought that this short book was a masterpiece. Although Krafft never referred to Guido von List, it is possible that *Sprachgeist* owed something to von List's eccentric linguistic theories. See Max Dessoir, *Vom Jenseits der Seele: Die Geheimwissenschaften in kritischer Betrachtung*, 5th edit., 1920, pp. 236–7.

[2] Theodore Chapellier, the Belgian astrologer, recalled Krafft's dramatic appearance at the Brussels congress: 'Krafft made a theatrical entry, agitatedly and yet nonchalantly. One beheld a slim, short, dark-haired young man with a pale, sharp-featured face and ecstatic and virulent eyes. A sort of Spanish cape was loosely draped on his shoulders and he wore a monocle.'

Germany.' His proposition that only the Germans, with their predilection for involved metaphysical concepts, however nonsensical, would take to Typocosmy confirmed my own suspicions.

Herr Goerner had offered to organise a lecture evening for Krafft at Frankfurt am Main, but Krafft suggested regular visits. His modest financial requirements were outlined at considerable length. 'Experience has shown', he added, 'that my lecture courses create a demand for private consultations, i.e. for horoscope interpretation, advice about difficult problems, and sometimes personal psychological treatment, from pupils, also their relatives and friends.'

F. G. Goerner was an engineer by training and first became interested in astrology in 1926. A year or two later he was greatly impressed by Krafft's astro-statistical articles and wrote to him about them. They met for the first time at the Wiesbaden congress in 1931. In the meantime Goerner had decided to become a full-time professional astrological-cum-graphological consultant and began to train himself for this purpose.[1] He told me that Krafft regularly sent him copies of the 'Globus' psychological reports and that these provided useful guidance for his own work.

In 1934, a year after Hitler became Chancellor, Herr Goerner had so many clients that he needed secretarial assistance and recruited the services of a certain Herr Gerhard zur Horst. He was interested in astrology and was able to save Goerner's time by casting his clients' horoscopes for him. Many of them were theatrical people who suffered from stage fright or could not remember their lines. There was now also an extensive Jewish connection and Goerner had a steady flow of distracted individuals who wanted to know whether or not the time had come for them to emigrate from Hitler's Germany. Goerner's Jewish clientele soon became an embarrassment since it attracted the unwelcome attentions of the Gestapo. It must be remembered, too, that in 1935 the German professional astrologers began to find themselves in a difficult position *vis-à-vis* the authorities.

Krafft did not lecture at Frankfurt but made his first visit to Mannheim at the end of October 1935. It is likely that he also saw Count Keyserling at Darmstadt on this occasion. Thereafter he regularly (monthly ?) lectured at Mannheim to a small group organised by Goerner. These visits became part of a lecture circuit which included Lausanne, Zürich and Stuttgart. There were also occasional visits to Munich.

Herr zur Horst could read Krafft's shorthand and henceforth typed many of his articles. It was also Herr zur Horst's task to obtain official permission for Krafft's occasional public lectures at Mannheim. In a

---

[1] Herr Goerner's name is included in a list published in 1932 of nineteen German astrologers who had undertaken to abide by the rules for professional conduct prescribed by Dr Korsch's Central Astrological Office. See *Zenit*, April 1932, p. 3 of cover.

memorandum written for Herr Goerner in 1957 he recalled that there were occasions when approval was not forthcoming because of their supposed astrological content, even if it was not Krafft's intention to discuss astrology in the strict sense of the word. Herr zur Horst found it very difficult to explain these nuances since Krafft's connection with Goerner was automatically equated with astrology. On one occasion, when he and Krafft were at the *Bezirksamt* together they obediently changed the lecture theme to one less suspect. However, when Krafft began to talk that evening, two obvious Gestapo spies made their appearance and listened for a while.

Herr Goerner was one of Krafft's most enthusiastic and devoted supporters. Apart from organising the Mannheim lecture courses he also persuaded his friends and connections to subscribe to Krafft's *Wirtschaftsberichte* (Economic Bulletins). I have already mentioned that these were first printed on a duplicating machine in December 1935, i.e. very soon after Krafft began his regular visits to Mannheim. One subscriber was Goerner's friend Eduard Hofweber, a director of a local engineering firm. Hofweber was a close personal friend of Rudolf Hess. According to Herr Goerner, Hofweber regularly sent copies of Krafft's bulletin to Hess. In any event Hofweber's connection with Krafft became a matter of interest to the Gestapo some years later. Herr zur Horst mentioned in his memorandum that Krafft's activities at Mannheim after 1935 only added to Goerner's difficulties with the authorities.

Krafft attended Dr Korsch's international congress at Düsseldorf in 1936 but did not enjoy the experience. In a letter to Dr Rouhier, the proprietor of the well-known Librairie Vega (occult and esoteric bookshop) at Paris, he complained of Dr Korsch's 'morbid ambition'. 'This man, who is much more a lawyer than an *homme de science* . . . is possessed by a veritable "anti-personality complex", meaning that the moment that anyone achieves influence or prestige because of his own knowledge, culture or authority, Dr Korsch pursues him with petty and spiteful attacks. . . .' Krafft informed Dr Rouhier that henceforth he would have no further connection with any organised astrological movement.

The main reason for this letter to Dr Rouhier, however, was to announce his plans for an ambitious bi-monthly review to be called *Kosmologika*. At least a dozen copies of this document (dated 22 October 1936) were circulated to various friends. Among them was M. Theodore Chapellier, of Brussels, who produced it when I met him in January 1965. Nothing came of the *Kosmologika* project, but Krafft and Chapellier were soon involved in plans for the publication of the book that eventually became the *Traité d'Astro-Biologie*, although by the time the latter appeared in 1939 Krafft and Chapellier had long since gone their separate ways.

It must be remembered that all Krafft's previous efforts to publish a *magnum opus* had been frustrated, although more by his own incapacity to produce a full-scale work than from any lack of material.[1] Chapellier, who was a Theosophist, was the proprietor of *Uranus* (Brussels, No. 1, October 1934) and was currently publishing articles contributed by Krafft. By this time the astrological publishing situation had become tricky in Germany. It was this factor that undoubtedly led to Krafft's decision to produce a large book in French, although his best market was clearly in Germany where his name was well known, even famous, in astrological circles. Hitherto he had published very little in French.

Krafft's desire to appear as the author of an important work was largely due to the sceptical and, in his opinion, discourteous reception that he had experienced at the Zürich astronomical observatory late in 1936. I believe that it was this setback that led to his decision to leave Zürich and, somewhere in Germany, write the book that would at long last establish his reputation as a serious scientific researcher.

During the last three months of 1936 he had spent much of his time studying past records of variations in sun-spot activity. 'At the back of them I sensed the existence of a planetary cycle,' he told a correspondent. 'In fact, I then made a whole succession of discoveries by which the interplay of these cycles was satisfactorily explained. Overjoyed at having solved a puzzle that had exercised others for more than a century I hoped, after my rupture with the "astrologers' guild", again to establish a connection with official science, and at the same time fill the gap by which the actuality of cosmic influences on terrestrial events could be more easily accepted, because so many different effects have already been ascribed to sun-spots or even recognised.'

He took his documentation to the Zürich observatory on 23 December 1936 but met with a cool reception. The director told him that he had something better to do than to evaluate Krafft's alleged discoveries. After a heated argument the director said that he would get an assistant to look at the material 'sometime in the New Year'. The assistant visited Krafft in January 1937, refused to accept his conclusions and said: 'So many people have vainly tried to solve this periodicities puzzle, that I don't see why it should be you that cracks the nut.'

The first evidence that Krafft was now writing a book is a note written in the margin of a letter from Dr Ferrière (15 January 1937). Its provisional and unwieldy title was *De l'Astrologie par la Cosmobiologie à la Typocosmie*, and Krafft said that Chapellier would publish the first fascicule during the summer. It appears that Krafft himself was subsidising the publication, either wholly or in part.

Krafft married Anna van der Koppel at Zürich on 7 May 1937. Whoever else he informed, he said nothing about it to Dr Ferrière until January

---

[1] At a rough count Krafft published at least a hundred articles in periodicals between 1927–41. The importance of his work as source material for the whole area of the 'irrational' cannot be denied.

1939. There was a hint of their plan to leave Zürich in his long letter to Dr Bender of 4 June 1937. He had already told Bender that he and his wife hoped to spend a few days at Bonn, on their way to Holland, at the beginning of July, and Bender suggested that he might be able to arrange for Krafft to lecture there. Krafft was delighted and wrote: 'If the plans we discussed last year lead to a closer collaboration between us, and frequent visits to Bonn for myself . . . a development of this kind would be acceptable in view of my prospective "folding of tents" in Switzerland, and would be the first stage of a long, long journey that will first take us through Germany to Zeist, near Utrecht, where we propose to stay until the end of September. . . . You are now at least aware that the "Uranian" upheaval of the past eight or ten months has made me "mobile" and, if the opportunity presents itself, I am available for new plans and possibilities, even if some of my prospective "leisure" must be devoted to finishing a book for which my publisher has long been waiting.'

The Kraffts left Zürich on 25 June 1937 and made their way to Bonn via Munich, Stuttgart and Mannheim, where he had lecturing engagements. A duplicated sheet containing particulars of their itinerary was circulated to the many people with whom he was in contact. Their provisional programme included a stay at Zeist until the end of September and subsequent visits to England and France. This document stated that his next round-trip in Switzerland would probably take place during the second half of October and would include visits to Geneva, Lausanne, Zürich and Basle. A final paragraph read: 'For psychological readings and consultations the usual particulars of the place and time of birth are required, also specimens of handwriting from an earlier period.'

Krafft lectured at Bonn on 8 July 1937. A week or two earlier he had received a letter from Dr Bender containing a tactful hint that he should not enlarge upon his *Sprachgeist* theories. Dr Bender thought it unlikely that what he described as 'Word Magic' would be received with either interest or enthusiasm. While at Bonn Krafft agreed to participate in some future 'blind diagnosis' experiments, namely to write short studies of the horoscopes of individuals known to Dr Bender and his colleagues but not to himself.

During August there was a change of plans and Krafft wrote to Dr Bender to ask if he could recommend 'some isolated place in the Black Forest, somewhere that has not been corroded by civilisation'. Dr Bender, who was a native of Freiburg im Breisgau and knew every inch of the surrounding countryside, suggested the 'Hellhof' pension at Urberg, near St Blasien. 'It is run by two very cultured ladies of rather Anthroposophical leanings. Vegetarian cooking, beautiful surroundings. Perhaps you can make your nest in a little house close by. It was built by a painter and is now empty. I will ask them up there.'

The prospect of living at Urberg in a house called 'Hellhof' greatly appealed to Krafft because of the *Sprachgeist* implications. 'Hellhof' could be twisted to mean 'Höllenhof', literally 'Hell Court', with its Uranian-magical implications and, what is more, it was on the *Ur*-berg, the archetypal, primeval mountain. Later he told Bender that he had previously searched a map for 'names with the right kind of sound', and for a while had thought of Heilbronn (healing spring). 'But my wife thought that *our* place should be further to the south-east, which is why I considered Meersburg [on the Lake of Constance], as if I had a name with *b—r* in mind.'

The Kraffts finally arrived at Urberg towards the end of October 1937. Krafft was now busily engaged upon his book for Theodore Chapellier. The first fascicule had still not been printed, let alone published. The prospectus was not ready until *c.* March 1938, and then only after a lot of acrimonius correspondence had passed between Chapellier and himself.[1]

A prospectus and an unpublished essay were sent to Count Keyserling, who was not impressed. He wrote to Krafft on 29 March 1938: 'I have a very strong impression and, between you and I, Frau von Brasch has confirmed it from your handwriting, that you are trying to "force" things.[2] You should refrain from making dogmatic statements about matters that cannot be substantiated until you receive real illumination, independently of any tradition, like the Buddha achieved on the highest level. . . . I am completely convinced that your views on *Sprachgeist* are complete fantasies. And I doubt seventy per cent of the validity of what your Typocosmy promises to become, as far as I understand it. I urgently advise you to make the inward gesture of throwing all your papers into the waste paper basket and then write a book in French that will omit any of your past astrological conceptions. It is not the slightest bit certain that any kind of astrological or Theosophical conception has the slightest truth. Eighty per cent of the essay you sent me is based upon unproven concepts.'

Krafft affected to take no notice of these admonitions and wrote a silly letter to the Count about the latter's current astrological 'prospects' and attempted to defend his Typocosmy theories. Keyserling wrote to him again on 6 April and observed that Krafft did not appear to have understood his previous letter.

'I know that you are still suffering from a certain kind of Theosophical atavism . . . Allow me to inform you, on the basis of a metaphysical experience of which you have so far been ignorant, that the Theosophical

---

[1] The prospectus was for a book of *c.* 230 pages to be published in three fascicules: No. 1, Cosmic Influences on the Human Individual, Cosmobiology, Typocosmy, Nostradamus; No. 2. Psychological Types (by Dr Ferrière), Historical Rhythms and Periodicities; No. 3. Horoscope interpretation.

[2] Elisabeth von Brasch was a well-known Munich graphologist whose opinions Keyserling greatly respected. See his interesting article on graphology, 'Zum Handschrift-Lesen', in *Der Weg zur Vollendung*, May 1940.

type, as such, is an inferior one, and must be completely melted down if anything worthwhile is to emerge from anyone. Theosophy, with all its ready-made assumptions, belongs to the "make it easy" culture on which our world is going to ruin. . . . Without being aware of it, you gave me advice in a most patronising manner. But you are hardly qualified to do that. I can only remind you of my first letter. You really must take a different path if you are not to come to grief.'[1]

The Kraffts returned to Switzerland for a month in April 1938 and stayed for a while at the Villa Rose, where his mother was in a difficult and quarrelsome mood. In a letter to Mrs Butler (1 May 1938), who knew Krafft *mère* well, he mentioned that his mother had been made to realise once more that 'her power over me was broken'. Mrs Butler had asked him to cast her horoscope but (in English): 'I am not very keen on the simple prediction of future events and rather would prefer a gradual exposure of forthcoming rhythms and progressions than a five or ten year forecast of definite "facts". For Life does not pre-exist but *unfolds* in correspondence with cosmic *symbolism*, and everything else but interpreting such symbols, e.g. predicting events, would mean for me something short of black magic.' Krafft was fond of Mrs Butler and was therefore unwilling to 'predict' for her. I am sure, however, that he attempted prediction in many other cases, because that was what some of his clients paid for and expected, or because it intrigued him to demonstrate his skill.[2]

Krafft and his wife returned to Urberg in May 1938 and he continued to work on what he called his 'Brussels' book. During his leisure hours he built a roughly-constructed wooden cabin or summer house, from which there was a magnificent view of the Black Forest country to the south-east. He could not have used it very much that summer because on 17 August 1938 they left for France and, according to a duplicated circular, did not expect to have any fixed address until the end of the year. They were at the Villa Rose at the time of the Munich crisis. In a letter written to Count Keyserling he mentioned that he had been besieged with enquiries about the likelihood of a general war. They then went to the south of France and were at Grasse and Nice for a couple of months.[3]

By now the 'Brussels' book had foundered. An undated postcard to Dr Ferrière, apparently written in November 1938, announced that 'at 6.32

---

[1] The Count had already publicly criticised Krafft's *Sprachgeist* theories in his periodical *Der Weg zur Vollendung*, October 1936, pp. 43–46. Nevertheless, Keyserling respected his efforts to find something better than the old Tradition.

[2] Cf. the predictions he did for M. Tilea (see p. 176) and his Hitler prediction (see p. 169).

[3] Krafft went to Monte Carlo to visit Gabriel Trarieux d'Egmont (1870–1940), a well-known professional astrologer whose books *Que sera 1938?* and *Que sera 1939?* were being widely read. It was through Krafft that Trarieux d'Egmont began an exchange of letters with the Count. He is sympathetically commemorated in the first volume of Keyserling's *Reise durch die Zeit*, 1948, pp. 340–3.

a.m. this morning (Sun conjunction my Ascendant) I conceived a new plan to enlarge the Brussels book—a privately printed edition subsidised by *une admiratrice*'. His admirer was Mlle Marguerite Panchaud, the proprietress of the china and porcelain shop at Lausanne where he had lectured to his local group from January 1936 onwards. Chapellier's version of the debacle is described in the typescript of an article—it may have been published in *L'Horoscope* (Paris 1946, No. 9)—which he gave me in 1965: 'The publisher and the printer were swamped with a deluge of manuscripts covered with erasures, transpositions, footnotes, footnotes to footnotes, additions, underlines, cabalistic signs, etc. When a page was laboriously set up in type the proof came back crammed with deletions, transpositions, notes, etc. In the end the author, the publisher and the printer mutually sent each other to the devil. Two years were devoted to this tragi-comic adventure. . . .'

The Kraffts were in Switzerland again shortly before Christmas and returned to Urberg in February 1939. Work on the *Traité d'Astro-Biologie* now began in earnest. He told Dr Ferrière that it would run to 192 pages and be ready in May. 'What a task! But the book will be epoch-making because the Tradition's deficiences are evident almost everywhere.' On 13 March he wrote in English to Mrs Butler and told her that he was working anything up to fifteen hours a day. 'Meanwhile the police called upon this place during our absence because they had been told by some frantic fool that the hut might have some military purpose, especially because of its "dominating" situation 700 ft. above the valley, I suppose.' The hut was the small summer house that Krafft had built in June 1938.

The *Traité* was being set up in type, chapter by chapter, by another printer, L. Wyckmans & Cie., at Brussels. In March Krafft was worried because it had already grown to 210 pages and by the middle of May there were some three hundred. By the time that Krafft wrote the copy for his acknowledgments on 17 June the book amounted to 343 pages and when Wyckmans completed the printing on 30 June there was a total of 354 pages. Krafft received his first consignment of bound copies at Urberg at 2.40 p.m. on 20 July. He made a careful note of the time, probably in order to be able to cast a horoscope for the book's prospects of success.

Apart from Typocosmy, *Sprachgeist* and Nostradamus, the *Traité* contains the essence of Krafft's 'scientific' work and speculations since 1923. It was largely based upon his many periodical articles but there was a lot of new material. Letters written to Dr Ferrière, Dr Bender and Countess Keyserling while he was feverishly working on the book indicate that he was in a pronounced state of euphoria. Important 'new discoveries' were being made almost daily and, of course, they had to be included. It was as if Krafft had a presentiment that time was running short and that the work must be quickly published at all costs. He appears to have been completely confident that it would lead to immediate fame and recognition.

It is by no means easy to describe the contents of the *Traité d'Astro-Biologie*. The book covers an enormous amount of ground but in an apparently confused fashion. It consists, in fact, of a wonderful mishmash of fascinating statements and alleged proof of the existence of all manner of cosmic influences, periodicities, rhythms and so on. And yet it does not read like the work of a madman. My own conclusion, however, is that the *Traité* has no scientific importance whatever. Nevertheless, for the student of Krafft it is prescribed and even illuminating reading.[1]

The *Traité* was published at a most inopportune moment, for on 21 August 1939, almost exactly a month after Krafft first delightedly held the book in his hands, a musical programme on the German radio was interrupted and a voice announced that the German and Soviet governments had signed a non-aggression pact. This was just as much a surprise to Krafft as to everyone else in Europe and, I believe, in spite of 'the stars' entirely unforeseen by him. By this time he had adopted the attitude that the Germans could do no wrong.

A few weeks earlier he had advised Dr Ferrière 'not to believe a tenth of what is said about Germany. *There is so much that is positive here* that the manner in which my compatriots concentrate upon the negative points instead of accepting the truth and, indeed, admitting that the diagnoses and forecasts of the past six years were wrong, has been nothing less than infamous. Once again the work of the Freemasons and the Jews.' This, indeed, was the voice of Dr Goebbels.

Dr Ferrière did not agree. 'If only the [German] chiefs would disavow their sadistic and cruel underlings, that would be even better', he wrote. Krafft scribbled his reply in the margin: 'And it would be even better if our fellow-countrymen would reduce these stories to their correct proportion. You know how servile people are in Switzerland; the ridiculous charges they make to people doing research work in libraries and archives, etc. If you could see the "team spirit" here you would be in a better position to understand that the Swiss have something to learn from it. As for sadism, I've seen and endured it in Switzerland more than one would believe possible.'

The Kraffts had intended to leave Urberg early in September and to spend a few weeks at Zürich before going to the Villa Rose. Now, as he explained to Dr Ferrière on a postcard dated 26 August, they had decided to remain at Urberg 'because of the crisis'. Krafft wrote: 'I do not think that there will be a general war', as if to infer that the Germans would have a free hand in Poland.

About a fortnight earlier his friend Georg Lucht, who was an engineer by profession, spent a few days at Urberg. They had first met at the 1936

[1] It is possible that copies are still available from the original French distributor, Librairie Amedée Legrand, 93 Bde. Saint-Germain, Paris, 6me.

Düsseldorf congress and Lucht was now an earnest student of Typo-cosmy. In the memorandum that he prepared for me in 1961 Herr Lucht wrote: 'Those were portentous weeks, pregnant with fate. For us the question was whether there would or would not be a war. Krafft was at first optimistic. He thought that Germany would be able to surmount the crisis in a positive manner, as was the case when Germany occupied the Sudetenland and Austria. I did not altogether share this view, not only because Hitler's horoscope was badly afflicted, but above all because the horoscope of the German Reich, cast for 9 November 1918, had two strong Mars directions for 1939–40. Then a letter arrived from Munich from Dr Mrsic, an astrologer who was to be taken seriously. According to his calculations large troop concentrations were to be expected on Germany's eastern borders as from midsummer. He said that there would be danger of war, and that this war could probably not be averted. This letter made a very deep impression on Krafft. When I left we were both convinced that a "catastrophe" would ensue if the dreaded war were to spread.'

I imagine that Krafft must have cast a fair number of horoscopes, his own included, during those tension-ridden days. They cannot have vouchsafed any useful information or, if they did, he preferred to ignore it. From now on everything happened with a strange inevitability.

11

A Thousand Obscure Verses

Much that follows will be difficult to understand without some brief information concerning Michel de Nostredame (1503–66), the French physician and astrologer who was the author of a renowned collection of rhymed prophecies that have been reprinted time and again, and not only in French, ever since the first of them were published in 1555. Indeed, it is difficult to think of any other sixteenth-century French writer whose work has been so frequently reprinted or discussed in commentaries. Understandably, perhaps, the book known as the *Prophéties* has never been of great interest to scholars and, as far as I know, hardly anything has been published about its complicated bibliography since the appearance of a short article by Graf Carl von Klinckowstroem in 1913.[1] Krafft, who knew his Nostradamus literature extremely well, estimated that about forty different editions of the *Prophéties* were issued between 1555 and the end of the seventeenth century and as many again between 1700 and 1940. In this context he appears to have equated commentaries or partial reprints with editions of the original work. Be that as it may, Nostradamiana of all kinds, including periodical articles, is extraordinarily extensive and a lot more has been published since 1940.

The best of the early editions appears to be the one printed at Lyons by Benoist Rigaud in 1568, two years after Nostradamus's death, since this contains 300 prophecies that had not previously been published. The book is divided into ten *Centuries*, each containing a hundred quatrains or four-line verses, and every quatrain represents an individual prophecy. These thousand prophecies are not presented in any obviously chronological order and every one of them must be 'interpreted' separately. Many of them offer a number of possible solutions while others appear to defy any elucidation whatever. Generations of students of Nostradamus have wrestled with these fascinating verses and have read into them both the possible and the impossible. Time scales count for nothing and a quatrain that had a specific historical meaning for, say, a seventeenth-century commentator, will often have a completely different one for a Nostradamus researcher alive, for instance, today.

[1] C. von Klinckowstroem, 'Die ältesten Ausgaben der "Prophéties" des Nostradamus' in *Zeitschrift für Bücherfreunde*, Leipzig, 1913, pp. 361–72. This writer described twenty-five early editions published between 1555 and 1644. Krafft provided some useful information about the textual transmission of the *Prophéties* in his little privately-printed periodical *Nostra Damur* (No. 1, November 1940). The first serious study in English was C. A. Ward's *Oracles of Nostradamus*, [1891]. The only other English commentary that I would care to recommend is James Laver's *Nostradamus, or the Future Foretold*, 1942; Penguin reprint 1952.

Two typical examples follow.[1] The first is the famous quatrain (IX, 20) that has been widely supposed to refer to Louis XVI's flight from Paris to Varennes in June 1792. It reads:

> *De nuit viendra parla forest de Reines,*
> *Deux pars vaultorte Herne la pierre blanche,*
> *Le moine noir en gris dedans Varennes*
> *Esleu cap. cause tempeste feu, sang tranche.*

Mr James Laver's translation of this quatrain reads: ' "By night will come into Varennes through the forest [of Reines] two married persons . . . by a circuitous route (from *vaulx*, a valley and *torte*, tortuous), Herne, the white stone, and the monk in grey, the Elected Capet; and the result will be tempest, and fire and blood and *tranche* (*trancher*, to cut, to slice)." . . . But why the "Elected Capet"? Because Louis XVI was the first King of France to hold his position not by Divine Right but by the will of a Constituent Assembly. And he is flying through the forest by night, this elected king who is also a monk, or monkish by temperament . . . and he is dressed in grey (which we have seen to be the case) and the end of his adventure will be the *tranche* of the guillotine.'

Any attempt to pierce the sense of Nostradamus's verses is like trying to solve an immensely difficult crossword puzzle clue, and at the end of one's labours one can never be sure that the 'interpretation' is correct.

My second example is said to concern Napoleon I (I, 60).

> *Un Empereur naistra pres d'Italie,*
> *Qui à l'Empire sera vendu bien cher :*
> *Diront avec quels gens il se ralie,*
> *Qu'on trouvera moins prince que boucher.*

Mr Laver's translation: 'An Emperor will be born near Italy who will cost the Empire dear; when it is seen with what people he allies himself he will be found less like a prince than a butcher.'

Modern Nostradamus studies date from the publication of Eugène Bareste's *Nostradamus*, Paris, 1840, a book that attracted so much attention that it was reprinted twice in the year of its publication. Bareste's work was followed, among others, by Anatole Le Pelletier's *Les Oracles de Michel de Nostradame*, 1867, and the Abbé Charles Nicoullaud's *Nostradamus, ses prophéties*, Paris, 1914. At this point I will deal with Nicoullaud's interpretation of quatrain III, 57, because of its bearing upon the Krafft story. It reads:

> *Sept fois changer verrez gent Britannique,*
> *Taintz en sang en deux cens nonante an :*
> *Franche non point par appuy Germanique,*
> *Aries doubte son pole Bastarnan.*

[1] The texts are from the Benoist Rigaud edition, Lyons, 1568.

One cannot begin to attempt to interpret any quatrain without first trying to establish the period or even the year to which it might conceivably refer. Nicoullaud suggested that the first two lines of III, 57 implied that during a period of 290 years (*deux cens nonante ans*) Britain would change her ruling dynasty seven times. Thus a point of departure had to be found. He first thought of 1603, the year when James I came to the throne and added 290 to 1603. This suggested 1893, a year in which nothing of any importance occurred. Next he took the year in which Charles I was executed, namely 1649, and once again added 290, this time obtaining 1939. This latter date must now be equated with *Taintz en sang*, i.e. 'tinged with blood', which is certainly appropriate for the year in which the Second World War began, although Nicoullaud did *not* foresee that eventuality.

In 1921 C. Loog, a German postal official who lived in Berlin, published a little book with the title *Die Weissagungen des Nostradamus* (*The Prophecies of Nostradamus*). It was still in print (5th edition) in 1940. Loog claimed to have discovered some kind of cabalist or 'numerological' key to the solution of the quatrains. On the last page of the first edition Loog's publisher claimed that the author had revealed to him, under a pledge of secrecy, the 'code word' that would provide the essential clue for the interpretation of all the quatrains. This disclosure was made on 22 December 1920. In order to ensure priority of discovery Loog made an affidavit before a notary some weeks later.

In the case of the *Sept fois changer verrez gent Britannique* Loog followed Nicoullaud in taking 1649 as his starting point for the subsequent addition of 290 years, and proceeded to interpret the quatrain as follows: 'In 1939 there will be the last noteworthy change of dynasty in Britain. "Aries [zodiacal sign] will clearly have doubts about his protectorate Bastarnien." In the era of Tacitus the German tribe of the Bastarnae was on the other side of the river Vistula, hence in "Poland". Aries, the first sign in the zodiac, rules the East. Nostradamus therefore clearly indicates that in 1939 there will be a critical state of affairs in the revived State of Poland hand in hand with Britain's last and greatest crisis.'

So far, so good: Germany invaded Poland in 1939 and Great Britain declared war on Germany. But why had Loog identified this quatrain with Poland in the first instance? He found his clue in Le Pelletier's *Les Oracles de Nostradame*, 1867. But for his interpretation of III, 57 Le Pelletier took 1501, and *not* 1649, as his starting point. By adding 290 to 1501 he obtained 1791, which he equated with the French Revolution. Furthermore, it was he who identified the Bastarnae, a roving tribe which first appeared on the lower Danube in *c.* 200 B.C., with the territory east of the River Vistula, i.e. Poland. Thus Loog took his interpretative elements from both Le Pelletier and Nicoullaud and arrived at speculative although eventually strangely accurate conclusions that owed something to *both* sources.

Loog's work was issued by the Johannes Baum Verlag at Pfullingen in Württemberg, an obscure firm that specialised in the publication of rather messy occult literature. Indeed, his observations on quatrain III, 57 might well have been ignored if they had not been mentioned in a book published only a year later (in 1922) but which was nevertheless still being read almost two decades after. This was Dr H. H. Kritzinger's *Mysterien von Sonne und Seele* (*Mysteries of the Sun and the Soul*), which Frau Dr Goebbels, of all people, perused one evening in the autumn of 1939 and, as we will see, with some very unexpected results. This brings me to the story that Dr Kritzinger told me when I visited him at Karlsruhe in 1961.

'Oh yes, I was well-acquainted with poor Karl Ernst Krafft,' he said. 'Indeed, I was directly, although in a sense accidently, responsible for his ultimate arrival in Berlin early in 1940 to work on Nostradamus for Dr Goebbels.'

I had a miniature tape recorder with me and at that point switched it on. At Mannheim the previous day I had learned something about Krafft's activities after he came to Berlin, and now, quite unexpectedly, was to learn about the succession of coincidences that had brought him there.

'In 1939 I would have supposed that my book *Mysterien von Sonne und Seele*, which had been published about seventeen years earlier, would have been completely forgotten,' Dr Kritzinger commenced, 'but this was by no means the case, for the book was still being read. Now in that volume, which appeared in 1922, I included a chapter on Nostradamus and his prophecies and referred to a passage in Loog's recent book on the same subject. Loog had suggested that a certain quatrain [i.e. III, 57] indicated that in 1939 a major crisis in Great Britain would coincide with a Polish one. As far as I was concerned my reference to Loog's interpretation had almost catastrophic results. Not long after the outbreak of war in 1939 Frau Dr Goebbels, got hold of my book and was reading it in bed late one evening when she came across the passage in question. Dr Goebbels was already asleep, but she was so excited that she roused him and made him read it. The strange thing is that at about this time at least four people sent him copies of my book with the reference to the 1939 prediction underlined, so now he was rather interested.

'A certain Colonel von Herwarth, a retired army officer who had a job at the Propaganda Ministry, contacted me and said that Dr Goebbels wanted to talk to me. He told me that he would let me know when an appointment would be made for me to see him. Personally I was horrified at the prospect of this encounter because one never knew how any dealings with these top Nazi gentry would turn out. Thus when I left home on 4 December 1939 to go to the Propaganda Ministry I felt distinctly apprehensive. My wife told me that after I left she kept looking at the door, and wondered if I would ever return. I was with Dr Goebbels for exactly fifteen minutes, from 12.50 to 1.5 p.m. The meeting passed off far more easily than I had ever dared hope, but then Dr Goebbels could be very affable when he wanted to be. If he was pleasant to me, it was merely because he thought I had something up my sleeve that he might not be able to get from anyone else.

'He began by talking about Loog's now famous interpretation of quatrain III, 57, the one that begins *Sept fois changer verrez gent Britannique.* It was the manner in which this prophecy had apparently been fulfilled that impressed Dr Goebbels and others at the Propaganda Ministry. They could see a host of psychological warfare possibilities and obviously supposed that any Nostradamus expert would be able to provide other surprising instances for use for propaganda purposes outside Germany.

' "Have you got anything else on the same lines?" he kept on asking, as if I could shake one interesting prediction after another about Great Britain and the war out of my sleeve. "What's going to happen next?" was another question he asked. I said that I had no idea. But Dr Goebbels was insistent. "But surely since you understand the basis of the thing [i.e. Nostradamus], you must at least have an inkling," he said.

'I replied that I was only aware of what certain astrologers of my acquaintance were saying, and that I certainly could not vouch for the accuracy of *their* statements. I tried to explain that I had no personal interest in trying to predict the future and added that Nostradamus was a hobby of mine because of my interest in prophetic literature generally. For me the question was whether or not ancient prophecies had actually been fulfilled. At any rate, I eventually managed to persuade him that I certainly had no prophetic gifts myself.

' "Well, what have your astrologer friends got to say about the present situation?" Dr Goebbels asked. I quoted Herr Saenger's remark that Daladier, the French prime minister, would soon retire from politics. Saenger was a retired schoolmaster and was well known in Berlin astrological circles. "On what grounds did he make that prediction?" Dr Goebbels asked. I explained that it was on the basis of comparing Daladier's horoscope with Churchill's and those of other leading allied politicians.[1] Then Goebbels said: "Well, perhaps I can get something started. I want someone to work right through Nostradamus for me. Can *you* tackle the job for me?"

'I was flabbergasted but somehow recovered my composure. "This work can only be done by someone with plenty of spare time," I said, "and as director of a scientific research institute under the *Heereswaffenamt* [Army Ordnance department] I'm up to my eyes in work." Goebbels asked whom I could recommend as the best available Nostradamus

---

[1] It is more likely that Dr Kritzinger referred to Neville Chamberlain's horoscope. Winston Churchill was not yet prime minister.

specialist, so I suggested Loog. Then the meeting ended and I was relieved to make my escape with a whole skin.

'Loog was summoned to Berlin and came to see me. When he learned what it was all about he was distinctly stuffy. He didn't want to have anything to do with the business. However, during the past few years he had made a complete new German translation of the *Prophéties* together with a commentary and he left the manuscript with me. For Loog's sake I didn't hand it over to the Propaganda Ministry people but fobbed them off with the excuse that the material wasn't suitable for "processing" for psychological warfare purposes. This was probably true in any case. But they still insisted that they wanted a Nostradamus expert so I mentioned Krafft's name, and that is why he eventually turned up in Berlin. As far as he was concerned the ultimate results of his involvement in this business were nothing less than disastrous, but none of us could foresee that at the time. Krafft was a queer sort of chap, you know, and extremely ambitious. He had been stuck at Urberg in the depths of the Black Forest ever since the beginning of the war. This Nostradamus assignment was just what he wanted. . . .'

'And like the proverbial fly he walked straight into the spider's net?' I suggested.

'Unhappily, yes!' said Dr Kritzinger.

There are a number of references to Dr Goebbels' current interest in the use of astrology and bogus prophecies for propaganda purposes in the records of the secret daily ministerial conferences held at the Propaganda Ministry.[1] Half a dozen minutes made during a period of six weeks (30 October–13 December 1939) indicate that he was also keeping a watchful eye on the home front. On 30 October he demanded an immediate report on the contents of the surviving astrological periodicals and almanacs in order to be able to decide for himself whether or not they represented a public danger. At the 'Promi' press conference held the same day journalists were told to exercise great discretion when mentioning astrological predictions. On 2 November it was decided that in view of current rumours whose origins could be traced to fortune-tellers, clairvoyants and astrologers, Party offices were to be instructed to be on the alert. On 10 November he ordered that the astrological publications should be carefully examined for anything that could be construed as a prediction of the attempt to assassinate Hitler at the Munich Bürgerbräu beer cellar on 8 November. An astonishing prediction made by Krafft had aroused great interest in exalted circles in Berlin the previous day.[2]

On 22 November it was resolved that all fortune-telling publications

[1] See W. A. Boelcke, *Kriegspropaganda 1939–41 : Geheime Ministerkonferenzen im Reichspropagandaministerium*, Stuttgart, 1966.
[2] The story of this prediction is told in the next chapter.

should be banned. At the same meeting it was decided to go ahead with the preparation of a Nostradamus leaflet in French. On 5 December, the day after Dr Kritzinger's memorable meeting with Dr Goebbels, Dr Karl Bömer was instructed to consider the draft of the text for this leaflet with Colonel von Herwarth. The latter, it will be remembered, had approached Dr Kritzinger on Dr Goebbels' behalf. On 11 December Dr Goebbels asked for copies of all the 1940 astrological almanacs. Their sale was forbidden on the following day. On 13 December Dr Goebbels referred to propaganda based on astrological material and mentioned the excellence of the Nostradamus leaflet. He suggested that the horoscopes of leading allied personalities should be cast, presumably for psychological warfare purposes. There is no further reference to astrology or Nostradamus in the minutes until 27 March 1940. By that time Krafft had already been in Berlin for close on three months.

MICHEL NOSTRADAMUS
An apocryphal engraving (1622).

12

Krafft's 'Hitler' Prediction

The German-Soviet non-aggression pact was signed on 21 August 1939 and the Kraffts were still at Urberg on 26 August. Two or three days later they decided to return to Switzerland and arranged for a taxi from the near-by town of St Blasien to take them to Zürich, a matter of sixty miles. But when the car arrived the driver said he could only go as far as the border at Waldshut because the frontier might be closed at any moment and he might not be able to return. So they resolved to stay on at Urberg and await developments.

Krafft was in a difficult position. He felt that he had burned his boats in Switzerland and in any case had no desire to live there permanently. Dr Ferrière wrote to him on 4 September, the day after Great Britain and France declared war on Germany, and begged him to return. Krafft replied on 9 September and said that he could not endure the prospect of living in a country which had for years past been led by the nose by *joupins* (yids), and where he would no doubt be speedily locked up in prison. The presumable grounds for his fear were that he supposed that the Swiss security authorities already suspected that he might be a potential German fifth-columnist. To Dr Ferrière he now expressed the hope that he would be able to place his knowledge and abilities at the service of the 'unjustly abused and slandered Third Reich'. All this was written on a postcard. Dr Ferrière wrote to him again on 11 September. Krafft returned the letter to him on 20 September with his own comments scribbled in the margin. He mentioned important tasks that lay ahead of him. He said, too, that thanks to a favourable reaction on the part of certain highly-placed persons, he would now be in a position to further the cause of what he called 'our science' in Berlin.

A long letter dated 18 October 1939 that he wrote to his friend Mlle Marguerite Panchaud at Lausanne must have pleased the German censor-ship authorities, since it indicated that Krafft had completely swallowed the Nazi propaganda line. This is an extraordinary document, with fre-quent allusions to the machinations of international freemasonry and Jewry and warnings that it would undoubtedly be Switzerland's turn to be invaded if further unjustified criticisms of Germany's actions and policies continued to be printed in the Swiss press. He even advised poor Mlle Panchaud to read the *Protocols of the Elders of Zion*, a notorious anti-semitic forgery.

The clue to Krafft's violently anti-Swiss attitude is to be found in one brief passage. In Germany, he declared, personal ability and superiority were recognised and appreciated, while in Switzerland such qualities were merely scorned. It is clear, therefore, that in Krafft's opinion the land of his birth had never accepted him at his own valuation, while in Germany, given the chance, he hoped to achieve the recognition that he felt to be his due. His problem, however, was to find a suitable opportunity to show his mettle. It is not improbable that the first steps to that end had already been taken, for a few weeks earlier, probably just before 20 September, he had a promising meeting with his friend Dr Fesel.

Dr Heinrich Fesel (1890–1958) had originally been a schoolmaster. He was an accomplished classical scholar and knew some Sanskrit. He was also interested in astrology and was at one time a member of Herr Goerner's circle at Mannheim. When Goerner organised a study group for astrology and graphology there early in 1933 Dr Fesel, together with a certain Dr Brauch, assisted Goerner in instructing learners in these two arts. It was Goerner who originally introduced Krafft and Fesel to one another. Fesel later moved to Berlin but remained in touch with Goerner and never failed to ask for news of Krafft. He subscribed to Krafft's *Economic Bulletin*. Herr Wilhelm Wulff told me that it was Walter Schellenberg, the head of Section VI (Foreign Intelligence) of the *Reichssicherheitshauptamt*, who recruited Dr Fesel as a member of the RSHA. According to Herr Wulff, Fesel was far from being an enthusiastic National Socialist and speedily regretted his connections with Himmler's secret intelligence service.[1]

It is likely that Krafft had written to Fesel to enquire about the possibility of employment of some kind. In any case financial difficulties were already on the horizon. Latterly he had been living on capital or his savings but now it was urgently necessary for him to earn some money. The problem was that he was unable to practise professionally as a 'psychological adviser' in Germany. More accurately, what he could not legally do was offer so-called psychological advice on the basis of astrological deductions in return for payment, since professional astrology had been frowned upon in Germany for some years past.

Fesel, probably on the instructions of his superiors, arranged to meet Krafft at Titisee, a small holiday resort half-way between Freiburg and Urberg. The precise date of this encounter is unknown but it was undoubtedly very soon after war began. Fesel then agreed on behalf of the RSHA to make Krafft a monthly payment of 500 Marks in return for

---

[1] Dr Fesel was employed in Section VII, whose function was 'ideological research', e.g. the investigation of freemasonry, occultism, strange cults, etc. At one time it was directed by Professor Dr F. A. Six. According to Charles Wighton, it was 'the wastepaper basket of the RSHA. There the SS cranks whom even Himmler found too much, found shelter.' (Charles Wighton, *Heydrich*, Corgi paperback edition, 1963, p. 184.)

memoranda to be written by him. The choice of subject was left to Krafft's discretion but it is evident that these papers were to be on more or less the same lines as his *Economic Bulletin*, i.e. a mixture of political or economic comment and speculation with occasional references to planetary cycles and other astral phenomena.

It is difficult to assess why the RSHA should have been prepared to put Krafft on its pay roll, since anything he might have to say about political or economic affairs can hardly have been of interest to any intelligence department. Nor is it easy to believe that Dr Fesel's employers were prepared to pay anything for monthly 'predictions' based upon Krafft's astrological theories. My own view is that Fesel's people merely ¦wanted to keep a potentially useful agent on ice for the time being. The fact that Krafft had a Swiss passport was obviously advantageous to the Germans since it would allow him to travel more or less freely outside Germany, e.g. in France and the Low Countries. Krafft was careful not to accept this employment without first consulting the Swiss authorities in Germany. According to a memorandum written by Frau Krafft long after the war, and now deposited at the *Institut für Zeitgeschichte* (Institute for Contemporary History) at Munich, when Krafft visited Berlin in order to discuss the proposed work with what she vaguely called 'the department in question', he also called at the Swiss embassy and was informed that he would not be contravening Swiss laws or regulations. Fesel must have provided Krafft with a suitable 'cover' story because it is highly unlikely that Krafft would have been permitted to blurt out: 'I want to do some work for the *Reichssicherheitshauptamt*!' His arrangement with the RSHA was certainly finalised during October 1939.

That the memoranda that Krafft wrote for Dr Fesel's department were not particularly secret is implied by a statement of Herr Goerner's. His secretary, Gerhard zur Horst, typed the fair copies of the monthly memoranda for Dr Fesel, and Goerner himself read them. He recalled that Krafft's papers dealt with such subjects as the Polish campaign and its aftermath, the possibilities of military action in the west and various propaganda themes. On 2 November Krafft sent Dr Fesel a communication of a kind that the latter was by no means anxious to circulate at the RSHA headquarters in Berlin. In this he predicted that Hitler's life would be in danger between 7–10 November and actually used the expression 'possibility of an attempt of assassination by the use of explosive material'. Fesel filed the document and preserved a discreet silence for the very good reason that astrological speculations concerning the Führer were strictly tabu. There was to be a surprising aftermath. On 9 November 1939 the German public learned that there had been an unsuccessful attempt on Hitler's life. The previous evening the Führer and other members of the Nazi old guard had attended the traditional annual reunion at the Bürgerbräu beer hall at Munich to commemorate the 1923

Putsch attempt. Hitler and a few other important Party members left unexpectedly early to return to Berlin by rail. A few minutes after their departure a bomb hidden in a pillar directly behind the speaker's rostrum exploded, killing seven persons and wounding sixty-three others.

Krafft, who never knew when to let well alone, was pathetically anxious to draw attention to his astrological prowess and immediately dispatched a telegram to Rudolf Hess at the Reich Chancery at Berlin in which he referred to his original letter to Dr Fesel and stated that Hitler might still be in danger during the next few days. Some months later he gleefully told Georg Lucht that his telegram had 'exploded like a second bomb in Berlin'. The embarrassed Dr Fesel was forthwith ordered to produce the letter. It actually reached the Führer, who showed it to Dr Goebbels at luncheon at the Reich Chancery on 9 November.[1] That same day four officials from the Freiburg Gestapo headquarters fetched Krafft from Urberg for interrogation and on the following day dispatched him under guard to Berlin for further cross-examination. Herr Goerner told me that apart from satisfying the security people that he had nothing to do with the Munich business, Krafft was even able to convince them that accurate astrological predictions were possible under certain circumstances. He was then informed that he was free to return to Urberg. It was as well that he had asked the *Sicherheitsdienst* for a chit to the effect that it had nothing against him because, according to Professor Bender, when he arrived back at Freiburg the local Gestapo tried to arrest him again at the railway station. He probably took the opportunity to remain in Berlin for a few days. *Sterne und Mensch*, March–April 1940, reported that he had attended a meeting of the Academic Astrological Society on 21 November 1939.

On the same day that Krafft sent his rash telegram to Berlin, two British intelligence officers were lured across the Dutch-German border at Venlo and captured by Walter Schellenberg (who had yet to achieve his eventual eminence in the RSHA) with the help of an SS detachment. One of them was Captain S. Payne Best, whose account of his subsequent experiences was published in his book *The Venlo Incident* in 1950. Once again there were some unexpected astrological implications.

In the course of one of his many interrogations Best was asked about his connection with a certain Herr K. von H., who was an astrologer. A few weeks earlier a friend had dined with Best and his wife. Their guest was accompanied by her son 'who had come to The Hague from Berlin where he had a remunerative practice as a consultant astrologer. . . . Some-

---

[1] See W. A. Boelcke, *Kriegspropaganda 1939–41*, Stuttgart, 1966, p. 223, whose annotation is based upon the 'Nostradamus' chapter in Boris von Borresholm, *Dr Goebbels nach Aufzeichnungen aus seiner Umgebung*, 1949. While the substance of Borresholm's story is correct, he may not be a completely reliable source. Neither Lucht nor Goerner said anything about the letter reaching Hitler and it may have been written earlier than 2 November.

how or other the Gestapo had got on to this and had succeeded in ferreting out the man in question. He had at once been arrested and subjected to a thorough grilling for, as it appeared, he had been employed to work out Hitler's horoscope or whatever else astrologers do.'[1]

One Gestapo official—Best described him as 'a long and very beautiful young man with fair waved hair, tinted lips and cheeks, and pencilled eyebrows'—was very anxious to know what Best had arranged with Herr K. von H., the astrologer. Best said that he had arranged nothing with him and in any case hardly knew the man. His interrogator then said: 'Why did you tell Herr K. von H. not to return to Germany until *after the change of the moon*?' Best was flummoxed until he suddenly remembered that a German agent with whom he had talked in Holland prior to his capture had solemnly informed him that Hitler firmly believed that his enterprises depended for their success upon the phase of the moon at the time of their initiation. He recalled, too, that he had 'pulled K. von H.'s leg in a mild sort of way and had told him that it would be better if he postponed his own return to Germany until after the new moon or a few days later.'

When I read Captain Payne Best's book I felt that the initials K. von H. were vaguely familiar in connection with astrology. Then I realised that Herr K. von H., who had turned up at Best's home at The Hague with his mother, was probably none other than Baron Keun von Hoogerwoerd, a Dutchman who had taught Louis de Wohl astrology in Berlin in the early 1930s. At any rate, that made two astrologers who were arrested in Germany soon after the Munich explosion: Krafft and the Baron, although for entirely unconnected reasons.

An interesting account of the aftermath of the bomb attempt will be found in a recent book by Dr Hans Bernd Gisevius.[2] According to the author, who had his information from Arthur Nebe, the gifted chief of the German criminal police, Hitler, in company with Goebbels, Himmler and Heydrich, was convinced that the Munich plot could only have been staged by a well-organised group. One theory was that it had been organised by Otto Strasser (who was living at Herrliberg, near Zürich, at the time) with the help of the British secret service. Nebe, however, thought that this was nonsense. When he and Gisevius were on the run after Stauffenberg's ill-fated attempt to assassinate Hitler on 20 July 1944 he told Gisevius the following story.

Himmler, it appears, was so astonished at Nebe's scepticism in November 1939 that he summoned a member of his regiment of clairvoyants, in this instance a Viennese 'seer', who forthwith went into a trance on a couch in Himmler's office. The medium proceeded to describe the hazy features

---

[1] S. Payne Best, *The Venlo Incident*, 1950, pp. 60–61.
[2] H. B. Gisevius, *Wo ist Nebe?* (*Where is Nebe?*) Zürich, 1966. An English translation will be published by André Deutsch Ltd, London, in 1968.

of a certain Otto who, he said, was conferring with three well-dressed gentlemen in Switzerland. They were all talking in a foreign language. The gentlemen gave Otto some forged papers and a plan, presumably of the Bürgerbräu building.

Next, in order to establish closer contact with Otto, the medium said that he wanted to handle something from the wreckage at the Bürgerbräu. Nebe gave him a scrap of metal that had nothing to do with the bomb and the flow of useless information continued. The point is that Otto bore no resemblance to Georg Elser, the would-be assassin, who had contrived a highly-effective home-made time bomb without help from anyone else. That the Gestapo picked him up a few days later was largely due to a silly blunder or two on Elser's part, otherwise he might well have escaped undetected.

Himmler's gullibility was in many respects as great as Elser's mechanical skill and personal temerity, but then the *Reichsführer* was a notably silly man. Nebe told Gisevius that Hitler was fascinated by Elser's technical expertise—so much so, indeed, that it was Nebe's impression that Hitler supposed, on occult grounds that there was some mysterious link between Elser and himself.

Dr Kritzinger's memorable encounter with Dr Goebbels took place on 4 December 1939. Subsequent developments were not long delayed. Loog came and went and Krafft was summoned to Berlin for discussions since he, of all possible candidates, appeared to be the best qualified for the task of providing the Propaganda Ministry people with the kind of Nostradamus material that was theoretically required. He was not accorded the privilege of an interview with Dr Goebbels and was seen by Dr Fesel. The latter, as we know, was not employed in the Propaganda Ministry but the authorities may well have decided on security grounds that Krafft should be responsible to his existing contact man. Herr Lucht's memorandum made it very clear that the work had a 'top secret' classification.

On his way back to Urberg, probably on 18–19 December, Krafft spent a night at Mannheim where he had a long talk with Herr Goerner. Dr W. Gollner, a Stuttgart psychiatrist who was interested in astrology and had visited Krafft at Urberg in August 1938, was also present. Krafft told them about his prospective employment and mentioned that Dr Fesel had also suggested that he should undertake some kind of intelligence mission in the Low Countries. Neither Goerner nor Gollner was happy about any of this and both tried to persuade him to stay out of harm's way at Urberg. Krafft, however, was adamant and argued that here was the challenge for which he had long been waiting.

His friends were disturbed, too, when Krafft talked of reviving his *Who's Who in Borderland* project because, as they emphasised, this would be the surest method of attracting the attention of the Gestapo.[1] They were aware that any public identification with astrology or any other occult interests was likely to be increasingly dangerous. Krafft refused to take their objections very seriously because he was convinced that his influential contacts in Berlin would assume a benevolently protective role as far as he was personally concerned.

Dr Gollner wrote to me on 8 September 1961: 'Krafft completely and wholeheartedly believed in the powerful Uranian [magical] force that linked his own horoscope with the Uranus-laden quality of the ruling fascist hierarchy in Germany, and reckoned that it would be this force that would carry him to the top.'

The Kraffts spent Christmas at Urberg, packed their bags and left. Their destination was not Berlin but Eisenach, a small Thuringian town about 200 miles south-west of the capital. I do not know why they chose Eisenach, but in the event they never settled there. Krafft was in Brussels on 29 December, possibly on Fesel's behest, but there is evidence to show that when he and his wife did arrive at Eisenach, probably a few days later, they were unable to find suitable accommodation and travelled on to Berlin.

[1] Since 1934 Krafft had been intermittently planning the publication of a biographical directory of persons interested in astrology and other 'fringe' areas. A number of questionnaire cards were circulated shortly before the publication of the *Traité* in 1939.

13

The Affair of the Tilea Letter

The Kraffts arrived in Berlin during the first week of January 1940 and after spending a few days at an hotel found temporary lodgings at the home of their friend Carl Maria Holzapfel, a writer who lived in the Joachim-Friedrichstrasse in the Halensee suburb. Holzapfel was acquainted with some important Nazis.[1] Georg Lucht was also in Berlin and although a trained engineer was not yet involved in war work. When Krafft asked him if he would like to assist him with the Nostradamus work he gladly accepted. Lucht knew little or nothing about the problem of interpreting the quatrains but he was an efficient typist and it was secretarial help that Krafft needed most. Besides, Lucht obviously greatly admired Krafft, who liked a handy audience. They both attended a meeting at Dr Fesel's office and were required to sign a document recording their undertaking to preserve complete secrecy about their work and not to reveal, in any shape or form, anything they had ostensibly learned from Nostradamus or astrological investigations. According to Lucht, at this time Krafft was seeing Dr Fesel almost daily.

It was not long before Krafft began to make a few contacts of the kind that he had wanted for so long, namely with people of influence in the Third Reich. The incidents described below occurred early in 1940. Herr Lucht recalled them and Frau Krafft also mentioned them in the long memorandum that she left at the *Institut für Zeitgeschichte* at Munich after the war.

Krafft's friend Holzapfel arranged for him to be invited to a party held at the home of Arno Breker, a well-known sculptor who lived in the fashionable Grunewald district. Breker's work was greatly admired by the National Socialists, for whom he created many heroic pieces that exactly corresponded to their romantic conception of the appearance of 'Nordic' men and women.[2]

Krafft arrived late and while a servant took his hat and coat heard a piano being played in the drawing room or studio. The artiste was Frau Elli Ney, a famous concert pianist, who interrupted her performance when he entered the room. One of the guests was Dr Hans Frank, the Governor General of Poland, who was hanged at Nürnberg. It was he who dramatically introduced Krafft with the words: 'This is the man who accurately

---

[1] C. M. Holzapfel (*b.* 1890) was a departmental head in Dr Robert Ley's *Kraft durch Freude* organisation and the author of the adulatory poem 'Dem Führer', published in *Deutsche Bühne*, Jan.–Feb. 1934—in fact, a rabid Nazi.

[2] For particulars of Breker's work see Josef Wulf, *Die Bildenden Künste im Dritten Reich*, Rowohlt paperback edition, 1966.

predicted the attempt on the *Führer's* life!' As Herr Goerner remarked:
'Fame of this kind must have been very sweet for Krafft—public recognition at last!'

Later that evening he was invited to talk about the Nostradamus prophecies and, according to his widow, Dr Frank in particular was greatly interested in his remarks. Dr Bernhard Rust, the Minister for Science, Education and Popular Culture, was also present but failed to share Dr Frank's enthusiasm. Krafft told Lucht that Rust had reacted in a cold and almost unfriendly manner. Herr Goerner also had something to add to the record of that auspicious evening. Krafft is supposed to have shown Herr Breker's guests a 'Dynogram', i.e. a graphic representation of the astrological factors that would supposedly affect Germany during 1940, and to have suggested that the war should not be allowed to continue after the winter of 1942–3. Someone confidently observed that the whole business would certainly be over and done with by that time. For Krafft this must have been a memorable occasion.

It was Holzapfel, too, who arranged for him to visit Dr Robert Ley, the head of the *Deutsche Arbeitsfront* and founder of the *Kraft durch Freude* organisation, at his home one Sunday morning. Holzapfel worked for Ley and had mentioned Krafft's Nostradamus researchers to him. After a lengthy discussion Ley told Krafft that he personally believed in the existence of cosmic influences. Krafft later mentioned to Lucht that he scarcely expected an admission of this kind from a dissipated drunkard like Dr Ley. The Doctor hinted that he would like to own a good edition of the *Prophéties*. It happened that on 7 October 1936 Krafft had given Goerner a copy of the 1689 edition which he inscribed for him, so he wrote to Goerner to ask if he would be willing to sell it. A few days later Goerner received a letter from a member of Ley's staff with an offer of RM300. Herr Goerner was unwilling to part with the book and it was still in his possession when I met him in 1961.

The smooth progress of Krafft's work on Nostradamus was soon interrupted. This was at the end of January 1940 when he received a letter from a certain Monsieur Virgil Tilea, who was none other than the Rumanian Minister in London. They had first met at Zürich in the spring of 1937, shortly before Krafft folded his tents there and left for Germany. At that time M. Tilea was not in the Rumanian diplomatic service. His appointment to the London legation was made in December 1938 and he arrived in Great Britain in January 1939.

In the spring of 1937 M. Tilea's first wife was undergoing treatment at the Bircher-Benner clinic at Zürich and he accompanied her there. Dr Franklin Bircher suggested to M. Tilea that he might like to make Krafft's acquaintance. M. Tilea was not at all interested in astrology but nevertheless agreed, and when he did meet Krafft rather disliked him. M. Tilea told me that he found him mildly repulsive. Krafft said that he would like to cast M. Tilea's horoscope and this offer was accepted. M. Tilea did not expect very much from this curious and, to him, novel operation, but was intrigued a few days later when Krafft gave him some information about an event in his past life of which he could not possibly have had any prior knowledge.

About a year later the Tileas were once more in Zürich. Dr Franklin Bircher asked M. Tilea if he would like to meet Krafft again. M. Tilea said no, but then changed his mind. It had occurred to him to ask Krafft if he would be willing to collaborate in an astrological experiment. Krafft agreed to this and a few days later M. Tilea gave him photocopies of two specimens of handwriting and particulars of the birth data (i.e. date, time and place) of the writers, but without revealing the identities of the individuals whom I will call A. and B. Within a week Krafft provided information about both of them. In his written interpretation for A., Krafft suggested that the man suffered from a schizoid personality and remarked that according to his own experience this was often the case with people of partly Jewish descent. Furthermore, he predicted that A. would be unlikely to survive the month of November 1938. For B. he prophesied that while the subject at present clearly enjoyed a position of considerable authority, even eminence, he would experience a disastrous reverse in or about September 1940.

A. was Corneliu Codreanu, the Rumanian fascist leader and head of the anti-semitic Iron Guard organisation. Krafft had correctly pin-pointed his Jewish ancestry for his mother was a Jewess from Czernowitz, and his prediction also came true since Codreanu was accused of high treason and then shot 'while attempting to escape' on 30 November 1938. B. was King Carol of Rumania, who was obliged to abdicate in favour of his son Michael on 6 September 1940. The Germans occupied Rumania a month later. Hence the second prophecy was also eventually vindicated.

M. Tilea's diaries were not available in London when we discussed a draft of this chapter in May 1965 and he was unable to recall the date when he asked Krafft to prepare an astrological study relating to himself. He said it was in 1938 and it would be logical to assume that it was probably in December 1938, namely immediately after Krafft's Codreanu prediction had been fulfilled. M. Tilea told me that the accuracy of this prediction really impressed him. By now, therefore, he was curious to know what Krafft might have to say about his own future. This proposed astrological delineation was never delivered, although there are references to it in letters written by Krafft to M. Tilea. These are discussed in this chapter.

As I have already mentioned, M. Tilea arrived in London in January 1939. The Germans occupied Czechoslovakia on 15 March and within a matter of days began to make outrageous economic demands upon Rumania. M. Tilea, who was no friend of Hitler's Germany, thereupon perpetrated a diplomatic 'indiscretion' and revealed the outline of these proposed exactions to the British government. If the precise nature of Hitler's expansionist plans in the Balkans was not already evident to the British, it was clear enough now and the Government's attitude stiffened. The German-Rumanian Economic Treaty was signed on 24 March and a week later the British guaranteed to come to Poland's assistance in the event of a German attack. It seems that M. Tilea's intervention had a considerable impact on the formulation of British policy at the time.[1] The Germans were furious with him for letting the cat out of the bag and he was continuously attacked by name in German radio broadcasts.

When the *Traité* was published in July 1939 Krafft immediately sent a copy to M. Tilea, who was at that time understandably too busy either to read the book or write to Krafft. However, he was to be reminded of Krafft's existence soon after the war began when a letter from him arrived in London. Dated 26 September 1939, it was written in English at Urberg and had been mailed to M. Tilea's home address in Bucharest, whence it was forwarded by diplomatic bag. Furthermore, it was written very soon after Krafft's meeting with Dr Fesel at Titisee, when the latter agreed to put him on the *Reichssicherheitshauptamt*'s pay roll. It is unlikely that Krafft had omitted to mention his previous connection with M. Tilea to Dr Fesel, and my assumption is that he was instructed to remain in contact with him. It must be emphasised that M. Tilea was still a person of very considerable interest to the Germans, the more so since he was in London.

Krafft's letter began with a gratuitous hint that following Germany's easy victory in Poland, it would be advisable for Rumania to accept the idea of a 'new order', meaning German *Lebensraum* in the Balkans. 'When we met for the last time at Zürich,' Krafft began, 'you then seemed rather sceptical when I ventured that certain people [i.e. the Germans] had their best time still ahead of themselves, and that a new order in S.E. Europe was inevitable to come. Meanwhile you might have remembered our talks and your confidence in historionomic and cosmobiological laws should have increased.' Next he referred to his Codreanu prognostication: 'From Dr Franklin Bircher I was told past [*sic*] spring that you thought my information given about one of the two birthmaps [i.e. the horoscopes of Codreanu and King Carol] and handwriting was "inspired" by the knowledge of the man concerned. This was not so, and when I actually heard who he was, I was more bewildered than you probably were, about the tragic end of this patriot.'[2]

Krafft wrote to M. Tilea again from Urberg on 12 December 1939. In this communication, which was again written in English, he referred to a previous letter of his which no longer survives. He was still working on M. Tilea's horoscope but required some additional information.

[1] See M. Gilbert and R. Gott, *The Appeasers*, 1963.
[2] I asked M. Tilea about Codreanu's patriotism. 'He was a muddled visionary!' M. Tilea replied.

'In my last letter I had asked you a few complementary questions, in view of the working out of your birthmap, e.g.: the birthdates of your wife and both your parents (hours'not necessary in this case); also the (renewed) birthdate of the other person about whom you desire to have this horoscope done. Moreover, I had suggested that I would not only let you have a summary of the historionomic studies to be made, but a detailed exposure of them so as to offer you the opportunity to check my conclusions by your own judgement. How about that? (N.B. These detailed studies will have to be made in any case, so why [should I] not write them out completely?!)'

Krafft's theory was that a satisfactory astrological interpretation could only be achieved by comparing the native's horoscope with those of people particularly close to him, hence his request for particulars of the birth dates of M. Tilea's wife and parents. This letter was written a few days before he went to Berlin to discuss the Nostradamus project with Dr Fesel's department.

I have already mentioned that Dr Fesel is supposed to have invited Krafft to undertake an intelligence mission of some kind in the Low Countries. This may explain why Krafft's next letter to M. Tilea, dated 29 December 1939, was written at Brussels. There is little of interest in this document, which is in French, and I imagine that he wrote it for two reasons: firstly because it could be mailed direct to London without the knowledge of anyone in Germany; secondly to give M. Tilea a further reminder of his existence. In it he drew M. Tilea's attention to an article by R. H. Naylor, the well-known British astrologer, that he had obviously just read at Brussels in the November issue of *Prediction*, which was published in London. It is unlikely that he would have been able to see a copy of this periodical in Germany. Krafft liked Naylor and while at Brussels asked his agent Horicks to send him a copy of the *Traité d'Astro-Biologie*. Mrs Phyllis Naylor, his widow, recalls the book's arrival early in January 1940. Krafft had written a dedication on the fly-leaf and she told me in 1959 that both she and her husband wondered why the inscription appeared to have been written at Brussels when both of them supposed that Krafft was in Switzerland.

In this letter to M. Tilea Krafft mentioned that he hoped to be able to send him the promised astrological study by the end of January. 'You can always reach me at the old [Swiss] address,' he added, 'or via Mr Horicks, who is the Belgian agent for my book.' He said nothing about his impending move to Berlin. M. Tilea wrote to Krafft at his Swiss address at the end of January 1940. This letter, which reached him in Berlin in the middle of February, contained particulars, as requested, of the birth dates of M. Tilea's wife and children but those of his parents were not included.

So far Krafft's correspondence with M. Tilea had not given rise to any difficulties with Dr Fesel's department—my theory is that the *Reichs-*

sicherheitshauptamt had been in the picture since September 1939—but now he began to run into troubled waters. Krafft spoke to Dr Fesel about his intended reply to M. Tilea and showed him a draft. Dr Fesel said that he would have to consult his own chiefs. A week or two later Krafft called on Dr Fesel to collect his monthly salary and asked if any decision had been reached about the matter. Dr Fesel replied that the letter could be sent, but added that some alterations would be required. In its present form, he said, its tone was not sufficiently pro-German and he advised Krafft to paint Germany's military prospects in far more glowing colours. Finally, he emphasised that if Krafft were not willing to agree to this, permission for the letter to be mailed would be withheld.

According to Georg Lucht, Krafft was incensed and insisted that this was a private matter between Tilea and himself, adding that M. Tilea was not paying him for any professional services and that Dr Fesel's bosses had no right to exert pressure of this kind. Dr Fesel merely shrugged his shoulders and said that he would in any case have to keep the draft. For Krafft this was the last straw. He threw the banknotes that Fesel had just handed to him on the table and yelled: 'I haven't done any work for *your* department during the past month so here's your money. Furthermore, this draft is remaining in *my* possession!'

Whether he actually took the draft away with him I do not know, but he arrived home without his month's pay. The situation was tricky enough in all conscience, for apart from the fact that acts of defiance were always risky in Dr Fesel's department, the Kraffts now had barely enough money for their immediate expenses.

Frau Krafft's memorandum gives the impression that it was at this point that her husband severed his connection with the *Reichssicherheitshauptamt*. While his salaried employment may well have ceased, by no means the last had been heard of the letter. The RSHA decided that a reply was to be sent to M. Tilea and on its own terms. Herr Lucht informed me that he had to type a number of successive versions before Dr Fesel's chiefs declared themselves satisfied. The RSHA was evidently determined that the letter should reach M. Tilea without fail. It was typed in duplicate by Herr Lucht. One copy was dated 22 February but a note at the end explained that it was not ready for signature until 27 February. Krafft added a handwritten postscript in English: 'I take the opportunity of having this letter sent to you by a friend going to Rumania.' This friend was a convenient fiction. The letter was taken to Rumania by an RSHA courier and was mailed to Bucharest by registered post from Brasov on 14 March 1940. The envelope, which was addressed in Krafft's handwriting, bore the instruction: 'In case of absence, please forward by diplomatic bag.' The other copy, dated 14 March, went by ordinary mail from Berlin to Bucharest and was opened by the German military censorship. According to Herr Goerner, who heard about these occurrences from Krafft some two years later, Krafft was delighted with the 'cloak and dagger' business connected with the letter posted at Brasov.[1]

Krafft began his letter by apologising for his tardiness in replying to M. Tilea's communication which, he said, did not reach him until the middle of February, the delay being due to several changes of address. He mentioned that he had been invited to Berlin in mid-December for a discussion about Nostradamus and that for the past five weeks he had been working on a new edition of the *Prophéties* on behalf of a Society and in a connection with a 'government department'. He hoped that the book, which would contain a scholarly introduction, would be ready by the beginning of April and offered to inscribe a copy for M. Tilea.[2] In the meantime said that he would be glad to know if the book should be sent via the Rumanian legation in Berlin. He added that it would not be available in the bookshops 'so as not to provide fresh food for superstition', and that it would contain undeniable proof of Nostradamus's prophetic gifts.

After these preliminaries Krafft mentioned that he intended to prepare a fresh study of M. Tilea's horoscope and this would include deductions made on the basis of what he called an 'improved seven-year rhythm'. This rhythm, he explained, did not consist of exactly seven years but was one of seven years *minus* seven weeks, the starting point being the sun's zodiacal position at the time of birth. In terms of conventional astrological techniques this was a recent 'discovery' of Krafft's.

So much for the first page of a letter that ran to twelve large quarto sides, and which poor Georg Lucht was required to type and re-type until Dr Fesel's department was satisfied. Krafft now turned to an assessment of M. Tilea's personal position and affairs at that time. But the remainder of the letter, indeed the greater part of it, consisted of a highly-tendentious review of the current European political situation seen through German spectacles. This extraordinary communication was nothing less than an exercise, although by no means a subtle one, in psychological warfare.

It happened that M. Tilea was in Bucharest when the letter mailed at

[1] Herr Goerner gave me Herr Lucht's memorandum, which had been written specially for my benefit, on 8 July 1961. This document contained a detailed account of what had transpired in Berlin in 1940. A few days later I met M. Tilea in London and showed him this document. It was of considerable interest to him because hitherto he had been unaware of what had happened in Germany. M. Tilea lent me the letter dated 14 March, still in its envelope, that had been opened by the German military censorship, also the envelope mailed at Brasov. See the illustrations facing pp. 181 and 196.

[2] It seems that the publication date had already been delayed, for a postcard to his friend Dr Ferrière dated 19 February 1940 indicates that Krafft had expected the book to be ready by the middle of March. This presupposes that most of the material had been available *before* Krafft arrived in Berlin, but this may well have been the case since Krafft had been studying Nostradamus since the early 1930s and it is likely that he had been recently searching for possible allusions to the Second World War when he was still at Urberg. 'You will receive a copy,' he informed Dr Ferrière, 'and you will be astonished to read all the "Seer of Salon" was able to predict for our times. It is clearly not very reassuring for the British!'

Urberg b/St Blasien, Sept. 26th 39
Permanent address: Commugny
(Switzerland)

Dear Mr. Tilea,

When we met for the last time, at Zurich, you then seemed rather sceptical when I ventured that certain people had their best time still ahead of themselves, and that a new order in S.E. Europe was inevitable to come. Meanwhile you might have remembered our talks, and your confidence in historimmic and cosmobiolgical laws should have increased.

From Dr. Franklin Bircher I ~~was told~~ past spring that you had thought my information given about one of the two birthmaps and handwritings was 'inspired' by the knowledge of the man concerned. This was not so, and when I actually heard who he was, I was more bewildered than you probably were, about the tragic end of this patriot.

About two months ago I had ordered a copy of my recent 'Traité d' Astro-Biologie' to be sent to you to Embassy of R. at London, and I hope that you got the book which, I feel sure, will interest you in more than one respect.

Should you find time to read it I should like to know one day your appreciation of this rather unorthodox piece of work.

Meanwhile I am, with my compliments for Mrs. Tilea, sincerely:

K.E. Krafft:

11. Letter written by Krafft to M. Virgil Tilea, the Rumanian Minister in London, in September 1939.

12. The envelope was addressed by Krafft in Berlin. It was mailed in Rumania by Himmler's intelligence service on 14 March 1940.

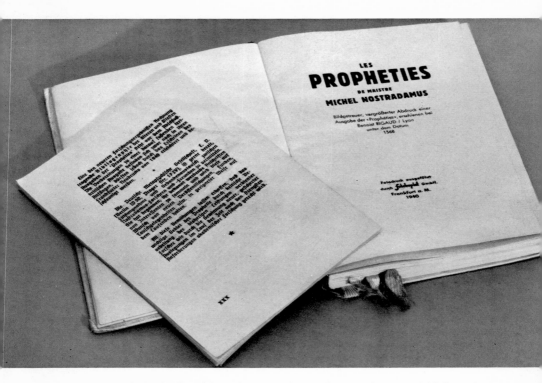

13. Krafft's facsimile edition of *Les Prophéties* of Nostradamus and his introductory pamphlet. The publication was secretly sponsored by one of Himmler's departments in 1940.

Brasov on 14 March arrived there. His mother had just died and he had returned to Rumania via Italy and Jugoslavia, carefully avoiding the shorter route via Vienna. He had begun to be suspicious of Krafft as early as the previous autumn, namely when he received the letter that Krafft had written at Urberg on 26 September, with its not very subtle allusion to a prospective German 'New Order' in south-east Europe. Again, apart from that propagandist passage, he wondered why Krafft had remained in Germany. It was for these reasons, he told me, that he decided to keep in touch with Krafft and answered his various letters, on the assumption that Krafft would sooner or later be bound to give himself away.

The fact that this last letter had been written in Berlin and then ostentatiously mailed in Rumania appeared to confirm two hypotheses: firstly that Krafft's employers, whoever they were, obviously wanted to make very sure that M. Tilea would receive this communication; secondly, that if Krafft, of all people, was in Berlin, then he was undoubtedly advising the top Nazis, possibly even Hitler himself. M. Tilea was prepared to believe that Krafft was a highly-gifted astrologer—his successful Codreanu prediction had shown that—and according to M. Tilea's information Hitler was known to believe in astrology. His colleague M. Raoul Bossy, the Rumanian Minister in Berlin, had reported as much and M. Tilea had read this interesting information in one of the secret intelligence reports circulated by the Rumanian Foreign Office to its embassies and legations abroad.

His suspicions were confirmed a week or two later when he visited Zürich on his way back to London. Mme Tilea was at the Bircher-Benner clinic for treatment and he was able to discuss the Krafft business with Dr Franklin Bircher. Dr Bircher was aware that Krafft was in Berlin and had also come to the conclusion that he must be working for the Nazis at a very high level. Realising that Krafft's letter represented nothing less than a barefaced attempt at 'brainwashing' on the part of the Germans, in order to make him have second thoughts as to the wisdom of his pro-British sympathies, M. Tilea wrote an ironical letter to Krafft from Zürich on 30 March 1940. In this he acknowledged the receipt of Krafft's recent communication and informed him that he had seen through his little game. The other copy of Krafft's letter, the one that had been mailed to Bucharest from Berlin on or about 14 March, was forwarded to London by diplomatic bag and reached M. Tilea there soon after his return from Switzerland. This purposeful duplication of the message confirmed all his previous suspicions. Furthermore, since Krafft *must* be working for Hitler, it only remained to persuade the British to take the necessary counter measures.

14
Nostradamus and Psychological Warfare

On my desk as I type these words there is one of the 299 copies of Krafft's facsimile reprint of the Benoist Rigaud edition of *Les Prophéties de M. Michel Nostradamus*, which was originally published at Lyons in 1568, two years after the death of Nostradamus himself. It is unlikely that any other piece of Nostradamiana ever had a more curious publishing history than this one of Krafft's.[1]

There is no doubt that when he and Georg Lucht began work early in January 1940 they set about their task with tremendous enthusiasm. By the end of February, however, Lucht was wishing that he had never allowed himself to become involved in Krafft's affairs. The business of the Tilea letter had frightened him. 'During those weeks we both had one foot in a concentration camp', he wrote. Early in March he received an offer of employment from the Siemens electrical concern at Berlin-Spandau and told Krafft that he would like to accept it. Krafft was furious and accused the hapless Lucht of wanting to leave him in the lurch with the Nostradamus work still uncompleted. So Lucht stayed on. But their collaboration was only to last for another two weeks. When Lucht typed the final version of the letter to M. Tilea he was already close to a nervous breakdown and Krafft was in a tense and irritable mood.

'During the last days of March', Lucht wrote, 'we had reached a stage of undisguised mutual hostility. Krafft accused me of being apathetic and kept on quoting the proverb about "striking while the iron is hot". I was terribly depressed but forced myself to produce a few lame and weary arguments to the effect that there wasn't even an iron to strike. I said that it would be a mistake for us to overestimate either ourselves or our influence. "It's we who are being made to dance to the piper's tune," I said, adding that our employers were simply exploiting us and making us pervert Nostradamus in a shameful manner for psychological warfare purposes. I said that I could not see any sense in it all—only nonsense.'

Lucht finally cut loose on 2 April 1940 and a fortnight later was officially directed to employment in an aircraft factory. In connection with his realisation that Krafft was being obliged to 'pervert' the sense of prophetic quatrains, which were in any case extremely difficult to 'interpret', I must refer to a passage in the tape-recording I made with Dr Kritzinger.

'After Krafft arrived in Berlin', he said, 'we met from time to time and discussed many of the quatrains together, but often without reaching any common ground. Here I must mention one critical factor: all that Dr

---

[1] See the illustration facing p. 181.

Goebbels wanted was propaganda material based upon Nostradamus' predictions. But Krafft and I both agreed that it would be an offence against the spirit, as it were, of Nostradamus if we tampered with his prophecies and if we did this he would bitterly reproach us from the grave. So we did our best only to provide material that appeared to be sensible and to the point.'

However, in a letter dated 24 October 1962 Dr Kritzinger mentioned that many of Krafft's interpretations were too 'far-reaching'. A case in point was the supposed meaning of quatrain v, 94, which reads:

> *Translatera en la Grande Germanie,*
> *Brabant & Flandres, Gand, Bruges & Bolongne :*
> *La traisue sainte, le grand duc d'Armenie,*
> *Assaillira Vienne & la Coloigne.*

During the summer of 1940 the interpretation of 'Grande Germanie' was strikingly evident. It could only mean 'Gross-Deutschland', whose armies now occupied Brabant and Flanders, Ghent, Bruges and Boulogne sur Mer. But who was 'le grand duc d'Armenie' and why should he attack Vienna and Cologne? Dr Kritzinger thought that he must be Stalin, who was born in Georgia, therefore in the neighbourhood of Armenia, where the meeting point of the Russian, Persian and Turkish territories lay in the Ararat Mountains. However, it was unthinkable at that time that Stalin should attack Vienna or Cologne so Krafft proposed a more acceptable and, to him, more logical solution. The 'grand duc' was clearly Arminius, chief of the German tribe of the Cherusci, who defeated three Roman legions in the Teutoburgian forest in A.D. 9. Now, by a curious analogical process, the 'grand duc' became the *Führer* of 'Gross-Deutschland' who sent his armed warriors to the Rhineland, and hence Cologne, in March 1936 and to Vienna when he occupied Austria in March 1938. Two years later his armies conquered Brabant and Flanders, etc. However ill-founded these speculations may appear, and they are typical of all attempts to interpret the meaning of the quatrains, it is evident that Krafft and Dr Kritzinger found them of absorbing interest.

But why did Krafft's backers agree to the plan, which must have been his own, of producing a facsimile edition of the *Prophéties* in a very limited number of copies together with a commentary to be written by him? For the purposes of psychological warfare fodder, which was surely their main interest, it would have sufficed to allow their tame editor to supply his own interpretations of an appropriate selection from the thousand available quatrains and then have them adapted or re-written by a hack propaganda writer who would certainly not have shared Krafft's reverent interest in Nostradamus and his work. However, if Krafft required a bait to make the task appear attractive, the concession that he should have a book to show for his pains was psychologically a sound move. Again, while he was to be allowed to sell copies to his friends, there was never any question of the book being freely available in the bookshops. A widespread public interest in Nostradamus and his prophecies was the last thing that the authorities desired, for they realised that no author was a better source for potential rumours, and if there were to be any rumours at all, then they would prefer to invent their own.

By the time Lucht made his departure on 2 April Krafft's commentary already amounted to 200 pages of typescript. According to Lucht he had made a number of astonishing deductions. Not so surprising, perhaps, was the one that pointed to the imminent invasion of Holland and Belgium by the German armed forces. But the security people objected to accurate speculations of this kind and by the time that someone had censored the manuscript practically nothing was left. Nor did the RSHA allow the book to appear that spring and it was not 'published' until December 1940.

As I have said, the facsimile reprint of the *Prophéties* was limited to an edition of 299 copies. There is no publisher's imprint and the title-page merely states that the text of the 1568 edition had been reproduced by photo-lithography by Fotokopist GmbH at Frankfurt am Main. Krafft's commentary had been so emasculated that it now required no more than a 32-page pamphlet, dated 12 October 1940, which was contained in a pocket inside the front cover. In this one has to search for the author's name, which eventually appears in small type on page 26. Indeed, anyone who might have read it at the time in quest of interesting speculations concerning Germany's future would have been disappointed, for all that Krafft was allowed to publish was an innocuous little essay on the problems that confront all who endeavour to interpret the quatrains. Who paid for the printing and binding? It will be remembered that Krafft told M. Tilea that the book was being sponsored by a Society in conjunction with a government department. According to Herr Lucht it was Himmler's *Reichssicherheitshauptamt* that footed the bill, with Dr Fesel acting as an intermediary. In reply to some queries that I sent him, he stated that the Propaganda Ministry was not directly concerned with this project and, as far as he knew, Krafft never met Dr Goebbels.

There is a clue to the identity of Krafft's mysterious Society on the very last page of his introductory pamphlet where there is an allusion to the Deutsche Metapsychische Gesellschaft (German Metapsychical Society), whose address was on the fourth floor of a house at Pragerstrasse 17, Berlin W50. The Society, it was stated, would be glad to arrange for contacts and exchanges of ideas between Nostradamus researchers. Furthermore, it was announced that the Society had begun to collect the addresses of people interested in Nostradamus and would keep them informed of new publications and opportunities for mutual discussion.

According to Dr Kritzinger, Pragerstrasse 17 was the address of Lt.-Col. Konrad Schuppe, a retired officer who was the Society's president.

He also said that he met Krafft there several times in order to discuss the possible interpretations of certain quatrains. Herr Wilhelm Wulff's impression was that the Society was formed on Goebbels's instructions and that its purpose was to identify people who were interested in Nostradamus.

Post-war German sources have so far revealed very little about the use of Nostradamus material for psychological warfare purposes. Walter Schellenberg recalled in his memoirs that in mid-May 1940, at about the time the German armies were crossing the Belgian frontier near Sedan, he was instructed to collaborate with the Propaganda Ministry in the production of material for dissemination in France by means of radio broadcasts and printed leaflets. I assume that the preparatory work had been done by Krafft some months earlier, although for security reasons he would not have been told very much.

Schellenberg referred to leaflets containing appropriately threatening quatrains from the *Prophéties* that were dropped from aircraft. Nostradamus was made to predict that south-east France would not be affected by the hostilities and Schellenberg claimed that the civilian population accordingly took to the roads in that direction, thus leaving the approaches to Paris and the channel ports less congested when the German armies got on the move.[1] I have searched in vain for copies of these leaflets, but have seen a small one which, on the basis of typographical evidence, was probably printed for the Germans in Belgium or France. This contained a dozen lines of doggerel verse attributed to Nostradamus but they were not based upon anything in the *Prophéties* and it is unlikely that Krafft had connection with this production.[2]

There was yet another German Nostradamus expert, who has so far not been mentioned. He was Dr Alexander Centgraf who, under the pseudonym Dr Centurio, after the war published *Nostradamus, der Prophet der Weltgeschichte* (*Nostradamus, the Prophet of World History*), Berlin, 1953. On page 70 of the fourth edition of his book (1960), he mentioned that during the cold winter of 1939–40 he received a visit from a friendly gentleman who described himself as a scholar. This man wanted to know if Dr Centurio thought that any particular quatrain referred to 'a lightening attack upon France'. He thereupon proposed four quatrains (Nos. 6–9)

[1] W. Schellenberg, *Memoiren*, p. 105.

[2] At Dr Goebbels' ministerial conference on 27 March 1940 it was decided that 'the Nostradamus brochure can appear in its present form'. This indicates that an earlier version (probably that of December 1939) had been replaced by a new one, possibly on the basis of material supplied by Krafft. According to W. A. Boelcke, *Kriegspropaganda 1939–41*, 1966, p. 304, by the middle of 1940 a total of 83,000 copies had been printed: 20,000 in French, 5,000 in Dutch, 10,000 in Italian, 10,000 in Serbian, 25,000 in Croatian, 5,000 in Rumanian, 5,000 in Swedish and 3,000 in English for dissemination in the U.S.A. See this source for other references to Nostradamus, the last dated 10 September 1940.

from the third 'Centurie'. I have often wondered if the 'scholar' was Krafft himself. Dr Centurio mentioned that after Paris was occupied by the Germans he was surprised to read in American newspapers that prophecies attributed to Nostradamus had gained a wide circulation in France during the previous months and that the French government had been disturbed by their insidious effect.

Dr Kritzinger gave me an interesting document in the shape of a photocopy of a 16-page duodecimo Nostradamus booklet with the title *Der Seher von Salon* (*The Seer of Salon*). This bore the imprint of Rota-druck Wilhelm Meyer KG., Berlin SW68, hence its German origin was undisguised. A German friend of his was surprised to find that a copy had been slipped into his overcoat pocket when he collected his garment from the cloakroom of a cinema at Tehran, Persia, sometime in 1940–1. Internal evidence indicates that the background material for this pamphlet was supplied by Krafft.

There is nothing like a war for producing illogical situations. There were the Germans industriously planning to undermine French morale with material culled from the *Prophéties*, while the French authorities, on their side, were subsequently busy banning Nostradamiana in order not to give offence to the Occupying Power. In November 1940 the censorship department at Vichy took steps to prevent the sale of Dr de Fontbrune's recent book *Les prophéties de Maistre Michel Nostradamus* because the author's commentary might upset the Germans.[1] Dr Kritzinger told me, too, that E. Ruir's *Le grand carnage d'après les prophéties de Nostradamus de 1938 à 1947*, Paris, 1938, was also suppressed 'on the grounds that his interpretations were too accurate'.

There were contemporary objections to the publication of commentaries on Nostradamus even in neutral Switzerland. In 1940 Les Editions Utiles, a Geneva publishing firm, issued a reprint of the 1649 Rouen edition of the *Prophéties* but without any interpretative apparatus. The publishers inserted a note to the effect that they had not been authorised to include a commentary nor, for that matter, to 'translate' the original text into modern French.

Lucht and Krafft parted company on 2 April 1940. In June Lucht received a letter from his erstwhile colleague. Krafft had temporarily moved to Nikolassee, a suburb in the direction of Potsdam, and invited Lucht to visit him there one Sunday. When they met Krafft told him that his connection with Dr Fesel's department was now a very loose one and that he was working as a translator at the *Deutsche Nachrichtenbüro*, the official government news agency. (He found this job through a chance meeting with a friend from Hamburg, a certain Herr Hoelken.) Krafft said that translating—it was mainly from German into French—was not

[1] Eleventh edition, 1958, p. 6.

particularly arduous work and that he thought he would be able to stick it for a few years.

Frau Krafft's memorandum mentioned that her husband had been his own master for too long to relish being employed in a subordinate capacity, but that this job at least did not involve him in differences of opinion (i.e. with the RSHA) and left him with some spare time for his Nostradamus studies. On 21 May 1940, for instance, he lectured on Nostradamus to an unusually well-attended meeting of the Berlin Academic Astrological Society.

A postcard mailed on 5 July 1940 to Dr Ferrière mentioned that he had made further 'curious discoveries' and that Nostradamus' 'pro-German sentiments' were becoming increasingly evident to him. This strange remark implies that Nostradamus had foreseen the Third Reich and the Second World War, but then Krafft thought that this was the case. As might be expected, a later generation of Nostradamus 'experts' have variously asserted that their hero predicted the first Sputnik, the Chinese communist revolution, the assassination of President Kennedy and so on. Every new generation finds something in the quatrains that seems to fit.

Krafft soon began work on yet another Nostradamus book. According to Frau Krafft's memorandum he received a telephone call during the autumn of 1940 from a certain Dr Wilmanns who, she said, was employed in the German Foreign Office.[1] Dr Wilmanns informed Krafft that he had the manuscript of a book on Nostradamus in his possession. He said that the work was unsatisfactory and wanted Krafft to correct and revise it. (This German obsession with Nostradamus is really nothing less than comic.) Krafft replied that he was too busy but Wilmanns was so pressing that he consented to read the manuscript. Later he returned it with a letter to the effect that the work was of such indifferent quality that it would have to be completely re-written, but emphasised that he had no desire to be saddled with the task. Wilmanns would not take no for an answer and once again Krafft found himself with a Nostradamus book on his hands. His facsimile edition of the *Prophéties* had not yet been published.

Georg Lucht continued to keep in touch with him. By this time, according to Lucht, Krafft had established some kind of contact with the Propaganda Ministry. When Lucht visited him late in 1940 he was shown some copy drafts and printed leaflets which Krafft said he had written for the 'Promi'.

Krafft introduced Lucht to Wilmanns early in 1941 and Lucht, too, was under the impression that Wilmanns was employed at the Foreign Office. Whereas Krafft's friend Dr Fesel sincerely believed in astrology, Wilmanns emphasised his own scepticism but told Lucht that his official

[1] Enquiries made on my behalf at Bonn revealed that there is no record of a Dr Wilmanns being employed at the Foreign Office at the period in question.

duties required him to interest himself in it. Wilmanns asked Lucht when the U.S.A. would enter the war. Herr Lucht was careful to give him an evasive answer and recalled that he was delighted to escape from this meeting with a whole skin. It is evident from Herr Lucht's memorandum and letters that after the affair of the Tilea letter he was always apprehensive that Krafft would land himself in trouble, and Lucht clearly thought that as far as he himself was concerned encounters with people like Dr Wilmanns were best avoided.

Apart from work on the book commissioned by Dr Wilmanns, Krafft was engaged upon other Nostradamus projects, but these were for his own pleasure and were connected with the private lecture course that he organised in Berlin. The first of these lectures took place in January 1941. Krafft chose his audience with care and was able to inform Dr Ferrière (on a postcard) that he was attracting an attendance of between sixty and seventy people. Yet another brief message mailed to Ferrière on 29 May recorded the continued success of his lectures, also the hope that henceforth he would no longer be bracketed among the astrologers who, he suggested, 'deserved to be extirpated'.

Georg Lucht was present at the inaugural lecture when Krafft's theme was 'The Prophecies of Nostradamus'. According to Lucht: 'As the talk proceeded it became increasingly fascinating, but at the same time more and more dangerous for Krafft!' Lucht was painfully aware that in January 1940 he and Krafft had been required to sign an undertaking that they would not discuss either Nostradamus or astrology in public, and he could already see Krafft as a candidate for the kind attentions of the Gestapo. They exchanged a few words after the lecture and Lucht asked Krafft if he realised what risks he was taking. Krafft merely laughed and said: 'Nothing at all will happen to me. This lecture has been registered with the police and certain people know all about the subject matter of my talks!'

Count Brockdorff, formerly Police President at Kiel but now on the staff of the *Kultusministerium*, wrote to Herr Goerner at about this time and suggested that he should quietly warn Krafft that he should end his lecture course because the Security Service was keeping an eye upon him. If Goerner communicated this advice to Krafft, he did not heed it. Indeed, he appears to have been unaware that even apparently innocent remarks might be misconstrued with dangerous consequences to himself. At the end of June 1941 Frau Krafft told Georg Lucht that Krafft was present at an informal gathering shortly before the Germans invaded Russia. There, on the basis of his astrological deductions, he referred to the imminent possibility of 'large-scale military operations in the east', which could only mean against the Soviet Union. Somebody informed the Gestapo, which immediately smelled 'high treason' but took no further action. As Lucht remarked, Krafft's astrological enthusiasms compelled him to communicate his supposed discoveries.

This semi-public lecturing activity of Krafft's seems to have been connected with the recent (December 1940) more or less private publication of the facsimile edition of the *Prophéties*. As I have said, this book was never available in the bookshops, but there is an indication that copies could be obtained from Krafft himself (price RM.30) in an article by him in the January 1941 issue of *Sterne und Mensch*. It was stated that orders would be forwarded by the journal's publishers. It appears, then, that these lecture events were intended to publicise the book within a strictly limited circle, but this queer public relations campaign did not end at that point. Krafft was now producing a little privately-printed 16-page octavo periodical with the title *Nostra Damur*, also a series of printed index cards containing analytical material relating to individual quatrains. *Nostra Damur* was intended for circulation to the 'Patrons and Friends of the 1940 Facsimile Edition of the *Prophéties*' and only two issues were published.[1] Krafft wrote the complete texts for photo-litho reproduction in his own highly-individual and legible handwriting and was thus able to avoid typesetting charges.

It will be recalled that Krafft had originally planned to preface the facsimile edition of the *Prophéties* with a lengthy Introduction, but this intention had been frustrated by Dr Fesel's department. One of Krafft's purposes in publishing *Nostra Damur* was to print some of the material that he had not been allowed to publish in the book itself, his plan being to present copies of the first three issues free of charge to all who had subscribed to the facsimile edition. However, while Krafft's interpretations of the quatrains were as speculative or hazardous as any others, before or since, *Nostra Damur*, with its carefully-written articles on the history of the textual transmission of the quatrains, was quite a scholarly little production.

The publication of *Nostra Damur* and the quatrain cards came to a sudden end in March or April 1941. Krafft referred to the matter in a duplicated circular which he mailed to his Berlin friends and connections in April.[2] In this he stated that although the third issue of *Nostra Damur* and the handwritten texts for the reproduction of thirty more cards were ready for the press, 'owing to the stringent restriction on printing—even when the paper has been provided by the customer—the issue of further publications of this kind has been rendered impossible for an indefinite period'. Reading between the lines, there is little doubt that he had been told to refrain from further publishing activities in connection with Nostradamus. Nevertheless, in spite of Lucht's fears, he had evidently not been forbidden to lecture, for in another circular he announced two talks, both of them illustrated with lantern slides, on 'Nostradamus as a Prophet of

---

[1] They are dated 8 November 1940 and 31 January 1941 respectively. He printed 600 copies of No. 1 and 500 copies of No. 2. See the illustrations facing pp. 212 and 213.

[2] See the illustration facing p. 197.

Greater Germany'. These were scheduled to take place at an address in the Nürnbergerstrasse on 28 May and 11 June 1941 at 7.15 p.m. Nürnbergerstrasse 24a was the residence of a Frau Petersen, one of Krafft's new circle of friends in Berlin. She had a music school and the lectures were held in a large room there.[1]

In his circular Krafft mentioned that there was every prospect that he would soon be able to import copies of what he called his 'Brussels' book for re-sale to his circle. It seems that there had hitherto been import control difficulties. This so-called 'Brussels' book was the one commissioned by Dr Wilmanns. According to Frau Krafft's memorandum, before it was completed he had a number of angry altercations with Wilmanns, who wanted him to 'cook' certain interpretations more positively in Germany's favour. Krafft refused to do this and at one point said that he was not prepared to allow his name to appear on the title-page. A compromise was reached when Wilmanns agreed that the quatrains which were the cause of the bother should be omitted.

The title of this book was *Comment Nostradamus a-t-il entrevu l'Avenir de l'Europe* and it was published, probably in February 1941, by Editions Snellew at Brussels. In the course of some 200 octavo pages Krafft discussed forty quatrains, including three upon which he proposed to elaborate in his Berlin lectures. The latter, he said, all pointed to the defeat of Great Britain. The 'Brussels' book was clearly designed for readers in Belgium and France and was an exercise in 'grey' rather than 'black' psychological warfare, since little or no attempt was made to disguise that it was sponsored by the Germans. While Krafft's interpretations were not specially subtle, they were not so obviously pro-German as to arouse too much suspicion. As a single item in an overall psychological warfare campaign the work was probably not without its value.

A brief summary of Krafft's treatment of one of the three quatrains in question may be of interest. It was the hundredth quatrain in the second *Centurie*.

> *Dedans les isles si horrible tumulte,*
> *Bien on n'orra qu'une bellique brigue*
> *Tant grand sera des predateurs l'insulte,*
> *Qu'on se viendra ranger à la grand ligue.*

For Krafft *les isles* meant Great Britain, and *predateurs* were the das-

[1] Letter from Frau Anna Endell (25 May 1966) who attended some of the lectures. According to Dr W. Schütt (in *Das Neue Zeitalter*, 16 December 1949) Krafft also gave lectures at his house and resided there in 1940–1. This must have been at Burggrafenstrasse 16. Dr Schütt recalled that Krafft was short of money early in 1941 and hoped for a further meeting with Dr Hans Frank, the Governor General of Poland, because he supposed that Frank would be able to provide him with useful contacts. He had met Frank at the famous musical party at Arno Breker's house early in 1940. Schütt also remembered Krafft's pleasure when someone at the Munich 'Brown House' (Party headquarters) commissioned him to prepare a study of Churchill's horoscope.

tardly British, i.e. people who rob and pillage. The *tumulte* in Britain would be horrible, worse than anyone could imagine. *Bellique brigue* was construed to mean total war, involving the whole population. The last two lines were supposed to explain why. 'The injuries that these [British] pirates have inflicted upon other nations will have been so great that Europe would range herself against Britain to put an end to her predatory acts.' Krafft said that ever since Dunkirk in 1940 the British had made feverish preparations to resist invasion. But their *levée en masse*, he continued, was not far removed from total chaos and the frenzied state of mind of Britain's populace was just as dangerous to national security as the enemy's imminent onslaught. It is interesting to note that Dr Wilmanns must have commissioned this book at about the time when the Germans were nominally intending to invade the British Isles.

The 'Brussels' edition contained an announcement to the effect that translations into German, English, Spanish and Rumanian were in the course of preparation. These were apparently never published but a Portuguese translation was issued in Lisbon in 1941 as *Nostradamus vê o futuro da Europa* by Edições Alma. This publishing house was probably operated more or less clandestinely by a propaganda unit under the control of the German embassy at Lisbon. The printing was executed by a firm that was ostensibly Portuguese but was certainly under German proprietorship. When I visited Lisbon in May 1962 I discovered that there was no copy of Krafft's book in the Portuguese National Library. There the officials claimed that since it was not in their possession it could not possibly exist. Within an hour I was able to find four mint copies at a secondhand bookshop, acquired them for the equivalent of 1s. each and made haste to fill the gap in the National Library's shelves. The curators appeared to be mildly irritated that I should have produced the book at all. My impression is that Krafft never saw a copy of the Lisbon edition.

In May 1941 Krafft had been employed at the *Deutsche Nachrichtenbüro* for almost a year. His employers were keeping him very busy, for on 5 May he sent a card to Dr Ferrière in which he stated that he had recently been working for thirteen hours at a stretch. But respite was not far off, he said, for he had been granted three months' leave and proposed to return to the peace and quiet of Urberg until the autumn. But neither Krafft nor his wife went to Urberg that summer, for five weeks later he was arrested.

15
The 'Aktion Hess'

At 5.45 p.m. on Saturday 10 May 1941 Rudolf Hess, *Reichminister* and first in line of succession after Goering in the event of Hitler's death, climbed into a Messerschmitt-110 fighter aircraft at Augsburg and set course for Scotland. Hitler learned the news at Berchtesgaden the following morning when Hess's adjutant arrived with a letter from him. It was now urgently necessary to find an explanation for his departure that could be plausibly offered not only to the German nation, but also to the world at large.

On the Monday morning when the *Führer* presided at a meeting attended by Goering, the Gauleiters and other leading Party functionaries, a suitable answer was found. The story now was that Hess was not only mentally deranged but had been disastrously influenced by astrologers. Walter Schellenberg recalled that it was Martin Bormann who persuaded Hitler to accept the proposition that Hess was mad, and it may well have been Bormann who took good care to involve the astrologers.

Dr Hans Frank, the Governor General of Poland, was present at this meeting and stated in his posthumous autobiography that the astrological thesis was already current before it began.[1] On 14 May the *Völkischer Beobachter* published an article that included the following passage: 'As was well known in Party circles, Rudolf Hess was in poor health for many years and latterly increasingly had recourse to hypnotists, astrologers and so on. The extent to which these people are responsible for the mental confusion that led him to his present step has still to be clarified.'[2]

In London on 14 May *The Times* printed some highly-speculative information received from its correspondent in Switzerland: 'Certain of Hess's closest friends have thrown an interesting light on the affair. They say that Hess has always been Hitler's astrologer in secret. Up to last March he had consistently predicted good fortune and had always been right. Since then, notwithstanding the victories Germany has won, he has declared that the stars showed that Hitler's meteoric career was approaching its climax.'

Schellenberg recorded that Heinrich Müller, the Bavarian ruffian who was head of Section IV (Gestapo) of the RSHA now gleefully went to

---

[1] Hans Frank, *Im Angesicht des Galgens*, 1953, p. 411.

[2] There is an intriguing reference to Hess's interest in occultism in Helmut Heiber, *Walter Frank und sein Reichsinstitut für Geschichte des neuen Deutschlands*, 1966, p. 806. During the early years of the Third Reich he applied for an initial grant of 12 million Marks and an annual subvention of 2 million Marks for his projected Central Institute for Occultism. Nothing came of this grandiose plan.

work. Warrants were issued for the arrests of Hess's adjutants, a number of his close friends and even his chauffeur. But time was required to plan the 'Aktion Hess', which was soon to lead to the arrests of hundreds of other people, with the astrologers at the top of the list. Schellenberg also remembered that Himmler, who had a weakness for astrology and mystical prophecies, viewed the intended action against the astrologers and clair-voyants with mixed feelings. He mentioned that it amused Reinhard Heydrich, the RSHA boss, to review Hitler's instructions with 'Gestapo' Müller in Himmler's presence in great detail. On one occasion Heydrich is supposed to have cynically compared Himmler with a certain German field-marshal, saying: 'One is worried about the stars on his epaulette and the other about the stars in his horoscope.'[1]

The régime took a number of steps in order to influence public opinion as far as occult beliefs or practices were concerned, but kept quiet about the wholesale arrests of the astrologers and occultists. In a decree issued to the Gauleiters above Martin Bormann's signature on 6–7 June 1941, the Churches and 'astrologers, fortune-tellers and other swindlers' were indifferently lumped together. In order to prevent the discussion of undesirable subjects the Propaganda Ministry issued an instruction on 24 June 1941 that 'public performances' were not to be allowed if they involved demonstrations of an occult, spiritualist, clairvoyant, telepathic or astrological nature. Public lectures on these themes were also forbidden. This ukase was followed on 3 October by a confidential circular instructing editors that henceforth no articles on these subjects were to be published. This document contained additions to the existing list of proscribed topics, i.e. the 'occult ray theory' (radiesthesia), absent healing (by prayer), and Georg Lanz von Liebenfels' Ariosophical teachings. On 26 November 1941 the Party Chancery circulated a confidential circular that recom-mended Party functionaries to read a recent issue of *Die Weltliteratur* (No. 8–9, 1941) containing articles describing the campaign against astrologers, Anthroposophists, clairvoyants and occultists generally.

In a memorandum written for Herr Goerner in December 1959, Herr Adolf Gerst, who was a member of the Karlsruhe Gestapo in 1941, men-tioned some additional categories, e.g. Christian Scientists, members of the Christian Community (an Anthroposophical religious sect), faith healers and even graphologists. Herr Gerst also listed psychologists and psychotherapists, but here my inference is that the Gestapo was only interested in people who, like Krafft, had no medical or other recognised qualifications. The point is that the Gestapo's net was widely cast.

The main wave of arrests in connection with the 'Aktion Hess' was made on 9 June 1941, almost exactly a month after Hess flew to Scotland. On that day the Gestapo went to work in every part of Germany. Herr Gerst's personal knowledge was confined to what happened in his own

[1] Charles Wighton, *Heydrich*, Corgi paperback edition, 1963, p. 226.

district, but evidence from other regions confirms his statement that most
of those arrested were released after a few days, or at the most three or four
weeks, but there were some important exceptions. 'Professor' Issberner-
Haldane, for instance, spent the remainder of the war years in custody.

Although all the astrologers were asked if they had had any connection
with Hess, by this time the question of whether or not he had received
astrological advice was of secondary importance. Herr Gerst made it clear
that for the authorities the real issue was that all these people were regarded
as potential political opponents of the régime. He wrote: 'Experience
showed that in countless instances information derived from graphological
interpretations . . . adversely affected the total acceptance of the National
Socialist *Weltanschauung* and hence influenced the stability of the home
front.'[1]

The Gestapo did not wait a month before arresting Herr Schulte-
Strathaus who, together with half a dozen other members of Hess's staff,
was taken into custody on 12 May. Ernst Schulte-Strathaus (*b*. 1881) was
a literary historian and Goethe expert. He had been on Hess's staff at the
Munich Brown House since 1935 and was in charge of the cultural-
political office. However, according to Dr Gerda Walther, who knew him
well, he was also Hess's local expert on 'occult' subjects, including astrology.[2] He was an enthusiastic amateur astrologer and was well known as
such.

Whether or not the Gestapo found Hess's horoscope when they
searched Schulte-Strathaus' office or home is not known, but there is no
doubt that he was suspected of having advised Hess that 10 May would be
a propitious day for his flight. A speculation known to comparatively few
in 1941 was given wide circulation in 1954 when a Munich journalist published a series of articles about the 'Aktion Hess'. Here Schulte-Strathaus'
connection with Hess was described with a wealth of inventive detail.
Schulte-Strathaus wrote to the man on 23 December 1954 and complained
of his distortions. In this letter he stated that he had never sought to foist
his own astrological views on Hess, furthermore that he had certainly
never suggested that 10 May would be a suitable day for his departure.[3]

It seems, however, that Schulte-Strathaus had mentioned a specific
astrological phenomenon to Hess in January 1941. On this occasion he
spoke of the prophecies that had been made in the past in relation to
'major conjunctions', namely the simultaneous presence of a large group of

[1] Herr Gerst's memory may have played him false. There is no evidence to suggest
that the graphologists were affected. In this context it may be noted that Himmler kept
a card index recording the names of all the people to whom he had made a gift of any
kind. Signatures from their letters of thanks were affixed to the index cards for graphological purposes.

[2] See Gerda Walther, *Zum anderen Ufer*, 1960, p. 473.

[3] Herr Georg Neidhardt gave me a copy of the letter when I was in Munich in 1962.
I never succeeded in meeting Herr Schulte-Strathaus.

planets in one sign of the zodiac, and had referred to those that had taken place in 1484, 1504 and, above all, to a very ancient major conjunction in the 'watery' sign Pisces which caused many people to expect a repetition of the Flood.

According to Schulte-Strathaus he had told Hess that an unusual major conjunction would occur on 10 May 1941, with six planets in the sign Taurus coinciding with a full moon, and had jokingly remarked that the presence of so many planets in one place might be sufficient to cause the earth to tilt on one side.[1] But in January 1941, he said, he had not discussed this forthcoming conjunction with Hess's horoscope and at the very most could only have mentioned in passing that, according to the rules in the astrological 'cook-books', 10 May 1941 might not be a specially favourable day for Hess. Finally he emphasised that Hess certainly never chose 10 May on the basis of astrological advice given by himself or anyone else, and that he had no personal knowledge whatever of Hess's plans. Herr Schulte-Strathaus therefore languished in prison because it was suspected that he might have been Hess's astrologer, and was not released until 1 March 1943.

In the course of my travels in Germany I asked about a score of astrologers if they could name any member of their 'guild' who might conceivably have advised Hess, but none of them had any plausible suggestions to offer. Then Dr Alexander Centgraf, with whom I had been corresponding, said he was a certain Dr Schmidt-Nabus, whom I was unable to identify. Later I found a fragmentary clue in Dr Rainer Hildebrandt's sympathetic biography of Professor Albrecht Haushofer.[2] He was the son of Professor Karl Haushofer (1869–1946), the celebrated founder of the science of political geography. Karl Haushofer had employed Hess as his assistant at Munich for a brief period after the First World War and the family had remained in close touch with him. The elder Haushofer has often been described as the sinister figure who was responsible for filling Hitler's head with grandiose ideas about German *Lebensraum* in the east, but long before 1939 he had realised that the Führer was a dangerous madman. His son Albrecht (1903–45) was professor of political geography at Berlin in 1941 and up to the neck in the affairs of the underground opposition to Hitler. He was murdered by the Nazis in 1945.

[1] Some readers will recall the countless newspaper paragraphs that were published early in February 1962 concerning the major conjunction in Aquarius that occurred at that time. The apparently senseless speculations of astrologers in all parts of the world were certainly given a lot of undeserved publicity. During the spring of 1935 Krafft's friend Dr Ferrière had been searching in the ephemerides for advance information of similar major conjunctions and had come across the one due at the beginning of May 1941. In a letter to Krafft he suggested that it symbolised 'a nest of vipers'. Krafft replied that he had first become aware of the 1941 conjunction some fifteen years earlier and added: 'The effects? Collective insanity? Flagellations?'

[2] Rainer Hildebrandt, *Wir sind die letzten* (*We are the last*), [1949], pp. 100, 111, 114.

By all accounts Albrecht Haushofer was an extraordinarily attractive and gifted man. Furthermore, like so many educated Germans of his generation he seriously believed in astrology. Dr Hildebrandt, who was his pupil and intimate friend during the war years, recalled his preoccupation with Hitler's horoscope and all that this document was supposed to imply. A letter that I received from Dr Hildebrandt also contained the information that Haushofer was a student of Nostradamus.

It will be remembered that Hess flew to Scotland with the intention of talking to the Duke of Hamilton, whom he expected to lead him without further ado to King George VI and Winston Churchill for discussions on a *modus vivendi* with Germany. According to Dr Hildebrandt, who appears to be a reliable witness: 'Hess's astrological foible strengthened his own conviction that everything possible must be done and hazarded in order to end hostilities without delay, because at the end of April and beginning of May 1941 Hitler's astrological aspects were unusually malefic. Hess interpreted these aspects to mean that he, personally, must take the dangers that threatened the *Führer* upon his own shoulders in order to save Hitler and restore peace to Germany. Time and again Hess's astrological "adviser" had told him that Anglo-German relations were threatened by a deep-seated crisis of confidence. . . . Indeed, at this time there were very dangerous [planetary] oppositions in Hitler's horoscope. Haushofer, who dabbled a great deal with astrology, seldom left his friend [i.e. Hess] without a hint that something unexpected could "happen" in the near future.'

The Haushofers, father and son, had been engaged for some time past in cautious attempts to establish contact with the Duke of Hamilton. However, neither of them had the slightest idea that Hess himself would fly to Scotland and the news of his departure flabbergasted them. Both the Haushofers were arrested, although in neither case were there any astrological implications. Also arrested, according to Dr Hildebrandt, was 'Hess's astrologer, a certain Dr Schmitt'.

Herr Wilhelm Wulff eventually clarified the Schmitt puzzle for me when he explained that the gentleman was undoubtedly Dr Ludwig Schmitt, a well-known Munich physician who was commonly known as 'Breath' Schmitt on account of his theories concerning the therapeutic effects of correct breathing. He was acquainted with Hess, who had a weakness for all kinds of 'fringe' medicine. Dr Schmitt was a keen astrologer and Herr Wulff encountered him at a number of pre-war German Astrologers' Congresses. He appears as Dr J. L. Schmitt, Leopoldstrasse 25, Munich, in the list of thirteen German medical men who practised astrology that was published in *Zenit*, May 1931. Herr Wulff met him after the 'Aktion Hess' in the cell block at the Berlin-Sachsenhausen concentration camp. Whether or not Schmitt was consulted by Hess prior to his flight is not known.

Geöffnet

Berlin-Halensee, 14.Mz.40
Joachim-Friedrich-Str.54
Ks/GL(2)

Lieber Herr TILEA,

Ihr Brief von Ende Januar ist mir erst Mitte Februar zugegangen. Die Verzögerung war zumteil verursacht durch mehrfache Ortswechsel während der letzten Zeit. Mitte Dezember wurde ich nämlich nach Berlin eingeladen zu einem Referat über NOSTRADAMUS. Bei dieser Gelegenheit wollten wir nach Eisenach in Thüringen übersiedeln, fanden aber dort keine Wohngelegenheit. So beschlossen wir, hierher weiter zu fahren, wo ich im Zusammenhang mit meinen kosmobiologischen Forschungen seit Jahren einen grössern Bekanntenkreis habe, und sich auch günstigere Arbeitsmöglichkeiten bieten als in unserm weltverlornen Urberg.

Seit fünf Wochen bin ich nun beschäftigt, für eine hiesige Gesellschaft in Verbindung mit einer Reichsstelle eine neue Ausgabe der Ihnen wahrscheinlich bekannten Prophéties von NOSTRADAMUS zu besorgen, mit einer wissenschaftlich-kritischen Einführung in das umstrittene Gebiet. Da ich mich damit seit zwanzig Jahren abgebe und schon vor Jahren viel darüber geschrieben habe, macht mir diese Arbeit viel Freude; und ich darf wohl sagen, dass hier das Beste und Gründlichste vorbereitet wird, was bisher je über NOSTRADAMUS und das Prophetische veröffentlicht worden ist.

Sobald das Werk fertig ist - ich hoffe Anfang April - wird es mir ein Vergnügen sein, Ihnen ein Stück zu dedizieren. Vielleicht schreiben Sie mir bis dahin, ob ich Ihnen das Buch durch die Gesandtschaft Ihres Landes senden darf, da es sich um ein kostbares Werk handelt, das nur in kleiner Auflage gedruckt werden und im Buchhandel nicht erscheinen wird (damit nicht daraus der Aberglauben neue Nahrung schöpft, - obwohl, oder gerade weil darin unwiderlegliche Beweise für die seherische Begabung von NOSTRADAMUS über Jahrhunderte weg erbracht werden). -

In Ihrem letzten Brief geben Sie mir wohl die Geburtsdaten Ihrer Frau und Ihrer Kinder, nicht aber diejenigen Ihrer Eltern. Gerade diese aber sind mir ein wichtiger Anhaltspunkt für die Beurteilung der Erbmasse, aus deren Grund das Einzelwesen wächst. Beispiele dafür haben Sie wohl in meinem "Traité" gefunden, wo ich im Kapitel VI gezeigt habe, wie in einer Familie (der unsrigen!) sich der Planet Merkur durch vier Generationen hindurch im selben Zeichen vorfindet. Ein solches Gestirn ist dann im Geburtsbild eines Nachkommen viel gewichtiger, als wenn seine Stellung im "Stammbaum" nicht vorgezeichnet wäre.

Eine andre wichtige Entdeckung, die ich noch bei Ihrer Studie mit-verwerten will, betrifft den verbesserten Siebenjahres-Rhythmus. Dieser umfasst nämlich, wie umfangreiche Erhebungen gezeigt haben, nicht genau 7 Jahre, sondern 7 Jahre weniger 7 Wochen; und der Ausgangspunkt ist für jeden Menschen der Stand der Sonne zu seiner Geburtszeit. Wenn also jemand im Frühling geboren ist, dann setzt sein Leben an einer andern (vorwiegend expansiven) Phase jenes Rhythmus ein, als wenn beispielsweise er im Herbst zur Welt kam.

Von diesem Rhythmus und seinen Phasen bezogen auf den Lebenskreis hängen wieder weitgehend die Reaktionen des Einzelnen

---

14. The letter that interested the British intelligence service. It bears the *Wehrmacht* censorship label.

Translatera en la grand Germanie,
Brabant & Flandres, Gand, Bruges & Boulogne.
La trève feinte, le grand duc d'Arménie
Assaillira Vienne & la Cologne.

("Prophéties", V.94)

"Der Waffenstillstand war eine Finte, der Friedensschluss
ein Betrug. Deshalb wird der grosse Führer vom Lande des
Arminius überraschend besetzen das Rheinland ("Köln")
und die Ostmark ("Wien"). In den Bereich Grossgermaniens
wird er überführen Mittelbelgien, Boulogne und Polen."

Mitteilung und Einladung

an die Förderer und Freunde des Frankfurter Neudrucks
der "Prophéties" von 1940
und ihren Bekanntenkreis

Nach mancherlei Verzögerungen ist vergangenen Monat in Brüssel eine im
vergangenen Spätsommer abgeschlossene Studie

"Comment Nostradamus a-t-il entrevu l'Avenir de l'Europe?"

erschienen, mit gegen vierzig ältern und neuern Deutungen aus den "Prophéties", darunter zahlreiche in den letzten Jahren in Erfüllung gegan-
gene Vierzeiler;

Nach Klärung schwebender Fragen betr. Einfuhr ausländischer Literatur
besteht die Aussicht, Exemplare dieses Werkes Nostradamus-Freunden ver-
mitteln zu können (150 S. - Pr.etwa RM 3.-).-

Dagegen sind Nr.3 des Mitteilungsblattes "NOSTRA DAMUR" und die Texte
für etwa dreissig weitere Karten mit Auslegungen druckreif geworden im
Augenblick, wo durch scharfe Einschränkungen im Buchdruck - selbst bei
vorsorglicher Bereitstellung von Papier und Karton durch den Auftraggeber -
die Ausführung weiterer Arbeiten in dieser Richtung auf längere Zeit un-
möglich geworden ist.-

Umso mehr werden es die Freunde der Grenzwissenschaften und der "Prophéties" begrüssen, wenn ihnen durch

Zwei Vorträge mit Schaubildern

Gelegenheit geboten wird, über den gegenwärtigen Stand der Nostradamus-For-
schung Verlässliches zu erfahren.

Die beiden Vorträge sind vorgesehen für je

Mittwoch, den 28.Mai und den 11.Juni 1941, Punkt 19 Uhr

im Haus ~~Augs~~burgerstr.24 A, Hochparterre rechts
(Ecke Augsburger Strasse, in Richtung Wittenbergplatz
auf der linken Seite;
U-Bahn: Nürnberger Platz; Strassenbahn: 92 und 98).

15. Duplicated circular issued by Krafft in Berlin
in 1941 to advertise his lectures and publications.

According to *Das Neue Zeitalter* of 3 December 1954, after the war Frau Maria Nagengast, a Munich astrologer, claimed that she received a letter from Hess in March 1941. He is supposed to have enquired which would be a propitious day for a journey abroad in the near future. She suggested 10 May 1941 and received RM.300 for her trouble. The lady's astrological expertise was clearly not sufficient to indicate that Hess's mission would fail and that he would still be a prisoner twenty-five years later. However, like almost everything else in *DNZ* this story should be taken with a pinch of salt.

Well-attested accounts of the experiences of individual astrologers who were arrested in the course of the 'Aktion Hess' are not very common, but those summarised below appear to be typical. In every known instance the Gestapo confiscated the victim's astrological books and papers, also all occult or other forbidden literature in their possession. Publishers' and booksellers' stocks were also seized. The precise number of arrests is not known. Estimates range from three hundred to a thousand individuals, including a fair quota of Party members.

Dr Gerda Walther was arrested at Munich on 9 June, not in the small hours as was the case with so many other victims, but later that morning at the *Wehrmacht* foreign postal censorship offices where she was employed. Dr Walther was not a professional astrologer. She was well known in international parapsychological circles as the former secretary and assistant of the late Freiherr Albert von Schrenck-Notzing, a noted investigator of the phenomenon of physical mediumship. At her interrogation she was first asked about her previous connection with the Christian Community, a religious sect associated with Rudolf Steiner's Anthroposophical movement, but the official soon turned to astrology.

'Suppose, for example, that a Negro, a Jew and an Aryan were all born on the same day and at the same time, would you make identical astrological predictions for each of them?' he asked.

Dr Walther realised that there was a racial implication and contrived an evasive answer that appeared to satisfy him. He was reading questions from a sheet of paper and soon they came to one that neither of them could understand. The official pushed the paper to one side with a show of irritation. 'They sent this from Berlin, but I really don't know what they want!' he exclaimed.

Dr Walther was taken to a local prison and interrogated again a few days later, this time by a certain Herr Mohr. He wanted to know if she had ever had the horoscopes of Hitler and Hess in her possession. She replied in the affirmative. 'Then how did you get hold of them?' he asked. She replied that in the past it had only been necessary to walk to the nearest newspaper kiosk to buy an astrological year book or similar publication. 'What is Hitler's horoscope like?' Mohr asked. 'Oh, very interesting, very unusual!' said Dr Walther, but was careful not to indicate in what respect, good or bad, the Führer's horoscope was peculiar. Herr Mohr contented himself with a grin. A few days later she was released after signing an undertaking not to disclose that she had been arrested or any circumstance connected with the event.

Another astrologer who was questioned by the Munich Gestapo—his name appears to have been Johannes Schrami—managed to make a copy of the fourteen questions that had been thought up in Berlin. Section VII of the *Reichssicherheitshauptamt* apparently had nothing better to do at that stage of the war than to analyse the replies to the following question-naire.

Secret State Police Munich, II G Special Commission, Brienner Strasse 50

1. For how long have you been interested in astrology and how did you come to the subject? Were you self-taught or did you receive instruction?
2. State the names of any well-known persons for whom you have cast horoscopes.
3. Are you a member of an astrological society? Have you any personal connections with leading personalities in the Reich and Party? What astrological literature have you read? What books do you own yourself?
4. Do you subscribe to any astrological periodicals? Have you actively practised astrology?
5. Have you lectured on astrology or given instruction to anyone? What systems do you use?
6. With what astrological circles are you regularly in touch, and how frequently?
7. Have you attended any astrological congresses, either in Germany or abroad?
8. What are the names of the astrologers of your acquaintance and with which of them are you in touch?
9. Do you believe that you can substantiate the validity of astrological interpretations?
10. In your opinion do planetary constellations determine human fate, and how do you account for free-will and hereditary factors?
11. Should members of different races (Aryans, Jews, Chinese and Negroes) born at the same place under identical constellations expect the same astrological interpretations? If yes, then do you not admit the racial requirements of fate?
12. Are you connected with occult or spiritualist organisations and have you participated in seances?
13. Have you been identified with other occult sciences?
14. What do you feel about clairvoyance and fortune-telling?[1]

[1] These questions were not posed to every astrologer arrested in the course of the 'Aktion Hess'. For example, A. M. Grimm, a well-known professional astrologer who

In the preface to the second volume of the post-war edition of his *Psychologische Horoskopdeutung*, Vienna, 1951, the late E. C. Kühr related his own experiences at Breslau on 9 June 1941. He was still asleep when four Gestapo officials arrived at his home. They searched his abode from top to bottom, told him that his library was to be confiscated and that he was under arrest. It happened that he had already moved most of his astrological books to a safe place so very little was found. Later the same day the Gestapo visited his publishers, the Regulus Verlag at Görlitz, which specialised in astrological and occult literature, and ordered the complete stock to be 'frozen' pending further instructions.[1] Gestapo officials also descended upon the printing office that was engaged upon the production of the second volume of Kühr's book and saw to it that the type was melted down in their presence.

Kühr was questioned at the Breslau Gestapo headquarters by a man who appeared to know something about astrology. He said: 'Well, what are *your* aspects like at the present time?' Kühr replied that Uranus was close to his Ascendant and the Sun was transiting his Saturn. 'In which House?' the Gestapo official asked. 'In the ninth,' Kühr replied. 'Then at the moment you should be surprised at nothing!' his interrogator observed.

Kühr was released a month later, but not before he had signed a declaration to the effect that he would not mention his arrest to anyone, contact any of his astrologer friends or former clients, either personally or by letter, or in the future practise astrology in any shape or form, or even refer to it in conversation. He was required to report immediately to the Labour Exchange, and forbidden to leave Breslau without the Gestapo's permission. Finally he was warned that the slightest infringement of these instructions would lead to his immediate incarceration in a concentration camp. When he returned home he discovered that the Gestapo had missed an extra carbon copy of the manuscript of his book and, in spite of the risk, had half a dozen photo-copies made which he sent to friends in different parts of Germany for safe-keeping. One set survived the war in the least likely place, namely in Berlin.

The wife of Freiherr Dr von Kloeckler was arrested at their home at Leipzig on 9 June. Von Kloeckler had resumed his medical studies after

---

lived near Munich, was not asked them. The portmanteau nature of the third question indicates that Herr Schrami could probably do no more than make some hastily scribbled notes. After the war the questionnaire was first published in *Das Neue Zeitalter*, 3 December 1954. The typescript copy of the same text now at the Institut für Zeitgeschichte at Munich was received from Herr Goerner, who did not mention its source, on 25 January 1960. While the *DNZ* text may well be genuine, its authenticity has not been established.

[1] The Regulus Verlag and the Baum Verlag at Pfullingen, which published C. Loog's little Nostradamus book, were both closed down by the Gestapo at this time. See Joseph Wulf, *Literatur und Dichtung im Dritten Reich*, Rowohlt paperback edition, 1966, pp. 273–4.

professional astrology became impracticable in 1935 and had qualified shortly before the outbreak of war. In 1941 he was employed at a hospital at Oschatz, some thirty miles east of Leipzig. Although formerly by far the best-known Leipzig astrologer, he was not arrested because his medical work was important to the war effort. The Leipzig Gestapo nevertheless summoned him for questioning. When he said that he must be sure of catching his train back to Oschatz in order to attend to two very sick patients, they graciously drove him to the railway station in an official car— but nevertheless kept his wife in custody for eight weeks.[1]

In June 1941 Herr Wilhelm Bischoff, who is now a professional astro-loger at Berlin, was serving in the ranks of an infantry regiment stationed at Trier. His astrological books and papers were taken by the Gestapo from his home at Saarbrücken. On 21 June Private Bischoff dispatched an angry letter to the Saarbrücken Gestapo in which he complained that it was outrageous that its officials should be allowed to plunder the pos-sessions of a soldier who was faithfully defending his *Führer* and *Vaterland*. Receiving no reply he wrote again on 25 August. A very senior Gestapo officer wrote to him on 17 September and peremptorily informed Private Bischoff that he could thank his lucky stars that he was now in uniform or the Gestapo would know very well how to deal with him. 'But I reserve the right to take appropriate measures against you after your release from the army,' *Regierungsrat* Hentsch concluded.

Dr Hubert Korsch, the president of the *Astrologische Zentralstelle*, the most important German astrological society, and editor of its organ *Zenit* until it ceased publication in 1938, was arrested at Düsseldorf. So, too, was Josef Loh, *Zenit*'s former assistant editor, who survived to tell what subsequently happened. The Gestapo already had a well-filled dossier for Dr Korsch and now they urgently wanted to learn the identity of 'Specta-tor', the author of an article about Hitler's horoscope that had been pub-lished in *Zenit* as far back as May 1931. 'Spectator' was, in fact, Josef Schultz, also of Düsseldorf, but although both Korsch and Loh were cross-examined for a fortnight, neither of them revealed his name. Dr Korsch was never released, and was probably murdered at the Oranienberg concentration camp near Berlin on 24 April 1942.[2]

Another victim of the 'Aktion Hess', and one whose path was soon to cross that of Krafft and F. G. Goerner was Professor Johannes Maria Verweyen (1883–1945), the incumbent of a chair of philosophy at the University of Bonn until his dismissal by the Nazis in 1934. He was born a Roman Catholic but left the church in 1921 when he became a Theosophist. Five years later he encountered that extraordinary character 'Bishop' James

[1] Information from Dr Otto Kellner, who was a close friend of the von Kloecklers.
[2] See Dr W. Koch, *Dr Korsch und die Astrologie*, a pamphlet published by Zenit Verlag R. Schumacher, Munich, 1956.

Wedgwood, from whom he received the orders of the Liberal Catholic Church, which was an appendage of the Theosophical Society. Verweyen was deeply interested in many varieties of mystical and occult thought, including astrology. He had rejoined the Catholic church in 1936.[1]

Gerhard zur Horst, who had been Goerner's secretary before the war, was arrested at Mannheim. Some of Krafft's papers were still in his possession and the Gestapo asked many questions about them. During his interrogation he noticed that a card index containing the names of Goerner's clients was on the table. The Gestapo appeared to be particularly interested in his own relationship with Krafft and also enquired whether he knew anything about their respective contacts with Hess's friend Herr Hofweber, who had subscribed to Krafft's *Economic Bulletin*.[2]

Now I come to Herr Goerner's story which I tape-recorded at Mannheim in July 1961.

Herr Goerner was not at his home at Mannheim on 9 June 1941, the day that most of the 'Aktion Hess' arrests were made. Since 14 May he had been staying at Gammelsbach, a village about thirty miles east of Mannheim. Early that morning his housekeeper telephoned to say that the Gestapo had been at his flat between 5 and 6 a.m. and had seized his books and papers. Then the line went dead and he realised that apart from the fact that his telephone was being tapped, the Gestapo now knew where he could be found. At 10 a.m. his friend Dr Jander, telephoned and said that the Gestapo had been at his home and advised him to return to Mannheim and sort things out with them.

Herr Goerner was apprehensive and decided to remain at Gammelsbach and await events. He did not have to wait for very long. At 2.30 p.m. that afternoon a police car passed through the village. 'That can only be for me!' he said to himself. Sure enough, it soon returned in his direction. A plain-clothes detective approached him and asked: 'Are you Herr Goerner?' He was quite friendly, Goerner recalled, and spoke with a broad Bavarian accent. He admitted his identity and was immediately asked if he had any books in the house. He replied that all his books were at Mannheim. He was informed that he was not under arrest but would be temporarily detained. He packed his few things and was driven to the Gestapo headquarters at Mannheim.

[1] See the short biographical study by Karl Kamps, *Johannes Maria Verweyen: Gottsucher, Mahner und Bekenner*, published in 1955 by the Roman Catholic Credo Verlag at Wiesbaden.

[2] I wrote to Herr Hofweber and asked if he happened to know what Hess thought of Krafft's bulletin. Herr Hofweber replied on 10 July 1963 to the effect that he had lost all his papers during the war and could remember nothing at all about Krafft's publication. He added that he had first met Hess when they served in the same fighter squadron in First World War, and bitterly blamed Sir Winston Churchill, who had in any case long since retired from active political life, for failing to agitate for his friend's release from Spandau prison in Berlin.

Upon arrival there he was shown into a room in which there were already a lot of people whom he knew. He noted, not without surprise, that the majority of them were interested in astrology or occultism. There was a long wait while one after another was summoned for interrogation. Some simple refreshments were provided: a hunk of bread and a piece of sausage. Eventually Goerner was interviewed by a member of the criminal police. 'What do you know about Hess's flight?' was the first question. 'Nothing at all!' Goerner replied. The man was not satisfied and the questioning continued for another one and a half hours.

A female secretary made notes of the proceedings. At about 11.30 p.m. the man left the room for a few minutes. 'Things don't look too good for you!' the woman observed. The police officer returned with a sheet of paper in his hand. 'This is a warrant for your arrest,' he said. 'You'll be leaving here shortly.'

While arrests and interrogations of this kind were taking place in all parts of Germany on 9 June 1941, Karl Ernst Krafft was industriously at work in his office at the *Deutsche Nachrichtenbüro* in Berlin. On Wednesday 11 June he was due to give the second of two lectures on Nostradamus and at the end of the week he and his wife intended to leave for their long summer holiday at Urberg. However, on Thursday 12 June two Gestapo officials arrived at his office and requested him to accompany them to his lodgings in the Burggrafenstrasse because, they said, they wanted to go through his books. The Kraffts had only recently moved there and the reason why Krafft had not already been swept up in the *razzia* of 9 June was that the Gestapo had not yet caught up with his change of address. When they arrived at the Burggrafenstrasse Krafft picked up his rare 1568 edition of the *Prophéties* and exclaimed: 'You mustn't take this!' Then, according to Frau Krafft, he proceeded to give the Gestapo officials an impromptu lecture on the importance of the book. They listened politely for a quarter of an hour until finally one of them said: 'Really, Herr Krafft, we *must* have a look at your books!' After a cursory inspection they invited him to accompany them to the Gestapo's Alexanderplatz headquarters so that a statement could be drafted. Before they left one of them said to Frau Krafft: 'He'll be back this evening.'

The 'Aktion Hess' drove astrology and all the other 'fringe' sciences or beliefs underground. But for every astrologer or occultist arrested there were dozens who escaped unscathed, particularly those who had never belonged to any organised group or who had not written for publication on these now prohibited topics. A secret memorandum circulated to top-level Party functionaries by the *Sicherheitsdienst* in July 1944 referred to reports received from informants in different parts of the Reich. The SD's watchmen 'had noticed a considerable increase in all possible forms of prophecy about the future course of the war' and mentioned the use of clairvoyance, astrology and numerology.[1] The two following anecdotes are offered without comment.

At Leipzig my friend Dr Otto Kellner's dentist, a certain Herr Gohlis who was a Party member, continued to practise astrology and 'pendulum swinging' with all his old enthusiasm. In order to discover whether or not the house in which he resided would be bombed, he cast the horoscopes of all the other tenants. He had previously analysed the horoscopes of all his patients who had lost their homes through British air raids and had drawn certain conclusions. Only one of his neighbours' horoscopes seemed to be unsatisfactory and the house survived the war unharmed except for a few bomb splinters.

Herr Reinhold Ebertin has told a somewhat similar story in connection with his mother, the late Elsbeth Ebertin, who was killed in an air raid on Freiburg im Breisgau in November 1944. 'My mother saw the crisis coming for she knew the horoscopes of many people living in the neighbouring houses. However, if she had left it would have caused a terrible turmoil and she would have been picked up by the Gestapo because people were saying: "As long as Frau Ebertin is here nothing very much can happen to us!" '[2]

---

[1] *Meldungen aus dem Reich: Auswahl aus den geheimen Lageberichten des SS, 1939–44*, edited by H. Boberach, 1965, p. 523.

[2] *Kosmobiologie*, Feb.–March 1966, p. 20.

16

Captain Louis de Wohl

There was a reference to the astrological implications of Hess's flight to Scotland in a newspaper article published in London on 22 May 1941, twelve days after his arrival. Herr Walter Tschuppik's piece on 'Astrology in Hitler's Service' cannot have been seen by more than a handful of Englishmen because it was printed in *Die Zeitung*, a weekly publication that was read almost exclusively by *émigré* Germans and Austrians.

According to Herr Tschuppik, soon after Hess's unexpected advent it was recalled that at an Astrologers' Convention held at Harrogate a month earlier a certain Mr Mawby Cole had predicted that a momentous historical event would occur on 11 May as the result of the major planetary conjunction due on that day. Cole himself was killed in the last great German air raid on London on Saturday 10 May 1941. Herr Tschuppik recorded that some journalists who were interested in the connections between occultism and politics called at the late Mr Cole's residence, were ushered into his study and were shown a horoscope for the Jupiter–Saturn conjunction and, 'even more remarkable, an American astrological periodical which also mentioned this fateful constellation'.

'One must remember that the ingenious Dr Goebbels had very quickly realised astrology's propaganda value,' Herr Tschuppik continued, 'since his ministry incorporates a special department called AMO (Astrology, Metapsychology and Occultism), and National Socialist astrologers send articles to newspapers all over the world in order to prepare public opinion for events upon which Hitler wants attention to be focused.' Herr Tschuppik suggested a direct connection between Hess's flight on 10 May and the major conjunction. Hess, he stated, had believed in astrology and in that respect followed the example of Hitler, who kept his personal astrologer at Berchtesgaden. Until recently the astrologer in question had been one Kraft [*sic*]. Kraft, however, had recently disappeared and the initiates were whispering that he had been murdered. His successor was Rudolf Ossietz, 'a young man of whom it is only known that he has daemonic dark eyes and black hair brushed back over his head'. The fictitious Herr Ossietz was made to resemble Krafft.

Herr Tschuppik next informed his readers that the gullible editors of popular American astrological periodicals had become the victims of Dr Goebbels and his AMO department. Indeed, he alleged that American astrological journalists had already twice unwittingly been of service to Hitler. The first occasion was during July and August 1940 when they had all prophesied England's imminent defeat. Rather later the Propaganda Ministry astrologers had predicted 'peace on 15 February 1941' and astrological periodicals in every country had followed this line without being aware that it was German propaganda. Herr Tschuppik observed that although Dr Goebbels's forecasts had frequently been incorrect, there was clearly a connection between astrology and politics and suggested that Hess's journey had been far more carefully planned, in an astrological sense, than the Propaganda Ministry would be prepared to admit.

While Herr Tschuppik's article contained a number of happy inventions, e.g. the AMO department and Rudolf Ossietz, it is conceivable that the Propaganda Ministry had, as he suggested, been planting articles in various popular astrological magazines.[1]

At about the time the arrests in connection with the 'Aktion Hess' were being made in Germany in June 1941, Captain Louis de Wohl, astrologer 'by appointment' to various British intelligence departments, had just arrived in the United States of America on astrological business. While de Wohl was subject to the Official Secrets Act and would therefore have been forbidden to discuss his work with any unauthorised outsider, I believe that Herr Tschuppik's article must have been based on hints passed to him by de Wohl, if only because the latter was one of the few people in German émigré circles in London who could have been aware of Krafft's existence.

The gentleman whom M. Virgil Tilea, the Rumanian Minister in London, presented to his influential British friends as someone well qualified, as far as he could judge, to 'counter' the supposedly formidable Karl Ernst Krafft in Berlin, had an unusual career behind him.[2] The late Ludwig von Wohl—he made some trifling alterations to his name when he came to England in 1935—was born in Berlin on 24 January 1903. In *I follow my Stars* he said that he was born at 7.45 p.m., but after the war informed a well-known American astrologer that the correct time was *c*. 3.30 p.m. It is not uncommon for an astrologer to publish an incorrect birth time in order to make it difficult for a confrère to 'meddle' with his or her horoscope—an act of 'preventive magic', as it were.

De Wohl was of Hungarian descent and partly Jewish. He was educated in Berlin and during the decade before Hitler came to power was not unsuccessful as a novelist, journalist and film script writer. He had a wide circle of acquaintances in Berlin and attended many social functions. It was at the annual Netherlands Ball, a 'white tie' affair held at the Hotel Esplanade in the late autumn of 1930, that he met a gentleman whom he

---

[1] I have not been able to examine any astrological periodicals published in the U.S.A. during the period 1939–41 and have therefore not been in a position to evaluate this material. A reference in *The Goebbels Diaries* to the dissemination of occult 'prophecies' for psychological warfare purposes is mentioned later in this book on p. 226.

[2] See de Wohl's autobiographical *I follow my Stars*, 1937. A brief but rather unsatisfactory account of the events of 1940–1 will be found in his *The Stars of War and Peace*, 1952.

described as an old acquaintance. The latter was none other than Prince Heinrich of the Netherlands (1876–1934), the husband of Queen Wilhelmina. The Prince introduced him to the Baroness Keun von Hoogerwoerd, a lady-in-waiting at the Dutch court, and she, in turn, called her son to meet him. 'Since you are a writer, I think that his profession will interest you,' she said. 'He's an astrologer!'

De Wohl described the Baron Harald Keun von Hoogerwoerd as a strong, thick-set young man in his early thirties. It is more than likely that he was identical with the mysterious Herr K. von H. who made a fleeting appearance in Captain S. Payne Best's book *The Venlo Adventure*, whom I have mentioned in an earlier chapter.[1]

The Baron was not well known in contemporary German astrological circles but may have had a 'society' connection in Berlin. That evening he and de Wohl discussed astrology. At first de Wohl was sceptical, but soon became interested and asked the Baron to cast his horoscope. A week later he received twenty pages of typescript, was fascinated by what he read about himself and was soon taking lessons from him. A year or so later, de Wohl recalled, 'I found myself being thrust into the position of adviser to my friends . . .'[2]

While Louis de Wohl had an obvious capacity for falling on his feet, there is little doubt that he was an imaginative and gifted man and, furthermore, quickly able to apply a considerable intelligence to the problem of making a living when he arrived in London as a refugee from Germany in 1935. Miss I., who was involved with his war-time activities, told me that 'he had the quickest working brain' that she had ever encountered. He quickly perfected his English and began to write books, and at the same time developed a clientele as a professional astrologer.

His post-war book *The Stars of War and Peace* begins with an interesting but inaccurate anecdote. It was Rudolf Freiherr von Sebottendorff (mis-spelled Sobottendorf in the German edition), he wrote, who warned Hitler not to attempt a *Putsch* in November 1923. He then suggested that when Hitler was in prison at Landsberg after the *Putsch*, Rudolf Hess reminded him of Sebottendorff's prediction.[3] Thereupon, according to de Wohl, Hitler began to study astrology and decided to enlist the help of expert astrologers in the future.

De Wohl claimed that in 1935 he was approached by a member of the Party who 'wore a smart uniform and had a lot of minions working for him'. This gentleman is supposed to have invited de Wohl to place his own astrological expertise at the service of Germany and its *Führer* and to have suggested that he should make contact with the appropriate office. De

[1] See pp. 170–1.

[2] Louis de Wohl, *I follow my Stars*, 1937, pp. 121–42.

[3] It was Elsbeth Ebertin who issued the warning in question. For an account of von Sebottendorff's indirect connection with Hitler, also of the Ebertin 'prophecy', see chapter 6.

Wohl said that he was not even aware that such an office existed. 'That's what I'm here for!' the Party member replied. But the prospective recruit gave an evasive answer and soon left Germany. This story about the smartly-uniformed Party official does not hang together. In 1935 the only member of the NSDAP who appears to have had any official responsibility for astrological affairs was Karl-Friedrich Schulze (1897–1964), who acted as a censor of astrological literature, his main function being to prevent the publication of the more vulgar kind of fortune-telling books.[1]

Louis de Wohl was introduced to M. Tilea during 1939 by Oscar Kaufmann, a Rumanian banker. De Wohl revealed his interest in astrology and M. Tilea told him about Krafft's Codreanu prediction. I do not know whether M. Tilea ever showed him the letters he received from Krafft during the last months of 1939, but he was given a copy of the one that caused Krafft so much trouble in Berlin in February–March 1940.

According to de Wohl (in *The Stars of War and Peace*), after M. Tilea disclosed the contents of Krafft's letter of 22 February 1940 to the British, it was he who suggested to M. Tilea the formula that eventually led to his own appointment as Krafft's watchdog in London. He said that he emphasised to M. Tilea that it was not of the slightest importance whether or not certain highly-placed British citizens believed in astrology *because Hitler certainly did*. Hence if he, de Wohl, were to make the same astrological calculations as Hitler's man, who was undoubtedly Krafft, he would immediately know what kind of advice the *Führer* was currently receiving and be able to inform the appropriate British intelligence departments. At this point, according to de Wohl, M. Tilea agreed to give him some introductions. However, it was M. Tilea who reasoned on these lines and, furthermore, a good many weeks passed before de Wohl became personally involved in the 'Tilea Plan'.

At this point I must interpolate a technical objection to M. Tilea's theory in as much as it related to predictions. As far as so-called predictive techniques are concerned, an astrologer has a choice of up to half a dozen more or less well-known methods. The fact that none of them has a strictly scientific basis is beside the point. Sometimes one or other of these procedures appears to 'work', but as often as not an astrologer produces complete nonsense. Prediction is astrology's Achilles heel. Logically, then, it would be necessary for an astrologer working in London to use the same predictive method as his counterpart in Berlin. But nobody in London was in a position to know which particular procedure, if any, was being used in Berlin.

The man with whom M. Tilea first discussed the Krafft business in London was Sir Orme Sargent, then a Deputy Under Secretary of State

[1] See the obituary notice by Reinhold Ebertin in *Kosmobiologie*, October 1964. According to Herr Ebertin, Schulze was replaced by a relative of Heinrich Himmler 'who possessed neither the technical knowledge nor the strength of character necessary for such an office'.

at the Foreign Office. M. Tilea outlined three salient factors: Krafft's impressively correct Codreanu prediction; his presence in Berlin and his supposed connection with Hitler; and finally the significant deduction that astrology could be used for psychological warfare purposes. I do not know what Sir Orme Sargent made of M. Tilea's proposition that an astrologer here could 'predict the predictions' that Krafft was allegedly making for Hitler in Berlin, but he understood the possibilities of the psychological warfare gambit. Accordingly some discreet enquiries were made concerning the abilities of a number of local astrologers. A little later Sir Orme Sargent regretfully informed M. Tilea that 'our astrologers appear to be rather pessimistic', and it was on these grounds that nobody could be recommended for the post of Krafft's 'double'.

M. Tilea came to the rescue. 'I know an astrologer who is not pessimistic,' he said. 'His name is Louis de Wohl.'

It was at this stage that M. Tilea introduced de Wohl to a number of influential people. During the summer of 1940 he was invited to meet Lord Winterton, Viscount Horne and Lord Dundonald. The latter sent him to the Hon. Mrs Margaret Greville, a renowned Society hostess. She, in her turn, is supposed to have introduced him to the Duke of Alba, the Spanish Ambassador, who immediately invited him to dinner. De Wohl said that Mrs Greville also introduced him to Lord and Lady Londonderry and Lady (Austen) Chamberlain. When de Wohl dined at the Spanish embassy on 28 August 1940 the Duke of Westminster and Lord and Lady Halifax were said to have been present. Lord Halifax was at that time the Secretary of State for Foreign Affairs. According to de Wohl's account of that momentous occasion, when the men were drinking port after the meal the Duke of Alba asked him to tell Lord Halifax what he knew about Hitler's horoscope. It was of no importance, de Wohl recalled, that he did not have a copy of the horoscope with him, for he knew it by heart. He said that he spoke for an hour and that from time to time Lord Halifax asked him questions.

In *The Stars of War and Peace* de Wohl wrote that he had no idea if Lord Halifax was in any way responsible for what happened subsequently, but mentioned that he was under the impression that Lord Horne had a hand in the business. Lord Horne wrote to him on 22 August and in this letter referred to their recent meeting at M. Tilea's house. He said, too, that he would discuss a memorandum that de Wohl had written for him with certain people. I gather that in this document de Wohl argued that the dates of all Hitler's major *coups* were related to planetary aspects that had previously been evaluated by his astrological adviser(s).

'Very soon', de Wohl wrote, 'I was introduced to a General and an Admiral—who they were and where these meetings took place is of no importance. It was not easy to find a niche for me. Neither the War Office nor the Admiralty could employ an astrologer.' He said that he did not wait for any official decision to be made but set to work on his own account in September 1940. Subsequently, he said, a niche was found for him in a 'Psychological Research Bureau', which had its offices at Grosvenor House in Park Lane. In the Swiss edition of *The Stars of War and Peace* de Wohl mentioned that this was one of London's best hotels.

For a long time de Wohl's pointed reference to Grosvenor House *Hotel* puzzled me. I inferred that the Psychological Research Bureau was his own invention and that its office was de Wohl's bedroom at the hotel. It must be explained that the Grosvenor House building consists of a hotel and a block of unfurnished flats controlled by the hotel company. The hotel itself is one of London's most luxurious establishments and it struck me that it was typical of de Wohl that he should locate his Psychological Research Bureau at a 'good' address. The answer was provided by Miss I., who was at that time a senior secretary in Sir Charles Hambro's office at the Special Operations Executive (SOE), the day before my manuscript was due for delivery to my London publishers.[1] She made it clear that de Wohl was now on SOE's payroll.

'Before de Wohl was taken on by SOE', she wrote, 'he was living in St John's Wood. He persuaded Charles Hambro (and Hambro persuaded other people) that he ought to live somewhere more central and, further-more, insisted that he *must* live at Grosvenor House. So SOE paid for an *unfurnished* suite (not just a bedroom) and I bought all the furniture for it.[2] The name Psychological Research Bureau was, as you supposed, his own invention and officialdom did not object. . . . I'm pretty certain that we did not move de Wohl into Grosvenor House until at least October 1940, probably later. I was very often at the so-called "Bureau", posing as his secretary. . . . I had, at that time, to go there to type his "reports" to the Admiralty and War Office, as his English, although good, was still a bit rocky as to grammar.'

I know very little about de Wohl's activities in London between the autumn of 1940 and May 1941. According to Miss I. his 'reports' were written for the Directorates of Military and Naval Intelligence but it is evident that these departments' interest in astrology and de Wohl did not last for long. Nevertheless, he seems to have had at least one influential supporter, but this gentleman was speedily posted a few thousand miles away from London when it was discovered that he was actually beginning to believe in astrology.

The Naval Intelligence department conducted some independent research in December 1940 or January 1941, when a member of its staff was told to make a small-scale investigation. My informant wrote: 'I went

[1] The late Sir Charles Hambro was then second in command at SOE.

[2] In connection with the unfurnished suite provided by SOE, it should be mentioned that the German air raids on London were already in full swing by the autumn of 1940 and even at Grosvenor House accommodation cannot have been outrageously expensive. In any case SOE worked with secret funds.

round with someone else to a certain number of mostly very unlikely astrologers to see whether, working on Hitler's horoscope, they produced a pattern which seemed, from German action or lack of actions, to work out parallel with the advice that Hitler might be getting from his astrologer. . . . I heard nothing of de Wohl and the atmosphere was not one in which I gathered that anyone thought that they knew what system would be used in advising Hitler—indeed, quite the reverse.'

The most sensible idea for de Wohl's employment came from Sir Charles Hambro, who commissioned him to furnish 'black' propaganda material for dissemination through SOE channels.[1]

According to Miss I., de Wohl 'obstinately insisted on continuing his "offerings" and sent astrological reports on German generals and admirals with the idea that the War Office and Admiralty would be forewarned (always supposing that Hitler *did* use astrology) "where the next attack would come", i.e. the locality where the C. in C. had "really good aspects" '. It is obvious, however, that nobody took de Wohl's unsolicited reports at all seriously.

Sir Charles Hambro decided to send de Wohl on an astrological mission to the U.S.A. The purpose of this visit must be considered in relation to the prevailing state of affairs in Europe. The Germans had overrun most of the Continent and were enjoying their initial successes in Russia. Japan was still biding her time and the U.S.A. was ostensibly neutral. It cannot be said that Great Britain's prospects of ultimate victory were specially bright at that moment. The German propaganda machine was certainly not inactive and Hambro was by now aware that astrologers and their beliefs could be used for propaganda or psychological warfare purposes. Krafft's letter to M. Tilea had clearly demonstrated that much. It is possible that the Germans had infiltrated American mass-circulation periodicals, such as *American Astrology*—there were half a dozen similar publications—with articles or readers' letters predicting an inevitable German victory. If not, some American astrological journalists may have done the job for them by drawing false astrological conclusions from current evidence of German military prowess. Hence the plan that de Wohl should visit the U.S.A., ostensibly as a private individual, and mount a counter-attack.[2]

The information published here is partly based upon an analysis of two

[1] At this stage of the war the Psychological Warfare Executive's 'black' activities were only just beginning. Sefton Delmer's famous 'Gustav Siegfried Eins' broadcasting station first went on the air on 23 May 1941, and the late Armin Hull, Delmer's 'black' printing expert, did not begin to operate until November 1941. PWE and SOE were separate entities although there were close links between them. For the early history, organisation and functions of SOE see M. R. D. Foote, *SOE in France*, London, HMSO, 1966, and Bickham Sweet-Escott's autobiographical *Baker Street Irregular*, London, 1965.

[2] It is unlikely that there was any connection between de Wohl's visit to the U.S.A. and the announcement in the *Völkischer Beobachter* on 14 May 1941 that Hess had been

memoranda written for me in 1966–7, the first by H., an old friend, and the second by Miss I., whom I eventually traced after a long search. H. wrote: 'My memories of the operations of Louis de Wohl are vague. During 1941 I was instructed by Sir Charles Hambro to attend to the organisation and administration of the American operation. A few weeks later I came to the conclusion that the project was senseless and asked to be relieved of the responsibility. Hambro's Chiefs of Staff secretariat then became responsible for policy planning and my section handled the routine work connected with travel and finance. Soon after de Wohl arrived in the U.S.A. he asked for "world-wide backing" for his astrological propaganda campaign. It was at his request that we arranged for "predictions" to be made in West Africa (from Lagos), also from Cairo. These achieved publicity in English language newspapers published in Africa. I recall seeing some hilariously funny press cuttings. I believe that de Wohl's plan was to "reach Hitler's astrologers" with direful astrological predictions, filling them (and, through them, Hitler) with doubts and dismay. The fact is, however, that I never attached any importance to de Wohl as an SOE agent for the dissemination of subversive propaganda. The project seemed to me to be too complex, too expensive, and too much open to charlatanism, to justify the time spent on it. I visited New York when de Wohl was there but did not meet him.'

Miss I. wrote to me twice in January 1967. H. had described her a year earlier as 'a top SOE secretary' but could not recall her name. 'I was already acting as liaison between de Wohl and any section of officialdom that might be concerned at any given time,' she recalled. 'The chief contact was a gentleman in the War Office.'

Miss I. was also sent to the U.S.A., partly as SOE's 'watch dog', but mainly to provide liaison services between de Wohl and a special British mission in New York. De Wohl had no contact whatever with this mission and probably never knew its address. Miss I.: 'This, in theory, was to avoid any American suspicion that Louis had *any* connection with British officialdom. To the American world I was de Wohl's secretary.' However, the American Office of Strategic Services was kept informed. According to Mr Bickham Sweet-Escott: 'Our friends in OSS were not impressed. I have no doubt that they thought that the de Wohl mission was a cover story for something infinitely more sinister. Perhaps indeed it was.'[1]

De Wohl landed at a Canadian port on 24 May 1941, and made his

---

influenced by astrologers, although the news must have confirmed Hambro's feelings that all astrological angles were worthwhile exploiting. It appears that de Wohl disembarked in Canada so soon after Hess's arrival in Scotland that there would hardly have been time to plan such a complicated mission. It is improbable that British intelligence immediately learned of the wholesale arrests of astrologers and others in the course of the 'Aktion Hess' in mid-June.

[1] Bickham Sweet-Escott, *Baker Street Irregular*, 1965, p. 147. Mr Sweet-Escott's surmise was unjustified.

way to Montreal, where Miss I. joined him three weeks later. There was an 'administrative muddle' and three more weeks later they had still not crossed the border into the U.S.A. However, they eventually arrived at New York and de Wohl got to work. The New York office was not very helpful, but arranged (probably through trustworthy inter-mediaries) for a Metro-Goldwyn-Mayer publicity man to organise a press conference for him. Miss I.: 'He had been hired to boost de Wohl, who had been briefed to make himself well known, during the first two months.' This led to a cinema news-reel interview. 'De Wohl made one short piece for a news-reel, which cut no ice. He looked like hell on the screen and the effort was not repeated.'

I had asked Miss I. to describe de Wohl's activities in North America. She wrote: 'Perhaps I should first tell you what the project was *supposed* to be. At fairly frequent intervals SOE were to send to the New York office items of black propaganda they wanted to appear in the American press, in the hope that they would go from there to Germany. All helpful details were to be supplied, but the ways of putting this over to the U.S. journalists was left to de Wohl. The underlying theme was "Germany is going to lose the war". In actual fact we never received anything from London, and the New York office swore they never received anything. When I returned to London a colleague swore that he had sent stacks of material, and the N.Y. office must have deliberately sat on it. Which side was telling the truth? Your guess is as good as mine.'

At this point I have slightly re-shaped Miss I.'s notes: 'De Wohl worked out astrological "maps" of various people he thought were of particular use to Hitler and then told select gatherings of journalists all the "astrological bad aspects" to which his selected victims would be subject during the near future, in the hope of giving the said victims an aura of "bad luck". He also tried to persuade ex-colleagues from UFA [Berlin film studios] who were in Hollywood to take an active part in anti-German propaganda. He worked on the same lines with a few American astrologers he could trust. Publicly and privately he tried to drive home the fact that it would be better for the United States to enter the war voluntarily than to be pushed into it. It seemed to me at the time, and still does, that what *could* have been an excellent piece of psychological warfare turned out, from lack of co-operation, into a fair flop. Initially the project was supposed to last two months—at the *outside* three months. Seven months after leaving England I began to get a bit restless . . . because it seemed to me that it had ceased to be of much use to the war effort.'

De Wohl, according to Miss I., had not been at all anxious to go to the U.S.A., because his current planetary 'aspects' were unsatisfactory, and undertook this particular mission because of a sense of duty. Many of his German refugee friends were already serving in the British army and he, too, wanted to make his contribution.

NOSTRA DAMUR

Über ältere und älteste Ausgaben der « Prophéties »

Irrtümer erweisen sich zuweilen zählebiger als eine noch so gut beglaubigte Wahrheit. Dies ist zumal dort der Fall, wo sich seit Jahrzehnten die Mehrzahl der Berichterstatter damit begnügt hat, bei Zeitgenossen oder Vorgängern das abzuschreiben, was diese ihrerseits aus zweiter oder dritter Hand umbesehn übernommen hatten. Unter solchen Umständen belegt Übereinstimmung der Behauptungen wenig mehr als die Bequemlichkeit oder die Kritiklosigkeit der Schreiber.

Die erste ernst zu nehmende Bibliographie der Schriften von NOSTRADAMUS veröffentlichte T. KELLEN). Einen weiteren Schritt zur Klärung der Frage der frühen Drucke der « Prophéties » bildete die Arbeit C. von KLINCKOWSTROEM's).

'Auf dem ersten Blick – so schrieb damals vKL. – erscheint nichts leichter als eine Beschreibung der ältesten Drucke der « Prophéties » des NOSTRADAMUS. Fast alle Biographen, die ältern sowohl wie die neuern, stimmen darin überein, daß er den ersten Teil

---

1) Börsenblatt f. d. deutschen Buchhandel (Leipzig 1904), 918-921.
2) Zeitschrift f. Bücherfreunde (Leipzig 1913), 361-372. - Mit zahlreichen Illustrationen.

16. One of the two issues of *Nostra Damur* published by Krafft in Berlin for private circulation in 1940–1.

17. The Portuguese edition of Krafft's *Comment Nostradamus a-t-il entrevu l'avenir de l'Europe?*

18. A faked German astrological magazine edited by Louis de Wohl for PWE in 1943. Copies were infiltrated into Germany.

19. One of half a dozen Nostradamus quatrain cards published privately by Krafft in Berlin in 1940–1.

The fact that the American Federation of Scientific Astrologers was due to hold an important national convention at Cleveland, Ohio, in August 1941 provided de Wohl with an excellent opportunity for meeting colleagues from every part of the U.S.A. His offer to lecture there on comparisons between the horoscopes of Hitler and Napoleon appears to have been accepted with enthusiasm.

While de Wohl's paper may not have been up to Krafft's exacting standards it was nevertheless a lively piece of work. After discussing, among other matters, Hitler's love life—here Eva Braun's violent death was at least presaged although de Wohl cannot have known of her existence —he turned to the Russian campaign, which was still only a few weeks old. 'Here, in my opinion, is the first major action of Hitler which could not have been countersigned by his astrologers. So far he has timed everything perfectly well,' de Wohl observed. But who were these advisers? De Wohl mentioned no names but called them 'the best astrologers in Germany'. Furthermore, he added, Hitler had 'persuaded Karl E. Krafft, next to Dr Alfred Fankhauser the best Swiss expert, to change his address from Urberg in Switzerland to Berlin'.[1]

All this was followed by something even more imaginative: 'But even the collaboration of German and Swiss astrologers was not enough for Hitler . . . he had their findings checked by the famous Geopolitical Institute in Munich. What is Geopolitics? It is an extremely clever combination of history, geography, military strategy and astrology—the latter science functioning as the time-keeper.' De Wohl was not alone in overestimating the importance of the Geopolitical Institute at Munich, which was conducted by Professor Karl Haushofer. The Professor 'was said to control a staff of two thousand strategists, physicists, meteorologists, engineers and economists who checked the information that Hess supplied through spies and other agents for Hitler's "strategic Index". This was just not so. Karl Haushofer ran the Geopolitic Institute with one assistant and a typist.'[2]

At this point de Wohl's powers of invention and, indeed, sense of psychological warfare techniques, became nothing less than inspired, for he now adroitly suggested to his audience that Hitler planned to bring the war to the American continent on the basis of astrological briefs supplied by Haushofer's staff. The Institute, according to de Wohl, had advised the *Führer* on the following lines:

1. It is always opportune to attack a country when the two major 'malefics' (the planets Saturn and Uranus) are in the zodiacal sign that 'rules' the nation against which war is to be waged.

---

[1] Krafft would have heartily disliked being rated second to Fankhauser, furthermore it is unlikely that many of the leading German astrologers would have put Fankhauser in Krafft's class. Again, de Wohl was apparently unaware that Urberg is not in Switzerland but in Germany.

[2] James Leasor, *Rudolph Hess: The Uninvited Envoy*, 1962, p. 44.

2. Saturn and Uranus would be in Gemini, the sign supposed to 'rule' the U.S.A., until the late spring of 1942. Hence a German attack would not be made (according to the geopoliticians) before that time.

3. Finally, in all circumstances the war must be contrived on foreign soil.

In connection with the latter recommendation de Wohl proposed that the Germans would probably use Brazil as a stepping stone for hostilities against the U.S.A. and produced astrological reasons to support his argument: 'Brazil is ruled by Virgo and therefore she, too, will be under the hostile influences of Saturn and Uranus from the late spring of 1942 onwards. America has always been subject to grave events when Uranus transits Gemini.' In view of the Americans' understandable dislike of the prospect of the 'shooting war' approaching their own continent, all this was very sound anti-German propaganda, especially when delivered to an audience that would be quick to grasp the 'technical' implications.[1]

While in the U.S.A. de Wohl staged a sniping operation against Krafft. It consisted of disclosing two fictitious passages alleged to be from the Tilea letter to an American journalist. His intention was that the extracts, when published, should be read by the press attaché or any other intelligence officer at the German embassy at Washington, and reasoned that the information would then be cabled to Berlin with the result that Krafft would speedily find himself in hot water. In an article published in *Heim und Welt* (20 August 1950) de Wohl denied that he had ever faked any letter or letters written by Krafft. He admitted, however, that he had given an American journalist two extracts from the Tilea letter and claimed that both were completely genuine. According to de Wohl, the passages in question implied that Krafft was not certain that Germany would win the war and that he thought there was a possibility that the *Führer* would suddenly disappear. 'That is what Krafft said. I have a copy of his letter to Tilea in my possession,' he wrote.[2] The fact is, however, that Krafft had never written anything of the sort in his letter to M. Tilea of 14 March 1940, and for two very good reasons: firstly he believed that Germany would win the war and secondly his letter to M. Tilea was written with the Gestapo literally breathing down his neck. It would have been as much as his life was worth to suggest that Hitler would suddenly disappear.

De Wohl remained in the U.S.A. throughout the second half of 1941 and returned to London in February 1942. In America, at any rate, the

[1] The Americans believed that Hitler had nefarious designs in South America. Cf. Roosevelt's Navy Day speech at Washington on 27 October 1941. He said that he had a secret map made in Germany by Hitler's government showing Central and South America as the Germans proposed to organise it. The German Government published a denial on 1 November and declared war on the U.S.A. on 11 December.

[2] I have not seen the original issue of *Heim und Welt* and have quoted from a typewritten extract kindly supplied by the *Institut für Zeitgeschichte* at Munich. My impression is that the 'leak' was made to the New York *Sunday News*.

Krafft legend had been effectively launched. In Great Britain he was still obliged to preserve a discreet silence.

'Later I was a British officer with the rank of captain,' de Wohl wrote in *The Stars of War and Peace*. The frontispiece shows him in uniform with a captain's badges on his shoulders. Early in 1966 Sefton Delmer produced a de Wohl anecdote which puzzled me at the time. He had it from the late Leonard Ingrams, a friend and colleague of us both. Ingrams, who was in a position to know about de Wohl's war-time activities, had told Delmer that de Wohl's commission was completely unofficial. According to Delmer: 'Leonard Ingrams and his friends at SOE put de Wohl through an elaborate fake commissioning ceremony as he was so anxious to be an officer.' I then wrote to the Ministry of Defence and asked for particulars of de Wohl's military career. The Directorate of Manning (Army) replied that 'there is no record in the army department that the late Louis de Wohl ever held a commission in the British army'. Somewhat later my friend W., who had been employed in a military intelligence department (not SOE) told me the following story:

'De Wohl was desperately anxious to be an officer in the British army,' W. said, 'and pestered the Colonel in charge of my section to the point of extreme exasperation.[1] To keep him quiet the Colonel said: "I've arranged it. You're a captain in the British army. Of course I cannot give you anything in writing. It's much too secret and, of course, you can't use the rank." De Wohl was overjoyed and promised total secrecy. However, unknown to us he bought himself a military uniform and was observed walking down Piccadilly looking just like an unmade bed. He was immediately told not to wear the uniform but appears to have disobeyed this instruction.'

Finally, Miss I. provided another and, I think, credible version: 'There was a "swearing in" ceremony, conducted *not* at SOE but at the War Office, by Brigadier N., or so N. told me. Louis had been solemnly promised a commission as a reward for going to the U.S.A. When he returned to London he reminded his contacts of their promise but nothing was done. Eventually Brigadier N. thought up a face-saving operation. Hence the "ceremony" and the manufacture of some kind of official-looking paper stating that de Wohl had "sworn allegiance to His Majesty" *and* verbal permission to wear uniform in London. After a few months Louis, being an optimist but no fool, realised that he was *not* going to get a commission and gave up wearing uniform. When he returned from the U.S.A. Hambro was "out" and so, therefore, except for the Delmer interlude, was de Wohl.[2] But he insisted for a time in continuing his reports to the War Office. . . . I think it fair to say that by the end of 1943 de Wohl had been

---

[1] This Colonel was the 'chief contact at the War Office' mentioned by Miss I.
[2] Sir Charles Hambro did not resign from SOE until September 1943.

snubbed out of any enthusiasm for personally assisting the war effort.'

It seems, however, that de Wohl was still kept on the payroll. My friend W., mentioned above, joined a certain branch of military intelligence early in 1943. W. told me that de Wohl was paid in cash from secret funds and that one of his colleagues periodically went to Athenaeum Court, a hotel in Piccadilly, for this purpose. The messenger complained to his Colonel that de Wohl insisted on 'gassing' for an hour on end about astrology. The Colonel said: 'Let him talk, keep him happy!'

It is possible that what Miss I. described as 'the Delmer interlude' was the last time that de Wohl was officially employed. As I mentioned in chapter 1, Delmer introduced me to him early in 1943. Our few encounters were all in connection with three faked issues of Dr Korsch's astrological periodical *Zenit*. De Wohl wrote most of the copy for these under Sefton Delmer's supervision. The technical work was executed by Armin Hull, Delmer's 'black' typographical specialist, whose work is mentioned in the latter's *Black Boomerang*. De Wohl cannot have provided a specimen of *Zenit*, which ceased publication in December 1938, or we would not have mistakenly called our publication *Der Zenit*. This explains, too, why Hull did not reproduce *Zenit*'s usual cover design, but asked Fräulein E., the gifted German type designer and graphic artist who worked in his unit, to prepare the version, which was certainly appropriate, illustrated opposite p. 213 in this book.

There were two octavo issues, dated January and March 1943, and a miniature 'Armed Forces Air Mail' edition, printed on very thin paper, dated April 1943. In Germany many years later I acquired a copy of the latter and a subsequent search produced copies of the octavo editions. The miniature one is by far the most interesting of the three, probably because the de Wohl–Delmer partnership was now getting into its stride.

The miniature edition, like its predecessors, was ostensibly printed at Görlitz-Biesnitz by the firm of Hans Kretschmer. It included typical advertisements for obscure patent medicines, also for books offered for sale by genuine German astrological publishers. I was amused to find that we had given Herr Reinhold Ebertin, now of Aalen, a free advertisement for his astrological periodical *Mensch im All*, which had until recently been published at Erfurt.

Our offering for April 1943 was aimed at U-boat crews and was probably printed about three months later. By this time Delmer would have known the dates when German submarines were sunk in April. Information of this kind was essential so that de Wohl's 'predictions' might appear to have been fulfilled. Our purpose was to persuade German U-boat personnel in the North Sea ports to ascribe to *Der Zenit* an omniscience it hardly deserved, to disturb their morale and spread rumours.

The predictions were on the following lines: '*1st April*, unfavourable for U-boats to go to sea; *4th April*, advisable not to go to sea if the Captain's horoscope is unfavourable; *9th April*, propitious for the newer types of U-boats but bad for the older ones; *20th April*, very bad for U-boats.'

This issue also included a lively and highly-subversive article headed: 'The 30th of June is near!' which suggested that the events of 30 June 1934 (the Roehm '*Putsch*') would soon be repeated, this time by rebellious SS leaders. The 'black' theme that Himmler's SS would ultimately betray the poor, trusting *Führer* and all truly patriotic Germans, was constantly in evidence in Delmer's work.

'The *Reichsführer* of the SS is now coming to a period when his cosmic constellations bode no good.' Nor, according to the stars, was life likely to be easy for his colleagues Herren Ernst Kaltenbrunner, Bruno Strecken-bach, Karl Wolff, Hans Prützmann, Wilhelm Rediess, Arthur Nebe and Erich von dem Bach Zelewski. The latter was brusquely attacked: 'He's the man whose pig-headedness resulted in the Russian break-through at Kursk when he refused to send SS troops to the front. The *Führer* still trusts him. He should sack him immediately!'

In 1963 Herr Wilhelm Wulff, the Hamburg astrologer, showed me an octavo *Zenit* which had been intercepted by the *Sicherheitsdienst* at Stettin and had reached Germany in a consignment of machine tools from Sweden. It contained the horoscopes of Admirals Doenitz and Raeder. At that time Herr Wulff was doing astrological work for Himmler, although with a pistol that was a great deal less than metaphorical pointed at his head. Walter Schellenberg ordered him to prepare a technical evaluation of our work because the SD wanted to know if the material was based upon correct astrological principles. Herr Wulff was able to inform him that this was the case.

De Wohl also supplied most of the copy for *Nostradamus prophezeit den Kriegsverlauf* (*Nostradamus predicts the Course of the War*), yet another 'black' production produced under Delmer's supervision. The authorship of this little book was ascribed to Dr Bruno Winkler, of Weimar, who in his Introduction thanked Dr Heinrich Lesse, curator of the ducal manu-script collection at Ratisbon, for the loan of a unique (but non-existent) Nostradamus manuscript.[1] The propaganda 'sting' is to be found in the commentaries to the German translations of fifty bogus Nostradamus quatrains that were composed in appropriately archaic French.[2] This project constituted an interesting exercise in the provision of subversive rumour material under the camouflage of an apparently innocent booklet.

[1] Bruno Winkler was the author of *Englands Aufstieg und Niedergang nach den Prophezeiungen des grossen französischen Sehers der Jahre 1555 und 1558*, Leipzig, 1940, yet another Nostradamus item. The title is quoted in W. A. Boelcke, *Kriegspropaganda 1939–41*, p. 304. His doctorate and connection with Weimar were probably invented by Delmer or de Wohl.

[2] See the quatrain and translation in illustration no. 22. According to the German translation: Hister [i.e. Hitler] who carried off more victories (prizes) in his warlike fight than was good for him; six [men] will murder him in the night. Naked, taken unawares without his armour, he succumbs.

The production of this Nostradamus item, which bore the imprint of the Regulus Verlag at Görlitz, a firm previously well known for its occult and astrological publications, fascinated Armin Hull. Since Dr Winkler had used an 'ancient' manuscript, Hull decided to reproduce it and asked Fräulein E. to hand-letter the texts of the sixteenth-century quatrains in a contemporary script. These were reproduced by line blocks. The German translations of the fake quatrains were set in *Fraktur* type, with the commentaries in roman type (see illustration facing p. 229). The booklet was printed on the thinnest available Bible paper and although it contained 124 pages weighed less than an ounce. It did great credit to the fictitious Herr Paul George who, according to the colophon (dated 15 March 1943), was responsible for its design. Hull told me that this project provided a pleasant change from the routine task of forging German ration cards or preparing yet another edition of Delmer's famous *Krankheit Rettet*, a handbook for would-be malingerers, which was constantly reprinted with different camouflage covers, e.g. for soldiers' song books, ballistic tables, pocket guides to Oslo and the like.

As far as I was concerned, de Wohl faded from the scene as suddenly as he had entered it. We met in a London street soon after the war and exchanged a few words, but I never saw him again. Indeed, it was not until after 1959 that his war-time career became a matter of interest to me. I wrote to him in May 1961 but did not receive a reply. A week or two later *The Times* reported his death in Switzerland at Lucerne on 2 June 1961.

The Captive Astrologers

F. G. Goerner was shown a warrant for his arrest at the Mannheim Gestapo headquarters shortly before midnight on 9 June 1941 and was then transferred to the local SS prison. Upon arrival there he was given a blanket and pushed into a pitch-dark cell, where two invisible companions soon identified themselves as amateur astrologers. During the course of the following week he was intensively cross-examined upon three occasions, the last time by a uniformed Gestapo official who wanted to know all about his local contacts.

On 16 June he was taken to the Schloss prison at Mannheim and in the course of subsequent interrogations it became clear that the Gestapo was specially interested in his connection with Krafft and, in particular, with other friends of Krafft's in Germany. They also wanted to know if Krafft and himself had had any personal connection with Hess. He told them that he had known Krafft for ten years and had taken a deep interest in his work. As for Krafft's friends, he suggested that whatever information he might be able to give must surely already be well known to the Gestapo. 'You're keeping quiet about something!' his questioner said threateningly.

On 16 August, exactly two months after his arrival at the Schloss prison, Goerner was taken to the administration block and shown a so-called 'red protective custody order' signed, he told me, by Reinhard Heydrich himself.[1] He was informed that he would now be transferred to a concentration camp near Berlin.

'And when you arrive there,' he was told, 'we'll have you face to face with your friends Krafft and Verweyen and hear what you have to say.'

Goerner was surprised to hear Professor Verweyen's name mentioned in connection with Krafft but kept quiet. Two days later, on 18 August, he was fetched from his cell, handcuffed to a tall Dutchman and taken to Mannheim railway station. The train journey to Berlin lasted three days, with overnight stops at prisons at Frankfurt am Main and Cassel. Eventually he found himself in the reception block at the Oranienburg concentration camp a few miles north of Berlin. Soon he encountered a number of old acquaintances, among them Dr Korsch and Heinrich Huter, but there was no sign of either Krafft or Professor Verweyen.[2]

---

[1] Heydrich was head of the *Reichssicherheitshauptamt*, by then an enormous organisation with seven departments, of which Section IV, the Gestapo, was one. I cannot understand why Heydrich should have bothered himself with signing this particular order.

[2] Herr Huter was the proprietor of an astrological publishing business at Leipzig. When I met him at Stuttgart in 1962 he told me that the Gestapo had already seized

About a fortnight later, on Saturday 4 September, the barrack-room door opened and a camp guard appeared with a man dressed in civilian clothes. 'Well, now we at least know where you are!' the civilian remarked. It appears that Goerner had been 'lost' in the course of an administrative muddle. The door slammed and he was left wondering what would happen next. He did not have long to wait. Sunday passed and on Monday he was taken to a *Reichssicherheitshauptamt* office in Berlin and shown into a small room. He was told to sit down. Four senior SS officers faced him across a large table upon which there were a lot of papers. Once again he was required to discuss every detail of his previous relationship with Krafft and they also asked questions about Professor Verweyen. The interrogation was lengthy and according to Herr Goerner the longer it lasted the more friendly his inquisitors became. They obviously knew a great deal about Krafft, and Goerner soon realised that the papers on the table must have been taken from him.

The interview took an unexpected turn when he was closely examined about Krafft's peculiar *Sprachgeist* ('Spirit of Language') theories and his juggling with the vowels and consonants of words in order to establish connections and meanings that had certainly never occurred to academic philologists. It then became clear to him that they thought that these arcane etymological speculations provided a convenient disguise for a cipher system and that they suspected that Krafft had been engaged in espionage activities. He did his best to explain Krafft's queer linguistic theories to them but they did not appear to be altogether convinced.

He was taken back to Oranienburg. Nothing further happened during the next seven weeks and he became increasingly despondent. His health began to deteriorate, but when he reported to the camp doctor he was sent away with a flea in his ear. Then, out of the blue on 16 October, he was summoned to the administration block and soon found himself being driven in a police car in the direction of Berlin. Eventually he and his escort arrived at the Alexanderplatz police prison. He was shown into a small cell—it was No. 102—and was alone with his thoughts.

When Krafft left his home in the Burggrafenstrasse in the company of two Gestapo officials on 12 June, one of them told Frau Krafft that her husband would be back that evening. When they arrived at the Alexanderplatz he was informed that the official who wanted to talk to him was not available and he would have to remain there overnight. He was allowed to telephone his wife and tell her as much, and was then escorted to a cell. However, he did not return home the next day or even the following one. Instead three Gestapo officials went there and took all his papers and a great many books. Frau Krafft asked them why her husband had been arrested but they told

---

40,000 books and pamphlets from his stock in April 1939. He was released from Oranienburg in January 1942.

her nothing. A fortnight later she was able to visit him briefly at the Alexanderplatz police prison and learned that he had not been shown a warrant for his arrest and had so far not been interrogated.

Krafft felt confident that one or other of his important Nazi contacts would come to his rescue and dictated a letter for his wife to send to Dr Hans Frank, the Governor General of Poland, whom he had met early in 1940 at the musical evening already mentioned. Frau Krafft was in due course invited to call upon a senior member of Frank's staff in Berlin. He asked her a number of questions and said he would send a report to his chief. At a later meeting he told her that he could do nothing to help either Krafft or herself. Next she wrote to Dr Ley, who was more helpful than his colleague Dr Frank, for some days later she received a telephone call from a Foreign Office official who told her to contact a certain Herr Ehrhardt, a member of the *Reichssicherheitshauptamt*, and gave her his telephone number. She also went to the Swiss embassy where she was informed that they would get into touch with the German Foreign Office. A long time passed before she succeeded in obtaining an interview with Ehrhardt and she did not see him until six months after Krafft's arrest. In the meantime Krafft and Goerner had already met at the Alexanderplatz police prison.

A couple of days after Goerner arrived there on 16 October a key rattled in the lock of his cell door. It opened and a warder barked: 'Bath parade; towel and soap; stand outside in the corridor and keep quiet!' Goerner stepped into the passage outside cell 102 and cautiously looked left and right. The doors of cells 101 and 100 were closed but that of cell 99 was slightly ajar. Then it opened and out came Krafft. There was a quick glance of mutual recognition but it was risky even to whisper a word of greeting. Under the showers they were able to have a hurried conversation.

'How long have you been here?' Goerner asked. 'Since 12 June,' Krafft replied.

They discussed their respective prison experiences. Krafft said that things might have been worse; his wife was allowed to visit him from time to time and to bring him vegetarian food, also a few books. The latter, he said, were nothing very special but at least helped him to pass the time. He promised to slip one to Goerner the next time they went to the showers. He kept his word and during the next few months was able to lend him an occasional book of a religious nature—Goerner recalled reading a paper-covered life of St Theresa of Lisieux—or a few newspaper cuttings, and on one occasion even a complete newspaper. He had to keep this printed matter hidden as he would have been in trouble if it had been discovered in his possession.

Goerner was not altogether surprised to encounter Professor Verweyen in the exercise yard one day. They were able to exchange a few words but a conversation was impossible. The weeks dragged by, punctuated only by occasional meetings with Krafft at the showers. Then, on 23 December 1941, Goerner, Krafft and Verweyen were escorted from the cell block to another part of the building and were taken to the same Herr Ehrhardt whom Frau Krafft had been advised to see on her husband's behalf. He did not have much to tell them, only that the State's case against them would be considered in January when a decision concerning their respective futures would be reached. But January passed uneventfully and a further four months elapsed before anything momentous occurred.

In the meantime Frau Krafft had managed to arrange an interview with Ehrhardt and had several more meetings with him during the next few months. On the first occasion he explained that until now he had been unable to find time to deal with Krafft's case. And in any event, he added, to review Krafft's work on the basis of the papers that had been taken from the Burggrafenstrasse represented such a complicated problem that to assess what it was all about would require a whole army of specialists. He did say, however, that he would be prepared to listen to anything she might like to tell him.

Ehrhardt mentioned that most of the arrested astrologers had already been released, but emphasised that the *Sicherheitsdienst* was of the opinion that Krafft was undoubtedly a star performer as far as astrology was concerned, even if he and his colleagues found it very difficult to understand why this should be the case. Furthermore, he said, because of Krafft's personal magnetism he obviously influenced people with whom he came into contact and hence represented a potentially pernicious and, indeed, dangerous element in relation to the National Socialist *Weltanschauung*.

Frau Krafft replied that her husband had always objected to being called an astrologer in the accepted sense of the word and totally rejected the fatalistic attitude common to so many of these people. Ehrhardt impatiently remarked: 'Then why on earth did he devote himself like a fanatic to astrology for twenty years on end if it doesn't serve any purpose?' He added that while Krafft may not have had any conscious plan, it was thought that certain medical men in Switzerland might possibly have encouraged him to disseminate anti-social ideas in Germany. Again he, Ehrhardt, could not understand why Krafft should forgo the security of Switzerland and be content with a very modest way of life in Germany. Hence his conclusion that he surely must be in someone's pay. Frau Krafft did not succeed in getting very far with Ehrhardt on this occasion.

Goerner was able to have a brief conversation with Professor Verweyen in April 1942. Verweyen said that he had sent Ehrhardt a letter to the effect that he had been informed in December that a decision about his future would be made in January but that nothing whatever had happened, and he would now be glad to have some information. Whether or not it

was supplied is not known, but on 24 May a warder told Goerner that
Verweyen had just been transferred to the Oranienburg concentration
camp. He was never released but was kept at Oranienburg until February
1945 when he was transferred to the notorious Bergen-Belsen camp. He
died there a month later on 21 March 1945.

In the meantime Frau Krafft was seeing Ehrhardt from time to time.
At one of these meetings, probably in the early spring of 1942, he was
more encouraging than he had ever been in the past. He admitted that he
had previously been sceptical about Krafft's good intentions, but now he
was prepared to suggest that he should be released. There would, however, be certain conditions. Krafft would be expected to keep his opinions
strictly to himself, and he certainly would not be permitted either to lecture
or contact any highly-placed Germans, such as Dr Frank and Dr Ley.
Furthermore, there was no question of him being allowed to correspond
with anyone outside Germany. He would be free to return to his old job
at the *Deutsche Nachrichtenbüro*, but only on condition that he had no
access to any of its top-level departments. Krafft could think and study
whatever he liked, Ehrhardt said, but he was not to discuss undesirable
subjects such as astrology and the prophecies of Nostradamus with anyone,
or write about them. Frau Krafft asked him if he thought that his proposals
for Krafft's future would be accepted. He replied that the advice of the
official in charge of any particular case was usually followed.

Ehrhardt's proposals if, indeed, he ever submitted them to his superiors,
were not accepted, and the next time Frau Krafft saw him, probably late
in May 1942, he told her that there was now a new plan, adding that his
own department was in touch with one of the ministries and that they
would probably be able to find a job for him there. Goerner would accompany him and work under the same conditions. Each of them would have
his own room, a warder would keep an eye on them both, take them to the
canteen for their meals and even for short walks.

But there was more to come: providing that their work was satisfactory,
he said, a further application for their release could be made after six
months, but their employment would nevertheless continue.[1] Frau Krafft
recalled that at that point she became worried and anxiously protested that
Krafft should not be obliged to undertake any kind of work that would be
against his principles. Ehrhardt reassured her. 'We want him to do
mathematical calculations. After all, he's a good mathematician, isn't he?
Furthermore, if all goes well, you'll be able to visit him three or four times
a week after working hours, perhaps even more often.'

Ehrhardt made it clear that in return for these concessions she would
have to comply with certain conditions. 'You are not to make any further
attempts to secure your husband's release,' he said. 'If you do, it might be

[1] Herr Goerner said nothing to me about the conditional prospect of release after
six months.

very unfortunate for both of you. Furthermore, you are to keep away from the Swiss embassy and you definitely must not correspond with anyone outside Germany.' Frau Krafft replied that she would willingly agree to all this but would like to send a few lines to her mother-in-law every month to prevent the old lady from becoming anxious. Ehrhardt remarked that even if *one* door were left ajar it might be dangerous, adding that if she wrote to Krafft *mère* it would be at her own risk.

Krafft and Goerner did not hear about these new plans until 5 June 1942, when they were taken to Ehrhardt's office. Goerner recalled that he sat at his desk and gave them a searching look. Ehrhardt informed them that certain information about them had been sent to another department. At this Krafft pulled a glum face. Ehrhardt next asked them if they understood trigonometrical calculations. Goerner told me that he grinned all over his face and happily replied 'yes!', while Krafft merely muttered an affirmative. At this point Ehrhardt announced that they would both be leaving the Alexanderplatz police prison within the next few days and would be given a job of work to do. He said that apart from Frau Krafft's efforts on her husband's behalf, other people had interceded in his favour, and this was the reason for their exceptional treatment. Finally he warned them that if either of them tried any funny business he would soon find himself back at the Alexanderplatz prison or the Oranienburg concentration camp.

A week passed and nothing happened, but on the morning of Friday 12 June, the anniversary of Krafft's arrest, the prison barber, who was a 'trusty', entered Goerner's cell. Goerner was surprised to see him since he normally only came once a week, and it was only a day or two since he had last given Goerner a shave. 'I've just shaved your pal, the chap in cell 99,' he said. 'You'll be leaving here this afternoon.' Soon a warder arrived and told him to pack. It did not take him long to put his few bits and pieces into a small cardboard box, which was the only luggage in his possession. The time passed very slowly for Goerner that afternoon and evening. Nobody came to fetch him from his cell and he became increasingly anxious. At last he decided to go to bed, and while he lay there waiting for sleep to come he recalled a series of apparently prophetic dreams that he had recently experienced. These seemed to suggest that he would soon be either released or transferred to some unspecified department in the Propaganda Ministry. He remembered, too, that according to one of these dreams he was not due to be set free until 13 June, and today was only the twelfth. Reassured, he fell asleep.

Goerner's prophetic dream was fulfilled the next morning, when his cell door opened and a warder told him to come outside. Krafft was already standing in the corridor. They were taken to a car that was waiting in the courtyard and set off in a northerly direction. In due course they arrived at a large office building in the Kommandantenstrasse. It had previously been part of the Muratti cigarette factory but now housed a branch of the Propaganda Ministry. They were escorted to a room where several well-dressed young women were busy typing.

'We sat there like a couple of poor sinners', Goerner recalled. 'The girls stared at us as if we belonged to some peculiar race of cattle. After all we had been through during the past year we can't have looked very presentable. Then a chap in civilian clothes appeared. He told us his name was Fritz Hirsch and that he would be in charge of us. He took us to the canteen for a meal and showed us our quarters, informing us that we could be together during the daytime but that we would be locked up in our respective rooms at 5 p.m. He said, too, that in the event of an air raid someone would fetch us to the shelter. This was a pleasant novelty because at the Alexanderplatz we had to stay in our cells.'

They had arrived at the Kommandantenstrasse on a Saturday morning but their new employers did not appear until after the week-end. Goerner said that he and Krafft had a meeting with three or four men, but he could only remember the name of one of them. This was a certain Herr Kurd Kisshauer who, he thought, had at one time been employed by the Zeiss optical firm at Jena in connection with the design of planetaria. They were told that in future Kisshauer would give them their instructions, collect their work and check it. By now it had emerged that the trigonometrical calculations mentioned by Ehrhardt were required in connection with the preparation and interpretation of horoscopes. Krafft was to be in charge of the work, while Goerner's function was to act as his secretary and assistant.

Unfortunately, Kurd Kisshauer died in November 1958 and I was never able to interview him. He was a convinced opponent of astrology, so much so, indeed, that he wrote several pamphlets attacking it. In Party circles, however, he passed for an expert on the subject. Herr Huter, the Leipzig astrological publisher, told me that he had come across Kisshauer in April 1940 when he was trying to procure paper for his publications. Kisshauer was then on the staff of Alfred Rosenberg, who was responsible, among other things, for the supervision of political education within the NSDAP. Since publishers' paper stocks were allocated on the basis of presumed national interest, Herr Huter did not receive any assistance from Kisshauer, who was probably the last man who would have been willing to help him.[1]

Goerner recalled that he and Krafft were delighted to have something to do after months of inactivity. 'The work was really very interesting,' he said. 'We were surprised, too, at the large amount of material that the

[1] Kisshauer was the author of *Sternenlauf und Lebenslauf*, 1935, in the Reclam paper-covered series. See also his 'Die Astrologie — eine Wissenschaft?' in *National-sozialistische Monatshefte*, April 1938.

psychological warfare department was able to give us: birth dates, specimens of handwriting, photographs and so on. We received data of this kind
for Timoshenko, the Russian general, also for many allied statesmen,
generals and admirals. We were also asked to assess the horoscopes of
some of the leading British generals and it was soon apparent to us that
they had tried out three different commanders in North Africa. Krafft
looked at the chart of the latest of the three. It was that of General Montgomery, who was born at almost exactly the same time of the year as our
General Rommel. Krafft remarked: "Well, this man's chart is certainly
stronger than Rommel's." '[1]

The fact that Krafft and Goerner were set to work at that particular time
must be considered in relation to a passage in *The Goebbels Diaries* (translated and edited by Louis Lochner, 1948). The entry for 19 May 1942
reads: 'Berndt has drawn up a plan demonstrating how we could enlist the
aid of the occult in our propaganda. We are really getting somewhere.
The Americans and English fall easily for that type of thing. We are therefore pressing into our service all the experts we can find on occult prophecies; etc. Nostradamus must once again submit to being quoted.'[2]
Berndt's plan was devised before 19 May 1942 and Krafft and Goerner
began work at the Propaganda Ministry building in the Kommandantenstrasse on *c.* 15 June. I have not been able to discover the names of any
other 'occultists' whose services were enlisted by the Propaganda Ministry.

It has never been clear to me whether Krafft was supposed to provide
'serious' appreciations based upon astrological deductions, or merely
material that could be adapted by someone in the Propaganda Ministry for
propaganda or psychological warfare purposes. According to Frau Krafft
he was soon in trouble because of his refusal to perform a specific task in
the manner required by his employers. Instead he presented them with a
paper containing his own views on the subject in question and Kisshauer
made a fuss. But for the most part, Frau Krafft wrote, he dealt with any
given piece of work in his own way and without taking too much notice of
what his 'clients' might or might not expect. To that extent, she added,
both he and Goerner took a personal interest in the work.

Copies of two papers alleged to have been written by Krafft at this
time were in Herr Goerner's possession when I saw him. He told me that
he had taken them with him when he was eventually released in April
1943.[3] They are of interest for two reasons. Firstly, apart from a curious

[1] Field-Marshal Viscount Montgomery was born on 17 November 1887 and Field-
Marshal Rommel on 15 November 1891. De Wohl studied their respective horoscopes
at about the same time as Krafft.

[2] Louis Lochner described Alfred-Ingemar Berndt as 'a rather stupid young newspaper man who enjoyed a meteoric career under Goebbels as a "yesman". He was one
of Goebbels's most trusted lieutenants.' Biographical details in W. A. Boelcke, *Kriegspropaganda 1939-41*, 1966.

[3] The two documents were available to me overnight when I was at Mannheim in
July 1961 and I was able to make a few hurried notes.

circumstance in connection with the horoscope of General Sir Claude Auchinleck, they represent such futile examples of short essays or background notes obviously written for psychological warfare purposes, that one can only wonder at the stupidity of the people who used Krafft's services for this purpose. Secondly, if Krafft was really responsible for these productions, he either had his tongue in his cheek or actually believed in his own nonsense.

One of the papers bore the title 'The Roosevelts—The U.S.A.'s Unlucky Star'. In this the writer accused President and Mrs Roosevelt of being under the thumb of Freemasons and Jews; Wall Street was the world centre of Jewish financial power and the Jews were conspiring to rob America of her freedom and independence, all in accordance with the *Protocols of the Elders of Zion*. The Auchinleck piece, dated 3 July 1942, and therefore written about a fortnight after Krafft and Goerner arrived at the Kommandantenstrasse, is of greater interest. They calculated the General's horoscope on the basis of a birth in Eire at about 9 a.m. on 21 June 1884. Auchinleck, however, was not born in Eire but at Aldershot. Later I requested my old friend the late John Connell, the Field-Marshal's biographer, to ask him about Krafft's suggested birth time. Sir Claude said that he thought he was born between 8 and 9 a.m. and wondered how Krafft had managed to get so close to the probable hour. But everything else that Krafft had to say about the General was nonsense. He was aware that Auchinleck was of 'Irish' descent, but did not realise that his connection was with Ulster and not the south of Ireland. 'Today, in his present position, Auchinleck serves the enemies of his mother country!' Krafft confidently wrote.

The initial honeymoon period at the Muratti building lasted only a couple of months and towards the end of August things took a turn for the worse. They were then transferred to what Goerner called 'an absolute pigsty' in the Köpenickerstrasse.

'This was not a Propaganda Ministry office,' he remarked, 'but merely a dumping ground for Krafft and myself. The building had originally contained stables but had latterly been used for storage purposes. Krafft's room was at the end of a very long corridor, about a hundred yards from mine.' At the Muratti building, according to Goerner, Krafft had been confident that all would go well, but now he began to be increasingly depressed and, above all, resentful. It particularly infuriated him, for instance, that his wife had been expressly forbidden to write or forward letters on his behalf. He himself dispatched several angry letters to Ehrhardt who saw Frau Krafft and told her that he proposed to treat them as private communications and not place them in Krafft's file. He advised her to warn him that further letters would not be welcomed, adding that Krafft should consider himself very lucky that she was allowed to visit him at all. Frau Krafft told Ehrhardt that she was surprised that her husband was expected to do astrological work and said she thought that the practice of astrology had been completely forbidden. 'That's true enough,' Ehrhardt replied, 'we don't want any astrology in Germany. His stuff is being used for foreign propaganda purposes.'

It was probably Krafft's realisation that his sole function was to provide astrological fodder for processing by hacks in the Propaganda Ministry that contributed as much as anything else to his subsequent nervous breakdown, for when he first arrived at the Muratti building he had supposed that he had something important to contribute to the German war effort. Symptoms of a kind familiar to psychiatrists now developed: he who had always been so talkative and willing to communicate became increasingly withdrawn and silent. According to Frau Krafft he embarked upon rigorous fasts, refused the small delicacies she was able to bring him and rejected any highly-flavoured food. Now he could not bear the sight of Goerner and studiously avoided his company. Nor would he leave the building on shopping expeditions with Goerner and Hirsch or even with Hirsch alone. (Herr Goerner told me that they were able to supplement their diet with fruit and vegetables purchased at a nearby shop.) When Hirsch went to Krafft's room early in the morning he sometimes found him sitting on the floor deep in meditation. Hirsch's friendly greeting received no answer and Krafft was obviously unaware of his presence.[1]

After a stay of about ten weeks at the stables the two men were moved again, this time to more civilised surroundings at a Propaganda Ministry building in the Lützowstrasse. When they arrived there on 7 November 1942 they were given rooms in the rear part of the house. A steel door separated their quarters from the 'Promi' offices at the front. Herr Goerner told me that Krafft specially asked to be housed on a different floor to himself. My impression is that Goerner hardly ever saw Krafft during this final period although he had occasional conversations with Frau Krafft, who had been allowed to join her husband. She was free to come and go as she pleased during the daytime but was locked in with the 'prisoners' at night.

With their star performer unable or, more probably, unwilling to work for them, the psychological warfare people lost interest in what Goerner described as their 'caged astrologers'. While they were at the stables Kisshauer had already reduced his visits to twice weekly. Krafft did no work at all at the Lützowstrasse, but Kisshauer asked Goerner if he would like to undertake some on his own account. Goerner said that he could not offer Krafft's expertise but would do his best.

'I was happy enough at the Lützowstrasse between December 1942 and April 1943,' he told me. 'I was not asked to do very much. There were

---

[1] When I read Frau Krafft's account of this period I was reminded of Krafft's interest in yoga exercises twenty years earlier at Geneva.

20. Louis de Wohl—a photograph taken in London in March 1960.

21. Herr F. G. Goerner—a snapshot taken by the author in Mannheim in 1961.

DC.

Cesfar quon luicte et fre au faict bellique
Attca poctez plus grand que luy le près
De nuit au lit six luy feront la picque
Nud sans harnois subit sans surprins,

Hister, der in seinem kriegerischen Kampf mehr Siege (Preise) davongetragen hat, als für ihn gut war; sechse werden ihn in der Nacht ermorden. Nackt, ohne Harnisch überrascht, unterliegt er.

112

Nostradamus prophezeit den Kriegsverlauf

Regulus-Verlag, Görlitz, N.=S.

22. Cover design and page from a British pamphlet (1943) with a German imprint.

plenty of astrological books and tables and I amused myself by comparing various periodicities. Fritz Hirsch used to take me with him on shopping expeditions. We'd arrange a rendezvous somewhere and then he would go off on his own for an hour or two. Of course we always returned to the Lützowstrasse together.'

While Goerner philosophically made the best of things, Krafft's persecution mania became increasingly worse—the Germans described it as a *Haftpsychose* or prison psychosis. In her memorandum Frau Krafft recalled a letter that he sent to a senior Propaganda Ministry official whose office was in the front part of the building. In this he accused the man of wanting to drive him into a corner so as to have an excuse for sending him to a concentration camp. It was degrading, he complained, that he, of all people, should be expected to supply vulgar astrological predictions. But now he would make a prediction that would very soon come true: a load of British bombs would fall on the Propaganda Ministry, a just reward for their shabby conduct. Frau Krafft managed to see the recipient that evening—it was their first encounter—and begged him to ignore the letter. He told her that the *Reichssicherheitshauptamt* would be informed that his department had no further use for Krafft's services.

Krafft wrote many other letters, all of which his wife refused to post for him. These were intended for the Swiss embassy, various friends in Switzerland and the sculptor Breker, whom he asked to intervene on his behalf with *Reichsminister* Dr Hans Frank. But one letter, which was addressed to Ehrhardt, was mailed. Krafft found his way out of the building one Saturday afternoon and dispatched it himself. He succeeded in returning to his room without being seen by anyone and told his wife that he was sure that 'God had made them all blind!' Poor Frau Krafft was aghast. The next day she saw Dr Fesel at his home and begged him to intercede with Ehrhardt on Krafft's behalf. Fesel told her that he would see his colleague early on Monday morning and asked her to telephone him at his office at 9 a.m. She did so and Fesel told her to come to Ehrhardt's office without delay. Fesel was present when she arrived there. Ehrhardt said that if he had so far acted with consideration, it was only for her sake. As for Krafft, he deserved no clemency whatever. Now there were only two alternatives for him: either a mental hospital or a concentration camp. Indeed, he should not have told her that much, he added, and Dr Fesel's intervention, too, had been highly irregular. Fesel asked: 'What would have happened if I had not intervened?' and Ehrhardt cryptically answered: 'You know what!'[1] A few days later, on 12 February 1943, two Gestapo officials arrived at the Lützowstrasse and asked for Krafft. He left the building in their company.

[1] I would have liked to have heard Herr Ehrhardt's own account of this interview but was unable to trace him. Frau Krafft's record of the conversation was written in the early 1950s, hence about a decade later.

Goerner learned of Krafft's departure the same day. Many weeks had passed since he had last seen him. Kisshauer had not put in an appearance for some time and for the next two months he remained at the Lützow-strasse in a state of anxious suspense. Early on 13 April an official from the *Reichssicherheitshauptamt* appeared and told Goerner to come with him. A short car ride took them to the Potsdamerstrasse where, much to Goerner's relief, the driver turned in a westerly direction. To the north their destination could have been either the Alexanderplatz or Lehrter-strasse prisons. Eventually the car stopped outside a house in the Meine-kestrasse. Goerner was taken to a large room and left alone, and noticed with some surprise that he had not been locked in. Soon he was escorted to an office where he found a very senior SS officer. He was informed that he was now to be released but would first have to sign a declaration to the effect that he had never been in prison or worked for the Propaganda Ministry. Goerner did not bother to read the document but hastily signed it and walked out into the street a free man.

He found his way back to the Lützowstrasse and saw the head of the Propaganda Ministry section there. He asked if he could continue to use his room for the next few weeks as he was unwilling to return to Mann-heim and had not yet made any plans. No objections were raised and Goerner remained there until August.[1] While in Berlin he attended a course of lectures at the Institute for Psychology and Psychotherapy. He paid a brief visit to Mannheim in August and then enlisted in the army medical service. By this time he heartily regretted that he had ever become involved in Krafft's affairs.

Krafft was taken to the Lehrterstrasse prison on 12 February. There he was deposited in an underground cell where fifty prisoners managed as best they could in a space barely sufficient for a dozen. Early in March he caught typhus and had barely recovered when he was transferred to the Oranienburg concentration camp. By now a physical wreck, he was admitted to the camp hospital. There was another Swiss prisoner at Oranienburg. He was M. Jacques Farjon, who was told that a fellow countryman was in the infirmary block. His informant said: 'He's a remarkably intelligent man but doesn't say a word to anyone. But I've told him you are Swiss and he would like to see you.' The following Sun-day M. Farjon met Krafft for the first time. He recalled this meeting in an article published in *La Tribune de Genève* of 1 August 1946. 'His expression was something quite extraordinary, it had magnetic force,' M. Farjon wrote. 'Beneath a large and intelligent forehead two deep-set eyes burned

[1] The fact that Herr Goerner voluntarily returned to the Lützowstrasse proved to be a source of embarrassment to him when he applied after 1945 for compensation for the confiscation of his astrological books and his imprisonment. In almost every instance the Courts refused to award damages to astrologers whose private libraries were seized in the course of the 'Aktion Hess' or who had been detained in custody.

with an inner fire—two dark eyes that held you and did not leave you, peering at you and seeming to penetrate your most secret thoughts.'

In the meantime Frau Krafft remained in Berlin and during the next eighteen months was able to make two brief visits to the camp. She saw her husband for the third and last time in the autumn of 1944. He was carried into a small reception room on a stretcher and a prison guard was present while they talked. He was obviously very ill and apparently aware that the end could not be far away. Appalled at his condition she managed to secure an interview with a certain Herr Krayenbühl, an SS officer who appears to have been Ehrhardt's boss, and begged him to release her husband on the grounds that he could hardly hope to survive long under the present conditions. Krayenbühl said: 'We naturally don't want him to die, but nothing can be done. If we set him free he will soon recover and then it will all be the same as it was in the past,' presumably meaning that Krafft would continue to be a nuisance to them.

Frau Krafft now realised that her continued presence in Berlin would be of no avail as far as her husband was concerned. The allied armies were already on Germany's western frontier, the Russians were overrunning East Prussia and the end of the war was in sight. She applied for permission to return to Switzerland but the Germans refused to allow her to leave the country. Eventually the Swiss consulate managed to secure an exit visa and she crossed the border at the beginning of November 1944.

A woman friend of Frau Krafft in Berlin had promised to send Krafft regular food parcels, but the one dispatched in time for Christmas 1944 was returned with the sparse information that he was no longer at Oranienburg and that a new address would be notified in due course. Frau Krafft's friend made energetic enquiries and eventually learned that he had been transferred to the Buchenwald concentration camp. It appears, however, that he never reached there but died *en route* on 8 January 1945. The death certificate, dated 20 January 1945, originated from the Weimar registry and was mailed from the Buchenwald camp. Frau Krafft did not hear of her husband's death until 13 April, when the news arrived in the form of a brief communication from the Political Department at Bern.

A sensational story was published in *La Suisse*, a Geneva newspaper, on 15 April. There it was stated that some years before the war Krafft had concluded (on astrological grounds) that an attempt would soon be made on Hitler's life and had warned the authorities, with the result that the Gestapo was able to prevent the assassination. The article continued: 'Aware of Krafft's extraordinary and indisputable gifts, Hitler was determined to employ him since he was well aware of the potential value of his services. Krafft agreed on condition that it would be on a part-time basis so that he could continue with his private work, and this proposition was accepted. Thus Krafft became acquainted with all the leading people in the *Führer's* intimate circle and, in particular, with Rudolf Hess.'

As we know, Krafft's Hitler prediction was not made some years *before* the war, but in the autumn of 1939. Furthermore, he never worked for Hitler and never met Hess, although he did have brief contacts with two important Nazi bosses, namely Dr Hans Frank and Dr Robert Ley. It remains to ask how *La Suisse* knew anything at all about the Hitler prediction, even if its suggested date was incorrect.

While it is unlikely that many people in Switzerland had any very clear idea of what Krafft was doing in Berlin in 1940–1, the fact that he was there and apparently involved in some strange activity connected with Nostradamus and astrology was not completely unknown. Dr Ferrière, for instance, was in possession of some bits and pieces of information and was in touch with a number of people who had known Krafft. The person who talked most, however, was undoubtedly Krafft's mother and de Wohl was therefore not the sole creator of the Krafft 'legend'.[1]

In 1940, according to Frau Krafft, the BBC broadcast a news item to the effect that Krafft was Hitler's astrologer. This transmission was heard at Geneva by an acquaintance of Krafft *mère* who thereupon visited the old lady at Commugny and said: 'So that's what your son is doing at Berlin. He's Hitler's astrologer!' In due course Krafft received a letter from his mother in which she mentioned the broadcast. In his reply he said that it was all very strange and inferred that the British must have learned about the Hitler prediction which he made in the autumn of 1939 and had drawn the wrong conclusions. However, there is no reason to suppose that anyone in London had any knowledge of this matter, and the BBC broadcast was undoubtedly based upon speculative background material supplied by de Wohl or one of his contacts after the arrival of Krafft's letter to M. Tilea.

It is clear from Frau Krafft's letter to Dr Ferrière that her husband had rashly mentioned the 1939 Hitler prediction in a letter to his mother, and had gleefully told her that he was in touch with influential people in the upper hierarchy of the Third Reich. Now Krafft *mère* was not only German by birth, but was also in every other respect fanatically pro-German, hence her pride in her son's ostensibly important work and connections in Berlin. As far as Frau Krafft was concerned, the trouble was that her mother-in-law had talked too much and, indeed, with a singular lack of discretion.

One rumour led to another. On 16 April, the day after *La Suisse* published its inaccurate article about Krafft, a (Swiss?) radio broadcast stated that a certain Krafft, who was named as Hitler's astrologer, had been found at Buchenwald and was in allied hands. Krafft's name was in

[1] My inference that Krafft *mère* had been indiscreet is based upon a letter written by Frau Krafft to Dr Ferrière on 25 September 1945.

the news again on 22 September when Reuter circulated a story largely based on information that can only have been supplied by de Wohl. Here it was stated that Krafft had been Hitler's astrologer and that de Wohl had been employed by the British for the purposes already described in this book. This interesting news item was printed in the *Basler Nachrichten* and other Swiss newspapers on 22 September, and now it was the combination of Krafft's and de Wohl's names that created widespread public interest in Switzerland and eventually in Germany.

A number of people who had known Krafft hastened to contribute brief personal memories to the *Basler Nachrichten*; all of these were critical and on the whole unfriendly. A reply in Krafft's defence by his widow was eventually published in the *Basler Nachrichten* on 10 November 1945. She emphatically denied that he had ever had the slightest connection with Hitler or Hess, but perhaps understandably did not refer to his employment in Berlin and his connection with the *Reichssicherheitshauptamt* before he found himself a job at the *Deutsche Nachrichtenbüro*.

By 1947 de Wohl must surely have learned that the Krafft legend, which was largely his own invention, had no foundation, but this did not prevent him from giving it the widest possible circulation. Consider, for example, the record of the interview with him that was published in the London *Sunday Graphic* on 9 November 1947: 'In Britain one of my best clients was an old customer of Karl Klafft [*sic*], Hitler's pet astrologist,' he was reported as saying. 'From him I learned Klafft's technique. I knew what his advice to Hitler would be long before he was summoned by the *Führer*. By 1940, as a Captain in the Department of Psychological Warfare, I was working closely to Klafft's formula, and it was obvious he would be advising Hitler to act. The *Führer* took that advice and swept into France.' By implication Krafft's 'old customer' was M. Tilea, who certainly could not have explained Krafft's 'technique' to de Wohl. De Wohl went on to say that after Dunkirk 'for the first time Hitler's belief in his Chief Astrologer was shaken, and from then on he began to rely more and more on his own intuition. *This intuition became the unknown factor in my calculations.* Up to the last Hitler believed in astrology, and the demand for my reports never ceased. More than once we forestalled some of Hitler's tactically unpredictable motives.' Miss I., however, made it clear that there cannot have been any demand for de Wohl's 'strategic' reports after the end of 1940.

De Wohl must have made a lot of money from his sedulous dissemination of the Krafft legend and a host of wordy but never very convincing accounts of his own alleged activities in London. In 1947–8 articles by him were syndicated in newspapers and periodicals all over the world and he became internationally famous.[1] Frau Krafft's letters of protest remained

[1] De Wohl subsequently abandoned professional astrology and became converted to Roman Catholicism. He wrote a series of religious novels that gained the approbation

unanswered, but she eventually extracted a reply from him after he had lectured in Zürich on 'Astrology and Psychological Warfare' in *c.* 1947. According to Frau Krafft he said that he proposed to let sleeping dogs lie and that he had no doubt of the nature of Krafft's pro-Nazi sympathies.

Taking their clue from de Wohl, the German gutter press and, in particular, *Das Neue Zeitalter*, a scurrilous astrological weekly, produced their own crop of Krafft–de Wohl stories. The series published by *DNZ* in 1949 was by far the most remarkable. Its proprietors commissioned someone to produce a fictional account of Krafft's activities in Berlin. It was alleged that it was largely based upon fragments of Krafft's diary, which they claimed to possess. The diary story was pure invention. This fantastic serial described meetings between Krafft and Dr Goebbels that never took place and featured an imaginary liaison between Krafft and a lady called Karin Markow. She was supposed to have been an intelligence agent in the pay of the British secret service who received her instructions from de Wohl. However, at the same time as *DNZ* was printing its weekly instalment of inspired nonsense, it also published extracts from letters received from readers who knew at least some of the truth, so fact and fiction now appeared side by side.

---

of the Vatican. These included *The Quiet Life*, 1950, with St Thomas Aquinas as its hero, *The Restless Flame*, 1952 (St Augustine), *The Golden Thread*, 1953 (St Ignatius de Loyola), *The Glorious Folly*, 1958 (St Paul), and *Lay Siege to Heaven*, 1961 (St Catherine of Siena).

18

An Unbelievable Alternative

The supposition that Hitler believed in astrology and employed astrologers was current from 1933 onwards. It is clear that many thought that
the only possible explanation for his uninterrupted and increasingly
threatening run of political successes and territorial gains was his access to
advance information obtained by paranormal means, of which astrology
was the most likely. The question preoccupied Dr Hans Bernd Gisevius,
who had better access to confidential or secret information than most of his
contemporaries, as early as 1934 when he and his colleague Arther Nebe
tried, but without success, to get to the bottom of the rumours that were
then circulating in Germany. Seven years later, when the 'Aktion Hess'
provided further opportunities for checking, a positive answer was still
not forthcoming.[1]

It is probable that stories about Hitler's astrologer did not begin to
circulate outside Germany until *c.* 1938. I have already referred on p. 181
to the secret intelligence reports, based upon 'information' provided by
M. Raoul Bossy, the Rumanian Minister in Berlin, which were circulated
by the Rumanian Foreign Office to its embassies and legations abroad. The
earliest reference to Hitler's alleged dependence upon astrological counsel
that I have so far discovered is in the London *Daily Mail* of 30 January
1939, hence about seven months before the war, where it was stated
that the *Führer* paid great attention to the advice of his personal
astrologer.

On 5 April 1939 the *Gazette de Lausanne* published something on much
the same lines: 'Nobody believes in astrology more than Herr Hitler. The
best clients of the International Institute in London are the private astrologers at Berchtesgaden. Every month they ask for new astrological
documents. This is because Herr Hitler believes in astrology. And he
proves it. It is not by accident that his *coups* are all made in the month of
March. Before striking, he chooses the most favourable time indicated by
the stars. And March is assuredly his best month . . . Whether or not
one mocks at astrology, the important thing is that Hitler believes in it.'

---

[1] Letter from Dr Gisevius to the author (23 March 1966). H. B. Gisevius (*b.* 1904)
joined the legal staff of the Berlin police in August 1933 at the time when its political
section became part of the Gestapo. Disliking Gestapo methods he soon arranged for a
transfer and eventually left the police service in July 1936 when Himmler became Reich
Police Chief. During the war years he was in military intelligence and was implicated
in the 20 July 1944 plot to assassinate Hitler. SS Gruppenführer Arthur Nebe (*b.*
1894) became head of the Reich Criminal Police in 1936 and was executed in connection
with the 20 July conspiracy in 1945. If Nebe, with all his RSHA contacts, could not
identify Hitler's astrologer, the inference is that there was no such person.

However, there was no International (Astrological?) Institute at London and no *astrologues particuliers* at Berchtesgaden.

On 12 July 1939 the *Daily Mail* reported that Dr Nicholas Murray Butler, the President of Columbia University, New York City, had affirmed that Hitler had a staff of five astrologers. This multiplicity of *Führerastrologen* turns up again as late as 1950 when Louis de Wohl told a reporter from the *Empire News* (3 December) that Hitler employed six astrologers. One of this regiment of hypothetical star-gazers was named a month after the war began in the London *Evening Standard* on 5 October 1939.

'The recent disappearance of Hitler's favourite astrologer, Elsbeth Ebertin, is reported from Breslau, says the Havas Agency correspondent in Zürich. She has not been seen since the start of the war. She enjoys a big reputation among German astrologers and is said to be one of the few persons who knows the exact hour of Hitler's birth.' The next day the *Daily Telegraph* printed the same story and added that Frau Ebertin had been 'head of a publishing firm with almost a monopoly of astrological publications in Germany'. However, I have no doubt that Frau Ebertin could easily have been found at her house at Bahnhofstrasse 7 at Weinsberg bei Heilbronn, about twenty-five miles north of Stuttgart. The connection between Frau Ebertin and Hitler suggested by the Havas correspondent at Zürich was undoubtedly based upon someone's vague memory of her famous Hitler 'prediction' of 1923, which has already been discussed in this book.

Walter Schellenberg was another who was convinced that Hitler believed in astrology. Consider, for example, his statement that after Hess's flight to Scotland 'the great interest that Hitler had previously shown in astrology changed to uncompromising antipathy'.[1] Schellenberg did not know him anything like as well as Fräulein Schröder, who was one of his private secretaries from 1933 until 1945, and she was convinced that he was not interested in the subject at all.

'There were popular rumours that Hitler allowed himself to be guided by astrologers before reaching any important decision,' she wrote. 'I must confess that I never noticed anything of the kind and the subject was never mentioned in conversation. On the contrary, Hitler refuted this by his firmly-held conviction that people born on the same day, at the same place and at the same hour, in no way had the same fate. From this point of view he thought that twins provided the best evidence. He always vigorously rejected the proposition that the fate of individuals depends upon their stars or constellations. Nevertheless, the prediction made by a Munich fortune-teller [i.e. Frau Ebertin] in the very first years of his struggle for power had greatly impressed him. It seemed that her predictions had

[1] W. Schellenberg, *Memoiren*, p. 160.

fulfilled themselves in every respect. But Hitler only spoke very ironically about this coincidence and considered the whole thing as a joke.'[1]

Some remarks made by Hitler in his private circle confirm his scepticism as far as astrology was concerned. Indeed, there is no reason to believe that his attitude had ever been any different. 'Superstition, I think, is a factor that one must take into account when assessing human conduct, even though one may rise superior to it oneself and laugh at it. . . ,' he said. 'The horoscope, in which the Anglo-Saxons in particular have great faith, is another swindle whose significance should not be underestimated. Just think of the trouble given to the British General Staff by the publication by a well-known astrologer of a horoscope foretelling final victory in this war for Germany! All the newspapers in Britain had to dig out all the false prophecies previously published by this eminent quack and reprint them before public anxiety could be pacified.'[2] The Führer had got his facts wrong. It was the Germans rather than the Anglo-Saxons who had been 'infected' by astrology. In Germany between the two wars there were more astrologers per square mile than anywhere else in the world.

Even after the 'Akton Hess' the Nazis were apt to use astrology and other 'occult' procedures when it happened to suit them. In this context I do not refer to the perfunctory employment of Krafft and Goerner in 1942 but to even stranger instances, such as the organisation of the 'Pendulum Institute' in Berlin. In the spring of 1942, when Krafft and Goerner were still in solitary confinement at the Alexanderplatz prison, a number of people assembled daily at a house in the Admiral von Schroederstrasse, near the Tirpitz Ufer in Berlin. Many of them had been arrested at the time of the 'Aktion Hess' and had been subsequently released, but now they were all involved in an occult undertaking that had been organised under completely official auspices.[3] One who was unwillingly involved in this business was my friend Herr Wilhelm Wulff, of Hamburg. He indirectly owed his own introduction to the Institute to Dr Wilhelm Hartmann, a Nürnberg astronomer who happened to be interested in astrology, with whom he was already acquainted.[4] When he arrived in Berlin he was surprised to find himself in the company of a

---

[1] A. Zoller, *Hitler Privat*, 1949, p. 76. 'The real author of this valuable book . . . appears from internal evidence to be Frl. Schröder.'—H. R. Trevor-Roper's Introduction to *Hitler's Table Talk, 1941–4*, 1953.

[2] *Hitler's Table Talk, 1941–4*, 1953, p. 583.

[3] I have only been able to find three sources of information about the Pendulum Institut: a series of autobiographical articles by Herr Wilhelm Wulff in the *Hamburger Abendblatt*, October 1948, three articles on 'Der Okkultismus im Dritten Reich' by Dr Gerda Walther in *Neue Wissenschaft*, 1950–1, and her autobiography *Zum anderen Ufer*, 1960.

[4] Dr W. Th. A. Hartmann (*b.* 1893 at Hamburg) became director of the Nürnberg astronomical observatory and planetarium in 1929. His *Die Lösung des uralten Rätsels um Mensch und Stern*, 1950, proposes a scientific basis for astrological beliefs.

representative collection of spiritualist mediums and psychics, radiesthetic (pendulum) practitioners, astrologers, astronomers and mathematicians. He told me that when he learned what it was all about he could not help laughing, especially as the State was now proposing to employ the very people it had recently persecuted.

The Institute was directed by Captain Hans A. Roeder, of the German navy. The British had latterly been destroying a great many German submarines, and in default of any scientific method known to the Germans that would enable the Royal Navy to locate the U-boats, it was thought that the British must be using a completely new detection technique. Roeder's theory was that British naval intelligence was identifying the positions of German U-boats at sea by employing pendulum practitioners. Roughly speaking, the pendulum 'operator' would be sitting in a room at the Admiralty in London with a map of the Atlantic ocean in front of him. He would then 'search' the map with his pendulum and at a given moment if all went well, the pendulum would begin to move or swing in a pre-scribed manner. Eureka, another German submarine found! A radio message would be sent, destroyers would hurry to the scene with their depth charges and the U-boat would be sunk.

But two could play at the same game. The purpose of the Institute, therefore, was to establish the nature of the required pendulum techniques and that was why Herr Wulff, Dr Gerda Walther, the Countess Wassilko-Serecki (formerly President of the Vienna Astrological Society), Herr Ludwig Straniak and all the others had been summoned. Once the British secret had been discovered, a series of short courses were to be organised for German naval personnel, who would be trained by the 'adepts' to use their pendulums against British and American shipping.

This rum theory appears to have originated at Salzburg where Herr Ludwig Straniak, a master builder, had claimed to be able to locate the position of a ship by holding a pendulum above a photograph of the vessel and then 'searching' a map with the instrument. Members of the German admiralty visited him at Salzburg and returned to Berlin with the impres-sion that his 'techniques' deserved further investigation. Thus Straniak became a leading member of the band of pendulum swingers at the 'Institute'. Herr Wulff recalled that although Straniak gave many impres-sive demonstrations of his skill, these merely indicated that his methods could be used for certain experimental purposes, although not for the one that was of primary interest to the German navy. For instance, he could unfailingly identify (with a pendulum) the exact position on a large sheet of paper that had previously been in contact with a small metal object, but that was hardly enough.

Daily for hours on end the pendulums swung over maps of the Atlantic Ocean and other seas, but apparently to no very good purpose. Dr Gerda Walther and Herr Wulff refused to take Captain Roeder's hopes and theories seriously and managed to make themselves scarce without too much delay. Dr Hartmann, the Nürnberg astronomer, also thought it was all nonsense. Those who remained soon began to suffer from nervous exhaustion and a little later the Institute was moved to quieter and more salubrious surroundings on the island of Sylt, perhaps on the basis that a little ozone would help the 'vibrations'.

The assistance of the occultists was recruited again after Mussolini was arrested by the Badoglio government on 25 July 1943. Hitler gave instructions for 'Operation Oak' for Mussolini's rescue on 27 July. The problem, however, was that the Germans had no idea of the Duce's whereabouts in Italy and when the Intelligence Service failed to produce any useful information the occultists were called in to help.

Schellenberg referred to this peculiar business in his memoirs. 'In this situation Himmler once again put his occult hobbies into practice,' he recalled, 'and even with a certain degree of success. He assembled some of the "representatives of occult science" that had been arrested after Hess's flight to England and shut them up in a villa at Wannsee. Clairvoyants, astrologers and pendulum practitioners were required to produce the vanished Duce's whereabouts out of the hat. These seances cost a mint of money because what the "scientists" needed in the way of good food, drinks and smokes was quite enormous. But, lo and behold, after a while a pendulum *maestro* said that Mussolini would be found on an island to the west of Naples. In fact the Duce had first been taken to one of the small Ponza islands that he indicated. It must be stated in all justice that the man had no contact with the outside world at the time of the experiment.'[1]

Readers familiar with Schellenberg's memoirs and H. R. Trevor-Roper's *The Last Days of Hitler*, will recall occasional references to an astrologer who was said to work for Heinrich Himmler. Schellenberg did not mention his name but Mr Trevor-Roper, whose information appears to have been based upon what Schellenberg told him after the war, called him Wulf. This gentleman was none other than the Herr Wilhelm Wulff mentioned above in connection with the pendulum institute. Unlike Krafft, who would undoubtedly have liked nothing better than such a position of apparent power and influence, Herr Wulff by no means welcomed his personal involvement with Messrs Himmler, Schellenberg, Nebe (the head of the criminal police) and other leading members of the *Reichssicherheitshauptamt*. Herr Wulff allowed me to read an early draft of his memoirs when I visited him at Hamburg in 1962. While he has kindly supplied me with certain material, it would be improper for me to anticipate his own story which will soon be published.

Just as there is an astrological anecdote in connection with Hitler's first major public appearance in November 1923, there is another relating to the

[1] W. Schellenberg, *Memoiren*, 1959, p. 301.

very end of his career. The source for this is the unpublished diary of Count Schwerin von Krosigk, Hitler's minister of finance. The diary and its author were captured at Flensburg in May 1945 and Mr Trevor-Roper used the document when he wrote *The Last Days of Hitler.*

A few days prior to 15 April 1945, when the diary entries began, Goebbels told von Krosigk that he had recently been reading aloud to the Führer from Carlyle's *History of Frederick the Great.* Goebbels came to the passage describing the king's despair at the imminent defeat of Prussia towards the end of the Seven Years War and his intention, if there were no change by 15 February, to take poison. 'Brave king!' wrote Carlyle (according to von Krosigk), 'wait yet a little while, and the days of your suffering will be over. Already the sun of your good fortune stands behind the clouds and will soon rise upon you.' On 12 February the Czarina died and the Miracle of the House of Brandenburg had come to pass. At this point Mr Trevor-Roper's text is followed.[1]

'At this touching tale, said Goebbels, "tears stood in the *Führer's* eyes". They discussed the matter to and fro, and in the course of the discussion sent for two horoscopes that were carefully kept in one of Himmler's research departments: the horoscope of the *Führer*, drawn up on January 30th, 1933, and the horoscope of the Republic, dated November 9th, 1918. These sacred documents were fetched and examined, and an "astonishing fact" was discovered, which might well have repaid earlier scrutiny. "Both horoscopes had unanimously predicted the outbreak of war in 1939, the victories till 1941, and then the series of defeats culminating in the worst disasters in the early months of 1945, especially in the first half of April. Then there was to be an overwhelming victory for us in the second half of April, stagnation till August, and in August peace. After the peace there would be a difficult time for Germany for three years; but from 1948 she would rise to greatness again. Next day Goebbels sent me the horoscopes. I could not fathom everything in them; but in the subjoined interpretation, newly drawn up, I found it all; and now I am eagerly awaiting the second half of April." '

Late on 12 April von Krosigk received a telephone message to the effect that Roosevelt had just died. 'We felt the wings of the Angel of History rustle through the room. Could this be the long desired change of fortune?' he asked himself.

Mr Trevor-Roper learned from another source that when Goebbels, who had just returned to Berlin from Küstrin heard the news during the early hours of 13 April he ordered a bottle of champagne for his companions and immediately telephoned the Führer. 'My *Führer*,' he ex-

---

[1] With Professor Trevor-Roper's kind permission I have used the 1962 Pan Books paperback edition of his work. There he pointed out that Schwerin von Krosigk had not quoted either Carlyle or the facts correctly. The Empress Elizabeth of Russia died on 5 January 1762.

claimed, 'I congratulate you! Roosevelt is dead. It is written in the stars that the second half of April will be the turning point for us. This is Friday, April the 13th. It is the turning point!' A fortnight later both Hitler and Goebbels took their own lives.

There is another astrological story connected with Friday, 13 April 1945, apparently improbable although it could conceivably be true. During the summer of 1962 I read the Nostradamus book, mentioned above on p. 185, by Dr Centurio. The author stated that in June 1944, when the British and American armies were crossing the Seine, he was summoned to Berlin by Eugen Hadamovsky, the head of the Reich broadcasting system, who told him that Dr Goebbels was considering the possibility of reaching an understanding with the allies and, above all, Great Britain. Hadamovsky is supposed to have asked Centurio if Nostradamus himself had provided any clues as to such an eventuality. Dr Centurio forthwith suggested that quatrain IX, 51 would probably meet the case. It begins: *Contres les rouges secte se banderont*. Centurio took this to mean 'an alliance against the red parties', i.e. an alliance between Germany and the allies against the Soviet Union.

'At the request of my chief,' Dr Centurio continued, 'I immediately wrote a brochure in English with the title *Nostradamus and England*. It was printed by a publisher in south Germany. Dr Goebbels's project came to nothing. . . .'[1]

Amused but by this time by no means surprised at this anecdote, I eventually established contact with Dr Centurio who turned out to be Dr Alexander Centgraf. We never met, but he wrote to me at some length in a brave attempt at English prose on 28 June 1962. He obviously knew a good deal about Krafft and had actually succeeded in visiting him and Goerner at the Lützowstrasse. He also had a number of conversations with Herr Hirsch, their 'keeper', probably early in February 1943.

Hirsch told him that Krafft was 'trying to feign a mental disorder and was eating much garlic and was taking hip-baths in a frying pan'. Some days later Hirsch informed him that Krafft would be 'fetched off', i.e. by the Gestapo. I also heard a version of this 'hip-bath' story from Herr Goerner. It appears that Hirsch had discovered Krafft sitting motionless in an empty bath or tub. He was probably doing his yoga exercises, but Hirsch did not realise this. It seems unlikely, however, that he was feigning madness. Dr Centgraf told me that he wanted to intervene with the

---

[1] The pamphlet was written under the pseudonym 'Nestor'. I have never seen a copy of it. Dr Centurio's story contains a number of discrepancies. Hadamovsky lost his job at the Propaganda Ministry in April 1942 and was transferred to the Party's propaganda department. It is possible that he saw Dr Goebbels for the last time in October 1943. Soon after he enlisted in the *Wehrmacht* and is said to have met his death in Russia in 1944. Hence it is unlikely that he instructed Dr Centurio to write a Nostradamus pamphlet in June 1944. See W. A. Boelcke, *Kriegspropaganda 1939-41* 1966, pp. 80-83.

Gestapo on Krafft's behalf: 'I tried to help him, but I did not succeed in advancing to the Gestapo.'

The person who drew Dr Centgraf's attention to Krafft's presence in the Lützowstrasse was an obscure astrologer named Bernd Unglaub. Before he moved to Berlin in the autumn of 1926 he was at Munich, where he made a modest income as a writer of predictive almanacs and astrological ephemera, such as *Race-course Tips, Lotteries and Speculation* (The Astrological Success Series, No. 1). The Bavarian police seized the first issue of his *Sirius Pocket Almanac* (1925 for 1926) and forbade its sale or circulation. I have copies of the 1927–8 editions, which were published in Berlin where the police were not so fussy. They contain articles describing methods for developing clairvoyant faculties and other occult nonsense. He even gave his readers two addresses in Germany where the Mexican 'hallucination' drug Peyotl could be obtained. Better still, he recorded that second sight could be stimulated by fixing the gaze upon a picture of the Master Morya, one of Madame Blavatsky's improbable Mahatmas. This procedure, however, was not strongly recommended since he could recall two cases of suicide caused by prolonged staring at the Master's countenance. Herr Unglaub was a typical member of the occult 'underworld': very silly and probably a little mad.

'A cosmologe Mr Bernd Unglaub lived in the Bülowstrasse 27 in Berlin and was the neighbour of my deceased mother,' Dr Centgraf wrote. 'In 1929 he had written a little book *What is, What will be?* In this book he had prophesied Hitler's seizing of might [power] for the year 1933, and for 1939 the Great War, bringing much unhappiness to Germany.[1] I had seen and read this little book myself. Later (1941) all of the copies were destroyed by the Gestapo. Unglaub originated from the Allgäu [district]. Already by 1922 he had heard speeches by Hitler, but he did not join company with him, "because I know his end!" he told me in 1940!! "What [i.e. when] will be the end?" I asked. "May 1945," said Unglaub. Now Unglaub was arrested by the Gestapo on account of defaitismus. At the many requests of his despaired wife I went to see the competent expert of the Gestapo in the Albrechtstrasse in Berlin, where much courage was necessary. Now Unglaub was released and the Gestapo did no more trouble and pursue him.'

Dr Centgraf saw Unglaub for the last time on Friday, 13 April 1945: 'He came from the *Reichskanzlei*. Hitler had sent for him, to learn what he should do. Unglaub had spoken out for himself, very clever.'

At this point it is necessary to re-examine the background evidence, such as it is. Schwerin von Krosigk's diary entries began on 15 April. I think that we can assume that it was during the first week in April that Hitler and Goebbels spent a happy hour looking at horoscopes. Goebbels

---

[1] Herr Unglaub omitted to send a copy to the Deutsche Bücherei at Leipzig and it has therefore not been possible to check Dr Centgraf's statement.

told Hitler that Roosevelt's death was 'written in the stars' during the early hours of Friday 13 April. By inference, then, this is the one known day when Hitler might conceivably have decided that he wanted a little astrological information, e.g. to confirm Goebbels's suggestion.

But *did* the *Führer* say: 'Fetch me an astrologer immediately'? In beleaguered Berlin at that time it would certainly not have been very easy to produce an astrologer at the drop of an SS *Obergruppenführer's* hat. One can picture the adjutants feverishly enquiring around the *Führerbunker*: 'Can anyone here recommend a good astrologer? We must have one immediately!' Somebody may have known Unglaub, someone may have fetched him. In any case the Bülowstrasse was not very far from the Reich Chancery.

Unfortunately Unglaub did not survive to tell his story to any British or American intelligence officer, or, in later and quieter times, to reporters from *Der Spiegel* or *Stern*. He died on 21 July 1945 of cancer of the tongue —'as if the Gods were envious,' Dr Centgraf remarked.

As for the name Unglaub, translated literally it means . . . *un-belief*. Whether or not this Unglaub story is true, it is one that I personally find very difficult to believe. And yet so many strange things occurred during the era of the Third Reich that even this incredible confrontation of the *Führer* and Bernd Unglaub might have happened. Finally, while I have destroyed the Krafft 'legend', I may well have replaced it with an equally *unglaubliche* (unbelievable) alternative.

19
Postscript

I regret my inability to end this book with a neatly-wrapped parcel of definite conclusions. The available evidence suggests that information can be deduced from a natal horoscope, but I cannot explain why this should be the case. I have referred to at least three apparently accurate predictions made by Krafft, but I still find it difficult to believe that astrologers can forecast anything correctly except by chance or possibly some form of clairvoyance. In any case most predictions are expressed in such vague terms as to be worthless. Newspaper astrology is obviously nonsense from start to finish, and even the astrologers are mostly prepared to admit this.

It is hardly surprising that scientists have been unwilling to investigate the astrologers' claims. The whole area is so confused that it is difficult to know where to begin. Thus the endeavours of Professor Hans Bender and his colleagues at the Institute for the Border Areas of Psychology at Freiburg i. Br. are to be welcomed. There the inquest has been within the framework of a far wider parapsychological research programme. However, the Freiburg enquiry is still far from completion, and so far very little has been published on the subject.[1]

I have already mentioned Bender's blind diagnosis experiment with Krafft at Bonn in 1937. Similar but more extensive tests were made during 1944-5 with Thomas Ring, a highly-educated astrologer with psychological training. In his preface to the first volume of Ring's *Astrologische Menschenkunde*, 1956, Bender indicated that the positive results obtained with Ring persuaded him to continue the investigation on a larger scale. During 1952-4 Bender made contact with *c.* 150 German astrologers, including a number of professionals, who were invited to participate in two kinds of experiment: blind diagnosis tests and matching horoscopes to life histories.[2]

Bender discovered that the majority of the astrologers tested offered 'stereotype interpretations', meaning ambiguous generalisations which might or might not apply. The results of the matching tests were dis-

[1] Some preliminary information will be found in H. Bender, 'Astrologie und Aberglaube' in *Neue Wissenschaft*, 1964, 1, supplement to *Zeitschrift für Parapsychologie und Grenzgebiete der Psychologie*.

[2] Matching tests: the astrologer receives detailed biographical notes and descriptions of the personalities of up to half a dozen unidentified individuals, also their horoscopes. The astrologer is asked to allocate the horoscopes to their respective owners. A sociological study based upon the Institute's correspondence with these astrologers will be published in *Zeitschrift für Parapsychologie und Grenzgebiete der Psychologie*, vol. IX, 1, 1967.

appointing, but the blind diagnosis interpretations of natal horoscopes offered by three or four astrologers were impressively accurate and more or less identical in content. The hypothesis that the successful astrologers were possibly clairvoyant was ruled out, because all gave chapter and verse for their deductions, which were clearly based upon the Tradition. Bender was able to follow their arguments much as if each of them had been required to record all the successive stages required for the solution of a simple mathematical problem. There was, then, an astrological foundation for every statement. It is impossible to explain why a few astrologers succeeded and the others failed. Bender continued to experiment with the skilled practitioners and one of them, Herr Walter Böer, a schoolmaster, worked at the Institute on a full-time basis during 1963–4.[1]

Academic psychologists have developed a number of procedures, including certain well-known 'test' techniques, e.g. those associated with the names of Rorschach and Szondi, for evaluating and describing the nature of an individual human personality. Hence, given agreement on terminology, it is possible to make a detailed assessment of a person's psychological make-up. While Herr Böer was at the Institute Professor Bender and his colleagues interviewed and tested a number of subjects and the written records were deposited in a locked safe. Herr Böer was asked to interpret the horoscopes. He had no knowledge of their identities and had no access to the papers in the safe. His working data was restricted to particulars of the date, time and place of birth. A proportion of the subjects were neurotic or maladjusted while others, for control purposes, were ostensibly 'normal'. In many instances Herr Böer was able to match the conclusions of the psychologists with surprising accuracy.[2]

If we are prepared to admit that a natal horoscope can provide valid psychological information, it is necessary to ask who is qualified to extract and use it. It is evident that very few astrologers, no matter whether amateur or professional, can match the skill of a Böer or a Ring. Furthermore, the average astrologer is without psychological or psychotherapeutic training and is hardly qualified to offer advice. While it is theoretically possible for trained psychologists to learn the elements of astrology, there is no guarantee of their eventual proficiency. The particular kind of skill demonstrated by Herr Böer and a few other German astrologers appears to require a certain kind of intuition, and in its absence very little can be achieved. I have already mentioned that some Jungian analysts examine

[1] Herr Böer uses the conservative von Kloeckler system of interpretation, which he learned before 1939. He is not an occultist and his attitude to astrology is unusually objective. He has a good all-round knowledge of modern psychological theories and is a first-class literary stylist. His interpretative essays are far more readable than those of Krafft, whose prose was often tedious or pompous. Herr Ring also writes well.

[2] During a brief visit to the Institute in July 1964 I read the papers relating to a recent test and noticed how correctly Herr Böer had described the personality of a young Italian worker who had been in trouble with the local police.

their patients' horoscopes. Professor Bender told me that he is acquainted with a number of qualified practitioners who use astrology for psychodiagnosis, and said that they are careful not to advertise the fact. Their reluctance to divulge their interest is understandable, because even in Germany astrology still has a very indifferent reputation in respectable circles.

If astrology itself requires investigation so, too, do the astrologers. A score or more of detailed case histories would undoubtedly provide some extremely interesting (and sometimes devastating) information. A somewhat similar enquiry was made at Professor Bender's Institute by Dr Gerhard Sannwald, who examined a representative group of individuals who claimed to have had parapsychic experiences.[1] Professor Bender referred to Sannwald's work in a paper on 'The Psychology of Gifted Subjects' which he delivered at the International Parapsychology Congress at Oxford in 1964.[2] Summarising Sannwald's conclusions, Bender said that in the case of the 'gifted subjects' heightened imaginative activity was linked with a weakness of the ego and a lack of self-confidence. These people experienced difficulties in social adjustment and contact. Hence the external world represented a threat, and ego defences were reinforced by magical procedures or intellectual constructions which attempted to explain the source of the anxiety. Divinatory techniques, such as playing cards, the pendulum, the interpretation of dreams and astrology were employed in order to foretell the future. The 'gifted subjects' supposed that their inner world was more 'spiritual' or 'subtle' than that of ordinary people.

Dr Sannwald's discovery that some of his 'gifted subjects' dabbled with astrology did not surprise me. For many it provides an attractive and at the same time vehemently rationalised escape from reality, also a compensation for feelings of inferiority or an incapacity to deal successfully with merely terrestrial problems. Again, I have encountered innumerable 'esoteric' astrologers who claim, although without any apparent justification, deep spiritual insight.

I am prepared to admit that there are ordinary, sane and completely respectable individuals who believe in and practise astrology. They are at one end of the spectrum. At the other end there are the obvious cranks and a quota of unmistakable lunatics. It appears, however, that the cranks and the crackpots greatly outnumber their more level-headed brethren. As a class professional astrologers tend to be rather unsatisfactory people, although there are some whom I like and trust. Nevertheless, I am inclined to be suspicious of the motives that persuade anyone to adopt this

---

[1] Dr Sannwald's investigation covered 70 women and 16 men, most of them between 15–65 years of age. 71 per cent were unmarried. A numerically and in other respects similar control group was also examined, i.e. people who made no claims in respect of such experiences.

[2] Professor Bender kindly gave me a copy of his typescript.

unfashionable method of earning a living. In Europe one can ignore the probability of high earning power, since professional astrological work is seldom generously remunerated. It is said that some American astrologers make a lot of money, but it is doubtful whether they are any more skilled than most of their counterparts on this side of the Atlantic. Professional astrology seems to appeal to people who are unsuited to conventional employment and who, at the same time, derive great satisfaction from intervening, as it were, in the lives and problems of others. Some of my professional astrologer friends do this with tact, caution and a sense of responsibility, but the average professional is often a psychological misfit. Nevertheless, these 'magicians', good, bad, and indifferent, meet an identifiable public demand.

The Krafft case history throws light upon a typical situation, namely an obsession with the irrational. I was reminded of Krafft while reading Dr Wolfgang Treher's psychiatric study of the personalities of Adolf Hitler, Rudolf Steiner and Daniel Paul Schreber.[1] Treher refers to the delusions of grandeur frequently demonstrated by schizophrenics and the tendency of those suffering from this mental illness to assume a prophetic mantle. Krafft was probably schizophrenic, and if we accept Treher's arguments it is conceivable that many astrologers and occultists are un-diagnosed schizophrenics. In Krafft's case one can point to his persistent and obsessive belief that he had made outstandingly important scientific, philosophical and cultural discoveries (e.g. Cosmobiology, Typocosmy and *Sprachgeist*), his compulsive desire for an audience and for opportunities to communicate his 'message', his brutality (to his 'patients'), the creation of a personal 'sect' (the Typocosmy study groups), and finally his disproportionate belief in his own genius.

L. Szondi, a major psychiatric authority, observed that patients with incipient schizophrenic tendencies were particularly identified with metaphysical problems, Theosophy, Hinduism, occultism and spiritualism.[2]

In the immediate or near future we can expect to hear more on the subject of planetary influences, not from astrologers (schizophrenic or sane) but from scientists whose indifference to the traditional astrological thesis is nothing less than total. It is unlikely that many of these people have heard of Krafft, let alone read the *Traité d'Astro-Biologie*. An exception is M. Michel Gauquelin, at present a member of the staff of the French *Centre National de Recherche Scientifique* and attached to the Psycho-physiological Laboratory at the University of Strasbourg. M. Gauquelin

[1] W. Treher, *Hitler, Steiner, Schreber: Beiträge zur Phämenologie des kranken Geistes*, 1966 (published privately by the author: 785 Emmendingen/Baden, Hochburgerstrasse 58). D. P. Schreber (1842–1911) wrote a classic personal case history of insanity which is well known to students of psychoanalytical literature.
[2] L. Szondi, *Schicksalsanalyse*, 2nd edit., Basle, 1948, pp. 305–9.

(*b.* 1928) was still in his twenties and studying psychology and statistics at
the Sorbonne, when curiosity led him to examine Choisnard's and Krafft's
astro-statistical experiments. A conscientious inspection of the *Traité*
indicated that Krafft had offered no serious statistical evidence, but had
argued on the basis of what Gauquelin described as 'suggestive diagrams'.
It appeared, too, that Krafft's statistical techniques were quite primitive.
He attempted to reproduce some of Krafft's 'experiments' but the results
were negative.[1] Unable to make any progress on the lines indicated by
Krafft, he began a new research project based upon a collection of birth
data that eventually amounted to 50,000 dates assembled in French civil
registries. Using this material he subjected every department of the astrological Tradition to statistical analysis but with negative results. He was,
however, surprised to discover an unexpected statistical phenomenon. In
the course of analysing the horoscopes of 25,000 European professional
men he noticed statistically abnormal groupings of certain planets, i.e. the
Moon, Mars, Jupiter and Saturn, close to the Ascendant and *Medium
Coeli*. He was inclined to mistrust this evidence, for what it was worth,
because of what he called its 'pseudo-astrological' flavour. He checked and
re-checked his mathematical calculations but they did not appear to be
incorrect. A process of elimination eventually led him in the direction of
a genetic hypothesis and a theory of planetary heredity based upon the
statistical evaluation of 30,000 horoscopes of parents and their children.[2]

The planetary heredity theory explained Gauquelin's initial findings in,
roughly speaking, the following manner. The influences of the Moon and
some of the planets operate at the time of birth and accelerate or induce the
actual birth process. Furthermore, there is a tendency for children to be
born under cosmic conditions that are analogous to those that prevailed
when their parents were born. This fact, according to Gauquelin, can be
demonstrated in the case of the planets nearest to the Earth, namely the
Moon, Venus, Mars, Jupiter and Saturn. (He did not mention Mercury
in his memorandum.) A natural birth is presupposed. The implications
of this discovery were obscure. At this point he re-examined the horoscopes of his 25,000 professional notabilities in the light of scientific
typological and genetic theories. It is accepted that in the case of any
individual human being, his or her 'type' is linked with genetic factors
transmitted by the parents. Gauquelin suggests that there are hereditary
factors, probably of a chemical nature, which not only provide a child with

---

[1] Detailed accounts of the early stages of Gauquelin's investigations will be found in
L'influence des astres, étude critique et expérimentale, Editions du Dauphin, Paris,
1955, *L'homme et les astres*, Denoël, Paris, 1960 and *L'hérédité planétaire*, Denoël,
Paris, 1966. His *Cosmic Clocks and Human Life* is announced for publication by Henry
Regnery, Chicago. The information in this chapter is based upon an *aide memoire*
received from M. Gauquelin in January 1967.

[2] Choisnard and Krafft both believed in planetary heredity. Gauquelin came to the
same conclusion but by a different and, indeed, more sceptical route.

a particular kind of temperament, but 'trigger' the birth under a specific cosmic constellation. Theoretically, then, a birth time could provide a useful indication of a subject's biological or psychological type. A scientifically satisfactory method for 'interpretation' has not yet been developed. It would clearly exclude the necessity for intuition.

Gauquelin proposes that the 'planetary heredity' theory offers a non-astrological explanation for the practical ability manifested by a proportion of his professional men. They possessed gifts or followed a vocation which permitted them to succeed brilliantly in their chosen careers. In short, the planetary positions at the time they were born indicated genetic dispositions.

In his *aide memoire* Gauquelin mentioned others who are working on somewhat similar lines and who, like himself, are members of the International Society of Biometeorology and the Society for Biological Rhythm. Frank A. Brown, professor of biology at Northwestern University at Evanston, near Chicago, has demonstrated that living beings regulate their rhythm of life according to the movements of the Sun and Moon. Maki Takata, professor of medicine at the Toho University at Tokio has observed that the composition of human blood varies with the cosmic constellations. Giorgio Piccardi, professor of physical chemistry at the University of Florence, has employed ingenious chemical tests to demonstrate that planetary influences affect the water content of human cells. Gauquelin mentioned in passing that information transmitted by artificial satellites has indicated that interstellar space is not empty but permeated with an infinite number of waves and corpuscles which emanate from the stars and affect our planet. Hence, he observed, the intuition of the old astrologers was correct and every fibre in a human body is connected with the cosmos by invisible threads. At that point he and the astrologers part company, because he rejects any part of the traditional astrological thesis, no matter how cautiously presented.

It is difficult to know whether or not there is a road that will eventually connect the areas latterly investigated by Professor Bender and M. Gauquelin. For instance, could there be a cosmo–genetic explanation for Herr Böer's particular skill? The answer to this and similar questions may one day be provided by specialists in cosmic chemistry, biometeorologists and parapsychologists. I do not believe that we can expect much help from the astrologers and their Tradition.

INDEX

Index